Encomiums to this labor of love, a fe entanglement of scrutiny and joy. A full-throated documentary project of fascinating and newly inspired inter-generational poetics has sprung full grown out of the Jack Kerouac School Archive at Naropa University. With transcriptions based on notes and oral teaching from guests such as Jane Augustine, Joanne Kyger, Michael Heller, and Bernadette Mayer, as well as others from summer sessions, we encounter a host of generative surrealist women writers including Clarice Lispector, and modernists, Mina Loy, Gertrude Stein, Lorine Niedecker, as well as an elegant H.D. as seen through the eyes of Barbara Guest as encountered by Joanne Kyger. Did the woman have too much privilege? Is there such a thing as matriarchal language? Stamina and curiosity by the student-poets-scholars over 2 years of "Carrier Waves" (Zoom sessions) has led to this remarkable recovery and intimate response. Look to the Archive was the prompt and the student collective cohort, spear-headed by the indomitable Christina Chady, burrowed in. We started the BA MFA and SWP programs of Writing & Poetics nearly 50 years ago with a founding vision that we could build an archive that would resonate across a trajectory of consciousness. Work on this book seemed a powerful antidote through slog and mystery of pandemic time, of angst and loss, panic and sequester to some articulated agency around self-discovery, mysticism, dream, torqued language, identity, gender, race, class, sexual empowerment, queerness, disobedience, continuous present, whereby a struggling renascent poet feminism emerges. Brava to the students-poets-editors-scholars who grappled with disembodied voices. Head to heart to head to ear to oral nights to oculist witness, from reel to reel, reel to cassette, cassette to CD tracking, tracing dream and vortex, and wild mind dialects of head space and ludic place. Now we're up to the future with its fierce continuing opaline determination to be heard embodied in these texts and psyches. This is a great shimmering and useful handbook for younger writers/thinker. As Diane Lizette Rodriquez remarks: "The line of descent follows us."

Anne Waldman

***Embodied Unconscious* is the most inspired book** on poetry lineage ever to appear in North America. Doesn't it seem obvious now? That writers of the Jack Kerouac School should unearth voices from the trove of archives, write down what they hear their ancestors say, and respond with their own careful, cool gazes into the future? Almost every speaker here a woman—from Stein, Loy, Niedecker, their generation—to women who are changing poetry right now. Three generations of figures who pass the lamp of courage forward. As I read this collection, what echoes are Plato's words to artists: when the mode of the music changes, the laws of the state change too.

Andrew Schelling,
Jack Kerouac School, author of *Tracks Along the Left Coast*

Notoriously, American feminism in the 1970s trained its eye on the literary canon, rediscovering a body of work by female writers and fashioning a female ideal reader who resisted the "immasculation of women by men," as Judith Fetterly wrote in 1978. Yet, these correctives have just as notoriously needed correction as they threatened to reestablish the universal writer and reader—woman this time. The French theorists' psychoanalysis unsettled this universal (yet notably American) reader and writer by emphasizing bisexuality, desire, plurality, and diffuseness. In her talk "Gender and Language," Erica Hunt articulates two additional correctives from queer theorists and Black feminists: to consider "Gender as a set of signs which we tend to forget are arbitrary" and to "look at how race...informs our language." I see this anthology as an ongoing practice of restitution, recuperation, and revision. But more significantly and uniquely, this anthology, and the outrider lineage from which it comes, is a practice of refusal, a refusal of closure and reification that pushes language to its limits, as Jane Augustine says in her talk on Clarice Lispector. One of my favorite pieces in the anthology is a conversation (experimental women's writing is multivocal and participatory). Jane Augustine discusses H.D.'s mysticism, but Diane DiPrima and Anne Waldman occasionally interject so that I feel I am witnessing a convening straight out of H.D.'s mysticism—are these the three fates, a palimpsest of voices, the incarnations of Mary? Yes, probably.

J'Lyn Chapman

Embodied Unconscious

the feminine space of sexuality, surrealism, and experimentation in literature

An anthology from the Naropa archive

Edited and with an Introduction by
C. M. Chady

Spuyten Duyvil
New York City

ISBN 978-1-959556-45-9

Cover art is "Surreal Scene" by Mina Loy,

courtesy of Roger Conover, for the Estate of Mina Loy.

Library of Congress Cataloging-in-Publication Data

Names: Chady, C. M., editor. | Jack Kerouac School of Disembodied Poetics.
Title: Embodied unconscious : the feminine space of sexuality, surrealism, and experimentation in literature / edited and with an introduction by C.M. Chady.
Description: New York City : Spuyten Duyvil, 2023. | "An anthology from the Naropa archive" | Includes bibliographical references and index.
Identifiers: LCCN 2023034850 | ISBN 9781959556459 (paperback)
Subjects: LCSH: Women and literature. | Feminism in literature. | Poetics. | Surrealism (Literature) | Literature, Experimental--Women authors--History and criticism. | LCGFT: Literary criticism. | Lectures. | Essays.
Classification: LCC PN481 .E45 2023 | DDC 809/.987082--dc23/eng/20230928
LC record available at https://lccn.loc.gov/2023034850

Surrealism and the Unconscious:

Navigating Embodied Unconscious

a note on the text

C. M. Chady

What begins as a rupture, an opening, a gash through which light bleeds, carried within language. The resonance of a feminine space that ripples through every atom; every syllable transformed into action. The transfer of one's lived experience through the body, committed to writing, transmitted through lecture. Throughout this anthology, we experience how the writers, lecturers, and contributors within expand upon ideas of what creates a feminine space in literature and how we as well might cultivate it. These are ideas that arise not only of the mind, but through their embodied presence. How do women write a world that is not only through and of their body, but one that allows for an expanse of newness?

The anthology began with that opening of light, as somewhere in my chest I felt energy and potential rise and buoy. I first listened to Jane Augustine's lecture on H.D. interwoven with Hélène Cixous' feminist theory entirely enamored, both by my lack of knowing and the way in which that lack was filled and overflowed. Admittedly, this was my first encounter with H.D.'s work. The title and abstract had initially gained my attention, inspiring my curiosity of mysticism and feminism intermingling. Once I saw the clever ways she reclaimed and constructed a world that incorporated a feminine vision, I realized that this was much more than a chance encounter. The ways in which her world reconstruction occurred inspired me to think more deeply about the feminist theory I had encountered thus far, the women writers I had read, and moreover, those I had yet to discover. Even more remained to explore the impact and legacy of what it meant to write through language that emerged from women's experience, wrapped up in their physical and emotional experiences of sexuality, gender, and life in general. There was something much deeper, more involved, more embodied, more intimate to become immersed in that set the course for this anthology to come to fruition.

I set out to find additional accompanying lectures. Who should join the conversation? How might ideas from different lecturers, different writers across time and space come together to show how language has mobilized us through the twentieth century and into the twenty-first? While this began as an assignment for my MFA Creative Writing and Poetics during the Jack Kerouac School's Summer Writing Program where we were each asked to do an audio transcription from the archive and accompany it with an introduction, I found that it needed to become more than that. The archive had much more to say to us, and many of my fellow classmates felt a similar magnetism to the work they were encountering. During my search, many of Jane Augustine's lectures and classes during her time at the Summer Writing Program were among the first to emerge. Each was more eloquent and stimulating than the last as I began to craft the overall list for the anthology. I rounded it out with lectures highlighting recurring prominent figures such as Gertrude Stein and created space for women whose work has been vastly influential but somehow have not shared the same historic notoriety, such as H.D. or Mina Loy. Together, through their intricate and intersecting attention to linguistics, history, myth, and experience, they cultivate expressive feminine language.

The innovative and radical potential that resides within the lectures and work called to me to engage with them, to bring them together for this ongoing conversation. I wondered what it meant to cultivate a feminine space in writing and beyond. What form does feminine space and creation take? The answer pleasantly is that it does not adhere to any singular definition, rather, it arises out of the need to write of, through, and by a feminine experience unique to each individual in a world that is vastly male dominated. Language itself is rooted in gender; all those who engage in the art of writing fall into implicit performance of words. Every act of writing is an act of unwriting and reorienting. The writers featured here showcase this mentality as they create new traditions in literature, traditions that pave the way for continued innovative work that too often do not receive the kudos credited to them.

It is by no means news to note that women have historically been underrepresented in literature, art, and beyond. The transcribers and I have held conversations outside what is printed about the anthology, its ideas, and its impact. Many of us noted that while the lectures and classes within highlight women writers of modernity, often times they are still given definition by the men who surrounded their work. With talks from the 70s, 80s, and 90s, we wonder to ourselves how far we have come. Will these women forever be defined by the men in their lives—their husbands, their lovers, their contemporary artists and writers—and the way their work arose by comparison to male traditions, or will they begin to hold their own space with their creative legacy as a beacon? Throughout the anthology, we recognize some of these moments of short fallings, of the habits of thought and speak we fall into, and we challenge them as a means to understand each writer through her work and radiant mind.

While this anthology certainly addresses this historic lack, it mobilizes further to showcase how modern women writers not only stepped into their craft, but how they shaped a realm of literature for their experiences to live. The modes of patriarchal traditions did not fit their narrative, did not give them the tools to write their organic self. What resulted was pure innovation, out of necessity and creativity. Gertrude Stein questioned the foundations of language and broke from any known conventions in order to create language to express female pleasure. H.D. reclaimed history, myth, and religion that have always centered around male narratives and reclaimed them in a feminine perspective. Mina Loy parted from punctuation, delving into forms that were novel that today we take for granted as commonplace. Especially during their times, their work departed from the norm, and consciousness followed suit. As their forms and content explored what it meant to be a woman writing woman, they constructed a new world that allowed for that conversation and expression to ensure. As Cixous notes, that women must write of themselves to inspire other women to write of themselves, and so the cycle continues and brings us to the contemporary day.

What I found most striking in listening to all the recordings, is how resonant their lives and creative works are with the modern day. They lived through wars and personal hardships. They loved and lost. They write into the atrocity and hope of humanity. They unleash new uses of language that expand perceptions of the world. Through each of their narratives, a gateway is opened where we might peer inside their lives and works for a moment and trace the. We feel time close in on itself; the past no longer seems so distant. The reflections and visions still hold their vibrancy and only continue to enhance their potency.

To make the content within the anthology more potent and urgent, its inception occurred in a time of uncertainty and anxiety. In the summer of 2020, we were forced to self-isolate due to the pandemic, the United States erupted in protest over continued police brutality, an election loomed on the near horizon after a tumultuous four years, and climate change became ever more pressing. Everything seemed to be happening all at once, and moreover, the "normal" that everyone seemed so accustomed to was disrupted and our ability to adapt to change challenged. We began to see the flaws in our institutions illuminated tenfold; we questioned how we treated each other and our essential workers. We questioned what it meant to make art when it felt like the world around us was imploding. All of this coagulated around the anthology. It became more urgent than ever to assess that ways that we might conceptualize our society, institutions, discourse, and creative endeavors differently. How could a time of upheaval allow us to see beyond the rigid linearity we were trapped in and see a world that operated more holistically and inclusively? What would it look like for the world itself to enter a feminine space that might open?

We held onto our own ponderings of the world, our position within it, our potential to change it, as we transcribed each of the works and wrote our interludes. It was ever more vital during this time where we could not be together in physical space, that we connected intellectually and emotionally. The anthology was a foundation of community within a creative lineage. We could be together even when we were apart assessing, discussing, and writing alongside voices from the past. Our conversations had a space to manifest that gave language to the experiences that we felt within ourselves, that had been felt throughout the years through others. Time seemed to repeat itself as we entered a new iteration of discourse and saw running parallels.

While the anthology contributors each took primary responsibility for a section transcription and its relative interlude, overall, we wanted to embrace a more feminine mode of exchange that emphasized community, collaboration, and horizontal organization. Our process mirrored the feminine space of literature we sought to evoke through engaging with the archive. We met a few times to discuss the ideas that were emerging from the archive, and how we saw them intersecting with our own lives and experiences in the present. This connectivity allowed us to view recurring and mingling ideas across the anthology among sections, just as an actual conversation might unfold. Concepts resonated across sections and evolved in their intricacies.

Moreover, each interlude itself is the result of approaching the writing as an act of conversing with the archived recording. Each interlude comes in a form unique to the person writing it, some more grounded and scholarly, others more experimental and conceptual. As contributors transcribed and listened, they were not only looking for the ideas that flourished from these sessions, but the ways in which they experience these ideas through their own creation, and moreover, life itself. How are ideas within the lectures still present within our lives? How are they embodied? Why are these recordings not just of the past, but very much of the present? The interludes as a result are each individual's conversation with the archive—their own resonance and interpretation contributing to an overarching conversation that started before our own lives began. We bring them forward in the conversation to see the ways in which women writers have been expressing their experiences, how their lives have fueled their creative work. They are our matriarchs and peers. We contribute to the lineage as it becomes us, forever entwining us with ideas of the past, present, and future.

As we wanted the anthology as a whole to reflect the spirit of the Jack Kerouac School's Summer Writing Program, where visiting writers and artists share through class, lecture, and conversation and sparks of creativity ignite something larger in collective consciousness, each piece of the anthology reflects this. The lectures share ideas from past SWP programming, the interludes show our interaction, and the writing prompts invite creation. We see ourselves inextricably linked as thinkers, writers, teachers, and students, both within ourselves and with one another. It is our hope that the anthology perpetuates the conversation and extends the legacy of our community.

During my time working with the anthology, I have felt the presence of women in the archive with me as I think and write. There is something about the Naropa Archive that fosters such immersive work. The audio recordings themselves are ever present, always waiting for another encounter. Every time I played the recordings, the room filled with voices from the past washing over me. I would often rewind to repeat a phrase that was particularly resonant, allowing the words to repeat, like an incantation. Experience of time stretched and circular. As Diane di Prima states in a following lecture, once a syllable is uttered, it is forever present in the atmosphere. Every word stretched thin into one unifying sound, like an *om*. Our language is in the essence of the airwaves, eternal in the ether. What was, is, and will be. Every word engulfs us. We are carried in sonic and language, cocooned as we catalyst the future. The lecturers pull writers from history, just as we pull their voices from the past into this present anthology. Together, we foster a continual conversation, one that shows how our ideas evolve and cycle. We are living on the same earth, breathing the same air, reading the same words, and writing our new visions. We are a connected lineage. By reading and engaging with this anthology, you too may join us.

Embodied Unconscious

What is in a name?

Linguistically engrained gender and sexuality

Interlude by C. M. Chady

As with all beginnings, we start with an introduction. An introduction and orientation to the self and environment. Who are we and who are we in relation to other people? Jane Augustine opens her lecture with the usual expected introductions from participating students, but then asks them to go beyond the surface recognition of *this is my name, this is who I am,* to recognize the underlying implications within a name. Much of this has to do with innate gendering within a name or the tendency toward a patriarchal lineage per most western tradition. As she states boldly, "Your name is a sexual identity."

As our name becomes a label to the self, we are inextricably linked to whatever sexual identity our name provides us, and thus, become tethered to it within society unless we navigate our ways around it. I was immediately struck by this, contemplating my personal relationship to my own name, as well as the reason my parents, especially my mother, were interested in my being named as I am.

My first name is Christina, which you may not know since I publish under C. M. Chady. The ending of "tina," the feminine "a" that pleasantly lifts at the end of the word, clearly and distinctly labels me as sexually a woman. It automatically gives you a vague silhouette of who I might be as a person, generally physical features you'd be expecting, what my position in society might be, perhaps even guiding you to jump to conclusions about my interests or style. However, had I written that my name was Christopher, your mind would race to the other end of the vague silhouette, generally guided by your expectations of who I might be as a man. Because my name has always been so closely and obviously a feminine version of an otherwise same name, it has always clearly labeled me as "feminine" and as "woman" when I go by my full name.

Yet, if you know me, you know that I do not. Since I was thirteen, I have gone by Chris, an androgynous nickname. At the time, I was merely finding myself, claiming a name that my younger self had not gone by, in order to forge a new way forward in identity. Yet by doing this, I unknowingly shifted people's expectations of who I was as a person. One of my friends who I met during high school theatre saw my name before she met me: Chris. She was expecting to be working with a guy, until I showed up and introduced myself. It's amusing to see the ways that even with a supposedly androgynous nickname still carries with it an inclination toward assuming if someone is a Chris they are more likely to be a male than female. If you're a woman abbreviating, you're likely a Christy, Chrissy, or Tina, something that maintains the feminine delineation. Even in classes as I grew up, there were more guy Chris's than girl Chris's, which I proudly triumphed. It was something about being myself while subverting their gendered expectations that gave me a strange rise.

And yet by going by "Chris," I was doing exactly what my mother had intended for my name to be able to do. I was able to sink into a world that was not entirely ruled by sex and gender—I could be anything and everything. Working in business, she knew that people might form expectations and stereotypes if I presented myself as Christina, but with Chris, I could cleverly navigate a system without the sticky labels—more precisely, a male-dominant system with subconscious prejudices.

I mention this story to uphold the gendered charge that language contains. Augustine delves deeper into its implications in her following class discussion. Yet it is not only within names, but across all of language, that gender and sexuality manifest, even below our conscious awareness that shapes who we consider ourselves and the world around us. We can either fall into the performance and assumptions of such language, or we can be brought to full awareness of how it operates so we can see the ways in which meaning and power have been created and upheld across language and society.

The writers discussed within this anthology work both consciously and subconsciously on the implications of a gendered language. Certainly, writing throughout the twentieth century, with the rise of feminism and push for gender equality, the impact of sexuality and gender on not only writing but life itself would have been ever present. As Augustine states, "Life and writing are not separate." The oppression and limitations faced in life were navigated and worked out through their writing. Many of them followed non-traditional feminine roles; some were lesbian or bi-sexual; others abandoned motherly roles in order to fulfill their life as a writer, a move that might be deemed more traditionally masculine or certainly less scrutinized by society for male counterparts. As they worked through a society where they lived through their sexuality and gendered experiences, so too do these influences enter into their encounters with language itself. Writing became a mode of de-creation and re-creation as they toyed with ideas of what a version of writing of and through a woman's body and experience would look like in the world. They were constantly constructing a feminine space outside of a patriarchal canon and language that simply didn't work.

Most impressive is the innovation that occurred because of these limitations. The women of this anthology no longer had language that suited what they were wishing to express, and so they created their own. For example, Gertrude Stein will explore how to present the female orgasm in text; H. D. will reimagine myth with matriarchal lineage. In each of their writings, in their own unique method, each is returning to the origin of language itself, how we construct words, how words have gained their meaning, how we can twist meaning upon itself for deeper understanding and expansion. This devotion to language's intricacies allowed for the blossoming of new era of philosophy. The women within this anthology are just the beginning of not only the new language, but the new mode of thought that was able to spring from this new language, to generate a more gracious and full understanding of how our realities are lived.

Our realities are shaped through language. Every word uttered—its connotation, its origin, its history—surrounds us with the lens through which we view the world. Becoming aware of this allows us to see the deeper workings within our minds, and moreover, allows us to break down more rigid or even oppressive modes of thought for that which is bursting with potential. The feminine space of language gifts us that space of expansiveness and inclusivity—so as we enter into the first section of the anthology, I invite you to experiment with a "beginner's mind," encountering the information as if for the first time. See what happens if you let your predisposition of language and assumptions of its functions fall to the side. Engage with the ideas presented in the lectures, feel how they resonate within the body, and reflect on how you have experienced it within your own life. Where are our walls of comfort and how do we see outside them to encompass an unending horizons? How can we too rejuvenate language to reflect our lives? The writers of this anthology have shown us the limitless nature of language if we are clever enough to see it. Through this act of living and writing, we forge new language and thought, and thus a new potential for reality.

Writing is inseparable from our lives; our lives inseparable from writing.

Gender/Self Contradiction

Lecture by Jane Augustine
July 15, 1991

Transcription by C. M. Chady

Jane Augustine: I would like to find out who you are. You read the catalog; you know a little bit about me, Jane Augustine, which sometimes is enough. I think a lot about names, too, as connected with the issues of this week. Your name is a sexual identity.

I know a Vietnamese girl who entered college and was under her Vietnamese name, and she was assigned a roommate who was male because the people reading her documents didn't recognize a Vietnamese name that is associated with women. She became very good friends with him, that man, but it was a typical confusion, and we don't usually think it's not the kind of thing that happens to English-speaking women who we know. Which usually, we know which names are male names or female.

(Students introduce themselves.)

It's fashion, particularly in the West and even in New York where I live in the wintertime, but in the West, particularly just to use people's first names. I'm a little uncertain about that as a practice. Remember that slaves in the south were never allowed to add a family name, and I think that that was a shameful deprivation. We'll come back to the question of the fact that it's usually your father's name, that last name that you've got in your family is identified by the father's name, and that raises lots of complicated feelings for mothers, but I like people to introduce themselves by their full name because it's a reminder, that you also have a Malaysian family and you come from something, and that's part of your identity. However you feel about it, how complicated that may be, however you dissociate yourself from it, because after all, you are not simply a representative of you. That name is part of it, but not part. So, we will come to the ambiguity of words and what that relation to words really is, which is the bottom line.

Nobody gave me a class list. But I think a lot about names, particularly for women.

Because I want to be radical, I want to go back to the root, and the root of the fact is that if you really look at your father's assertion as the identifying name for your family, who, of course, is just as much your mother's family as your father's.

So, I really wanted to start with that. And then I can turn off the tape recorder at this point—I really wanted to let you write for five minutes and use this.

(Students free write while recording is temporarily off. Afterward, students share their responses.)

Student 1: I hope I can read my writing. When I think gender, I think of separation. I also think of identity and I get angry. The marginalization makes me angry. When names appear, gender is immediately put into the mind. And no doubt I'll say it appears to be a man's world, by this I mean men dictate how things will basically be. The marginalization makes me think of the moment that typically women's voices are in the margin of man's dictates about gender, about sexuality. Another thought, however, comes to mind, and that is that women, many women, including myself, oftentimes feel comfortable being in the margin. I can say I feel comfortable today, however, when I write, when I teach, when I think, I like to be free of gender, sexuality, and all that stuff. I do believe each of us is part of both genders, that we each share maleness and femaleness. Finding our way in balance with this is the problem. Coming out of the margin is a problem for me and one I wrestle with. It interferes with my writing, it blocks my writing, it blocks my thoughts being...and then I stop.

Augustine: Did anyone else have similar feelings or the opposite? Women are a part of both genders...

Student 2: I had that feeling, but it's not the first thing that came to my mind. My quickest response to gender, sexuality, marginalization: the politics of sexuality and gender identity is a pervasive condition of patriarchy, which is a mild term for male supremacy. As a gay male I am an oppressed member of an intolerant society, but beyond my own daily struggle with sexual politics, I see the psychological, spiritual, emotional, and physical control non-males as a fundamental cause for the violence, environmental assault, and energy imbalance on our planet today. It is a hardy tradition, one that has been building for over 5,000 years, but this supremacy, or for that matter, any hierarchical system of dominance, is not inevitable and it's not the only condition in which humans live. For example, I believe the end of these old ways of thinking and being must become obsolete if we are to survive and if our planet is to survive.

Augustine: Thank you, it's a good connection. That the... It's even hard to find the right word. Patriarchy is the historical term, but I find the politics so touchy that I am often saying I can never say male supremacy, you know.

Student 2: Why? Too radical?

Augustine: Too... boogies. I'll get bumped off. I'll get shot down before my discourse is heard, so I tend to say male dominant society.

But yes. Do you want to read to us?

Student 3: Basically, it's kind of been said already, the only other thing I have in here is...

Augustine: But let's hear it in your own words, which are not quite like mine. We are establishing community.

Student 3: This is to bring up stereotypes that are associated with one's gender. That a woman writer is labeled a woman writer, not just a writer, as male writers are just writers. Stereotypes associated with women writers are abundant, such as the idea that when there are women writers, they write sentimental love stories, etc. The thing that I think would be brought up this week would be the most successful artists are white males, so we can analyze this as problematic, read into the open forefront, and something else that I think would be important to talk about, are there are clearly differences in male and female writing? What is untouchable for women want to write about the double standards. Like, for instance, the movie Thelma and Louise, women shoot someone and then the woman is fascist, whereas, Rambo killed 100 people and so on—the standards in that area.

Augustine: Yes. Okay. Are there even words you just kind of jotted down also, fragments and quick questions and issues that come to mind either. I'm paraphrasing you. Are there questions, are there really differences? Are there differences, and of course there are, because these women oppressed so we're talking about other things. But I think someone is still talking about their oppression, whereas men aren't. Some men are.

Student 2: And I think even straight men are oppressed by their own system. We're all oppressed by it, strangely enough...

Student 3: Yeah. I'm starting to see that come out now in the cover of *Newsweek magazine*. Did you see it? A month ago. It showed, men like a man on the front cover with no shirt on and like a tie and the article is about men doing sweat huts and going out into the wilderness, you know. Starting to deal with their own oppression.

Augustine: But are they? That's another good question.

However, that there is some kind of system going that is oppressive to individuals in their individual development as human beings and artists, since it seems hard to argue with. But on the other hand, that is a big generalization and it seems to me that there is a lot more going on than, yes, there is an oppressive system, but no, there's more going on in the world.

But I like the issues that you raised, and you implicitly raised the issue of success: what is success, what is a success for an artist? Where does that come from? What does that mean? Who decides it? And I think that's the issue.

Student 4: I'm just jotting down some notes too.

Augustine: Why don't you read them? You don't have to apologize and you don't have to call it writing, and maybe it's not. I felt this very strongly myself. Somebody says, *write,* and something else happens when somebody says, *talk*. I think we need to examine that transition because I think it's a very, very important part. Writing is related to voice and how you feel you can use the language for what you feel you have to do, particularly if you admire writers and want to want to be one, and are particularly moved by words, then there is a little bit of a paradox. So we don't need to apologize. And I would love to hear you in your own words.

Student 4: The issue here would be that of one sex type with preference in terms of one's place in society, the issue of being on the edge of society as a token member of the women and minorities in the world. The place in society gender scribes for man or woman by virtue of their respective sexes. Sex validity is a point of departure for discrimination were displayed and lived out of partnerships that are unsanctioned by marriage or society, marginalization of the periphery that bordered the outside, not quite a part of by virtue of race, gender, class, sex preference.

Augustine: I think that you are bringing up a good point that we will touch on later too that the extent to which the whole of society, all the institutions are geared to certain kinds of partnerships, not to other kinds of partnerships. This is not simply on the personal level, though institutionalized heterosexuality is something that Adrienne Rich particularly discussed first in her book, which she discussed it a lot, but in *Of Woman Born: Motherhood as Institution and Experience*. That title has always been useful to me because I feel that as a writer and as human being, I must champion experience, and institutions are guiding our experience and they will lie specifically for, in refusing to recognize that two people of the same sex may want to be together intimately and form a household.

The notion then that marriage, that horrible institution. I'm married; I've married twice. My present husband would say the worst thing I ever did to him was marry him. I said, all right, we'll get a divorce. But no, we like to be together and we're not having the children. We're not transferring property. And so, marriage, heterosexual marriage is a horrible, horrible institution. And it's very hard for individuals to make that institution what they want. It's very hard for a woman to marry a woman, (indistinguishable). I know women married to women and divorced from them, but they had to make their vows privately. And the same is true to men who want to be together and surrounding all the partnerships, well, I'll call them homosexual partnerships just to distinguish them from heterosexual, and that will include gay men and lesbians, just so it's easy to refer to. Unsanctioned partnerships. Our efforts to isolate individuals and you can be friends with someone of your own sex, but you better not be intimate.

One of the first points that I want to make in today's discussion is in relation to sexuality.

But Lorelai, would you read?

Student 5: Basically, I have the same thing.

Augustine: No, I don't think so. I think that we have ideas in common, but we have each, your word is your fingerprint.

Student 5: I just said margin, pushed aside, on the outside. Definition makes them genitalia and sex organs. I think of Christianity and Western thought on male-female roles, including one's sexuality, heterosexism, fear of sex, fear of the sexually free. Sex, is property a basis for ownership, monogamy, more fear and insecurity, how that shapes our lives our outlook or self-esteem. I think of feminism specifically women trying to change the way women are viewed and consequently view themselves, trying to break women out of the confinements of the male gaze. I think of politics, of the political language I used on this piece of paper and what those words mean in my everyday life and my daily experiences. Do those words make me stand up to the checkout clerk who calls me honey or an auto mechanic who refuses to believe that I can change my own oil? And then I stop.

Augustine: Thank you. Actually, obviously, we're hitting it, and that's what I would like to see happen.

The point that seems clearest in Lorelei's list of, would you read it, again, sort of starting from, well, not part of the text, but then you list sex, sexuality, definition by genitalia is a nice list in there. Would you read that list again?

Student 5: I'll start from the beginning. I'm not quite sure where you want it to start. I said: margin pushed aside, on the outside, not part of the text, not looked at, directly ignored, gender masculine-feminine, dividing, separating, not mixing. Definition based on genitalia, on sex organs. I think of Christianity and Western thought on male-female roles, including on sexuality, heterosexism, fear of sex...

Augustine: Heterosexism as established by Christianity. That's very important. Wilton mentioned the environment and violence, social violence, the influence of religion.

Fear of sex, fear of the sexually free. Sex is property and basis for ownership, monogamy, more fear and insecurity, how that shapes our lives, our outlook, our self-esteem.

And you use the word feminism. For many years, I taught a course on the basic feminist books at the New School and one of the assignments that I always gave sort of early in the semester... We can still play this game, it's fun. You're sitting around with a bunch of people and you dropped the word feminist or feminism in some casual way. You're just talking with someone. You don't even go so far as to say, I'm taking a course with a feminist writer or a course in feminism. But you just say that some idea is feminist, or that you're interested in Feminism. Then I say, hold onto your hat and watch how people react. Okay, I wasn't doing that in 1975 and the people are still doing it. And I still get very funny reactions just from using the word Feminism.

Okay, here I am. I'm a feminist scholar and writer, and I will say more about it, this connection in this afternoon's panel on Shakespeare's sisters, but the first thing that I am doing with you—I have a Ph.D., I have spent my time dedicating myself to writing.

Student 4: And I think you're talking about feminism and dropping that word, in other words, that even more people get more upset about. You know, if you were to say "gay" in certain circles, even that word, which I used to commonly in writing in my own generation, but it's as though it's impolite. It's as though you said something that's offensive (another student interjects, agrees) Exactly! It's very offensive.

Augustine: Sex determines everything that we... sex and gender have some bearing on almost every aspect of our experience. I say, almost, because I think it's very important to understand that there is something that is not under the thumb of genderized thinking, which you have all one way or another emphasized as separating you off, separating us off, separating us from one another, from our chosen friends and partners, from our own identity and self-esteem and self-understanding. Gender issues are in the air and they're very divisive and there is something that is not. I am asserting in this course description, the gender self-contradiction, I am asserting that there is something in the self that need not be contaminated by gender thinking, and I am going to stress how what we think is due to a very large degree, our experience, and yet we need also to be aware that we are constructing our thoughts in a particular way and that there are many forces urging us to construct our thoughts about gender and gender relations. We need to examine what those forces are and how they impinge on our actual understanding of ourselves as human beings and therefore as writers. Life and writing are not separate. I started you out by quick-thought first writing so that you would be very close to your own voice.

We... You do not want to be separated from. You don't want to separate your writing self and your real self and the gender thoughts that are that come to us often get in the way. So, but what I had been seeing as happening, and in my own quick writing, and as we were talking, I realized that I am expressing continually my own hesitations, the words I feel I can't use, the difficulties that I encounter as I start to write. Well, I wrote a doctoral dissertation on H.D., and I framed that within the context of the feminist literary critics' desire to get better readings of women writers. But actually, I didn't say that in the dissertation, and in fact, my original dissertation supervisor, a famous man in New York circles, he had liked me very much as a student and he approved my idea to write a doctoral dissertation on Henry James, and when I switched to H.D., he wrote a series of maneuvers, dumped me, told me I had to find another supervisor, and furthermore, I had to find a phony excuse... I could not... fortunately, the famous man was retired so I could go to someone else and say X is retired now, and he doesn't want to supervise students, so would you please, Professor Y, who happened to be a friend of mine, who happened to be sympathetic to the general area of women in Modernism, so

I could begin to write what I wanted to write about, a lesser known women instead of canon, a canonized man. Well, this is a story which could be told by many and has been told many women who want to earn a living and survive and contribute to the job of women living and surviving and being read writers.

I wanted to tell another story. Just in early June, I went to a reading by a lesbian poet, a poet who is a lesbian. I'm not sure that it's quite right; I don't quite like that identity. It's a little bit like a woman writer, but Joan Larkin is a wonderful poet and a good person who was giving her reading. She told a story that she had been at the conference in San Francisco sometime last winter, I think called Outright, I believe. It was a conference of gay and lesbian writers in San Francisco. So the conference took place in the Hiltons, some large hotel in San Francisco where there were all kinds of people coming and going, and Joan was stopped by some other person who was staying in the hotel, who said something like, "I don't understand what's going on here. There seems to be some kind of group of writers? Can you tell me what this organization is that's what's meeting here? And it seems to be called Outright, what does that mean?" And Joan said that she sort of stammered and said, "Well, actually, it's a group of gay writers," and she said afterwards, she was telling the story in the course of her reading, she said, I couldn't...I was ashamed afterwards. I couldn't really say lesbian. It's still difficult for me, she said, to put that identity on herself.

And I think that she was feeling that that was something that would separate her from the world, the human world, by making so fixed the category of gender that, while at the same time that she doesn't want it, she's quite open. She's been married. She teaches at Brooklyn College.

There was that difficulty, there was some kind of forbidden word, and it was a loaded situation, even for someone who has dealt very thoroughly with her sexuality, who has come out, but who is still pained by the separation. So I feel that we have an identity problem.

Student 4: Sometimes the different people separate and there's no reason for it. When I think in my mind, of why it should be that everybody has to segregate off their own group. It's nice sometimes to be obviously among one type or whatever you want to say, but I think that the notion that everything is so divided according to groups and this in and out feeling, I think it's ridiculous. I don't even understand, it's like the dominant society, which is heterosexual and a part of the, you know, both work and corporate whatever dictates, it seems like to me, to every other grouping that you're pushed out here on the periphery, and just by virtue of a difference.

Augustine: Yes, the difference is, actually, whenever anybody feels like using it against you, they do. And why does different have to equal separate, different from what?

Student 1: And why does it have to be sexual? I think, *This is my friend Mary, she's heterosexual.* We never said that, right? Or this is John... It's like I have one of my best friends as well. I have to say he's gay so I can use the point here. But my husband for a while, until I said John is gay, it was a problem, and I thought, why? I don't know why that is. I mean, I just really, I don't know why. Well, I do know why, this is the way society is. Why is it okay for me to have a friend, a male friend who is gay, but it's not okay for me to have a friend who is not gay unless he is sexually involved? I mean, we have to get to the basis of sex, you know? So let's not talk about John the person, let's talk about his sex habits, and then we can get to the you know.

Augustine: Why do you think that is?

Student 3: It's control. It started a long time ago, I don't know when exactly, but we wanted heterosexual couples to procreate in the dark bedroom and keep this up for population reasons. Yeah, and that's simply what it is. It's to keep the world.

Augustine: Oh, well, we need to have more people on the planet. We would like people to be born. People need to be parents.

Student 3: And that was considered the job, moral job to do.

Augustine: Yes.

Student 3: In order to keep order in society, and if people were sexually liberated, they'd be going out and they'd be liberated in other ways as well...

Augustine: Sex is anarchic. It's individual. It does not consider… sexual attraction, actually, has to be highly regulated. So societies… one of its beginnings was to regulate. The society is very interested in how it's reproduced and what is reproduced. Ideas are reproduced. But women were simply property for a long time under... the patriarchy is very, very ancient too. It's also hard to say where patriarchy came from or whether there was ever a matriarchy; the only evidence is mythological, and that evidence is largely negative. When Marduk defeated the Goddess of the Sky Tiamat and stamped her out, we have some mythic evidence that a matriarchy base decides.

Student 2: But there's evidence that there's a non-patriarchy, with the absence of a matriarchy like the Adam Creed?

Augustine: Yes.

Student 2: Where there was no hierarchical... of cooperatives, partnerships society, instead of a dominant society based on...

Augustine: In isolated cases.

Student 2: Fair enough.

Augustine: Because we know we don't have to have patriarchy.

Student 5: There are Native American societies that are matrilineal and that have power shares between men and women. What the men and what women is dictated differently, but it's an equal power share.

Student 3: In African too, some parts of Africa, very small, but there are parts where the women are the ones who are the judges and stuff. If men have done something wrong, like swore at someone, or you know, raped someone or did something they weren't supposed to, women dress up in a traditional costume and go and take the person out of their hut and scare them. Yeah, they are like the Supreme Court.

Augustine: Well, we know that there were, the biblical evidence is that there were women judges in ancient Israel, Deborah (hard to distinguish on audio) the judge was the (hard to distinguish word). There were some concept of justice and that the whole thing could be journed fairly. In the very earliest written records of the temples in Asia Minor, there was differential feeding, women were given less food from the common storehouses 10,000 years ago, the records of the distribution of grain, that men got more women.

And it seems to be possible that 10,000 years of differential feeding may account for the genetic difference that women are in general, statistically smaller in body. The biological argument has often been that men dominate because women are smaller and that has transformed women into property, and the purpose of having the woman was to reproduce your male self in order to hand your wealth and extend your life. So this sense of the woman not having a true self, but being a piece of property like the animals.

Well, yes, the woman is a piece of property to produce the children who are property. That depersonalization of women is very ancient, very ramified, and it has the particular consequences that I wanted to just give you some information about in terms of contemporary psychoanalytic theory, particularly. Now, probably all of you have heard Freud's famous statement, it was really a question, what do women want? It's a wonderful question because it implies that all women were to him enigmatic and that he could not possibly imagine that women could want what men want.

If you think about Freud's Oedipus complex, the Oedipus complex is the situation in which the male child, growing up, begins to emulate the father but eventually finds the father a competitor. Freud's theories of infantile sexuality really apply only to male children: the male child falls in love, wants to possess the mother, sexually, and wants to kill the father, and Freud's feeling that these were the emotions of an infant he felt reflected in the Oedipus myth, which was the basis of Socrates' play. Freud thought that on the basis of civilization was the evolution of the young man through the Oedipus Complex to discover his incestuous wishes towards his mother and his desires, murderous wishes for his father, and having recognized and conquered both of those impulses, he could then have an integrated ego or self which creates culture and civilization.

I'm oversimplifying it, but basically that notion has pervaded Freudian psychoanalysis and all of the psychological theories and systems that have followed.

Many of these systems of thought, ways of thinking about the psyche of this older person have contributed and continue to contribute to the notions that there's masculine and feminine appropriate behavior for men and women, and that if you start studying those prescriptions for appropriate behavior, for masculinity and femininity, you see that.

Masculine and feminine behavior is the ultimate form of control that we talked about. And the prescription of what psychological femininity is enough to drive any right-thinking man right up the wall. Because all of those prescriptions for femininity would forbid me from being here to talk to you, and I might have been here 30 years earlier, if I had felt the first group. Took me a long time growing up in the 40s and 50s, to realize the problem. I did not know myself. I did not know myself, period. I did not know how I had it.

Raised by perfectly loving parents who appreciated my intelligence and to downgrade it, ignore and fail to act on all of my sources as an individual, which are nothing special. They are the sources that are going on.

But conventional feminine, conventional ideals of feminine behavior, the appropriate behavior for women are very intuitive to the right (indistinguishable). Virginia Woolf said the first thing you must do is kill the angel in the house, the loving mother who takes care of you. And the angel, of course, is Christian. It's a Christian reference. It shows the degree to which patriarchal religion has contributed to our... Well, religion is a source of ultimate authority. Religion has really been supplanted, if there's cultural backdrop and Christianity and Judaism, it's really been supplanted by science and particularly psychoanalysis, so I'm circling back to the notions of the self as presented by Freud and in contemporary literary critical theory.

In France, particularly, the issues of gender have been discussed. I want to give you a source book which has a brief excerpt from Jacques Lacan, the psychoanalyst literary critic who is the one in the past 20-30 years, he's dead now, but he is a chief formulator of the psychoanalytic approach to literary criticism. He says the nature of things and the nature of words are the same, and that women are excluded from the nature of things, definition of genitalia, and therefore, they're excluded from the nature of words, therefore they don't know what they're saying and furthermore, he says they don't know.

This is not in the excerpt that I will give you, but he says women don't know themselves. In other words, a woman cannot be philosophically a subject.

You know what I mean by the word subject? Philosophically means, the one who possess the subjectivity, who knows one's self capable of knowing one's self. So after the modern period French, psychoanalytic literary theory says all life is a text, and women, by the nature of the text that the nature of things, are excluded from it. Fundamentally, this idea is based on Freud's original notion that women don't participate in the Oedipus Complex and therefore are not makers of culture.

Maddening beyond belief to anyone who *thinks*, to any woman who *thinks*, and we all *think*, but we have also been told that we are total feeling.

Now, the Buddhist detail I'm also going to discuss with you because it's detailed and thought provoking. The Buddhist position is that emotions are actually a highly charged form of thought. The Western dichotomy between the thought and feeling is not recognized in Buddhist psychology, which comes from a completely different base.

Emotions are highly charged thoughts. Which is what they are. They are so highly charged that we feel them through our whole body—lust, rage, and fear—but they are conceptualized. Our minds make them just as they make our more rational thoughts.

But you should be as writers, familiar with the basic way in which elegantly, intellectually, the patriarchal status quo was reinforced by philosophical thinking based on the developments of psychoanalysis.

As for principally in France, interpreted by Jacques Lacan, but combated by, opposed by, three women philosopher, literary critics, Hélène Cixous—I'll tell you more about these women as I give you this source—Luce Irigaray and Julia Kristeva.

I'll tell you a little bit about each of these women. Hélène Cixous is the most radical and least acceptable to the male establishment of these writers. She is bisexual. Actually, her more recent writing, *The Book of Promethea,* which has just been translated, is the story of her love for another woman, very involved with how you write about it.

Cixous is also of very mixed ancestry. Born in Algeria, which was a French colony, and she's partly Jewish, partly a little European. She wrote an enormous doctoral dissertation on James Joyce. She is a novelist and playwright as well as a literary critic. Her most philosophical work on women, what I'll give you an excerpt from is called *The Newly Born Woman*. That's the translation in English, and it's a little paperback. I'm giving you references so that you can follow up if you are interested in. Luce Irigaray... Oh, I guess I should say, Cixous is head of the center for, I don't know how to translate it, a center for research on women, I guess is the best translation. I can't remember it in French, at Vincennes actually it's now called Saint Denis. It's the University of Paris, number VIII, Roman numeral eight.

Vincennes is the campus on which the great student general strike of 1968 took place. 1968 was an important year. (Student asks something, indistinguishable.) I don't know. Perhaps there is a history of 1968.

I mean, there were student strikes in Germany, the whole city university, the whole University of Paris, beginning with the campus number eight at Vincennes which is on the edge of Paris. The students were revolutionaries and were fed up with the old teaching system. They were fed up with all the colonial attitudes, the Cold War attitudes, the anti-sex, anti-freedom attitudes everywhere. That was the same year the People's Park happened in Berkeley, where the students were equally fed up. It was the year that students shot at Kent State. And all the universities, they were sitting when the students struck. It was a year of accumulated fury for all of the really gross and unexamined patriarchal dominance with its nationalist semi fascist ideas.

The '50s and McCarthyism and isolations in this country and the civil rights movement was a reaction against that. '68 was also the year when the civil, the Civil Rights Movement actually had begun a little bit before that. The student riots since 1968 were really, in this country, following the Civil Rights Movement.

Student 3: I don't mean to interrupt or correct, but the students were shot in the '70s, actually.

Augustine: In the '70s? Okay, you're right, thank you.

A lot of things happened in '68 and I should not be historically inaccurate, but the continuing... You can remember 1968 as a worldwide year. Yes. Other things happened in '69 and '70, the People's Park continued, and the Kent State shootings were in 1970.

As I was thinking it, I thought that, it doesn't seem that it all happened in one year. It's not that simple, but essentially it started in '68, and one of the results of that is that the whole Pari Huit, Paris Campus Number Eight, was dismantled and moved out of town to Saint Denis. Some people still referred to it as Vincennes, and it is now actually at Saint Denis, there is a center for Feminist research there. I mention that because there's not, we don't really have an equivalent in this country. The French feminist critics have more standing, even though they oppose an establishment of male critics. They still have more standing.

They have more voice than American Feminist theoreticians who are still working to develop their voice. Let me say a word about Luce Irigaray, in this connection, she was teaching at Vincennes when Jacques Lacan was teaching there.

She taught there, and she wanted to introduce a course in which woman offered a critique of the Freudian-Lacanian position from the woman's point of view, and they fired her. Lacan got her fired so that she could not teach that course, which would be an intellectual examination of the assumptions. So she has written two books...she's written a lot more than that, but I think the ones that are easiest to get in translation are Speculum, that's the Latin word for mirror, and I'll say more about the mirror. *Speculum of the Other (Woman)* and she put the "Woman" in parentheses.

The idea of woman as other is very important, and it's a kind of way to summarize the sense in which women feel different, separated, marginalized, outside, because male-dominant thought establishes, takes men as the norm, and these are heterosexual white old men. But there is this conceptual norm out there, and it is, again it's a thought, it's an idea, it's not a fact, and we will have to look at it as an idea. So maleness is the norm, then femaleness is abnormal. So the man is the one. Since what distinguishes men from women is possession of a penis, symbolically the penis is the phallus and one of the summaries of Lacan's position is the phallus is the supreme signifier.

Now signifier is another philosophical term, is used a lot in discussing words, language, and the signifier is what endows something else with meaning. The Lacanist signifier then is a word, and the signified is what it means. The signifier embodies and presents meaning. So the phallus is the supreme signifier. Some theoreticians have tried to say that that's really not the same as penis, that there are phallic institutions and phallic ideas which are not necessarily associated with men, but it all really boils down to the phallus as the ancient symbol for male. It can get abstracted and changed around, but it comes back to that, to genitalia, finally. The phallus is the supreme signifier, which is another way of saying women don't, in this theory, women don't have words, we don't have language. They can't endow something with meaning, and that's because they don't have subjectivity or a self or a thinking mind that can produce.

Okay, I've been very abstract. Give me questions on that.

Student 3: It just makes me really angry.

Augustine: It flies in the face of experience. Women think, just the way men think, little girls and little boys, however, they are taught to behave differently.

Consciousness in each of us, human beings, human consciousness, operates. Its content begins to accumulate along gendered lines, but we have a fundamental consciousness, which is a tool and we all learn to talk. Every human being can speak. We also know the multiplicity of languages. We also know, this is a big theme in Adrienne Rich as well that people can be forced to shut up.

The stories that I was telling in the beginning, Joan Larkin, brave and strong and fully identified as a lesbian, cannot say to a casual person in the hall of a hotel in a public situation, "I am lesbian." For good reasons—that shuts down something.

Student 2: Can I say something about that? I think going all the way back to something you said about labeling someone as gay and also her problem in identifying herself as a lesbian. I think the heterosexual need to label gays and lesbians and women and men is very much associated with their need to control because knowledge is associated with control, and anything that messes with those definitions shows them that they are not in control shows them how much that they don't. So if someone's sexuality isn't defined and it's ambiguous, everything is unknown and everything's out of control to that person. To give them that label is for them to say, oh, that person, is this, everything that I think about gay sticking on that person, and that's what they are, I think.

Augustine: Yeah. Thank you. You're right. These are power systems.

Student 2: It's giving away power for, to have said *lesbian* at that point would have been giving away power.

Augustine: I think that she also, there are also, as always, in my thinking about, should I say, *patriarchal, male supremacist* when I'm trying to talk, I say *male dominant* because I would like people to hear me.

So this is the identity dilemma. If your identity is... So, we have it in the world generally today. The Croatians want not to be identified with the Slovenes, but it was quite wonderful. The mothers of the Yugoslavian, the Yugoslavian soldiers, said, *Stuff!* You can't go out. It's like a National Guard from Illinois stepping over the border and shooting people in Indiana. That's why Kent State was such a scandal, that you could on the basis of this group is odd, so far out, so away from us, we have to kill them. But of course, you can't kill an idea.

That's why we have to deal with rules and ideas, but national identity has seized many people and it's a desire, I want to say I have this identity and I'm going to present it. It sells books to publicize us writers, and so there's a very strong sense in which one wants to say that, one does not want to be silent, one does not want to say. One does not want to be silenced, so one wants to say, I'm a woman, I'm a feminist, I'm a writer, I'm a thinker.

Or one wants me to say *this is my sexual identity*, although heterosexual people don't have to say it, it's almost more embarrassing to be heterosexual than to be homosexual, because the institution, heterosexual relations are very corrupt. (Student interjects, adds "homophobic.") They are homophobic. Yes, I was, when Wilton (student 2) was talking I was thinking that on my own campus, Pratt Institute in Brooklyn, there is...Straight men have tremendous fear of gay men, and it can get ugly. Heterosexual relations are really corrupted. Straight men generally regard women as prey, something to be conquered, something to be won over.

Student 4: Another notch in the bedposts.

Augustine: Yes. Yes. Something that you want to get something out of it.

Young women don't always lose. As a general prevailing, but it's a corrupt attitude. Sexuality, in its genuine form is the feeling that when you meet someone, you'd like to attract them to you, and that's based on something genuine, which is our uncertainty in ourselves. Because actually, the desire to have that strong identity, I believe, comes from a desire to go to fend off fear, to fend off uncertainty. It is very difficult to be uncertain.

It's nice to be able to say, I have such-and-such as sexual identity. I have such-and-such national identity. People often feel this way about their family. It's important for some people to say, oh, I'm... my family's Italian, my family's Irish, I'm proud to be Irish, I'm proud to be Italian or whatever. One wants to say these things in order to enhance oneself, one's sense of the family, a lineage, a connection. What was valuable in our human tribe, our little tribe, the family, and our larger tribe, our town, our ethnic grouping, whatever their accomplishments were. The problem is the corruption, is that right now, the identity, identification has this negative side, which is which is to separate, to make an enemy out of every other identity.

Now, this is what you were saying earlier. Why does different mean separate? Well, that's a political statement. Actually, we all live on the same planet. We are not separate. Wilton had the right idea that, well, the establishment of a norm, the creation of the differences, particularly gender differences between men and women, contributes to violence and to abuse.

Student 4: I was going to say the same thing though, also with her not being able to say, "I'm a lesbian," I think there's a fear of violence there. I mean, there's all this gay bashing, and she just has such a fear...

Augustine: Sure, and so one corner of Joan Larkin's mind was, I don't want to be attacked. I don't actually know. I don't want either...verbally or physically... I don't want... I'm responsible for all my friends too, where there are a whole bunch of us meeting here. I don't want...

Student 2: Or even psychically, the unspoken, you are unacceptable to me.

Augustine: Hostility.

Student 2: Horrible.

Augustina: Just like dealing with that day, you know, it's too much. She's already had a bad day.

Student 1: I just don't want to deal with this.

Augustine: What I want to do is give each of you a source. I will go over it very briefly with you, but there's one passage that I want to read with you.

I have, this is for you to ponder and there's some writing ideas, and I hope that you will write before Friday and I'm talking about the self. Page one, selection number one, from *Speculum of the Other (Woman)* by Luce Irigaray.

"Woman is a common noun for which no identity can be defined. Woman is not to be related to any simple designable being subject or entity."

Now, Irigaray knows that women have subjectivities. She's saying it's different from men's, and it is certainly socialized differently or verbalized differently. I'm not sure. I don't think the process is any different, but that passage is complex and involves her using irregular grammatical forms and unusual sentences. In my reading on Saturday night, I will be following this theme and this usage of the term Jouissance, appears in Irigaray. It also appears in Cixous on the next page.

Jouissance is the French word. It really on the most literal level it means sexual pleasure. But the connotation is sexual pleasure as experienced internally by a woman. It's related to joy, but one of the great difficulties of the whole masculinist theory that women do not have subjectivities, women do not create meaning or culture, therefore, women cannot even speak, is that women don't know their own sexual pleasure. That's another idea of Lacan's.

And you know, the Victorian stuff. Women don't experience sexuality and women don't experience sexual feelings was something that patriarchy has wanted to say for a long, long time.

Student 1: That way, they can control and conquer, right?

Augustine: The woman is a piece of property. If she has her own sexual feelings, she might tell you to fuck off. She may tell you to go away. She may not like you, but she better be from the patriarchal point of view. She's got to be in a slot. She's got to be in your category. She's got to be your mother and take care of you. She's got to be your wife and take days and take care of the kid. She's got to be your mistress and give you sexual pleasure without creating any demands or troubles. She's got to be your daughter, and one of the uglier forms of gender, the violence of gender differentiation, has been the feeling that women, your daughter's your property, too. And that's why we see so much father-daughter incest. Discussed now, it's been happening all along. It's a consequence of the property theory. And, of course, it is the ultimate corruption of heterosexuality. Cases of incest are older men, father figures, uncles, feeling that they can use, as a piece of property, the younger child, the young girl, the daughter, the naive. Older men also molest small boys. It is not nearly as nearly as much because the homosexual relations are still a little bit outside the pale, even if incestuous. But the male dominant family is a particularly ugly organization when it when it permits sexual abuse. There's an incest taboo, but somehow that doesn't matter when the father uses the daughter.

So we don't identify people particularly as heterosexual, but I consider it's admitting to social corruption, to say I am heterosexual, although actually it shouldn't. Nobody should be made to feel ashamed of whatever their natural response is.

Student 2: What were you saying about incest? I'm not sure I'm with you at this point.

Augustine: Well, the emphasis story has always held a lot of power to the imagination because Oedipus inadvertently did the thing that is unthinkable, anthropologically, sociologically, a son had sexual relations and children with his own mother. That destroys the whole structure of the family. You don't know who's related to whom, you don't know who's in authority. The daughter, who's in Roman Polanski's film Chinatown, that the daughter is a sister as well. (some indistinguishable input from students) You can't, well, you can't control it. You can't manage anything. It really is socially unmanageable if, and it is genetically unmanageable, biologically unmanageable, because of the genetic interactions. In other words, anthropologists put it this way. We say when you marry, you have to mate, to reproduce. You have to do it ex-ogamosly. That is, you marry outside of your tribe. You do not marry your sister, your cousin, your aunt. It's built into the biological system. That is to say, genetically, those matings produce defective offspring and eventually kill off the rest.

So just biologically, reproductively, you have to marry outside of the tribe. But the family is still potentially a good organization. Parents, children learn how to be people from the people who take care of them. And they're usually the people who produced them; women do still feel closely with their children. I have four children.

Student 1: I want to ask a question about the incest equality when the father and his son, okay, or the father and the man and the young boys. Do you think that society under the system looks at that as a more awful situation than the father and the daughter?

Augustine: Yes, I think so. Right. A father who makes his young son have sex with him is more unacceptable. It doesn't happen as often. A father who makes his daughter have sex with him, well, that's his natural impulse. It's all part of sexuality.

Student 2: I just want to point out here, I've been working on this issue for about six months. I'm working on a book about female perpetrators, and it's a real problematic situation when you start talking about mothers seducing their children. At one study that I read last month, I reported 43 percent of all sexual abuse is at the hands of mothers. You know, I mean, there are going to be people totally up in arms about that. But then again, if you think there are two things going on there, mothers are the primary caregivers of children and their children are mostly exposed to mothers or to women. You know, this increases your chances right there dramatically. Another one is that almost all perpetrators are victims, and so we pass down the abuse to these women. Who is, in the end, answerable to this.

Augustine: One very important reason for our, apart from success as a writer, so being a writer is to tell the truth about how things are so that we can break down the patriarchal dominance and gender ideas. In order to break downs power structures that are injurious to individuals. If mothers are abusing, many mothers to abuse their children, not merely sexually, they beat them up. We want to change our notions of power because there are a lot of institutionalized notions that when you want to do is get power over other people in order to ruin them. To destroy them, to control them, to make them do what you want them to do, whether they want to do it or not. In other words, to take away their humanity, their subjectivity, interfere with their consciousness. That's what power really, finely is. Power is the power over somebody, to make somebody else, to destroy somebody else. And that is a corrupt definition.

The opposite of that kind of corrupt power is to be dedicated to the benefit of all sentient beings, which is the Buddhist philosophy.

Writing should break down the patriarchal structures.

It's also difficult in studies, by the way, to know what prejudices initiate the study.

Women do have all the feelings that men have, and since there are the dominant institutions oriented toward power. Power over other people, power to make other people do to de-, to objectify them, to turn them into objects. It's to use your children to, and on your property, to use them sexually or use them as slaves, servants. (Hard to distinguish) ...just to make other people do what you want, to make someone, to destroy someone else's subjectivity instead of it being lived. And we want to change that, and that's why we have to change institutions. We can't start changing institutions from any other place, other than starting with ourselves.

The degree to which anybody has been marginalized is, well, it's very hierarchical. Outside, marginalization means outside the club. It's a fraternity, fraternities exist in order to keep people out, want to keep out. It matters who you keep out, not so much who you take in.

That's not a good view of the world. It's not helpful to individuals. And so we have to get to starting with ourselves and what we think of ourselves and we have the identity problem in proposing a super strong identity. Well, I guess maybe that leads to the formation of a fraternity, or separation. It is a question. How, what kind of identity we have, what kind of self. Possibly there are dozens of selves that contradict one another.

Anyway, read the Irigaray. The next page is also from Irigaray, quoting Lacan, which kind of summarizes the problem we are in.

Student 3: When did he write that quote?

Augustine: Well, he died in 1981. He wrote this text in reply to Lacan was written in 1975. He said it in a seminar in 1975, his twentieth seminar. He said women don't know what they're saying, that's the difference between them and me. And the full quotation is at the bottom of the page. "There is no woman who is not excluded by the nature of things, which is the nature of words. And it must be said that if there is something they complain a lot about the moment, that is what it is, except they don't know what they're saying. And so it the difference between them and me."

That's the mentality that women, the woman writer is up against, and I simply included it because the whole chapter is in the other book, by Irigaray, I give you one title, *Speculum of the Other (Woman)* and *This Sex Which is Not One*.

I've given you two of Cixous, one very famous. On page five, section four, my numbering is in the upper right-hand corner. Page five has a chunk from

Julia Kristeva on language theory, but it also has a section from what's called the Heart Sutra and the basic contradiction, just for you to think about is the form as vengeance. But on page six, I would like just to read over this dialog with you so that you can begin to think about it.

Shariputra is the fall guy; he's always the one who asks the dumb questions, and historically, around the 8th century AD, apparently, there was living in a city in India—Vaisali—a very insightful man named Vimalakirti and this whole sutras; it's a collection of stories called The Teachings, the Holy Teachings of Vimalakirti. The materials are written in Sanskrit. Now, typical Buddhism of this period, is a bit like, still exists, I'm afraid, in some Buddhist organizations, institutional Buddhist churches, that women have a lower birth. They're not able to achieve as much as men. Okay, I've been giving a lot of psychoanalytics, this is just the ancient Asian way of expressing the same idea and in theological terms. But this is the problem. Shariputra has been talking with this woman. Now, obviously, what she was, was a very smart woman who was sitting around with all the other people studying and listening and learning about the largeness of the mind. The human mind can... it is completely creative. There is really no limit.

And yet I've been isolating these social situations where I can't find the word or Joan Larkin can't find the word, we're hesitating, pulling back, but actually there is no limit. Every word in the universe is available to us. And the woman is called here, a goddess, because she's so, so insightful. This picture has elevated her and the things that she's saying are very brilliant. Well, Shariputra, typical religious Buddhist guy, thinks, well, if she's she really is a goddess and she's here manifesting in a woman's form, why doesn't she change herself to a man form, which would show she had really achieved enlightenment? And so he says Goddess, what prevents you from transforming yourself out of your female state? Although I have sought my female state for these 12 years, I have not yet found it. Reverend Shariputra, if a magician were to incarnate a woman by magic, would you ask her what prevents you from transforming yourself out of your female state? No. Such a woman would not really exist. So what would there be to transform? Just so, Reverend Shariputra, all things did not really exist. Now, would you think what prevents one whose nature is that of a magical incarnation from transforming herself out of her female state? There upon the goddess employed her magical power to cause the Elder—Elder's just as venerable—The Elder Shariputra, to appear in her form, and to cause herself to appear in his. Then the goddess transformed into Shariputra, said to Shariputra transformed into the goddess, Reverend Shariputra, what prevents you from transforming yourself out of your female state? And Shariputra transformed into the goddess, to a woman, replied, I no longer appear in the form of a male! My body has changed to the body of a woman. I do not know what to transform!

The goddess continued. If the Elder could change, again change, out of the female state, then all women could change out of their female state. All women appear in the form of women in just the same way as the Elder appears in the form of the woman. While they are not woman in reality, they appear in the form of women. With this in mind, the Buddhist said, in all things there is neither man nor female. And the goddess released her magical power and each returned to his ordinary form. She then said to him, Reverend Sahriputra, what have you done with your female form?

I neither made it, nor did I change it. Just so, all things are neither made not changed. And that meant a lot to me—I had not changed. That is the teaching.

Well, I'm going to leave you. I have enclosed some poems, attached. And I didn't put anybody's name on them; some of you might know who they are.

Student 2: Different people?

Augustine: They are all by different people. They are all by well-known people. Some are male and some are female. And the only message, at the bottom of page eight, poetry should be precise about the thing and reticent.

Are all of you writing poetry or are some of you writing prose?

(Some students mumble they are writing prose. Quiet responses.)

I've also included some ideas about things you could write about, but you might want to think more, we could say more right now, about the story, I call this the Sex Change Sutra, there are five or six other places in this Mahayana literature where similar conversations take place. The female form is changed. What's the message? In our terms that this is the Buddhist message is that all things are... they're not made and they're not changed, making of things—birth and death—are inceptions. It's the way we have to see how things go.

But what's the message about males and females? You have to kind of demythologize and translate that into these terms. For somebody now it dramatizes to say, if he does, he looks he doesn't have his male body anymore, and he doesn't know where he is or what his.

Student 2: It seems like the form of male or female exists, but as we're just born into bodies, we can never—I'm thinking of Plato now—we can never attain a form. A form is an abstract idea.

Augustine: Plato's cave was the idea that our forms were sort of partial and simplifications of some permanent ideal.

Is there something beyond the male and female parts, that's what it is. There is neither male nor female. Male and female are ideas. Now, they happen to be attached to physical manifestations. And so, is one's body one's self? Is the self an essence? So this is a big question in feminist theory and it's the one I'm dealing with and I'm dealing with it via the Buddhist text because nobody has done that yet.

Student 1: Is the self an essence?

Augustine: An essence. Essence again, is a philosophical term. If it's in essence, you can never get away from it. There is nothing beyond.

But my own position is all things are neither made nor changed. It's a way of saying there aren't any essences. There's no fixed essence, no fixed self, no fixed soul as in Christian theology. There's no identity you can put your finger on, but maybe that's hard.

The poems I have given you because there is no self in them and I have taken off the identity of the writers.

Student 3: I'm thinking of a piece of art with no self, and you don't mean like baggage, do you? There's certainly no baggage in it inherently, just the way they see something because of who they are, they see that blue sky.

Augustine: Is there... Yes, well said. There's no... The way the self appears in these poems is through its...baggage, so to speak, in your word, what it drakes, how it flows, the objects he sees.

Some of these poems are from the early 20th century movement called Imagism, and some from the early 20th century from the movement called Rejectivism. Those are just convenient labels for certain things that happened, and I offer them to you so that we can talk about them next time after we've had a chance to think about them or talk about them any time if you want to follow me and come to set up an interview. The uncertain self can nevertheless capture a moment of attention to what is out there as an anchor.

What that means in writing and writing poetry, it really means that a specific image, a specific thing seen, heard, is something resembling firm ground on which to start writing, but the writing is independent from the self; that's why I've taken the signature of the author off.

I should say, I noticed one poem is untitled, the titles are in caps, (lists them, hard to heard), there's another poem untitled, but it in parentheses above "river, marsh, droughts, and in flood moon light with sight of no land."

Ideas for writing. Can you bring us some writing on Friday? A new something. I have raised a whole lot of questions. Exactly when and how you were a marginal, exactly when and how you are not marginal. I said write something, taking off, okay, completely vague. You don't have to do all of these, any of these. You can... All I mean is, it's not so scholarly explication of classroom, whatever. It's poem, short story, a vignette, a composition related to these things.

I'm suggesting research your name, beneath that name is also going to be a slide show. Oh, yes, I guess I should just say my reading, for your interest, I write a lot of poems out of this tradition of looking at the object, which is an Oriental, an Asian tradition, but these are Western writers. The reading that I would be giving on Saturday night, we'll have slides on a screen, the room will be dark, and I will be reading from a possible manuscript, from an ongoing work call, *Tongue in the Dark,* which is the way I'm working tradition of concrete poetry. I've been influenced a lot by Jackson Maclow, this year, and by the artists Kurt Schwitters particularly, the collagist and the concrete, the international concrete movement, which was popular in the 60s and is now considered unfashioned. I still do it as a way of working out feminist meanings.

A poem, you see, is any formation of black letters on white paper. (Students asks for name clarification.) Kurt Schwitters, one of the founders of Dada, which was one of them, along with Italian futurism, one of the most revolutionary artistic movements of early [twentieth century]. Dada led to French surrealism. It's a mixed media form based on the premise that a poem is any configuration of black letters on white. I will be dealing with a lot of these themes. The theme of the shifting itself, or the split subject, it's another term from Julia Kristeva. The split subject is, the split between, I guess, Joan Larkin and what she knows about herself and the fact that she can't say she's a lesbian. The split between what I know in my own consciousness to be my own self and what other people out there say I am or should be or should do or should think. That's the problem. We have all been influenced by patriarchal, male-dominate ways of thinking, and they will come out even in such ways as you thinking that you don't want to quite read aloud what you wrote.

So I give you this to ponder and to talk about and to think about and keep and to write something in relation to for Friday, and we'll talk more and this is just for you to keep.

A Spiral Across Space and Time: The Life of H.D.

Interlude by Emily Trenholm

As I listen to this lecture on H.D.'s biography, I feel as if I'm being led down a wayward path towards a fixed point, a predetermined conclusion. Joanne Kyger echoes Barbara Guest's words and seems to have a specific thesis in mind—H.D.'s identity is portrayed as one-dimensional, and it's not an entirely flattering portrait. By the end, Kyger is rushing so quickly that she has forgotten to mention one of H.D.'s lovers, seemingly exasperated by her "soap opera" of a life—in my view a feminist life, one as open as her male counterpoints. Afterwards, reading *Trilogy*, I feel as if I'm feeling my way out of a labyrinth I didn't know I was held in. In the way a spiral allows you to enter and exit with a completely different orientation, I am given space to see her anew. Her work echoes the forms of her life, but in a way that is expansive and departs from any fixed point.

I'm reminded of these forms during a lecture on the goddess Sophia by English mythologist Sharon Blackie. Blackie delves deeply into the past traditions of Europe to bring more holistic, pre-colonial thought into the present—much like H.D. She spoke of the anima mundi "[which] is inside us and we are inside it. Psyche is in us, but we are also in psyche. There is no separation." The anima mundi, or world soul, communicates in images, speaks to us in dreams—and in poetry. I begin to sense that H.D.'s life may have been as paradoxical as her work. But perhaps paradox is not quite the right word. Perhaps more like in mysticism, opposites are held in tension by a third element. This tension as we shift between separateness and union with the world soul.

While considering her two main biographies, is it possible that she is neither fully the mystical poet master of Robert Duncan's *The H.D. Book*, and the privileged free spirit of Barbara Guest's biography *Herself Defined,* but both?

Though this lecture quotes the latter, they are best considered together; if Duncan addresses the mythic, timeless self of H.D., and Guest addresses the particular necessities of her material life, both belong. And considering both is a powerful act that opens up the narrative of what the identity of an artist—or a woman—can be.

Guest's book and this lecture also consider H.D.'s life with a new focus on her privilege as a wealthy white woman. It feels necessary and redemptive to consider the effects of wealth and whiteness on the art world, because they're still painfully felt today and needing to be countered by transparent narratives like this one. To discuss her identity intersectionally, it's important to also note she was a bisexual woman, and that at the time queerness was strongly suppressed. What if we can equally (and perhaps mystically) hold the vantage point of H.D.'s time, and hold this multiplicity? Because what could be a more feminist, queer act? For a woman to match a male artist of that era in ambition, mobility, and openness in love and sex. To be a poet, magazine writer, actress, patron, as well as mother. As Guest's title suggests, she seems like a woman who lets no other person or society at large define her—and thus limit her. What if her life—like the themes of the mundane and sacred, the mythic and particular, masculine and feminine—is another of her collaged creations that celebrates multitudes?

~

Isis, Mary, Eve, The Lady. As they shape-shift into and out of each other in H.D.'s *Trilogy*, my own unconscious responds, as a psychic flame blooms in my heart. As I read about the mystical elements of the Moravian church she grew up in, I realize why. Blackie describes our individual experience of the anima mundi as our "inner imaginarium." As I read of holding candles in a hollowed-out orange, the image in my head is coring dozens of apples and placing beeswax candles inside. A dark silent room, flame reflected in crystal. Children holding apples to chest, some looking down, some ahead, ahead always shifting as they follow the spiral inward. My imaginarium echoes H.D.'s, a thread woven across time. A cosmic form in which she and I walk the same spiral and our spirits cross like shadows in the candlelight.

An apple, as in Eve. An orange, as in the ancient Great Goddess whose very body is the world. H.D. describes Freud as Janus, the two-headed god that looks both forward and back. But H.D. seems to fit this description more: "the figure of Woman as poet, mystical seer, and god," who weaves elements of both past and future, showing that "differences are also...affinities that, with enlightenment, can ignite love rather than war, creation rather than destruction" (VII-IX). Her images ignite an inner knowing from my own experiences; the power of myth is its ability to make connections across space and time. Or, time eternal may move in spirals.

The cross becomes again a flowering tree. The Tree of Knowledge shifts into the Tree of Life. The Moravian Church was also named "The Order of the Grain of Mustard Seed," after the parable told by Jesus, in which the smallest of seeds grows into the tallest of trees. Seed as in intuition, or the potential of the unconscious. It was a church that valued Gnosis, personal spiritual knowledge, with an emphasis not on dichotomies of sin and repentance, but illusion and enlightenment—which are not so much opposites as fluid stages of human consciousness. And as H.D.'s poetry illustrates, "Gnosis can be as wild as Eros" (Jarnot).

Anthroposophia, goddess of the wisdom of being human. These memories emerge from a community where I lived which was born as a philosophical cousin of the Moravian Church, like different mustard seeds from the same tree carried on the wind. Both recognized that the human body is the modern sacred space and personal gnosis is the Word made flesh—an evolution of Sophia into Anthroposophia. And maybe most importantly, the human imagination is the place where eternal forces come into form and shapeshift out again. I experience this shapeshifting in the ancient Egyptian myth of the Goddess who swallows the sun in the west and gives birth to it in the east; in an Easter sunrise service that celebrates both the rebirth of the Mother of the Word, and of Jesus "in [whom] there is no male or female" (Campbell 181).

I remember walking in the dark through a field with fossilized manure piles and drifts of melting snow to a group at the top of the ridge, the heart chakra of five-hundred acres of pasture, marsh, and prairie. I turn and join them in watching the tree-topped horizon as a faint white smudge appears, that liminal space of pre-dawn, a silence where everyone tries to sing the light back into form.

As Joseph Campbell reminds us: "[The] female [is] the giver of forms. She is the one who gave life to forms and she knows where they came from. It is from that which is beyond male and female. It is from that which is beyond being and nonbeing" (181). H.D. bridges the female poet as giver of forms and the non-dual ground of all being out of which life emerges.

And if the red cloth hanging in the Moravian church evokes both the red of menstruation and the feminine bleeding of who some mystics call "Mother Jesus"? It hangs behind a simple wooden altar as I sit in a small group of people on folding chairs. Two figures in red walk down the aisles on each side of us, their gaze focused on the cloth. Each word said just like before and just like now and just like always.

~

Robert Duncan experiences H.D.'s work like a prayer, a longing, an offering. His memories of first being read a poem of hers resonated with my own—"Falling in love, a conversion or an obsession these were close to what the poet knew in the poem, seeing the world in the light of a new necessity. An in-forming" (6). But also, through a sense that she possessed the memory of multiple lifetimes, as if each poem expressed both me and not-me simultaneously, bringing me into a third state—of becoming.

H.D. is a weaver of time as well as a nexus for internal and external worlds. My favorite detail of her life that Kyger includes is when H.D. miscarries a child after hearing of the sinking of the Lusitania leading to World War I. She is so attuned to the larger currents of history and the precipice of death of her time that she feels it all in her own body, an uninterrupted spiral of feeling. To follow H.D.'s poetry is to follow this spiral inward then out, with apples in hand, a "re-lighting of the flame of womanly vision," a journey to the "self-out-of self." And to follow the spiral of her life is to do the same, in congruent motion.

American Women in the Experimental Tradition: H.D.

Joanne Kyger
July 8, 1991

Transcription by Emily Trenholm

Joanne Kyger: I'm going to read again from some biographical notes. Most of these are taken from a biography, the only biography existing now of H.D. by Barbara Guest, who's also a poet herself from the New York School of Poetry. Anne Waldman mentioned her yesterday; she's a friend of Frank O'Hara's and Don Allen's, and she wrote a biography of H.D. published in 1984. Have any of you read that book? It's called *Herself Defined*. Okay, great. This will be all news to you. This is a biography, which is an interesting literary biography. She doesn't really discuss H.D.'s poetry at great length, but she discusses H.D.'s life, and H.D.'s life reads a little bit like a very grand soap opera. Also sometimes it seems like a grand movie. It's like a great movie script to her. It summarizes a bit. It has a lot of the social ins and outs. Her life is a very emotional one in many different ways. You'll see some familiar characters will enter and reenter and enroll in Imagism. On page two of the Xerox here is a synopsis again of Richard Aldington's statement on Imagism, and at the very end is the excerpts from *Helen in Egypt*, which we'll listen to the tape of that which she records in 1955.

Hilda Doolittle was born in Pennsylvania, just like Gertrude Stein. She was born on September 10th, 1886, and her childhood was spent among the Moravia community in Bethlehem, Pennsylvania, which was the sect to which her mother's family belonged, and it was in this spirit of the Moravians that Hilda Doolittle grew up.

It was a city, Bethlehem, Pennsylvania, founded in 1741 by the Moravian brethren who had come via Saxony to America from Moravia. Briefly, the Moravians were bound to exercise constant love to one another and to other religious sects. Faith is a direct and supernatural illumination from God who is Christ, the fountainhead of all love. Once you are awakened, it is your duty to share this grace with others—hence their missionary zeal. H.D. wrote about the influence of this church upon her: "I must have the absolutely pure mystical Moravian pietism or poeticism or hard-boiled Freudian facts." This was her spiritual balance, the pure mystical Moravian and the hard-boiled Freudian facts. Later she becomes a disciple of Freud's.

Hilda's mother Helen Wolle is from this tradition, but she marries outside to Charles Doolittle, a widower with two children from Puritan stock and a professor of astronomy, and they were married in 1882. Hilda is the second child and only girl of four children. When H.D. is nine in 1896, the professor gets a job at the University of Pennsylvania and becomes Flower Professor of Astronomy, which was a chair, very famous—and notice the similarity between Amy Lowell's brother, who is also an astronomer—and he is the first director of this famous observatory. They get a large house on three acres surrounded by working farms and houses. At this point, it's an extended family of nine people, it's a big household, in Upper Darby, Pennsylvania—for those of who know Pennsylvania. And she makes friends, Hilda does, even though she's kind of out in the countryside with the two neighboring girls, one of which remains as a significant friend through her life.

She goes to the Friends School, the Quaker school, in Philadelphia, and then for one disastrous year at Bryn Mawr, where she is a day student. Her yearbook describes her, as she was when she first met Ezra Pound, as someone with "a face with gladness overspread, soft smiles by human kindness bred." Her tastes were literary and leaned towards the classics. She loved basketball. She was five feet eleven. She was tall for a woman of her time.

Her height always embarrassed her. She gradually got into kind of a slumped way of moving her body. From the yearbook also, it says, "Hilda is studying astronomy, principally because she found it so convenient to look right into the stars without using a telescope." Great high school kind of humor. An accurate, quirky forecast of the later H.D.

A melancholy description of herself in 1909 says, "She was a disappointment to her father, an odd duckling to her mother, an inopportune, overgrown un-incarnated entity that had no place here." She decides she needs a twin sister and finds a friend and loved one, Frances Gregg, two years older than H.D. Frances Gregg is a person to remember who keeps constantly moving in and out of H.D.'s life, and they become confidants. She demanded a kind of emotional, subjugation and idealized relationship from her first deep love—and this was Frances Gregg. While at the same time Frances would be exposed to the most candid criticism and arbitrary desertion. Frances made exits and entrances in H.D.'s life until her own death during World War II, when she and her mother were killed during a bomb blast in London.

Then there is a relationship with Ezra Pound. Before meeting Pound is like B.C. and A.D. She meets him when she is 15 years old, a schoolgirl at a Halloween party where he is dressed like a Tunisian prince. (laughter) When she is 19 and coming to Bryn Mawr, she becomes his, quote, "disciple," along with William Carlos Williams, and he turns them on to his interests and puts down all of 19th century poetry. The Troubadours Provence, William Morris, Swinburne, Yoga, Latin and Greek poets, he teaches. He gives her brie...he cultivates her taste, they go on picnics, he gives her brie cheese. She says, "Ugh!" He says, "You have no palate." And she says, "What's a palate?" So she's with the sophisticated, debonair Pound.

She makes friends with Marianne Moore, who's at Bryn Mawr, at that point it continues, with whom she corresponds all her life. Marianne Moore says, "I remember her eyes, which glittered and gave me an impression of great acuteness and were sunny and genial at the same time. I remember her seeming to lean forward as if resisting a high wind. Her social charm, her bedrock reliability." She drops out of Bryn Mawr because she fails English and because it is either Bryn Mawr or Ezra Pound. She also writes flirtatious letters to William Carlos Williams, now interning at the French hospital in New York City and signs her letters H.D., her first use of initials as her identity. She writes him she is engaged to Ezra Pound. Ezra gives her a ring and has Sunday dinner with the Doolittle's, where he reads his poetry to their confused wonderment.

Then the engagement is broken, and he gives the ring to someone else, although never through his life ceases caring for H.D. and he awakens her as a poet. He goes to Europe and has two books published and writes to Hilda, and those two books published that I mentioned were the ones that Harriet Monroe finds and buys and takes back and asks him to be the foreign correspondent for *Poetry Magazine*, *Persona*, and... I forget the other name right now.

So Hilda leaves for Europe with Frances and Mrs. Gregg. Her friend Frances and her mother, supposedly for four months. But H.D. stays forever. They are entertained in Paris, although Frances writes, "Any party that included Hilda was prone to end in deepening gloom and a general physical and emotional haze." She's a very emotional person, as you'll soon find out, struggling with these powers and insights into her own self and her own sexuality. In London, despite her Americanness, she is taken up. But Frances is too impetuous and forthright for the British and so the Greggs go home and Hilda stays on with Ezra Pound, who takes her around.

She was quite beautiful. The only fault the English found with her face was her nose, which they considered too short for elegance, thought to be American. Her height here was an asset. She could be refreshing and charming and, in her snobbishness, knew toward whom to direct her charm. Her father sends her money to live on. She becomes...She's in fashion. Greekness was everywhere, and she looked the part. She could be seen either as a Greek maiden or a Greek god. People enjoyed long conversations about purity and simplicity, looking up to the Greek constellations in the heavens as they did so.

Then she meets Richard Aldington in 1912 when he is twenty and she is twenty-six. From an English middle-class background... Yes, she's the older woman already. From an English middle-class background, he writes poetry and works as a sports reporter, at this point. He gives her Greek books to read that aren't too difficult. He believes her poetry to be the finest of their era and writes articles about her for a little review magazine.

They get rooms together across from Ezra Pound, at this point in 1912, and she becomes one of the Imagists...they kind of get their little location together, and they all agree upon three principles, the Imagist principles: direct treatment of the subject, allow no word that's not essential to the presentation, and rhymes and rhythms to follow the musical phrase rather than strict regularity of the iambic beat, and group forms, including T.E. Hulme, who actually initiated what would be recognized as Pound's Imagist ideas at a meeting back in 1908.

Then in the middle of all this, Frances Gregg shows up again. She's come back with a celebrity lecturer, Louis Wilkinson, as a husband. Pound dissuades H.D. from going on the honeymoon with them. She's just married, she has her husband, and H.D. wants to go on the honeymoon with them. Pound says, "Don't do that."

Frances Gregg, on the other hand, does not like Richard Aldington and says that he has the manners of an innkeeper's son. She says, "I hate him. I think him under the surface unclean."

If you read a lot of the writing and commentary at this time, there's a use of people as being clean, somehow clean, and the way that their ideas are clean or if they're direct. People who are unclean means they're kind of not physically unclean, but some are messy and some sort of lack of honesty, maybe. Richard Aldington says he felt Ezra's Imagism was forced upon both H.D. and himself as the publicist of his movement. But there was H.D.'s writing—concrete, pure tense. From Ezra Pound's letter to Harriet Monroe: "Objectivity and again, objectivity. Nothing you couldn't say in circumstance... nothing you couldn't say in some circumstance. And the stress of some emotion as some emotion. Actually say simple speech." And sends H.D. off to be published by her. And since these are first, her first published poems are "Hermès of the Ways," "Orchard," and "Epigram," which are fairly often anthologized and are in the library in *Selected H.D. Poems*. From then on, she has no problem being published in the new publications of the era. She's instantly there.

H.D. and Aldington go to Paris in the fall of 1912 and see what's going on there. Gertrude Stein has just published *Tender Buttons*. Hilda's parents arrive and they travel to Rome, Capri, Florence, Venice, and upon returning to London a year later, Richard Aldington and H.D. are married with their parents and Pound as witnesses. Then Amy Lowell comes to town to find out about Imagism. She has H.D.'s poems and *Poetry Magazine* and decides her own poetry is also Imagist. She took to the Aldington's at this point, especially H.D. At this time, H.D. was indeed in bloom. Richard A. describes her in those days, "To look at beautiful things with H.D. is a remarkable experience. She is a genius for appreciation, a severe but wholly positive taste. She lives on the heights and never wastes time on what is inferior." (Background noise, audience laughter.) That's her, H.D. talking. "She responds so swiftly, understands so perfectly, relives the artist's move so intensely that the work of art seems transformed."

Ezra then gets married himself to Dorothy Shakespear and H.D. writes, "Yes, Ez is married. But there seems to be a pretty general consensus of opinion that Mrs. E has not been, quote, 'awakened.' She is very English and cold." Pound goes on to Vorticism, but H.D. keeps to her Greeks. John Cournos, poet and journalist joins them. They are a threesome. They thought of themselves as reincarnated delegates from a past more poetic and more beautiful than anything that had ever existed. Their mission was to rescue literature from more than two thousand years of perversion. They expected to inspire each other.

Pound gets the Imagists published: Aldington, H.D., Flint, Amy Lowell, Joyce, Pound, Ford Maddox Ford, John Cuornos, Allen Upward. They were outsiders, not part of the British establishment and promoted by an American, Ezra Pound, the great hustler. Amy closes in and has a special dinner (we talked about this before) and her rooms at the Barclay with the Aldington's, Pound, Ford Maddox Ford, D.H. Lawrence, etc. The war is just about ready to happen, but an elegant scene goes on during this time with a power struggle going on. Amy wins and takes off with manuscripts and the promise of three anthologies, a promise of a future. "You've got this writing. I'll give you a future for it because I'll publish it." As I said before, these anthologies appear in 1915, 1916, and 1917, and she pays the contributors. Amy says of H.D.'s work, "There are people who find this poetry cold. In one sense it is—for in it is this something of the coolness of marble. How sad, the loneliness of it. A poet's poet." She establishes H.D. in America.

H.D. discovers she is pregnant the day war is declared, and they move next door to the Lawrence's, the D.H. Lawrence's at Hampstead Heath. D.H. Lawrence says about Hilda, "She is like a person walking a tight rope. You wonder if she'll get across. This is the intensity that she's living at." She has a stillborn child, and she blames it on the sinking of the Lusitania. For some reason, I guess she took this very hard. She develops an almost pathological fear of getting pregnant again and refuses to have physical relations with her husband, who then himself has a few affairs. And we're getting off on the soap opera now. Then Richard Aldington goes off to war, and she finds a little place by herself and writes, writes, writes. She's into her writing. "I am too intense, too burning." Her first book *Sea Gardens* is published. She has a long relationship with D.H. Lawrence. Very intense. Some of that written in her book *Bid Me to Live*, which is a novel of hers, and it's a dialogue of the duel between D.H and H.D. with heavy emphasis on the genius, separate from the other characters.

"Aaron's Rod," which is D.H. Lawrence's story, tells his story of that particular time. They don't actually probably have a romantic physical affair, but it's a very intense affair of emotion and spirit and their artistry. Well, then this guy named Cecil Gray comes on the scene and H.D. decides that she's going to go live with him in Cornwall. This is in April 1918. Richard Aldington is still at war in France. Cecil Gray is twenty-three years old and at this point, H.D. is thirty-two and unlike anyone else he has ever known. He's just taken with her. He's just something like this...and she's a distressed, excitable woman, but he loves her. She works well there with him in Cornwall, but then finds herself pregnant and decides she doesn't love Gray, who is destined to become a distinguished music critic.

They part, she runs away, and never sees him again, nor does her child, except once in later years.

She, meanwhile, has been getting passionate letters from Aldington in the war in France, and she writes and tells him she is pregnant. He says he'll stand by her and then changes his mind and says she must take care of herself and her child without relying upon him at all. But at this point, she has met another other, a young woman of twenty-four who called herself Bryher. She has heard of and read H.D. through Amy Lowell's writings and has written to her, and they meet for tea out in Cornwall in 1918, July 17, a historic date for them. This lonely young woman falls right in love with H.D., and she wants to travel with her, to take her to Greece, to take her to America. She threatens suicide unless H.D. gives her the strength to go on living. She has tons of money, her father being a shipping magnate and probably the wealthiest man in England at this time. H.D. throws in her lot with Bryher. She writes her long poem "Hymen."

Her child is born March 31, 1919, and named Frances, after Frances Gray. Frances Perdita to be known henceforth as Perdita. She desperately needs a father's name for her child and so uses the last name of Aldington, which outrages Richard. Then she makes a bargain with Bryher that if she never threatened suicide again, she will live with her and offers Bryher a chance to bring up the child exactly like a little puppy. I love that quote in there. "Yes, you can have it and you can raise it just like a little puppy." Well, Bryher actually turns out to be a very good mother.

Bryher's father owns many ships and newspapers. Sir John Ellerman is his name. They live in great affluence. Bryher grows up intelligent, rebellious, and furious she was not a boy. She wanted to inherit and direct her father's business. She wrote splendid adventure stories—which were published—in which a lone boy faced by danger would conquer all. As long as H.D. lived, she was idealized by Bryher as her heroine. Although, as Thornton Wilder observed, it didn't stop her, Bryher, from looking like Napoleon and acting like Napoleon (laughter). They decide H.D. would present herself as a chaperone to the Ellerman parents, an older woman who could safely lead Bryher out into the world. They put the baby in the nursery and take off on travels to the Sicily's and then to Greece with Havelock Ellis.

Has everybody heard or anybody heard of Havelock Ellis? Havelock Ellis did the first sexual studies of aberrant behavior...must have been out by this time. It's a very classic in the world of sexual behavior, psychological sensitivity. He's a very strange dude who has a crush on H.D. One of the things in Barbara Guest's biography is her "Rainbow's Dream." You read this kind of poem and the "Rainbow's Dream" seems to be if he lays on the floor and she pees on him or something like that. And you think Havelock Ellison and H.D. and you go, oh no (laughter). He is nervous, and she at this point realizes that the three of them are not going to travel anymore. The trip to Greece is idealized but heavy on H.D., who has a kind of nervous breakdown there with Havelock Ellis and everything else, and Bryher has to bring her back to England over land and they then decide to visit America. They both bob their hair and take off with Perdita in 1920, on H.D.'s thirty-fourth birthday. They land in New York City, which Bryher decides New York City is barbaric and arrogant. She meets Marianne Moore and begs her to come to England away from this barbaric land. She later gives Marianne Moore money from the Bryher fund. Bryher was always very generous with her money to artists. William Carlos Williams, an old beau of H.D.'s, introduces them to Robert McAlmon.

In comes Robert McAlmon. Robert McAlmon who, remember in the last class, he's the person that publishes Gertrude Stein's *Three Wives*. Robert McAlmon, a young man from the Middle West, son of a Presbyterian minister. He is soon to marry Bryher, a marriage of convenience which will give her freedom as a married woman. They visit H.D.'s relatives in Monrovia, California, and Bryher insists she is a distant cousin of H.D.'s in an effort to shield what their actual relationship is. A kind of highpoint out there, they see Mary Pickford on set making a movie. But Bryher is still disappointed in the U.S. Returning to New York City, she marries Robert McAlmon with the understanding she would take care of the marriage and household finances. They would live in Europe, and she would be free to travel. Headlines shriek in the newspaper: "Heiress Weds Unknown."

The three writers—and they call themselves "Our Menagerie of Three, is the best menagerie"—take care of the child. They take care of Perdita and write with occasional sulking thrown in. Many think the marriage unusual, including Marianne Moore and Amy Lowell, who both write H.D., insanely curious. What's the scene? Why marriage? However, they are both focused with their literary interests and eventually Robert McAlmon publishes between 1922 and 1933 with his Contact Editions Ernest Hemingway, Gertrude Stein, Ezra Pound, Nathaniel West, William Carlos Williams, H.D., Julia Barnes, Bryher, Mina Loy and his own books.

All these writers were unknown at the time except for H.D. and Pound. This using Bryher's funds is accomplished by setting up his own press, Contact

Publishing Company. He supported the James Joyce's who are in Paris at that time, writing what he's writing, with Bryher's contributions, George Antheil, and also picks up the Bar Cafe tab all around. These are years in Paris...and thus his book he's written called *Being Geniuses Together*, which he writes with Kay Boyle, which is an account of those times. I read a little bit when he describes his relationship with Gertrude Stein in the last lecture. These are years in Paris around Sylvia Beach's Shakespeare and Company, with a famous bookstore, that later goes on to publish James Joyce's *Ulysses*. These were his golden years before he wandered back into the American desert in the late '40s and faded away. An account of these times with Kay Boyle called *Being Geniuses Together*.

Paris is one of the places they touched down in besides London and Switzerland to avoid taxes. One of the reasons they go, because she has such a large inheritance. So Paris and Switzerland to avoid taxes for Bryher, so she establishes a residence in Switzerland and eventually builds a house there. During this time, when McAlmon and Bryher were away—and they do travel together and have their interests in common, they're companions—H.D. finds herself a young squire by the name of...it's more soap opera-like, right?... Harold P. Collins, who is twenty-three years old. He's just smitten with H.D.'s sophisticated and useful thirty-seven years. In return for the intensity and excitement of her presence, and introduction to her friends, he gets to edit all her poetry, find reviewers for her work and writes fifty pages in *Modern Poetry*. His book, *Scholarly, Appreciated, Sensible Work: A Commentary on H.D.*

Bryher and H.D. then travel to Greece, to Venice, to Egypt. In 1923, they arrive at the opening of King Tut's tomb. From now on, Greece and Egypt will form an axis for H.D., joining in her last book *Helen in Egypt*. She writes, "We pray you Egypt. By what perverse fate has poison wrought with knowledge given us this, not days of trance, shadow for doom of death. A passionate grave thought, belief enhanced, ritual returned and magic."

Back in Paris, William Carlos Williams, her old friend, visits with his wife in 1924. Williams doesn't really understand her relationship with Bryher, and he writes about this in his own autobiography, *William Carlos Williams*, which is a wonderful book to read, if you've never read it. It's from his point of view. But we have H.D. saying in a letter, "By the way, I thought Williams most banal. Don't tell him so. And Florence we all thought was too silly. She tried to carry on like a movie fan and it didn't become her. It was so futile with a husband in the background, coming on like a sophisticated European." This is H.D.'s sophistication, looking at poor Flossy trying to have a good time in Paris.

Back in London, Frances Gregg and her mother entered her life again, down in their social scale, sharing one room. But Frances is writing and introduces her to Kenneth Macpherson, old, licentious and sweet, sweet, sweet. He falls in love with H.D. and leaves Frances Gregg, who is trying to awaken his imagination and further his career. He's a young Scotsman. H.D. is now forty and her collected poems have been published in America and she feels more collected. So starts an affair with Kenneth.

"What can I do for you?" She is truly in love. From *Red Roses for Bronze*, her work:

> O let me say the things
> that Thetis said
> to him when he grown to lustihood
> of warrior grandeur :
> let me be the lover-mother,
> lay again
> your head, here, here;
> ...
> see I tell
> and tell and tell the same thing over again,
> over and over
> in monotonous tone,
> I love you,
> love you,
> love you,
> dear-my-own.

He writes, "I have glimpsed your spirit beyond you and watched and wanted. Then suddenly I was shielded and loved. It was more than I could believe or bear. Please, if you can, stay near me." She comes home with him by moonlight across the rooftops to let him into her rooms. Bryher is watching across the street (laughter).

Bryher is getting tired of McAlmon's carrying on, drinking parties, giving drinking parties. Kenneth decides he must attract Bryher, too, if he is to continue his relationship with H.D. He succeeds so well that Bryher asks McAlmon for a divorce and eventually marries Kenneth Macpherson—talk about a triangle. (Audience member: a quadrangle.) Kenneth at this point gets into photography. This furnishes him with a safe future and also the expanse of time to continue his affair with H.D. They remain friends throughout his lifetime. They are companions. He can keep up with her restless pace—Bryher's—through their marriage and his bisexuality is also an asset. He writes kind of Bronte-esque novels garnished with silver-tipped walking canes, expensive suits, and villas.

The three take a honeymoon trip to Vienna and Bryher meets Freud. At this point, Macpherson, Kenneth Macpherson starts shooting a film. This is the beginning of a sort of cinematography and Bryher starts *Close Up* magazine, which is an instant success and goes on for six years until 1933. Here are reviews of experimental films, psychoanalysis as a theme, Sergei Eisenstein. They show films in Berlin. This was a... if you ever can see copies of this... a very beautifully done magazine and something that nothing had...not yet treated cinematography as an art form.

Audience member: What's the time span on that?

Kyger: Six years until '33, so it's be like '27, seven and six, or thirteen. So 1927 to 1933. They do *Close Up* magazine. It's large, beautifully printed. They make films and H.D. has parts in these films and she loves being an actress, and she looks good on the screen. You can see some in H.D.'s biography by Barbara Guest, you can see some photographs in there and she does indeed look very striking and very beautiful.

He's in the movies with her. "H.D. has parts and loves being an actress and looks good on the screen," she writes. But then there is a little side thing here. They make this film over a series of years. She writes to Berlin—she's back in London now—that she is pregnant by Ken Macpherson. And Kenneth writes back—this horrible thing, I think—writes back that she must under no circumstances have the pup—I mean, they seem to think of their children as puppies somehow—and must come to Berlin to have an abortion. He says, "Brave, handsome, beautiful, sad, noble, furry, dignified kitten," that's H.D., "Hurry up, hurry up and come and have that star or star fish or star maiden or whatever it is removed." So she immediately goes to Berlin and Bryher takes care of the abortion. She recuperates by seeing the sights in Berlin and going to the zoo.

She's still in the movie. She's compared to Greta Garbo and treated like a star. They produce a well-known movie at this time called *Borderline* in Switzerland with Gavin Arthur—who later arrives during the hippie times in the Haight-Ashbury as the famous astrologer—with Gavin Arthur and Paul Robeson and his wife and H.D. so they make this movie together there with H.D. doing her usual flirtations. Laurie Lenya is there at the time and says the most important thing in the film is H.D.'s work and she should do nothing but films. But these are, of course, are being privately financed by Bryher and they're more art films of a psychoanalytic kind of nature. They are not, of course, like what's happening with the tradition of filmmaking in the United States, which are movies for commercial consumption.

But the British don't like the movie *Borderline*. Too Germanic. But so Bryher decides it's been good training for her...this is an interesting comment... making movies has been good training for her because "it taught me speed in my writing. Not to hang about looking at my characters in a novel, but to get them moving and to try to fix a landscape in a sentence as if it were a few feet of film." Interesting way of seeing what you've done as an influence on writing.

Kenneth and Bryher build Kenwin in Switzerland, which is a Bauhaus house, a cubed eccentric affair—the only modern architecture around which has now been declared a landmark. It's a kind of a sterile looking place. But at that point Bauhaus was, of course, "the modern form"—which H.D. uses as a retreat in the years to come. This place called Kenwin, there's a picture of it in H.D.'s book...and a place for her daughter Perdita to come home to. Perdita is officially adopted by Bryher and Kenneth Macpherson. A glimpse of the early Kenwin can be found in H.D.'s short novel *Nights*, which she wrote under the name of John Helforth. I don't think it's been reprinted, I haven't ever read it. Macpherson always refers to it sometimes as when she's in there writing the novel, "Garbo is in there writing."

So onto Freud. A quote from Kenneth Macpherson: "Oh, that awful cat," I think he's calling her a kitty here. "Oh, that awful cat. She has got in, hasn't she? She'll be unbearable. A pupil of Freud. She'll live on that until she dies." Kenneth Macpherson wrote to Bryher in March 1933, "H.D. said she needed to see Freud because she wanted to 'dig down and dig out, root out my personal weaknesses, strengthen my purpose, reaffirm my beliefs, channelize my energies.'"

She becomes his patient and people in Vienna. She writes a book about that too, Freud. Bryher foots the bill and it's expensive, but Bryher's father, by this point, has died and has left her several million dollars. At that point, it's hard to know—translated like eight hundred million dollars or something at this time in the '30s, so she can kind of afford it (laughter).

He finishes her analysis in December 1934. Freud gives H.D. a dignity, a confidence, and her writing becomes freer, but she was not healed as a person and needs to have a psychiatrist in attendance all her life. She goes back to writing, "If I can get across the Greek spirit at its highest, I am helping the world and the future. It is the highest spiritual neutrality." She is reaffirmed in her identity as a poet.

They go back to London and lease a new flat together, she and Bryher in 1934. They lease a flat in London with room for Bryher and H.D. together. When the war starts, Kenneth spends those years in New York and stays on after the three of them visit together.

They go to New York City—and that's when H.D. meets Norman Holmes Pearson, who becomes her mentor and assumes this major role and being in a strategic place in the academy and therefore able to enrich her career. A friend, confidante, an admirer and given power of attorney over her and her work. In 1938, Richard Aldington finally gets a divorce from H.D. so he can marry, has a child of his own is on the way. She relives this whole thing with Aldington and becomes hysterical and paranoid and euphoric and writes letters but recovers, and they remain friends throughout his life.

The Second World War begins, and H.D. and Bryher spend the time together in London. They stay there during the war, writing, helping and muddling through, taking care of themselves. Simple things like learning how to boil water. It's very funny, there's a little paragraph in there about, "How do you do it or how long do you wait? If it goes bu-bu-bu, does that mean it's ready?" (laughter) Because these women have been always taken care of. They're not cooks, you know, they're not *Hausfraus*.

At this point, they become friends with the Sitwell's, which is an important and admiring friendship with Edith, Osbert, and Sacheverell. H.D. at this point becomes obsessed with someone called the Air Chief Marshal and Fighter Commander, Sir Hugh Dowding. He was her war monument and the Achilles of *Helen in Egypt*. He believes in life after death, giving lectures about astral heavens.

He comes to see her because she's written him, saying that she had received messages of where bombs were to fall. He tells her to be careful, that beings of a lower order could get into communication, dealing with these astral bodies. To be careful because you might get...you're not getting what you think you can get, you could get into something that could really start to... She turns to the Society for Psychic Research and Table Tipping. She writes some long poem "The Walls Do Not Fall." Well, spiritualism was in England at that point. London was highly practiced and participated in it.

Bryher at this point settles an income on her of about two million dollars, plus a yearly income on H.D. Plus, H.D. has money from her own family wisely invested. Yet she continues to think of herself as impoverished, fearing to spend money. She and Bryher have been together for twenty-two years and really her only extravagances are the theater and flowers. She always has fresh flowers in her apartment, daily flowers, and you can feel that ambiance in her poems at times.

This is about when her old friend Frances and her mother are killed in a bomb attack. "Much poetry is published during the war because it took less paper," —this is what Barbara Guest says. "And the people bought any book available for something to read." She completes "Tributes to the Angels," "The Flowering of the Rod" in 1944. All part of her *Trilogy*. Bombs continue to fall. This is a devastating time and place in London. They live a simple life, standing in line for food. Then after the war is over, H.D. has a nervous breakdown, a mental breakdown, and is hospitalized and put in a clinic in Zurich and has shock treatments. It's like she held herself together through this time of incredible necessity, and once it was over, she just got unglued. They kind of keep it a secret and they tell her friends that she has meningitis and Bryher takes care of everything and kind of smooths it out. She finds H.D. a hotel to stay in Switzerland to which she moves in the winter of 1946. It's a very handsome place near a park where she stays for the next [tape cuts out temporarily].

...threatenings of suicide is always very ongoing. Enthusiastic and active intellectually and physically.

Now begin during these six years when she's in this hotel, begin her prolific years when she writes *Helen in Egypt* and "The Sword Went Out to Sea," a prose story full of extraterrestrial themes, still not published, but very spacey. She has no day-to-day domestic problems. She takes her meals at the hotel. Her room is straightened daily while she is at a local cafe or coffee. She has nothing to do but write. All legal and literary details are taken care of by Bryher and Norman Holmes Pearson. And her daughter goes to the United States. She writes "White Roses and Red." Aldington, Richard Aldington, her former husband is living nearby, and they start up a correspondence and he becomes her adviser, and Bryher helps him financially and also his daughter. She writes "The Mystery," a story about the early Moravians and their leader Count Zinzendorf. She goes to New York and visits her daughter, Perdita, who has now become Mrs. John Shaffner, whose husband is a literary agent, and they have four children who become writers and artists. It seems like Perdita has a very healthy life with a family and doesn't seem to have any of the emotional difficulties that her mother had or even from being raised in this very unusual way.

At this point, she reads Pound's piece *Cantos* sent to her by New Directions, and she begins her own book of cantos, *Helen in Egypt*. "I never went to Troy, only a phantom went. What's this? Then did we toll in vain. There simply for a cloud." She finishes the cantos in 1956 and says in a letter to Bryher that Helen was her alter ego, that only through Helen did she remain alive.

She makes a recording of *Helen in Egypt* in a studio in Zurich in fall 1955. It's the one we'll listen to later. After that, realizes she needs prose introductions to each section. It is a mature way back stylistically to the early H.D. She is among the scenery and props of her youthful writing: scarves, sheathes, sandals, flowers, island, sand, and ships. An older Helen wandering with her sandals securely strapped now. What were her feelings towards the people who appeared in her life and what her effects are on others? She discusses it in this.

In 1947, Bryher flies off to America to divorce Kenneth Macpherson, who is then living with Peggy Guggenheim among her collections of paintings. Peggy Guggenheim and herself, the grand Guggenheim heir and also a great connoisseur of art and a great patron of art. Kenneth Macpherson doesn't really want a divorce, but Bryher is learning to be independent of both he and H.D. Good for you, Bryher. She's busy at this point writing historical novels. You can still find Bryher's novels sometimes in public libraries that have books from the '30s and '40s and '50s. One of the books she writes at this point is called *Beowulf,* which is the historical life of Beowulf and eleven more until 1971. She's very prolific, and they don't really sell because, as people say, there's no sex in them. This is still the male hero just during these great adventures, but no violence and no sex.

Bryher has another meeting then with Marianne Moore. What she says about Marianne Moore at this time, "Marianne Moore terrified me." (And we'll be reading Marianne Moore) "She terrified me. She was so very queer about her mother. The mother was thought to be dying of cancer and in such agony. Marianne wanted the doctor to do something, as the mother could neither eat nor speak and could eat nothing, and Marianne could not eat because if her mother could not eat, now she will only eat her mother's diet, raw vegetable juice."

She visits Hilda's brother, where she finds H.D. has about a million dollars in the bank that he has invested for her. Bryher writes H.D., "I'm afraid I'm rather shocked and almost a little angry. You have over 50,000 pounds tucked away in good American dollars and you never spend any of it. Now, you could buy yourself a car and hire a permanent chauffeur or have a maid. You must try to give people a bit more and larger tips. For heaven's sake, start spending some money. You can't take it with you."

After all this time in which H.D. has been totally supported and taken care of by Bryher, she has this stash back there. Bryher doesn't know what to say. "Get a car. Give people larger tips." Bryher continues to be generous and gives Kenneth Macpherson a villa in Capri and then outside Rome and then in Siena, where he dies in 1971. And at this point, he has become a great interior decorator. At this point, Bryher takes up with a funny elderly guy, Dr. Schmideberg. He's a kind of rote type of guy, and he's a great drinker, interested in psychoanalysis, and amazingly an elegant companion. She calls him "The Bear."

H.D. does not want to return to London again after the horrors of the war, and she never does. She continues to stay on in Switzerland. When H.D. is sixty-seven in 1953, she has an emergency operation and they remove a section of intestine and she is moved to a sanatorium for recuperation where she stays for the next eight years, a refuge for those who cannot manage life on the outside. She loves it there. It's a very elegant place run by Swiss and staffed well, and she loves it there and the people there. She goes to the cinema in Zurich. The food is good.

During this time, she makes a final visit in 1956 to Yale, a historic occasion where she is greeted as a celebrity with the press. She is seventy years old then. Robert Duncan comes to meet her. She is given tribute at Yale by Saint-John Perse, Elizabeth Bowen, Djuna Barnes, P. Boyle, Flossie Williams, William Carlos Williams, Thornton Wilder. Three thousand people attend this homage to her. That's when she meets Denise Levertov and becomes interested in her poetry among the young writers of that time.

She goes home to work on a piece called *Hermetic Definitions*. Back to the sanatorium, the Villa Marina. The sanatorium is sold in 1961, and she's moved to a hotel in nearby Zurich by Bryher. She has a stroke and dies in the hospital, September 1961 on the twenty-seventh day. The day before she died, H.D. received her publisher's copy of *Helen in Egypt*, which Bryher placed in her hands. She was buried on Nisky Hill in Bethlehem, Pennsylvania, with her family's graves. A few years before her death, H.D. had written to Norman

Pearson words that could be used as her own epitaph: "I think I did get what I was looking for from life and art." And then some more epitaphs from selected poems: "So I may say 'I died of living, having lived one hour.' So they may say, 'She died soliciting illicit fervor.' So you may say 'Greek flower, Greek ecstasy reclaims forever one who died following intricate song's lost measure.'"

This biography of H.D. has been criticized in some ways for treating her life on a very real level. My own feeling of reading it was that H.D. had been put on such a pedestal. I was around Robert Duncan during the time when he was writing his work on H.D. and she seemed way beyond, untouchable, in this insane perfection, and reading this book about her, well, we do see who she was, how she was really taken care of. Not to say that anybody that was that well taken care of could pursue their writing without the extraneous details of life that we all need to take care of. It helped me in some way put her in better perspective.

A Rose is a Rose Unless it is a Sea Rose

Interlude by Amy Bobeda

In the following lecture, Jane Augustine introduces us to the origin of Objectivism, through the contrast of Imagism and Objectivism in the writing of H.D. and Lorine Niedecker. Augustine draws us through H.D.'s poems, most notably "Sea Rose," as examples of Objectivism and Imagism—the sparse use of image standing for what it is, like the infamous Stein line, *rose is a rose is a rose*. We explore this sparse representation through the lens of two female poets who lived vastly different lives straddling the first half of the 20th century, when few women were distinguished as *poets*. H.D. was born the year Emily Dickinson died; Niedecker was born thirteen years after Dickinson's first posthumous collection was published. While the aforementioned Stein and Dickinson have been canonized and referenced, H.D. and Niedecker remain in a quiet place of American poetry waiting to be discovered by women in search of poets who mirror themselves.

Alongside Augustine's meandering biographies of H.D. and Niedecker's journeys as women poets, she also emphasizes their external relationships with men and nature. We see the influence of Ezra Pound and Sigmund Freud as pillars of support, allowing H.D.'s work to unfurl and flourish. Similarly, we find place as a distinct inspiration in the sparse words of Niedecker, who Augustine suggests lived a rather 'uninteresting' life. This may make the woman poet ask *what constitutes an interesting life?*

In recognizing the depth of the poetic life of H.D., we must also recognize the influence of men whose personal histories have clouded their work in our eyes. In a sense, H.D.'s work was born from the triad of herself, Pound, and Freud. While an anthology on feminism and specifically a lecture leaning into the life of the female poet rather than her work, a full encounter with the way Pound and Freud shaped H.D.'s world may not take center stage, although its presence persists and should be noted. Simultaneously, it's important to note the importance and influence of Pound, despite his moral transgressions. As Augustine says in the lecture, Pound's three rules of Imagism (direct treatment of the "thing," no unnecessary language, and writing as a musical phrase rather than metronome) "set the tone for 20th century poetry," which directly influences H.D.'s use of images, likely also prompted by the symbolic nature of growing up in the Moravian Church—the oldest remaining sect of Protestantism. Poet Robert Duncan writes in *The H. D. Book* of the German reformist Count von Zinzendorf who greatly shaped the Moravian Church, "created rituals and wrote hymns in which a new religious language emerged that brought out the associations of sexual and spiritual images. The spear, the wound, and the flow of the blood from Christ's side were deliberately related to the penis, the vagina, and the menstrual flow.[1]" It is said that his church created a hole in the wall covered in red cloth for children to enter, symbolically entering the wound of Christ, which was also the womb (tomb), which was also the wound of humanity. The depth and visceral quality of Moravian images must have contributed to H.D.'s Imagism beyond the simplicity of roses being roses. Metaphor, it seems, was steeped in her from an early age. This feminine and masculine triad of H.D., Freud, and Pound returns us to more ancient balances of masculine and feminine, rather than a trinity of father, son, and spirit we've grown accustomed to in the patriarchal age.

In H.D.'s "Hermes of the Ways," Augustine remarks on the line, "I know him/of the triple-path ways/Hermes," as an indicator towards H.D.'s balance and commentary of masculine, feminine, and her bisexuality, but also speaks to her process in the liminal space of mystic experience. As mentioned by Augustine, much of H.D.'s work, especially that on Greece was born from her visions and later analysis with Freud, which bolstered her belief in what was seen, rather than dismiss it. This speaks strongly towards the centuries of pressure for women (and men) to dismiss numinous experience in favor for the divine to transmit solely through the church. H.D., fortunately, lived otherwise. In this way, the triple-path speaks to the above, the below, and the space walked in between, as Hermes, like H.D. was a traveler, a moderator between the seen and unseen worlds.

---

1 Duncan (449)

Augustine's encounter with Niedecker's work focuses both on the pastoral—nature encounter, synonymous with H.D.'s, as well as the use of persona, adopted by both women, but prominently lived in Niedecker's *Thomas Jefferson* or *Mary Shelly*. She considers the persona as a way for us to be someone other than ourselves—perhaps an empowering escape for these women. Simultaneously, it could be seen as the female poet's ability to travel across the world and through bodies, empathically living the experience of those outside herself. Regardless it opens the possibility to be ourselves and others simultaneously bridging worlds and realities through the strength of imagination.

While Augustine returns to woman's experience in the work of both poets, there is little correlation to the female body, and the experience within the female body rather than the female body in relationship with society. In the pastoral and persona, we may miss the depth of experience held within the body. We read the *Sea Rose* as a rose at sea, and miss the images, the multiplicity like Zeizendorf's side of Christ representing many things at once. The arid scent of sea rose could move the poem into the space of menstrual, miscarriage, and post-birth experiences. Perhaps we find similar nods in "Thomas Jefferson," Niedecker's talk of seedlings based on a letter Jefferson wrote to his daughter. At some point we must feed the poems through our bodies and the innate femininity that traveled through H.D. and Niedecker as they wrote and read these works. In what ways were their use of Imagism to code the experience of the feminine (an act women have been partaking in since the origin of human culture) and to what degree are they employing imagism in the way a male writer would?

As Augustine self-titled the lecture *Imagism, Objectivism, and Women's Myth,* she notes the lack of work in myth towards the end of the lectures. (She will return to it in the next lecture of this collection.) Of course *Helen in Egypt,* she calls H.D.'s "personal mythmaking" yet the lecture itself creates a certain myth of these poets, living somewhat isolated imaginative lives with minimal personal struggles outside of motherhood (or almost motherhood), and marriage, yet something of this myth dismisses the mystical and mythic way H.D. and Niedecker saw the world, building their own worlds with a few words per line, the Hermes of their time, the conduit for the triad of earth, spirit, and the female body. They did not walk the traditional patriarchal feminine or masculine path, but rather chose a third—devising the otherworldly experience of the imagist female poet.

Imagism, Objectivism, and Feminism

Jane Augustine
July 8, 1987

Transcription by Amy Bobeda

Jane Augustine: I'm glad Anne said what she said about the vision of this program. This is the first year that I have taught at Naropa, but I've been a student of Trungpa Rinpoche for twelve years, and I consider that sitting practice and his teachings have been the major way for me to open my own intelligence and become a scholar poet, so I hope that some of that clarity that is his will come through today. I wanted to use my large topic *Imagism, Objectivism, and Feminism* as a way of organizing and clarifying some of the points that we've been talking about all along in relation to your own writing practice, the context of this talk is your writing, what you can use so, there will be an emphasis on that.

First, I want to give you a brief outline of today's session to help you categorize your thoughts. First will be a section of history on Imagism and Objectivism. Second, a biography of H.D. principally, since Anne has already taught a class on Lorine Niedecker, you know more about her. Third, reading of the poems which you have in the handout. Fourth, development from short to long poems in both H.D. and Lorine Niedecker. And fifth and last, construction of myth. We won't get to that last section completely today in any case, so section five will continue on Thursday evening in the joint class which Anne Waldman, Diane di Prima, and I will conduct together on the long poems of H.D. *Trilogy* and *Helen of Egypt*, her fully constructed myths. I wanted to give you that outline so that you would be clear about how I'm proceeding, and I've organized the handouts to fit in that outline.

I want to say one preliminary thing about my title *Imagism, Objectivism, and Feminism*. Feminism is not a political term here, it's shorthand for—the shortest way I could figure out to say—that we will be concentrating on the experience of the woman poet, as we must when we look at poets who happen to be women. H.D. which is short for Hilda Doolittle in case you don't know—so I want to say, for women here, students writing, you should be aware of the facets of these poets that reflect women's experience, as we should. For you men here, you have an opportunity to open your mind and see what is vital and interesting in women's experience that informs the art of women. I wanted to make clear what I meant by feminism in my title, but I suppose at this point *Imagism* and *Objectivism* may not be terribly clear either.

To begin on the historical: fundamentally, Imagism as a movement began in England in 1912. Ezra Pound was the major theorist, but there were a group of poets around him, principally, H.D. and Richard Aldington, who later became H.D.'s husband, and some other people T.E. Hulme, F.S. Flint, and John Gould Fletcher; you don't need to remember all of these names particularly. The reason I've given you on top of your pile of readings is there is a statement in the first part of my essay on Lorine Niedecker *The Evolution of Matter, Lorine Niedecker's aesthetic,* in that there is a restatement of Pound's Imagist definition and the rules. So, I call your attention to that part of this opening paragraph, "Ezra Pound's *Imagist Manifesto* inspired poets to produce their own poetic incarnations of his theory as much as did his own practice of translating and annotating Chinese and Japanese poems and forging the *Cantos* out of imagistic elements and techniques." Pound's familiar imagistic rules now follow, so note those.

"An intellectual and emotional complex in an instant of time" —now you've heard that before in these talks I think. He also gave a set of three rules. One, direct treatment of the thing. Two, to use no superfluous words. Three, to compose and sequence of the musical phrase, not the metronome. I want you to pay attention to those three rules because in some way they have set the tone of the entire practice of the 20th century in poetry in all sorts of different areas that's gone and a whole lot of different directions, lots of different ways to express but that's fundamentally where it all began.

Objectivism, briefly, was born, so to speak, in 1931. Louis Zukofsky made statements in the sixth movement of a "Poem beginning 'The" and in his essay, "An Objective." You'll hear more about Louis from Michael Heller this evening, but I call your attention to the statement. Maybe you have heard it but here it is for you to refer to:

An Objective: (Optics) — The lens bringing the rays to a focus. (Military use) — that which is aimed at (use extended to poetry).

That definition is a scientific definition from *optics,* and science important to the Objectivists. Use extended to poetry, "*Desire for what is objectively perfect, inextricably the direction of historic and particulars,*" and then he adds, "*Writing occurs which is the detail not mirage of seeing, of thinking with things as they exist and of directing them along a line of melody.*"

You'll see that the whole opening passage of this essay of mine shows there is a distinct line between those three rules of Imagism statements of Objectivism. One more point, there's a distinction that's important between Imagism and Objectivism. They don't exactly follow each other because Imagism as a movement was international. It began in England among English speaking people, but it's kind of connected with Europe, so it extends into Modernism later on, and we'll talk about Modernism at another point. Objectivism is an American movement rooted in America, but the person who holds those two parts together is William Carlos Williams. You heard Allen [Ginsberg] talk about the short imagistic poems of Williams, and they are imagistic, a very clear practitioner of Imagism, but he didn't live in Europe, he wasn't involved with the Europeans. He had a little love flirtation with H.D., knew her in college and so on, but he also had his own way of developing his work, and so he's like the trunk of a tree Imagism and Objectivism kind of branch off from him in terms of technique.

Okay, enough history.

(A student asks question about Objectivism; precise question is indecipherable.)

I think they read them, but I'm really talking here about the point of view of the writer. Objectivist writers are rooted in the American scene. The Imagist writers who developed into the Modernist movement combine different languages and cultures and link themselves with the arts.

So, with that background of general theory I would really like to get to H.D. and the particular focus on the woman artist which comes in connection with her work. She had a very interesting life. She was born in 1886, last year was her Centennial. She was born in Bethlehem, Pennsylvania. Bethlehem got its name because it was founded by Moravian Christians, a visionary eighteen century sect founded by Count Zinzendorf. Her mother was Moravian and that was important in H.D.'s development. Her father was a New Englander and an astronomer, which is also very important in H.D.'s development. Her father became director of the Flower Observatory in Philadelphia, and they moved from Bethlehem, Pennsylvania, to Upper Darby which is closer to Philadelphia in the middle of her teens sometime. In 1905 or so, she met Ezra Pound who a student at the University of Pennsylvania. She went to Bryn Mawr College for a year, a year-and-a-half maybe, but dropped out in 1906. It was either go with Ezra or get a conventional education and she couldn't—Pound won essentially. They were engaged to be married at one point.

The story of that is told in her novel. (Holds up a photo of H.D.) This also shows you that H.D. was very beautiful—very much like a Greek goddess this photo, with a band around her hair, beautiful nose, and down cast look. She's very classic in appearance and that became her... (Student asks for title of novel.) The title of this novel, as written by H.D, was simply *Her,* and it was reminiscent of Gertrude Stein since *her* which is an objective form of the pronoun becomes the subject of the sentence. New Directions couldn't hack it and they said, well you've got a call it *Hermione* but we'll will capitalize *HER*. This book was not published for many years. It is a fictionalized account of her love affair with Ezra Pound, but also her love affair with a woman named Frances Josepha Gregg.

The fact that H.D. is bisexual is I think quite important, especially in the way that she works out her characterizations in her novels and is part of a lifelong desire to unify experience, to reject and refuse separateness. To refuse oppositions between male and female, war and peace, art and science, and that desire for unity is what finally leads her to the completion of her personal myth in *Helen in Egypt* which is the great book published in the year of her death 1961. She was born in 1886 and died in 1961.

You can see from the cover of this that some wise person noticed that *Helen in Egypt* in this poem is a reconstruction of the beautiful H.D. herself. This figure from a Tuscan tomb has the fine profile and classic look that H.D. herself had and were integrally part of her spirit. But H.D. and Ezra Pound did not get married. In fact, she had a sort of nervous breakdown in order, because she couldn't trail behind him, couldn't be his muse. In 1908 he went off to Europe with his own ideas about changing the world through art. You'll hear more about that when Allen talks about Ezra Pound. And in fact, he did change the world of poetry. When he left, H.D. said he left a kind of vacuum, but France Greg filled this vacuum like a blue flame, with a blue flame. But in 1911 H.D. went to Europe herself, and in 1912 was she was the instrument of the founding of the Imagist movement.

I'll say more about the Imagist moment after I just outlined what happened the rest of her life. She married Richard Aldington in 1914, and she had a stillborn child in 1915 which disturbed her greatly. She published her first book *Sea Garden* in 1916, and Richard Aldington joined the Army and went away during World War I. When he came back on leaves at various times, he started love affairs with various women, especially a woman named Dorothy York, and H.D. was enormously wounded by this betrayal and more or less separated from him.

While he was away in 1918, she had a brief love affair with a man, a musician named Cecil Gray and became pregnant. In the fall and winter, January of 1918 and February of 1919, she was in the late stages of her pregnancy, and she got double pneumonia was extremely ill. The doctors said she would not live. She or the child would certainly die, probably both of them and in this desperate state a woman friend came to her, a woman named Winifred Ellerman, who became known as the writer Bryher. Bryher's father was the richest man in England, John Ellerman; he was a shipping magnet. Bryher came to H.D.'s rescue got her to London from cold chilly Cornwall, got her doctors, saw to it that she had the right medical care.

In March of 1919, H.D.'s daughter Perdita was born. Perdita, you'll member from *A Winter's Tale* Shakespeare, *Perdita* means "lost one." H.D. and Perdita lived and the lifetime companionship of H.D. and Bryher began. Bryher took

H.D. to the Scilly Isles off of England in 1919, where she had her first mystical experience. One that she refers to as the *jellyfish experience.* She later recounted this to Sigmund Freud who psychoanalyzed her in 1933. Bryher and H.D. traveled to Greece in 1920 where H.D. had a second very powerful mystical experience which she calls *The Writing on the Wall.* She saw certain kinds of symbols and they gave her signals about what she felt she had to do as an artist. She was writing poetry prolifically—I'm not going to give you all the dates that are listed in the collected poems—and she also began to write prose, a novel called *Palimpsest.* Bryher became a person who financed the Arts and founded a magazine called *Contact.* Bryher married first a man, these are two marriages of convenience for Bryher, Robert McAlmon with whom she edited *Contact,* and then she married him and then she married Kenneth Macpherson who was a filmmaker, and in 1931 H.D. made a film called *Borderline* with Paul Robeson, and Paul Robeson's wide—a fascinating film, which I've seen, hard to get—a silent film, but H.D. was very much involved in that time with mixed media.

Student: What year was it made?

Augustine: 1931, I'm sorry. *Borderline* is its name in relation to marginality it both race and gender.

In 1933, H.D. feeling that she was blocked in her writing, went to Sigmund Freud in Vienna to be psychoanalyzed, and this psychoanalysis transformed her life, essentially, because she felt that her work with Freud validated her mystical experiences. She later recorded, actually she took some notes at the time kept in a kind of journal but put them all together in the book called *Tribute to Freud.* It's a wonderful and fascinating book and for our Thursday evening class I have handouts from *Tribute to Freud* as well as from *Trilogy* and *Helen in Egypt.*

During the War, the Second World War, H.D. wrote a memoir of her childhood called, *The Gift,* which exists in published form but very cut down from what, edited from what HD actually wrote. In 1951 [she wrote] a novel on her Moravian background, a novel called *The Mystery,* which is unpublished and that's the focus of my own work on her. The great poem, though, of World War II written between 1944 and 1946 is called *Trilogy.* It's really three book-length poems. Put together that book exists in paperback. It's one of the great long poems of our time and everyone should have it I think. In 1961, the year of her death, *Helen in Egypt,* which is really the culmination her lifelong attempt to be involved with the Greeks and to rewrite *The Iliad* in the way that Pound rewrote the Odyssey, was published. That was in 1961.

Helen in Egypt retells the story of *The Iliad* but from the point of view of Helen not from the point of view of Achilles. We'll have more to say about that on Thursday evening. Another collection of poems *Hermetic Definitions* was published by her literary executor Norman Holmes Pearson also in 1961 after her death. She had a very interesting life and with that outline, I'm ending the biographical section, but I want to you to hear the details of the imagist movement because it's one of the most important moments in modern literary history.

This is how Imagism began—in September 1912, Hilda Doolittle arrived in Europe, and one day she met Ezra pound at the British museum, and this is how the story goes. She put her books and gloves away and pulls out a notebook and hands it to him, he reads, "*Hermes of the Ways,*" Hilda's poem, suggested by an invocation to Hermes by a poetess Anyte who was in the Greek Anthology Pound had first introduced her to. Why dryad—this is good—dryad is a tree nymph and this was Ezra Pound's nickname, pet name, love name, for Hilda Doolittle. He takes out a sharp red pencil changes a word here are there crosses this one out. He rereads the poem and then the next one, another poem based on a translation from a Renaissance book he had also given her then there is *Orchard.* Pound is really pleased. She is a model pupil more than she is a poet. The scornful exacting teacher is now certain of this. Reading "*Hermes of the Ways*" he again takes up his pencil and signs the poem *H.D. Imagist.*

That's the way it actually happened. He was a publicist for Imagism and sent these poems to be published. For all of his sense of his male dominance of her artistic career the fact is that she had a direction of her own and a feeling of her own that really makes her the all-important Imagist practitioner. Her practice of Imagism is closer to the rules than anyone else's, but the Imagist moment in history is an important one and so we should now see what these poems actually look like that. That brings me to the *Sea Garden* collection.

Student: Was that the first time she was referred to as H.D.?

Augustine: Yes, I guess I should ask as a little footnote about why Ezra Pound changed her full name Hilda Doolittle to H.D. It is the first time that she had begun to use those initials. In 1912, George Bernard Shaw's play *Pygmalion* was playing on stage at Coven Garden, and if you remember from *My Fair Lady,* which is the modern remake of *Pygmalion,* the flower girl heroin was a terrible Cockney accent is Eliza Doolittle, and she is remade by Professor Higgins into an acceptable upper-class person by their reconstruction of her accent. It's a completely wrong image for H.D., besides "Doolittle" is a kind of ridiculous name for somebody as energetic and applied to poetry. It had deeper psychoanalytic and psychological ramifications for H.D. because after she took the initials H.D., she invented a whole series of names for herself, both as writer and as character in her novels which are very autobiographical. So sometimes she called herself H.D. Aldington, sometimes she called herself Delia Alton. She has male pseudonyms, John Halforth is the name she used in the 30's. She refers to herself, often the names begin with an *H* she is the model for Hipparchia in her novel, *Palimpsest.* There's a dual character male, two characters, a mother and a son, Hedyle and Hedylus in her novel called *Hedylus.* The name has the H in the D in it; she has a character Henry Dona—H-D—in the novel *The Mystery.* So she played with her name continually from that time but that liberating moment was when she took those initials and got rid of that schoolmarm-y funny stiff name which didn't suit the tall elegant—she was a beautiful dresser too, very stylist too—H.D. was right for her.

(Student asks about the name change.) She didn't do it herself at first, but all the rest are hers. Pound was a very important influence and editor. You gotta hand it to him. You'll hear more about Pound from Allen, but Pound edited TS Eliot's *Wasteland.* He knew how to tell people how to cut.

(Student asks about translations.) I think there are very loose. I think that the things she read in the Greek anthology were merely inspiration. She also translated *Euripides.*

But just to give you a little more of Pound's ideas and influence in terms of

Imagism, there are some interesting statements. Objectivity and again objectivity and no expression, no hindsight, beforeness, no Tennysonian-ness of speech, nothing, nothing that you could have been some circumstance in the stress of some emotion actually say. Now that is Pound. He's using the word "Objectivity" in another place he says of poetry, this is what it's got to be, "*Objectivity. No slither. Direct. No excessive use of adjectives. No metaphors that won't permit examination. It's straight talk, straight as the Greek.*" He's actually referring to H.D.'s poems, which appeared in *Poetry Magazine,* in January of 1913, really launching her career.

I'm going to read "Hermes of the Ways." I was just not able to Xerox everything and I kind of caught up the first pages of the book *Sea Garden.* This is the photographic duplication of the actual volume that was bound in red. The opening poem in *Sea Garden,* we're looking at "Sea Rose."

> Rose, harsh rose,
> marred and with stint of petals,
> meagre flower, thin,
> sparse of leaf,
>
> more precious
> than a wet rose
> single on a stem—
> you are caught in the drift.
>
> Stunted, with small leaf,
> you are flung on the sand,
> you are lifted
> in the crisp sand
> that drives in the wind.
>
> Can the spice-rose
> drip such acrid fragrance
> hardened in a leaf?

The image is clearly looking at a particular kind of rose. The title "Sea Rose" establishes a landscape of the sea, and this is not rhymed. There's no comment.

(Student asked when it was published.) 1913. The book *Sea Garden* was published in 1916, or approximately 1913 was when they were written. There's also something else you're going to see in all of these early poems of H.D., a tension between what is easy and pleasing and familiar which would almost be the rose as a symbol as it's always been used as symbolic of women, of femininity, of beauty and whatever. But this rose is tougher and yet it's stunted and it's flung about and it has an acrid fragrance. So within the directness of the image we get still some hint about roses in what they have meant, but what H.D. is doing especially in these very first poem actually is beginning a project which is a lifelong. The attempt is always to go out, go farther. Adventure over the sea.

And I think I'll skip over to "The Shrine," because we see the beginning of her mystical interests as well as the construction of the imagery of the sea, which later on, through psychoanalysis with Freud, she began to see in more primal terms the sea is identified with the mother, and here it's the literal sea which is a wide space, limitless. Dangerous. And in contrast to the land. And she watches over the sea. The shrine is on a steep place and difficult to reach and dangerous but these are all the things that attracted H.D. And yet there is a as scene here—

> Are your rocks shelter for ships?
> Have you sent galleys from your beach?
> Are you graded, a safe crescent,
> Where the tide lifts them back to port?
> Are you full and sweet,
> Tempting the quiet
> To depart in their trading ships?
>
> Nay, you are great, fierce, evil —
> You are the land-blight.
> You have tempted men,
> But they perished on your cliffs.

Your lights are but dank shoals —
Slate and pebble and wet shells
And sea-weed fastened to the rocks.

It was evil — evil
When they found you,
When the quiet men looked at you.
They sought a headland
Shaded with ledge of cliff
From the wind-blast.

But you — you are unsheltered,
Cut with the weight of wind.
You shudder when it strikes,
Then lift, swelled with the blast.
You sink as the tide sinks,
You shrill under hail, and sound
Thunder when thunder sounds.

You are useless:
When the tides swirl
Your boulders cut and wreck
The staggering ships.

This is both imagistic and mysterious. You can see this shore and yet you feel that it is far beyond. That the shrine is a dangerous, mysterious place. It is rock.

And poem ends, I'll skip over to part four.

But hail —
As the tide slackens,
As the wind beats out,
We hail this shore —
We sing to you,
Spirit between the headlands
And the further rocks.

Though oak-beams split,
Though boats and seamen flounder,
And the strait grind sand with sand
And cut boulders to sand and drift —
Your eyes have pardoned our faults,
Your hands have touched us;
You have leaned forward a little
And the waves can never thrust us back
From the splendor of your ragged coast.

I think there are many things in this poem which are not to be accounted for by the Imagist tenants, and it's very interesting that H.D. has always been talked about as errant crystal, slight poems, finely chiseled. This is much more a recognition of tension, danger in the literal sense, the sea will beat you against the rocks, but this is hymn to a spirit. And the defining of that and working out of that spirit takes her a whole lifetime. Next to this, "Midday" is much more what we think of as imagist technique.

The light beats upon me.
I am startled—
a split leaf crackles on the paved floor—
I am anguished—defeated.

A slight wind shakes the seed-pods—
my thoughts are spent
as the black seeds.
My thoughts tear me,
I dread their fever.
I am scattered in its whirl.
I am scattered like
the hot shriveled seeds.

The shriveled seeds
are split on the path—
the grass bends with dust,
the grape slips
under its crackled leaf:

yet far beyond the spent seed-pods,
and the blackened stalks of mint,
the poplar is bright on the hill,
the poplar spreads out,
deep-rooted among trees.

O poplar, you are great
among the hill-stones,
while I perish on the path
among the crevices of the rocks.

On the imagistic level, so to speak, you can say that it's a description of a terribly hot day. You can see the light and sense of touch, often there is a physical weight in H.D.'s imagery. I'm scattered, like shriveled seeds, there is this imagery again of obstruction, shriveled, beaten down, blackened. By contrast practically a phallic symbol, "O poplar, you are great," there's a tree. This is the tension in the most submerged way between the sense of herself as a struggling artist, the struggle of existence; and the opposite of that the ease speaking out, the ease of growing up on high of being seen and being great. And so, I think in a very hidden way these objects are not translatable exactly, but one can see the tension that is felt between small and great as a projection of the mind of the women artist and the male spirit.

(Student asks question.) I thought that would be a too allegorical way of reading it. I'm simply pointing out that Imagist technique works, that is the thing itself is enough. I'm trying to think of the line— "the natural object is the adequate symbol—the natural object is the adequate symbol." What I'm showing is not how things symbolize so much as meaning adheres in objects always, and that these poems in their imagistic technique demonstrate that with great clarity.

Let's look at "Sea Violet" as a final take. This very submerged hint, the way H.D. words with flowers—we've seen the "Sea Rose," now we see the "Sea Violet."

The white violet
is scented on its stalk,
the sea-violet

fragile as agate,
lies fronting all the wind
among the torn shells
on the sand-bank.
The greater blue violets
flutter on the hill,
but who would change for these
who would change for these
one root of the white sort?

Violet
your grasp is frail
on the edge of the sand-hill,
but you catch the light—
frost, a star edges with its fire.

This is the positive view. The white violet is small, it's humble, but it catches fire. That's the other side of H.D.'s power.

Of the original poems that Pound praised, I want to mention the one called "Hermes of the Ways" to read you a line of it because Hermes becomes one of the most important figures in H.D.'s future. Hermes has been identified for us as Mercury the Roman god, but Hermes is also Hermes Trismegistus. Hermes thrice powerful is identified with the Egyptian God Thoth, the inventor of writing. Hermes is a shape changer. H.D. never kept the same name, she didn't choose the same pseudonyms. She changed shape. Hermes is like the Trickster figure African folklore. Like Coyote in American Indian folklore. How does coyote look? Well he looks just like a man. Trickster figures change format will and Hermes of the Greek is that figure who changes at will with whom H.D. profoundly identified. So, "Hermes of the Ways," begins this way—

The hard sand breaks,
And the grains of it
Are clear as wine.

Far off over the leagues of it,
The wind,
Playing on the wide shore,
Piles little ridges,
And the great waves
Break over it.

But more than the many-foamed ways
Of the sea,
I know him
Of the triple path-ways,
Hermes,
Who awaiteth.

Dubious,
Facing three ways,
Welcoming wayfarers,
He whom the sea-orchard
Shelters from the west,
From the east
Weathers sea-wind;
Fronts the great dunes.

Wind rushes
Over the dunes,
And the course, salt crusted grass
Answers.

Heu,
It whips round my ankles!

Hermes of the triple pathways. He who waits. Dubious, facing three ways. I want to stress that the sense of doubt is important in H.D. "Facing three ways," for H.D. I think is to face the female way/feminine way, the masculine way, and the unity of the two of them which is expressed in her bisexuality, as well as in the final versions of her myths in which there are enormous identifications between male and female.

"Hermes of the Ways" —so there's a Greek landscape already set up which is the ground for her entire life project and there's that sense of struggle, obstacle, and there is the utter clarity of the objects in the landscape: the flowers—poppy, rose, violet—and the motif of Hermes the shapeshifter who really shows that H.D. did not invest in any one sense of identity and all her name changes go along with that. She's dubious of a fixed identity; she changes. But the important thing from the point of view of language is the tightness, the clarity of use of the image, which is in fact the conduit of the extended myths of herself which characterize her later work. She builds up her late poems from a series of images modified by her thought, because I suppose that a thought itself actually becomes an object for her. Also, the images become Mystic images, actually seen in her mind coming from another dimension later.

I would like to compare I show you some similarities and differences between H.D. and Lorine Niedecker. You have a packet of poems of Niedecker's. You have already been introduced to Niedecker by Anne. On this Xerox, these are just taken out of the book by Lorine Niedecker called *From this Condensery.*

I'd like you to look at the little poem that begins without a title, a student:

> *A student*
> *my head always down*
> *of the grass as I mow*
> *I missed the cranes.*
>
> these crayons fly in a circle ahead
> said a tall fellow.

Well this is witty with its kind of accent—the man who made the word cranes into two syllables— crayons—but you can also see a reflection of this doubt about the self and modesty, reticence, in Lorine Niedecker's condensation. There's also a contrast here between head down in the grass studying, studying the grass. But you see the scene: she's mowing the grass and some cranes flew overhead in a circle and she missed them. The contrast is between being a student head down, she's kind of criticizing herself, I missed the cranes, *I didn't see what was in the sky, the vision overhead.* The poem, incidentally, is a rhyming poem. The First "as I mow" rhymes with "tall fellow."

It's very... there's no comment. She leaves it to you in contrast to see that it is some kind of comment on herself. At the top of the left of the first page, "So this was I," She's looking at a photograph of herself—now, when we look at photographs of ourselves we are confronted with our own fixed identity that's some moment in which somebody actually said, "Here you are."

so this was I
in my framed
young aloofness
unsuspecting
what I filled

eager to remain
a smooth blonde cool
effect of light
an undiffused good take,
a girl
who couldn't bake

How I wish
I had someone to give
this pretty thing to
who'd keep it—
something of me
would shape

The syntax is Objectivist syntax. The condensery here is "I wish I had someone to give this pretty thing to keep it and would shape something of me." This is a poem about being a woman, "I wish I could stay young and blond and a nice conventional girl." Lorine Niedecker was very fair and shy and lived in an uneventful life in Fort Atkinson, Wisconsin, having been married for a few months in 1930 and nobody knows who he was or what his name was even. And then marrying again in 1962 a man named Al Millen, and writing poetry all of her life. So this a poem about, which is beginning to develop the sense which is submerged in Niedecker comes out only cautiously once in a while, but shows us that her woman's experience is what's vital to her.

This is the point that I developed and you can read it for yourself in the essay called, "A Woman Poet Specifically." But, I will call your attention to the poem that I quote at the bottom of the page. Niedecker is listening to a bird—there are a lot of bird names in her poems, she's often the small bird. Niedecker says in listening to the wood Pewee:

> be alone
> throw it over—all fashion,
> feud.
> Go home where the greenbird
> is—the trees where you pass
> to grass.

That's her manifesto, and that's her advice to poets. Be alone. Throw it over. All fashion—women are fashion conscious, that comes into her poem "*Winter Green Ridge*," which I'll talk about in a minute.

"Throw it over, all fashion, throw it over all feud." —Don't carry on feuds. "Go home where the greenbird/is—the trees where you pass/to grass."

One thing that these two poets, H.D. and Lorine Niedecker have in common is, first of all their compression—great similarity in the line compression, condensation which makes for intensity. Less is more. Water rises higher in a narrow pipe.

(Student asked Niedecker's birth and death dates.) Lorine Niedecker's dates are 1903-1970. Thank you, I should have—I was kind of counting on the fact that Anne had talked about Lorine Niedecker and I didn't spend a lot of time of her biography but her dates are 1903 to 1970. So, Niedecker, just as firmly as H.D., obeys the injunction *no extra words*. Another point that you can clearly see is that in both poets there is what I would call a version of *pastoral*—natural world is the subject. H.D. reshapes the natural world, the flowers, the violet, the rose, the pear tree—which I think we're actually from her parents Garden in Upper Darby, but she turns it into the landscape of Greece. Whereas Niedecker is much more literal actually recording what she saw and heard around Fort Atkinson, Wisconsin. Nevertheless, there's a continuing motif there. Third, there is some hesitation and ambivalence about women's conventional roles, at the same time that there is great sympathy for women as in Niedecker's poem "Who was Mary Shelley." Niedecker had no children. H.D. had a child who died and a child born under difficult and ambiguous circumstances. And yet Niedecker writes a sympathetic poem—

Who was Mary Shelley,
what was her name
before she married?

She eloped with this Shelley
she rode a donkey
till the donkey had to be carried.

Mary was Frankenstein's creator
his yellow eye
before her husband was to drown

Created the monster nights
after Byron, Shelley
talked the candle down.

Who was Mary Shelly?
She read Greek, Italian
bore a child

Who died
and yet another child
who died.

This poem incidentally, illustrates a fourth point that I would like to parallels between H.D. and Lorine Niedecker, and well, I would say it is the technique of the persona. That is, putting on a mask. *Persona* is the Greek word for mask—it was the actual face mask that the actors in comedy and tragedy held up in front of their faces to show they were no longer whatever particular Athenian but that they were Zeus or Oedipus or whoever. The masks also were amplifiers like megaphones. So the term *persona* has the word *person* in it, but it's also the technique of identifying with someone else. The Mary Shelley poem is not a not a strict example of it, but I'll give you a strict example. The persona that you might try sometime—it's a useful disguise that you might try. Be someone else. Lorine Niedecker often decides to be someone else. In her long poem "Thomas Jefferson," which is in many sections, she shifts back and forth between being Jefferson and commenting on him. But here's one part.

The poem "Thomas Jefferson" begins this way:

I
My wife is ill!
And I sit
          waiting
for a quorum

Another one:
Part IV
Latin and Greek
my tools
to understand
humanity

I rode horse
away from a monarch
to an enchanting
philosophy

Now, that's almost like saying "throw it all over." That's Lorine Niedecker disguised as Jefferson. The persona technique, this mask that you put on first is a way of escaping from being drawn out of yourself, being someone else. Niedecker identifies with Jefferson, she becomes Jefferson in order to write this poem.

VI
To daughter Patsy: Read—
read Livy

No person full of work
was ever hysterical

Know music, history
dancing

(I calculate 14 to 1
in marriage
she will draw
a blockhead)

Science also
Patsy

This is extracted from a letter Jefferson wrote to his daughter very much condensed in the Niedecker style, but this is Niedecker speaking as the man Jefferson. H.D. often uses the persona and the poem that you have in front of you in another chunk, "A Dead Priestess Speaks," is a persona poem. This is now the longer and middle H.D. where she is applying Imagist techniques to developed the longer poem, and in it she's also developing and through the disguise is able to say things she couldn't say otherwise. This Priestess we find out is called Delia of Meletis. So, H.D. is assuming a persona again in her Greek landscape but now she's almost inventing a character in a drama, so her personal myth is enlarging.

"A Dead Priestess Speaks"

I
I was not pure,
nor brought
purity to cope
with the world's lost hope
Nor was I insolent;

I went my own way,

quiet and still by day,
advised my neighbor
on the little crop
that faded in the sudden heat
or brought my seedlings
where hers fell too late
to catch the first
still summer-dew
or late rain-fall of autumn;

I never shone with glory
among women,
and with men,
I stood apart,
smiling
they thought me
good

Far far far
in the wild wood
they would
have found me other
had they found me
who no man yet found
only the forest god of the wet moss
of the deep under ground
or of the dry rock
parching to the moon
at noon
I folded hands when my
hands lifted up a moment
from the distaff
I spoke of luck that got our
ardent son dictatorship
in a far city
when I left my room it was to
tilt a water jar or

fill a wine jar with fresh vintage
not too ripe
I gave encouragement
and sought
do you like this pattern of the helm
of Jason's boat
a new one with the olive
I smiled, I waited
I was circumspect
oh never never never write
that I missed life or loving
when the loom of the
three spinning sisters stops
and she the middle spinner
pauses
while the last one
with the shears cuts of the living thread
then they may read the pattern
though you many not
I
being dead.

I think that there is significance in the fact that Lorine Niedecker chooses the mask of Thomas Jefferson, she can stop being Lorine Niedecker... a quiet... and speak with authority and identify with a great thinker, a traveler, a man of power, a man with ambivalence; she can stop being herself. But that's just as true for men, obviously. That you can also choose a persona and it need not be a persona of the opposite sex. In this poem that's "A Dead Priestess," H.D. is a woman, but she is a woman who it's a way that she can express an ambivalent attitude which she perceived in society toward the woman who says she is a mystical, who says she's going to be a priest, and that she's going to have religious power because traditionally in society religious power, mystical power is attributed to men. Lots of men have decided, you know, "I'm going to go off, I'm going to go to Japan and study Zen for twelve years, I'm going to go to the mountains and be a hermit," and everybody says, "Gee, that's admirable. That's a really terrific thing to do." But, if a woman says, "I'm going to leave the kids, I'm not gonna do the dishes anymore, I'm gonna go to the mountains and mediate," everybody says, "What's the matter with you? Why aren't you staying home and taking care of the kids?" so there's a—

(Student interrupts with persona question.)
Yes, the persona is a marvelous device. You can choose anybody!

(Diane di Prima speaks, inaudible.)

I think that Diane is quite right to point out that you should be aware that some figure haunts you and will descend on you and you should take that voice—in fact what you will do is say, "I'm going to sound like that person does not sound like me, those are not my thoughts." It's a release from egotism and a release from convention and conventional behavior and it's a conduit to the development of a deeper theme. The persona poem in H.D. leads to the construction, the reconstruction, of the entire view of women in Western civilization. This is the point that I'd like to end with today, but I feel very lucky because Anne and Diane will join me on Thursday evening and we will continue to show how H.D. developed the full myth of herself in *Trilogy* and *Helen in Egypt. Trilogy,* I'll give you a capsule line into *Trilogy,* in *Trilogy* H.D. reclaims and redesigns the figure of our Lady, the Madonna, and the muse. That is, she's reworking Christian tradition. In *Helen in Egypt,* H.D. redesigns secular tradition of *The Iliad,* in which Helen is blamed for the war. She's an airhead. She's a beautiful woman; all those Greeks died for this, a face. In *Helen of Egypt* there is a complete reconstruction of the figure of Helen, Helen was the name, was H.D.'s mother's name and *Helen in Egypt* is written after the psychoanalysis by Freud, which freed H.D. to understand her identification with her mother. So we will talk about women's myths, actually the tail end of my title for this course. We could say that on Thursday evening the topic will be related to those books *Trilogy* and *Helen in Egypt*—bisexuality, mysticism, and language—on Thursday evening. And I have three handouts to give you which I'll put up here on the table. One from *Trilogy*, one from *Helen in Egypt* and one from Tr*ibute to Freud.*

Conjuring the Infinite Imaginary

Interlude by C. M. Chady

"Woman must write herself. Woman writing herself will go back to this body that has been worse than confiscated, write yourself. Your body must make itself heard. Then the huge resources of the unconscious will burst out. Finally, the inexhaustible, feminine imaginary is going to be deployed."

— Hélène Cixous, *The Newly Born Woman*

During a time when the world is in upheaval from global pandemic, institutional racism, climate catastrophe, to list only a few crises facing humanity, I find myself pulled into a similar framework by which H.D. wrote her poetic collection *Trilogy*. Written during World War II while living in London while the city was being bombed, with the external overwhelming and devastating, she noted in a letter to Norman Holmes Pearson that, "The orgy of destructions...to be witnessed and lived through in London, that outer threat and constant reminder of death...drove me inward." Instead of succumbing to the ongoing violence, surrendering self to its obliteration, she turned to her work which embodies the transformative and evocative nature of the Word and its ability to shape reality. She fully embraces the ability and necessity of the Word, of language, of its social exchange, to initiate and create change. In the face of death and devastation, in turning inward, she carves out what knowledge her body holds of language to manifest experience.

H.D.'s work is riddled with complexities of the interplay and interweaving of mind and body, myth and history, and of a bisexual self. In order to appreciate the depth and richness of her poetry, in Jane Augustine's lecture, focusing on *Trilogy* and *Helen in Egypt,* she utilizes theory of French feminist critic Hèléne Cixous to serve as a lens that illuminates these intricacies. With additional information and robust discussion from Diane di Prima and Anne Waldman, the three women illustrate the profound influences that H.D. pulled from in myth and history in order to construct her works. By pulling heavily from alchemy, Judeo-Christian tradition, Egyptian and Greek mythologies, she conjures the past into the present, pulls these vast traditions together to integrate them into something new. Often through etymology, through origin and evolution of language itself, she shows the ways in which words unfold throughout time, how the very essence of language can be utilized in an alchemic nature to transform and change. It makes sense, especially given the dark time that H.D. was writing *Trilogy,* that she illustrates how change in language can be mapped which illuminates subconscious constellations of association, as well as the ability to continue to create and transform meaning through its constructions. As Augustine discusses throughout her lecture, this word play and punning is key to H.D.'s work. She often links words based solely on their sound or based on their root commonalities that immediately showcase language's ability to unfold in an alchemical way.

As suggested, *Trilogy* was H.D.'s means of turning inward to herself. Throughout the lecture, with attention to Cixous' theory, Augustine emphasizes that ways in which H.D. was writing through herself, through her body. As Cixous states, "Women must write herself." H.D. writes not only through and of her body, but incorporates myth and history into a new narrative centered around the values of the feminine experience. She resituates women as the agents of change, the beholders of the future. With one section she discusses within her lecture, she highlights the way the H.D. describes Mother Mary, Mother of Christ. She states (in *Trilogy,* "Tribute to the Angels," Poem 32), "She [Mary] bore/none of her usual attributes;/the Child was not with her." Here she is no longer fulfilling the childbearing and rearing role that a patriarchal society has limited Mary to. A couple poems later, in Poem 38, H.D. elaborates on what Mary carries instead, "She carries a book but it is not/the tome of the ancient wisdom,/the pages, I imagine, are the blank pages/of the unwritten volume of the new." The books of ancient wisdom call to all books that were written before, that have carried society to its present day, that have created its morals and values, which in the time of H.D. situated in the violence of World War II, are failing. Instead, she carries a book full of "the blank pages/of the unwritten volume of the new." Mary, the Mother, carries the future yet to be determined. It is open and pristine, waiting to be recorded.

On one account, this points to H.D.'s belief in the power of words to be transformative. Words create the world, as Augustine also discusses in depth in her lecture. With the yet unwritten book, it is up to the present humanity to write the present and future. She holds the ability to carry and perpetuate what is set forth within words. From another angle as well, H.D. herself, through *Trilogy* is writing the very book that Mary holds unwritten. She is writing the volumes of the new through this collection, a conjurer of hope, of a different future. H.D. collects traditions of the past and appropriates them into a feminine agenda, spinning a history that has long been written solely by men to suit a patriarchal society. She does not omit what came before, but shows it through a new perspective, a new purpose, one that it not exclusive. By reconstructing past narratives that have limited the feminine experience, she opens potential in the present and future away from rigid linearity of solely the masculine. Her dynamic work shows how the present is formed by layers of overlapping potential.

Augustine continues to delve into the complexities of H.D.'s work. In using Cixous as a lens, she delves into their common bisexuality, and how H.D. writes this duality of being into the fabric of her poetry. Because she identifies as being attracted to both sexes, she also feels within her the stirring of both male and female characteristics, oscillating between them, both equally vital to a sense and construction of self. Writing characters that are both female and male representations of themselves, of different sides of a coin, highlights the bisexuality of being as opposed to the monosexuality. More generally, she is adapting masculine traditions into the realms of her work, which is neither entirely the old masculine tradition, nor entirely feminine. It is a weaving of the two to create a new, harmonious space. As Cixous says, "Woman is bisexual," highlighting the nature of women to be open to plurality, as opposed to linearity, the ability to encompass versus exclude. Because her work implements these expressions of bisexuality, there is not a notion of a fixed self, rather it is constantly shifting and evolving, which also allows for new ideas and concepts to be welcomed, rather than rejected. One can incorporate these ideas into a new version of the self to continue to shift and integrate these multitudes. Augustine aptly depicts instances of expressing bisexuality through language within H.D.'s work throughout her lecture, leading through the examples and professing through her interpretations.

Augustine's lecture goes much further than to discuss "Mysticism and Language," although the title is a hint at understanding the core of H.D.'s writing. She discusses the alchemic transformation and potential available in language through H.D.'s poetry and Cixous's theory. The melody of these works alongside her own scholarship shows the revolutionary vision of women, how their minds form a new foundation build on knowledge harnessed from within their being, from writing woman as women. They create a paradigm shift, a focus on the potential of the feminine, of the bisexual, of the openness that is tethered to the essence of humanity and its power through language to transform, even amid destruction. The legacy of H.D.'s work has carried throughout the twentieth century, into the twenty-first so elegantly and aptly because what she writes of and how she constructs it are still relevant to how we interact with our world today. Even with feminist theory opening new avenues of engaging with the feminine and the woman's body that were liberating in expressing an experience of an entire half of humanity, we are only in the nascent stages of realizing the impact and significance of opening ourselves to new version of histories, new potentials of a future. With the reconstruction of only partially told histories, woman's narrative becomes fuller, her purpose more reflective of how we experience our lives. As we consider how to approach the future amid so many crises for humanity, it is vital to tap into the essence of the inexhaustible feminine imaginary, as Cixous calls it, in order to create new visions of the world.

H. D.

Mysticism and Language

Jane Augustine
(Anne Waldman
and Diane di Prima in company)
July 9, 1987

Transcription by C. M. Chady

Diane di Prima: Good morning.

Anne Waldman: So this is basically Jane's class, as you know, and we're just here as guardians.

Jane Augustine: This is a joint class I couldn't do without my guardians. I'm very happy to see everyone here again because it's very nice to have this opportunity to continue discussion. We began with the short poems and the images technique, which H.D. laid down early in her life, is the technical basis for what she does later, but now we're going to try to tell you something about her long poems. We've given you a taste in the handouts, and I think that it's very important to contemporary poetry to know these long poems. They've inspired Robert Duncan himself, a very great contemporary poet, in his own poetic meditations, so the depth of H.D.'s mystical thinking is very far-reaching, and in these long poems, as I've said, in her long poem *Trilogy* and in *Helen in Egypt*, I believe that H.D.'s major project is to construct a myth of woman. Now of course I'm using myth in the sense of a large construction of meaning, larger than that which is derived from science or from everyday observation. H.D. wanted to unify the fragments of her life. She wanted to see a unified world—"world unity without war" is the phrase she uses in her novel *The Mystery*. And at the heart of divisiveness is the division of gender between male and female, but many other divisions are healed by her word "magic," so it's delightful to have Diane here who knows a lot about magic and healing. That's what I think is going on in these poems through the medium of language.

To open this discussion, I would like to read part of an essay, a study, that I had made. The way that H.D. uses language as the conduit or the way she sees language as the conduit to mystical experience. It is the word for her that matters. But the way I go about this actually is to begin with a manifesto to women writers by one of the best known of contemporary French feminist critics, Hèléne Cixous, who has written an extensive study of James Joyce and whose writing is very filled with puns, word play, and language intricacies. She'll lapse into English and German in the middle of her French, and so she is an inspired writer herself and is very interested in women's writing particularly, for which there is a French phrase, L'Escriture Feminine. That's a little hard to translate, you wouldn't translate it "feminine writing," believe me—it's translated something like "women's writing," but since French is a language that has a feminine gender constructed into certain words, there is a way that she can pun and play. So she's a critic that I like very much, and because of her particular puns, coinages, ways of approaching language, she's particularly applicable to H.D. and H.D. to her. And because of H.D.'s interest in language and mysticism, I refer to her as having a "Modernist mysticism."

So, L'Escriture Feminine—is it a hope or a fact? The French feminist critic Hèléne Cixous, in an essay called the "Laugh of the Medusa," issues a manifesto: "Women must right through their bodies, they must invent the impregnable language which will wreck partitions, classes, and rhetorics." I'll read that again because I think that it's something that you can take seriously, meant to, but she's writing from point of view of women. "Women must write through their bodies. They must invent the impregnable language that will wreck partitions, classes, and rhetorics."

In "Sortie," Cixous's long essay in *The Newly Born Woman*, she reiterates, "Woman must write herself. Woman writing herself will go back to this body that has been worse than confiscated, write yourself. Your body must make itself heard. Then the huge resources of the unconscious will burst out. Finally, the inexhaustible, feminine imaginary is going to be deployed." I think that's a wonderful manifesto. I would like to see "the inexhaustible feminine imaginary" come out. "The huge resources of the unconscious" will come out if you write from your body.

This is Hèléne Cixous. Now I'm going to apply it to H.D. because I believe that practice of L'Escriture Feminine existed before the theory, and theory is therefore profoundly validated. I believe that aspect of this imaginary has already been deployed by H.D. in her late works *Trilogy* and *Helen in Egypt*. A key sentence in *Helen in Egypt* reads, "She herself is the writing. She herself *is* the writing." This is not a metaphor, but a statement of essence, and therefore a linguistic paradox. How can a writing and a self be identical? "She herself is the writing," suggests that Cixous's program has been carried out and implies the question that arises in one's mind, how *does* a woman actually write through her body? Or write herself?

Cixous is clearly not a biological reductionist. She's not talking about anatomy is destiny. She's not prescribing content or method. The body is the seat of the unconscious which is impregnable, and of course, impregnable is a pun. Impregnable means, "that which cannot be made pregnant—physically" but it also means, "that which cannot be destroyed."

So, the impregnable unconscious in woman's body parthenogenetically produces impregnable language, but how and where? What language can simultaneously inscribe woman's physical body and the unconscious, which is not physical?

H.D. found this problem central, this is a central problem that she grappled with. In a way, it is the old philosophical problem of the mind/body split. But actually, she is dealing with it more existentially. She lived that split in quite a powerful way, and we see it in her imagery. Toward the end of her life, she saw that writing the body equals writing history. Writing the unconscious equals writing myth. But myth and history are not separable. Mind and body are not separable.

So, when she is trying to unite myth and history, mind and body, the bridge that she uses is speech. You probably have heard in more than one discussion of Buddhism, of the basic triad—body, speech, and mind. So a key feature of her language in her late poems is puns, coinages, word play, double meaning, inventions, words laden with multiple connotations, words building up what I call spiritual palimpsests, overlays of spiritual meaning.

H.D.'s late thought and writing centers on word linkages by sound. You have some of these in the passages that are selected from *Trilogy*. She manipulates names, gender, etymological definitions by sound. She has a mystical vision of the power of the Word. Her theory of language is that the Word is both the sign and the signified Word and what it refers to. Word and referent are inseparable. Therefore, Word has a kind of body, a kind of substance. It is not just an accident or an instrument of rational mind, which in H.D. would be seen as a characteristic of the masculine world. Masculinism and rationality have a kind of link. So this view of the Word, with a capital "W," actually begins in *Trilogy,* which was written during World War II during the bombings in London, and in it she—she suffered a lot during those bombings but came to believe that the power of life was stronger than the power of death, and the theme of *Trilogy* is resurrection. But she saw that the power of the Word to create was greater than the power of the sword to destroy, and this Word with a capital "W" is the Christian logos— "In the beginning was the Word" and the Word was with God and the Word was God—that line is repeated by her but she's pulling it out of conventional Christian context altogether. It's not a transcendent word or a metaphor, it's actually the words that we actually use.

"Poem 10" of *The Walls Do Not Fall*, which you all have front of you, repeats the question often asked of the usefulness of art during the war—what good are your scribblings? H.D. answers, "*We take them with us/beyond death.*" The Word can conquer death. She conflates St. John, the author of the Gospel of John, which begins with, "In the beginning/was the Word," but she combines him with Hermes Thoth Mercury. Because her tradition is more magical than Christian, though my particular study at this point is to show that there is a Christian element which she has drawn on from her childhood. At this point in her life she's going back to recreate a sense of union with her mother, which is what you can read about in the selections from *Tribute to Freud.* She began to feel that connection.

So she's taking St. John and putting him into a context that is indeed more important for her, the hermetic, the one dominated by Hermes, the shape-changer. She also takes seriously the idea that a word is a thing, and she even eludes to the notion that every sound ever made theoretically vibrates forever. The indicated flute or lyre notes on papyrus parchment are magic, indelibly stamped on the atmosphere somewhere forever.

(Diane di Prima and audience members talk; words indistinguishable.)

di Prima: That's the theory of the astral, and also the sense that the word is a thing—she had been doing ritual and angel magic for years by this time and the word is creative of this world in that tradition. It makes this actual—there are many levels of reality but we call this one the "actual" world, let's say—and the word itself is creative of actuality.

Waldman: It's forms, so the hermetic tradition is completely related to language as its process, as pure form.

di Prima: There's a sense that you pull from this astral to here by the means of the word. The Word is a conduit to bring things, to precipitate them out into manifestation.

Audience member: How can you know this experiential?

Augustine: Through ritual, and I would say through poetry.

Waldman: I was going to talk about that later, talk about her inspirations in terms of being a writer and all of us being writers and how it's kind of a model for ritual process in terms of one's own practice.

Audience member: So it's every sound that resonates...

Augustine: Yes, it's every sound that resonates, and actually she goes on to say it is not just words but phonemes within words, so that the next section...

Audience member: Where the does noise go?

di Prima: It's not noise.

Augustine: It just exists.

Waldman: It's transformation.

Augustine: The theory of the astral light, which she would be been quite cognizant of, says that every thought form, and definitely every act and every spoken thing, exists on that other plane and can be drawn on at will and the reason why, for example, meditating on traditional forms like the Tree of Life produces a bigger effect is because so many people have built up that thought form and it has that much more consciousness built into it, but that everything is there. The broken stuff is there, and what they call "lower astral" is more of just a confusion and then the more organized and will-invested images and so on contain more organic unity. And she would have been playing with all of this.

Let me go on to show you a little bit more about her theory of language. I don't want to cut off discussion, but I also want to direct it.

H.D. asserts a personal approach to the eternal realities that would be the meditation that Diane is speaking of. But she lays it down in the poems, which you will find, there are some breaks in your handout, but "Poem 39" on the page that says "540" at the bottom, "We have had too much consecration,/too little affirmation,/too much: but this, this, this/has been proved heretical/too little: I know, I feel/the meaning the words hide;/they" —that is words— "are anagrams, cryptograms,/little boxes conditioned/to hatch butterflies..." Now, you know that the butterfly is the traditional symbol for resurrection and transformation. So the "Poem 40" continues, for example: Osiris equates O-sir-is or O-Sire-is. Osiris, the star Sirius, relates resurrection myth and resurrection reality through the ages.

Now, that's a kind of word play with sound. It's the sound that links "Osiris" the name of the god, who is the god of the Nile, the flood, spring, the god who is the twin or Isis—male/female twinned figures, and for her there is a pun on the word "relate" because "relate" means "to connect to things," but it also means "to tell a story." And you would address a god as "sir" or "Sire," but you also know that god is one of the names for being, which is conveyed by the verb "is," and so there's an anagram in "Osiris", "O sir is'" and you turn that around and you get the star Sirius, the dog star, which was also associated—it's a winter star—associated with the drowning of Osiris and when the Nile floods, which is beneficent, which brings the summer. The Dog Star is the one that follows Orion, and Orion is a winter constellation, so actually Sirius is seen early in the evening as summer comes on. No that's not true, in the morning. It may be different in Egypt.

So, "Poem 42," well, "Poem 41" on this same page— "*Sirius:/what mystery is this?*/you are seed,/corn near the sand,/enclosed in black-lead,/ploughed land./*Sirius:/what mystery is this?*" and this, the "S" sounds—serious, mystery, is this—are all for her actual connections, and she repeats, Sirius, "you are drowned/in the river,"—that's Osiris or—"the spring freshets/push open the water gates./*Sirius:/ what mystery is this?*/where heat breaks and cracks/ the sand-waste,/you are a mist/of snow : little white flowers."

"Poem 42"—"O Sire, is this the path?/over sedge, over dune grass,/silently/ sledge-runners pass./O, Sire, is this the waste?/unbelievably,/sand glistens like ice,/cold, cold;/drawn to the temple gate, O, Sire,/is this union at last?" So the words are a conduit, a connection, a union.

di Prima: Another thing she's referring to there, probably, is the tradition that Isis, and therefore probably by association Osiris came from Sirius, which was the old Egyptian belief that they stated that they came from the star Sirius, which feeds into a lot of stuff people have been looking at recently like the Dogon myths which include traditions about a watery planet that goes around the star Sirius, the Dogon without telescopes or writing knew that Sirius was a double star long before we did. They've known it for hundreds of years. But that's modern. In her day, it was simply that Isis, and probably Osiris therefore, came from Sirius, some kind of tradition that Egypt came from another star to the earth.

Augustine: The mystery of how we got here. She has—I call these incarnational etymologies; it's my own term, but in the second part of *Trilogies,* a set of three books, the first one *The Walls Do Not Fall,* which is the one we've been quoting from, the last poem in *The Walls Do Not Fall* says, "*possibly we shall reach haven,/heaven.*" And haven and heaven sound alike so they are connected, they are really together. The similar sounds create semantic linkage for H.D. even if linguistic science shows no linkage, which has nothing to do with linguistics necessarily. Although sometimes, actually, etymology as a science conforms to some of her observations.

di Prima: There is a name for that—Fulcanelli the modern alchemist wrote a great deal about this kind of punning, and in a book called *Le Mystère des Cathédrales,* which is probably a follow up to "In the Shadows of the Cathedrals" that she was...(someone else speaks indistinguishably)...yeah, and what he calls it is the "Phenetic Kabbalah," and he follows things like the works Ariadne through meanings that lead through Sirius again, and the Dog Star, and so on.

Augustine: Phenetic Kabbalah, okay, we can call it Phenetic Kabbalah. It doesn't matter what we call it. In some way that's the idea that words have power of substance. They have flesh. They're incarnate, that was my way of thinking of them. They have power of substance as a kind of flesh that lives beyond death and regenerates life.

In Book Two of *Trilogy,* called "Tribute to the Angels," there's a Phenetic Kabbalah or incantational etymology in "Poem 8." This whole book is based on spiritual alchemy, alright? There's an analogy between alchemy and the poetic act for H.D. And she is summoning the angels—there are seven of them—and each, I won't go into detail, but each of them represents a spiritual force. Birth, death, war, change—and each has its characteristic color, its characteristic planet, and that's all based on the material that we know she read. But I wanted to call your attention especially to the poems involving the etymologies of "mar" and "mara." There is an analogy between alchemy and the poetic act.

di Prima: And of course, Hermes is the Lord of Alchemy.

Augustine: Hermes is the Lord of Alchemy, which is the hermetic art. But also his name is "Thoth," and as Thoth the Egyptian god he was credited with inventing writing, so he is the Lord of Speech. But I'm wondering if...yes. Look on the page that says "552" at the bottom, at poem number eight.[2] "Now polish the crucible" —that's the alchemical crucible in which the transformation of dross to gold will magically take place. This is a spiritual transformation for H.D. "Now polish the crucible/and in the bowl distill/a word most bitter, *marah,*" —the Hebrew for bitter; "a word bitterer still, *mar,*" —now that's just the plain English word, to mar something, to ruin

2 In *Trilogy,* "Tribute to the Angels," "Poem 8."

it. "sea, brine, breaker, seducer,/giver of life, giver of tears;/Now polish the crucible/and set the jet aflame under until *marah-mar*/are melted, fuse and join/and change and alter, /mer, mere, mère, mater, Maia, Mary,/Star of the Sea,/Mother."

Now, this string you can probably see. "Mer" is the French word for sea. "Mere" is a double word. It means a lake in Anglo Saxon, but it also means mere, slight, or small, and she means both. "Mère" with the accent grave is the French for mother. "Mater" is the Latin for mother, from which the French is taken actually. "Maia" is the goddess, she's the mother of Hermes, but also the goddess of the May, so she is associated with Mary, who has become Queen of the May. "Mary" is our mother. "Star of the Sea" if you translated that back into Latin, "Stella Maris," mother. And the sea, psychoanalytically is associated with both the unconsciousness and the mother, and as we will come to *Helen in Egypt,* you will see that that figure Thetis, the sea goddess, the mother of Achilles, is very important, becomes a double of Helen. Helen is finally unified with her mother.

di Prima: And "Star of the Sea" is traditional, alchemical imagery for a certain stage in the process when the first matter has finally, what they say, "conceived spirit" in the crucible, a kind of stellate pattern appears on the matter, and that's the star of the sea. And Ripley's text says, "Watch carefully, for thou shall see the day star arising with deliverance." She would have been cognizant of these texts.

Augustine: True. (to audience) Yes, you had a question? (Audience member asks question, indecipherable.) And plays on that word.

Waldman: And mirrors too.

Augustine: True...wonderful to have all these additions. This text though moves from the...what's happening is that H.D. wants to convert to bitter experience, to use it, to make it something less bitter. So she says in the next poem, number 9, "Bitter, bitter jewel/in the heart of the bowl,/what is your color?/what do you offer/to us who rebel?/what were we had you loved other?/what is this mother-father/to tear at our entrails?/what is this unsatisfied duality/which you cannot satisfy?"

I think that there is the continual struggle in H.D. between what has been described as her father's science and her mother's art. Alchemy is that union; poetry is that union. And this is the double sidedness of H.D. that I feel is connected with her bisexuality.

In "Poem 10", the star Hesperus appears, and that star is—and also the word mirror comes in, and glass. "In the field-furrow,/the rain water/showed splintered edge/as of a broken mirror,"—Very imagistic line, by the way—"and in the glass,/as in a polished spear,/glowed the star Hesperus,/white, far and luminous,/incandescent and near,"—Union of opposites—"Venus, Aphrodite, Astarte,/star of the east,/star of the west,/Phosphorus at sun-rise,/Hesperus at sun-set." That's just plain old astronomy. Venus is sometimes the evening star and sometimes the morning star—it's not a star, it's the planet that we name for Venus.

But she picks up that name in the next poem, "11." "O swiftly, re-light the flame/before the substance cool,/for suddenly we say your name/desecrated; knaves and fools/have done you impious wrong,/Venus, for venery stands for impurity,/and Venus as desire/is venerous, lascivious,/while the very root of the word shrieks/like a mandrake when foul witches pull/its stem at midnight,/and rare mandragora itself/is full, they say, of poison,/food for the witches' den."

This is what happens in H.D. happens continually. She has to acknowledge that there's a lot of negativity about women, especially sexual women, women who are, whose spirit is presided over by Aphrodite or Venus. They are often considered witches. And this very interesting passage, she says, "the very root of the word," well the root of the word "Venus" and "venery" and "venerous" is "ve," and she says the very root of the word "shrieks"—"veee" —it's a mad idea, but that's what she says, and that's what it is. The very root of the word "shrieks like a mandrake pulled at midnight," which is an act of witchcraft and viewed with suspicion, but she then goes on in the next poem to recuperate. "Swiftly re-light the flame,/Aphrodite, holy name,/Astarte, hull and spar/of wrecked ships lost your star,/forgot the light at dusk,/forgot the prayer at dawn;/return, O holiest one,/Venus, whose name is kin/to venerate, venerator. " So she, by etymology, in the words themselves, transforms that whole name of Venus which stands for lust and bad sex, in a whole negative, masculinized tradition, is turned around to become something true, something powerful, and the become the actual guiding star, the true star.

di Prima: I wanted to point out one or two other things here. One is this polished spear with the glass brings in the grail. Reading these things you have to read them on all the levels you possibly can at once. And then, in the Kabbalah, the third place on the tree, as you know, is Binah, which is called "Bitter Mother" and is called the "Bright Mother"—Ama is "Bitter Mother, Ima with an "I" is the Bitter Mother having conceived, which becomes the Bright Mother, which then goes to the next female place on the tree, Aphrodite, which is Venus, the seventh place. So she's also playing with that, the bitter moving to the bright, is that stuff. The bitter sea is one of the names for Binah on the Tree of Life.

Waldman: The sense of all the dualities, always within the imagery with their resonances and in terms of the grail, the union of male and female, which is the whole intention of this, the whole work, the three-part work. And then the spear comes into it, and in the Freud section he's talking about Aphrodite without her spear, and he think of the lacking, of the lost section, things without their other.

Augustine: This is great. This is all true, and it fits. (Waldman: Mirror) and it's mirror, and it's... (Waldman: Mama) it's mama. And mama! Mama goes on in this poem to be linked to our Lady because in the, in mystical appearance of our lady, in connection with the angel Gabriel, and you will find on page "564" that H.D. in her alchemy has summoned other certain angels Uriel and Anneal particularly in another section, and she also describes the lady. She said in a letter to Norman Holmes Pearson that she spelt the name of the angel "Anneal" with two n's, not the way it's traditionally spelt, but she said, "I spelt it 'Anneal' because it links onto 'Anna,' 'Hannah,' or 'Grace'"—and those are Biblical tradition. Anna is the mother of Mary, and "Hannah" is a variant of that same name, but also is traditionally called "Grace."

In the same passage of this letter to Norman Holmes Pearson, her literary executor and friend, she says, "The lady that has come instead, has appeared as a result of this alchemy, is the troubadour or poet's lady," and she actually appeared to H.D. in a dream. Her presence—female—is key to what H.D. called the poem's "Light Motif," protection for the scribe. The scribe in this case happens to be particularly female, but not just female. Protection for any scribe, for the poet. She's not the limited Christian Madonna. H.D. had this to say, "I distinctly link the lady up with Venus, Anneal, with the moon, with the pre-Christian Roman Bona Dea, with The Byzantine-Greek Church Santa Sophia, and the double "S" of the Santos Spiritus. That's a Meranian reference, but it's the Holy Spirit, essentially. Instead of a child in her arms, the lady carries a book, whose pages are the blank pages of the unwritten volume of the new, and the poet declares her psyche the butterfly out of the cocoon. So there is the reference now to her old Greek tradition, where psyche is the soul transformed and reborn.

(Indecipherable questions and comments about Sarasvati.)

di Prima: ...the priestess card, Sarasvati...(More discussion from her and other individuals, indecipherable.)

Augustine: So in the next two poems, they are beautiful evocations of our Lady, which is what is being transformed here. "We have seen her/the world over,/Our lady of the Goldfinch,/Our Lady of the Candelabra,/Our Lady of the Pomegranate,/Our Lady of the Chair;/we have seen her, an empress,/magnificent pomp and grace"—that might be a reference to the Taro— "and we have seen her/with a single flower/or cluster or garden-pinks/in a glass beside her;/we have seen her snood/drawn over her hair,/with her face set in profile/with the blue hood and stars;/we have seen her head bowed down/with the weight of a domed crown/or we have seen her, a wisp of a girl/trapped in a golden halo;"[3]

I think all of these evocations of our lady are meant to show that she is the universal woman, and she also has many names in "Poem 31," but none of these suggest her as "I saw her" although we approach possibly something of her core beneficence in the gracious friendliness of the marble sea maids in Venice, who climb the altar stair at Santa Maria Day Miracle or we acclaim her in the name of another in Vienna Maria von dem Schnee (snow in German), Our Lady of the Snow. These are linkages from other languages and other names for the universal mother.

3 In *Trilogy*, "Tribute to the Angels," "Poem 29."

She then uses language in Poem 32 from the transfiguration of Christ. "For I can say truthfully,/her veils were *white as snow,/as no fuller on earth/can white them*." That's the description of Jesus in the time of the transfiguration, but, that poem ends, she "bore none of her usual attributes; the Child was not with her."

"Poem 33" begins, "Hermes took his attribute/of Leader-of-the-dead from Thoth/and the T-cross becomes caduceus'/the old-church makes its invocation/to Saint Michael and Our Lady/at the death-bed; Hermes Trismegistus/ spears, with Saint Michael,/the darkness of ignorance,/casts Old Dragon/into the abyss."

It's based on a dream...

Waldman: Which she, in fact in the selections from the *Freud, Tribute to Freud,* the analysis, the dream comes forward, and he interpreted it of course as a mother fixation, as some kind of problem. There's the dream of the light and then the dream of the princess.

Augustine: I'm not sure that they're the same dream, but I think it's the same theme.

Waldman: Same thing of the mother, sort of coming...

Augustine: Appearing.

Waldman: She needs to deal with all this ground of almost male energy and patrons and invocations, to sort of move on to the bisexuality, which was a constant theme with her analysis, and there's a link there.

(Audience member asks a follow up question about Freud and his view of her as the daughter; not fully distinguishable.)

Well, I think that it was more than that. She was working with him as male, and we were talking about this earlier. She came of age in this poem, but she was actually in her seventies when she wrote *Trilogy,* [di Prima politely corrects] Oh sorry. She died in her seventies, but wrote this in her sixties.

di Prima: She was in her fifties when she wrote *Trilogy*.

Augustine: But *Trilogy* is after the psychoanalysis. She wrote it about 1944, you can figure it from when she was born.

Waldman: That's the year it was published.

(Audience member asks a question, indecipherable.)

Augustine: Yes, in which the figure of a woman appears. And the poem is an elaborate on of all of those, of the suggestions that came to her. It's a recreated woman. It's a woman entirely positive, and strong, and it is a woman freed from the patriarchal role for our Lady, which was just to be the mother of somebody, and she has a book in her arms, the blank pages of the unwritten volume of the new, which indicates what H.D. thought of herself as doing and she found her own soul revived, resurrected, after the war. And that renewal, I think, is absolutely the new born person. For me, this newborn person links to all the names that H.D. used for herself. When somebody is newborn, they get a new name for themselves, and it's not like anybody else's name. But this state of mind is one that H.D. continually works with, her fluid identity, it can't be fixed. She used a dozen or more pseudonyms for herself over the years as a writer. She could never pin down herself in any one mode or character in her novels, so she...it's almost onomancy. She creates a new name, there is a new self, and I think this is the way in which she was writing herself, because she believes in the magic of the eternally inscribed word. Yes.

di Prima: It would have been for her too, the tradition from the Golden Dawn, the magical tradition, that at each stage of initiation, you took a new quote "magical motto," which was a new name that is not at every stage of the ten steps, but at many of the stages you took a new name which somehow encapsulated your intent at that point, and she saw life every much as a series of initiations as she passed through various processes that would have also been an inducement from, and I'm not saying it's the only one, but an inducement or a tradition for by you changed your name. In fact, if you read any of the account of those people they all go by those funny initials that stand for Latin or Welsh or whatever mottos they took as their names at any point in their development, kind of like the American Indian tradition where you take different names at different points in your life.

Augustine: In the novels that H.D. wrote, her *Bid Me to Live,* which are really highly autobiographical, she names herself in various ways, and often she has a male twin. In *Palimpsest,* the first novella where Rome has a heroine named Hipparchia, there's a visionary moment in which her lover sees her as a boy, Hipparchius, and in her novel *Hedylus,* there is the mother is Hedyle and the son whose name is Hedylus, that novel is particularly… the son is sort of the artist's self of H.D. and the mother, the female motherly conventional world-weary person, but the two characters represent the two sides of H.D.

In her novel *The Mystery,* there are also duplicated figures. One of them Henry Dohna, who is an actual grandson of Count Zinzendorf, and Elizabeth, which was the name of H.D.'s grandmother. So she sees herself in these paired characters. And so in her prose, there is a sense of a union of separate, contradictory male and female impulses, and it's expressed through these characters and through what I call a "mythic twin" motif, and that is clearly an expression of her bisexuality. Freud referred to her as the "perfect bi"—that is, the perfect bi does not try to repress either side. She was, and it was very clear from the details of her biography, that all of her life she was attracted to and fell in love with both men and women. This has a corollary in her refusal to choose between her father and her mother, between science—her father was an astronomer, looked at the stars—and there is much imagery related to astrology as well as astronomy in her writing. So she was not going to forsake her father, and Freud himself became a kind of father to her, which is a theme of very important sections in *Helen in Egypt.*

Now, one reason that I chose to pick the French critic Hèléne Cixous as a person to talk about H.D. is because Cixous is bisexual and she says, "Woman is bisexual." And actually, that is anatomically or biologically true. Cixous says that it's an advantage at this time, historically it's easier for women to annihilate differences, and that's what H.D. wanted to do. Annihilate differences. Women in general can open up, men in general are trained to aim for the Cixous has called, "phallic monosexuality." And Cixous actually makes a manifesto, or an artistic program out of bisexuality. She says, "Bisexuality is the location within oneself of the presence of both sexes." And she says "It is essential to thinkers, and artists, and those who would create new values. There is no invention possible if you don't have an abundance of the other, or a variety, inside of you, separate people, thought people, whole populations issuing form the unconscious. The springing up of selves one didn't know." That language is almost H.D.'s own language, and she says, and I just read it in a letter that she wrote to her friend Silvia Dobson, "We have many selves," and everything that we are reading in her poetry and prose right now shows how she felt that we had many selves, which is the same thing as no self perhaps. "The springing up of selves one didn't know—our women, our monsters, our aliases."

To have many selves and to be shifting selves, changing selves all the time would be the same as not having a fixed notion of oneself, cast in a particular conventional role. I think that the self means a bisexual self, and self means the same as the word. Language is bisexual. The logos is bisexual, not monosexual. Bisexuality is the essential nature of writing through the body, not only because... (Someone interrupts, indistinguishable.) Me, me. (Audience member speaks again, indistinguishable.) I have many selves. Yes, yes, I've got all of them. And it's just a coincidence that Hèléne Cixous has the same name as H.D.'s mother.

Well, the language is a conduit to the unconscious, the unconscious contains these thought people, separate people, the other, stuff we don't know, which comes, springs up, "the springing up of selves one didn't know—our women, our monsters, our aliases." (Audience member says, "Our friends.") Our friends. The point is that, I conclude, language is bisexual, the Logos, this Word with a capital "W" that H.D. is talking about all the time is a bisexual entity. It is not monosexual. Bisexuality is the essential nature of writing though the body, not only because it accesses the unconscious but also because it is the nonexclusion of a different or a sex.

(Audience member asks a question about Cixous.]

It's well, we would say in English. Hèléne. And H.D's mother's name was Helen, as in Helen of Troy.

(Audience member asks indecipherable question.] One novel is called *Palimpsest*. H.D. was very fascinated by the idea of a palimpsest. You know what a palimpsest is?

Oh, well, a palimpsest is a sheet of, originally a papyrus or a thin sheepskin on which (Audience interjects for clarity.)—parchment—which was made from sheepskin originally—on which a text was written. Paper, papyrus, or parchment was so valuable that often something that was considered unimportant was more or less eradicated. Something else was written over it. (Diane di Prima offers insight into wiping off parchment, audio indistinguishable.) You can kind of scrape the surface and then write another. But for H.D., this became a spiritual principle of memory, essentially (Waldman off-mic, "layers") layers of memory, one on top of another, but the one underneath is never completely obscured. Sometimes you can scrape, but you can't—you can take off the top layer of the writing, but not the deeper impression. She wrote a book called *Bid Me to Live* as an epigraph from Herrick... *Bid Me*. I'm sorry. There is a there was a novel written in 1928, recent, just very recently reprinted was out of print for a long time called *Hedylus*, and the woman character is named Hedyle. The names are obviously deliberately chosen because they've got an H and a D in them. That's just that's just characters in her novel, that's not counting the pseudonyms that she wrote under that she signed her manuscripts with.

(Audience member asks question about Cixous.) I'm sorry, I should've done that from the start. Actually Cixous, it's not a French name at all. She is Algerian-Jewish. That makes it worse. But she's a French feminist critic right now. She's alive and well right this minute, probably arguing with a bunch of people in Paris right now.

Yes, yes. (Audience member asks a question, indistinguishable.) How can it be monosexual? (Audience has a follow up thought/question, indistinguishable.) Fully, fully—language springs and...

Waldman: No language wasn't invented by the patriarch. (di Prima, off mic, mentions syntax.) This is syntax.

Augustine: I'm suggesting that the multiplication of cells from the unconscious, as for H. D., facilitated by words which are literal conduits they create and transform, and so they are the way that new selves arise. And selves, of course, come in masculine and feminine form. Normally, male and female, and it might come in animal forms and a few other forms too, certainly spiritual forms for H.D.

There are many other forms, but writing through the body has to be comprehensive. It has to be. This is a quotation from Cixous. "Writing through the body for women means nonexclusion, for a man as well, means non exclusion of a difference or a sex." And H.D. has that same idea of union—nonexclusion of a difference. Don't let anything hold back your mind. And in fact, nothing can hold back your mind. And you are the resources of your unconscious or more profound than you know and transcend, but include gender distinction.

And by the way, Cixous would know the Kabbalistic, and dual tradition. Cixous writes a lot about male and female figures, Amazons.

di Prima: Aleph, at least, at least for that far back, meditation on repetition of revolving the letters of a single word until it becomes a door into some kind of realization is a Kabbalistic practice. And then became for the Christians meditation on a short piece of the text. And you see that in the mystical Christian writers. But actually, on the single word is in the Kabbalah, you know, at least from the twelve hundreds. What were you going to ask? (Audience member asks question, difficult to distinguish, about sexuality, language, and the body.)

Augustine: I, you incorporate it... Language comes out of you and is not. And it is not, it doesn't exclude anything. Cixous actually plays around with that a great deal. And she'll you know, she'll do...

(Audience member asks if Cixous is a translator.) She is. There are translations of, and the most accessible work of hers, which I am referring to, is in *The New French Feminisms,* plural, edited by... Is it? Well, Isabelle de Courtivron and Elaine Marks—Elaine Marks is a friend of mine.

Do I have to spell that too? Isabelle de Courtivron …(Audience member interjects, indistinguishable.) Bisexuality—it means falling in love with both men and women, not excluding. It means just falling in love. (Audience members are interjecting, indistinguishable.) So it's not hermaphrodites... It's easy to say.

But we're talking about a mystical theory, actually. We're talking about the mysticism of H.D. finally, and this notion of the bisexual incarnate person, dual persons, impose spiritual palimpsests are close to reincarnations. And as we go into *Helen in Egypt*, there are many, many more blurrings of the lines between mother-father, mother-daughter, lover-mother. And in that, in *Helen in Egypt*, there is the phrase, "She herself is the writing, and she is there called a hieroglyph." Now, you know that a hieroglyph is a pictorial representation, which is both a thing and the word. So that notion is very deliberately chosen as central to *Helen in Egypt*, which was originally called "Helen and Achilles," where there was an opposition between Achilles as a male principal and Helen as a female principal and that that evolved into *Helen in Egypt*. Egypt, incidentally, is not only the land of Hermes Thoth, but it is the alternative to and synthesis of the spiritual worlds of Greece and Rome, which were opposed. H.D. plays a lot with this imagery. Greece is the land of beauty and the land of woman. Rome is the land of war. The land of the soldier. The man that sometimes associated with her husband, Richard Aldington. Greece is the point. Pardon me, Egypt is the third way of the Hermes of the three ways. (Audience member speaks, indistinguishable.)

Yes, that. Yes, right. A more primal source. Yes, which H.D. visited with Bryher and the dedication to *Trilogy* is, makes that important.

di Prima: In that blurring. It's interesting that in *Helen in Egypt* there are points at which Greece becomes the male principal as opposed to Troy, which it is for us a lot also. I mean, Greece raises female as, and when compared to Rome, but it is it is the masculine principle when you compare it to Troy, which the Romans and some put down as a sybaritic civilization. The men wore soft robes and oils and so on. So actually, in losing Troy, we lose a certain aspect of our bisexuality. She plays with that, too, I think. Don't you?

Augustine: Yes, yes, absolutely.

Everything you're saying is a wonderful expansion. I mean, I only have one paper and one angle. (Audience member asks a question, indistinguishable.) Biologically, every one begins female in the womb after the moment of conception. So we have the edge somehow because we're, we don't get altered genetically.

di Prima: Compensation. Because half of the chromosomes are ours. (Augustine and others laugh; audience members continue to ask question, indistinguishable. It is roughly about language and sexuality.)

Well, actually, I think it's a good question to go on asking yourself. But language, in this case I'm equating language with Logos with a capital "L." That is the ultimate creative principle that in the beginning was the Word is not a trivial statement. It is the idea that everything we see—material—everything that is manifest was created by a Word. Now...(di Prima interjects briefly.) chanted into being. Yes. So that's a very big concept. Therefore, there cannot be anything left out. You can't, it can't belong to one sex and it can't exclude the other whatever side of the fence you happen to find yourself on in this, can these constellations of energy, which actually, you know, we really don't exist. We are consecrations of energy, not actual physical substances. So the Logos has to be bisexual.

Since the world was chanted into manifestation, we are exactly living in an enchantment. Right? But not in the negative sense of what delusion or illusion is my—the other Maya.

(Audience questions.)

The Kabbalah says that the letters were formed as black flame on white flame and flame also makes a sound. [Audience member continues with question, indistinguishable.]

Augustine: Sure. All... Something's going on spiritually behind language, are we...?

(Audience member asks a question, indistinguishable.)...and meaning?

Well, I think the mysterious thing is that H.D. actually sees those as unified, and that's where the magic comes. You can't quite sort out the sound, the utterance, the articulation from the meaning.

She includes... That's why the puns are possible. That's what makes the puns work. That's why puns are what they are. And that's deeply and profoundly linked with all the kinds of things that are going on in our practice of poetry right, right now. (Audience members asks a question, referencing the idea that a language is a virus from outer space.) A virus from outer space? Well, maybe. But still. Still we're doing it. Maybe toes came from Sirius also.

This... Luce Irigaray wrote a book called—which is translated, it's the same pun in French—*This Sex Which Is Not One.* And she's referring to women. When we say it in a casual phrase, this sex, which is not one, women don't exist as a second sex. They're kind of abnormal. They're a variation on the proper theme, which, has been projected by the male dominant culture as the man. But what she also means is this sex, which is not one sex—it's two or three or twenty-five multiple identities and shifting selves, which Irigaray also develops. She's also a wonderful writer. In French, the French feminist criticism is taken much more seriously and much more publicly, generally discussed. That's very helpful and nice. Those women critics are taken as seriously as their male counterparts.

(Audience member asks if they think about ideas more.) They do think about ideas more.

(Audience member asks a question, indistinguishable.) Well, naturally, it is kind of a dangerous word. Everyone can do it. Everyone participates in this, but everyone doesn't because we live in an asymmetrical or skewed culture at the moment, which is male dominate and therefore imposes certain, almost apriori, mental limitations, both upon men who have their own ideas about themselves and women who have in general more complicated and limited ideas. In *Helen in Egypt,* H.D. is making a deliberate effort to counteract the male mythology which backs up the *Iliad.* Helen caused...you know, the face that sank a thousand ships and launched a thousand ships less and sank (Someone mentions something, she perhaps misspoke, laughs.) Whoops—and burned the topless hours of William Malas, wonderful lines.

And so we should talk about *Helen in Egypt*.

di Prima: Just wanted to say that everybody can access all these selves and everybody who steps out of that system does. What happens with women is it happens that our actual physicality pins us in a way that man's doesn't. Between the fact that we come up against childbirth and menstruation and menopause in a very real way, we look at our insides every month when we see when we bleed. Right? So that if the way in is in fact through the body and the body is what leads us to the unconscious, which Wilhelm Reich and so on would also agree with, then we're pushed up against the wall and invited into that space and a much more graphic, palpable way on a constant basis. You could say that men's physicality, male physicality, is that too with sexuality, but it's a little... I mean, when you're carrying your first child and you know that you could die, you're up against it in a particular way. So you're up against your physicality. You have to make friends with it if you're going to integrate enough to write.

Waldman: Well, this is why she's so extraordinary. It's quite unusual at this time that her life and work were so integrated and the sort of depth of her study of herself through this hermetic definition, which is the title of one of her other books, is quite incredible in that. And then drawing on these, all these images of transformation in the *Trilogy* is great. You should actually read the whole three-part section, which is in this Collected Poems, which is also in a paperback. And it's incredible process of a whole life. And actually coming to this realization and working through the male, I mean, grounding in the male before she can get to the bisexual word, moving into the, you know, the union of the two. And it's...we haven't really talked that much about the music in the language. It would be wonderful for you to maybe get together and read some of this aloud, because there's a real transformation in the very carefully chosen language. And these, the words really start to, I don't know if you could hear it in that one section, really resonate off each other.

"Now polish the crucible/and in the bowl distill"—crucible, distill—"a word most bitter *marah,*/a word bitterer still *mar.*" And it's just incredible. "Sea, brine, breaker, seducer." Just that move from sea brine breaker seducer. "Giver of life, giver of tears./Now polish the crucible"—repeating that—"and set the jet aflame/under till *marah-mar*"—You get that till distills still—"are melted, fuze and join/and change and alter/mer, mere, mère, mater, Maia, Mary,/Star of the Sea,/Mother."

It works in a you know, like an incredible resonant, amazing shape, which is what it's talking about, is the process is the objects and you know, some you've gotten all this talk this week in and analysis of your poems. I wrote this poem and said, Giver of Life, you'd cross out "the word life." It's too general as you know, there's something else going on here. It's not that simple, which is what she presents as not to be dualistic with the hope that this female investigation and journey and process. So the poem is the thing. It's talking. That's also the resonance and magic of the words as they are moving together, making these amazing new combinations which actually sort of spark one's own process to move from this to that to the other.

And then the poem, really the whole *Trilogy* actually starts to build and build through this incantation, the whole Amen-Ra thing. Amen-Ra, which is this transpersonal male and then reborn as the sun. And that in itself is one of the most universal motifs of transformation. That move... it's shamanic, really. Then Amen-Ra becomes Aries the Ram. So these moves through these, you know what he called them, they're like luminous details that we've some of us have talked about and many way that that intent. But I just want to bring it back to the language, so we don't get too lost in the ideas that which are always... You can read this on many levels. You might know nothing. You might not know who Isis is and that, or Osiris, and O-Sire-Is will start to work on you and enter you in this incredible way and maybe make you want to investigate it further. But in and of itself, it has a magical process going on.

di Prima: I think we have to understand that all of the long poems, the last poems of H.D. are magical rituals that she actually intended—*Trilogy*—Jane and I were talking about this at the picnic—to renew, in some sense, the world after the war. Well, as she intended, Helen, in some sense, for me to heal her life, to make a sanity of all the movements and all the different impulses of her being. And as she used hermetic definition as a shamanic right to lead her through into her death, she used Lionel Durand as the angel that goes before for her own dying. She gave birth to him and the end of that poem. She gave birth to the angel of her death. You have to understand that these were real for her. They weren't just thought, they were actual ritual. Actual magic is what she's doing. And this magic on this plane.

Waldman: Anti-war poem. I mean, you can do it that way starts. It's a real anti-war. It starts out in this kind of destruction and ruin and these images of chaos. And so combining ancient and modern root and bringing things from these diverse times into, through her into an active—it's incredibly active poetry, ritualistic in that way. And then these images, she's constantly evoking these images of resurrection and healing. And then conjuring up and invoking precedent presences and deities and saints and so on and invoking them, inviting them into the poem. They become these actual forces, because they resonate with our history and experience. (Audience member interjects, indistinguishable.)

That gave you that. (Audience member continues to speak, indistinguishable.) No. It's an incredibly brave poem too. (Audience member continues, indistinguishable.)

Well, she certainly worked out of her...(Audience member continues.) Eidolon is a great word she uses.

Augustine: She uses it at the end of *Helen in Egypt* and of the identities are even more of shifting and unified. I believe that she wrote every day of her life.

Waldman: Writing every day, in the morning. And keeping a dream notation. (Audience member speaks, indistinguishable.)

Augustine: I said, yes, but that's not to say it's not spontaneous.

Waldman: One more thing just on this *Trilogy*, because that's the poem I've been studying more than *Helen*, but the idea of this process and writing it in her elder years, and Diane and I were talking about menopause as a rite of passage, which men don't experience, where then you can become, I mean, you can get come to terms with your male energy too, beyond that, and she...

di Prima: And a lot of the Eskimo and other shamanic traditions woman can be a medicine woman or a witch or whatever you want to call it, until she bears her first child and then not again 'til menopause, because that energy is given over to something else, and when you take that energy back, she was in her 50s when she wrote *Trilogy*, so it would have been around that time, when you take that energy back you become very, very powerful and in a very different way than you could be in any other time.

Augustine: H.D., late in her life, lived in Switzerland in a... She broke her hip in great old age or she didn't really actually live to great old age, but she lived in a kind of sanatorium called Kusnacht. And it was reported, it is recorded, that people came to talk to her. They considered her a wise woman, a counselor. She actually did fulfill... (Audio cuts out momentarily.)

Trust a man a good bit younger than she named Dr. Erich Heydt, who now lives in Washington, D.C. and I've met him. He's very handsome and attractive and there was certainly kind of love between them. And so the background that we have of her psychoanalysis, which actually verified her strength, strengthened her in her sense that her mystical tradition was not so different from his, from Freud's, the preservation of all that we owe to Dr. Heydt, which I think is good.

We should perhaps say a little bit more about *Helen in Egypt* and the passages that you have in front of you elaborate on the creative and all embracive, all embracing quality of the Word. And we may see that H.D.'s rituals, which Diane has described, are that what she calls, that's what instructed her. And this is a scene which takes place on the Egyptian shore and Helen is speaking to Achilles.

"...'there is mystery in this place,/I am instructed, I know the script,/the shape of this bird is a letter,/they call it the hieroglyph;/strive not, it is dedicate/to the goddess here, she is Isis';/'Isis,' he said, 'or Thetis?' I said,/recalling, remembering, invoking/his sea-mother;/*flame,* I prayed, *flame forget,/forgive and forget the other,/let my heart be filled with peace, let me love him, as Thetis, his mother,*/for I knew him, I saw in his eyes/the sea-enchantment, but he/knew not yet Helen of Sparta,/knew not Helen of Troy,/knew not Helena, hated of Greece."[4]

4 *Helen in Egypt,* "Poem 7."

A little footnote on Helen of Sparta. Helen of Sparta is not Helen of Troy. At Sparta, Helen is a goddess associated with the trees. You will remember that Ezra Pound referred to H.D. as Dryad, a tree goddess. When Helen of Sparta is referred to, this is Helen who is dignified, who is worshiped as a goddess, not Helen, who is despised as the wanton ex-wife of Menelaus. So that distinction is important.

(Audience member asks question, indistinguishable.) Or Aldington? Yes, Achilleas might... The warlike figure is perhaps like the soldier Aldington. It's not good to read too tightly H.D.'s personal life into this. On the other hand, it was her own experience that she wanted to transform and integrate into a whole of the... She prays to Thetis. She becomes Thetis, in a way.

There are names alliterating on the syllable "is." I guess it's Book Six, "Cypris," I'm on page one seventy-eight. Again, the prose epigraphs are also very interesting. Sometimes they are repetitions of what happens in the poem, sometimes they are counterpoint and contrast, but the whole word etymology is given at the beginning of Book Six and the voice here is, actually the voice seems to speak for Helen. I believe that this is the voice of Helen of Sparta, not the voice of Helen of Troy. The voices she was hearing in her head, but it is the voice of the goddess, not the voice of the...the voice seems to speak for Helen. It is a lyric voice this time, a song rather than a challenge. It takes us back to Egypt but in a Greek mode, Isis is Cypris, Cytheraea, and Isis is Thetis, Amen.

(Audience member ask for clarification.) Aphrodite, yes. Yes, Cytheraea, Aphrodite came from the island, was born on the island of Cythera, according to one of the Greek stories. So there's an identification of the Greek and the Egyptian, but also an identification of Isis with the mother. Isis was not only the wife of Osiris, but she was the sister, and they had a child, Horus, the hawk-faced, under strange circumstances. So Amen Zeus is the father of Isis, Thetis, Aphrodite, Cypris. We cannot altogether understand this evocation. The rhythms must speak for themselves and the alliterations. Cypris, Thetis, Nephthys, Isis, Paris, Proteus, the legendary king of Egypt, as we have learned before, takes many shapes, like Hermes. Could he manifest as Achilles? If so, the question is not asked but implied. Could he manifest as Paris? Then could the two opposites, the slayer and the slain merge into one, and that one the absolute? This last question is implicit, but not formulated by the final phrase or strophe "Amen begot Amor." H.D. always plays with Amen, Amen-Ra, the father God of Egypt and the fact that "Amen" is the end of the Christian prayer, so be it, and sums up here Amen Amor, the initial alliteration is the rhyme or sound connection, which is that Logos.

di Prima: (Off mic but adds on to these ideas, mentions the Christos.)

Augustine: Amen. Amen. Cupid's father?

Oh, the word "Amor" then, we should perhaps look at intervening passages, but the final, in my language theory, the final union takes place in the union of the words. Let's see, look on page three-oh-one, section seven, which is very close to the end of *Helen in Egypt*. Helen returns the two voices and again, almost grudgingly, it seems, contrast that she had not known Paris in Egypt but she had said Paris's beautiful enchantment of the last Paris before Egypt. Paris after is Eros. L'amour, Eros is the God of love, L'amour. Yet there is no refutation of her final decision or choice. There is no before and no after. There is one finite moment. Is this the eternal moment of her constant preoccupation? La mort means death in French.

di Prima: Free sages. All the work hermetic definition, where of love is the death angel. But also that she uses that death as a door, that love is a door to her death.

Augustine: But also it seems that love and death are the ultimate contradiction. The ultimate opposition. And... (di Prima mentions something about Freud, but is off mic and difficult to hear precisely.) That's true. Well, I don't know.

Waldman: Finally, appreciate Freud through H.D.

Augustine: One does appreciate Freud much more through H.D., and it's almost a paradox and a tribute truly to H.D. that she understood when Freud said to her. She understood completely when he said, you have discovered for yourself what I have discovered for the race, and she took that as a validation of her mystical experiences, although he said the writing on the wall is your most dangerous symptom, and so on.

Waldman: A mother fixation.

Augustine: Mother fixation, desire for union with your mother in some way. H.D. went ahead and said yes, and finally concluded, yes, I am Helen. I am my mother. I am my own mother. I produce myself. I am the sea. I am the unconscious. I am Thetis, the mother of Achilles, the lover of Achilles, the original love.

di Prima: It goes to show every theoretician needs to cultivate a poet in order to make his theories valid.

Augustine: I had thought that it would be very fine if we actually simply read.

Waldman: Let's do the incantation.

Augustine: But be careful. (Audience is joking, laughing.) You should notice something...

There is no before, no after—there is one finite moment, and as often she, instead of making a statement, asks a question. She really will not make the assertion too firm or too fixed, which would also be to be too fixed itself, too fixed in concept. The eternal moment of death preoccupies her, but in some way, as in the end of *Trilogy*,[5] she says something extraordinarily beautiful and strange and down to earth.

"There is no before and no after," I'm on page three-oh-three. "There is one finite moment/that no infinite joy can disperse," —this paradox—*There is no before, and no after.* "There is one finite moment/that no infinite joy can disperse/or thought of past happiness/tempt from or dissipate;/now I know the best and the worst;/The seasons revolve around/a pause in the infinite rhythm/of the heart and of heaven." And then she concludes with Eidolon. Eidolon is both real and unreal.

Waldman: Like a phantom, but also totally real.

---

5 She misspeaks at this moment. It is actually at the end of *Helen of Troy*, not *Trilogy*.

Augustine: Real.

Waldman: They've all had that experience.

Augustine: E-I-D-O-L-O-N. It is the Greek word, image or ghost.

Waldman: Image.

Augustine: Actually image. And that is a fundamental, back to the fundamental, paving stone of H.D.'s language.

di Prima: The alchemical tradition of the eidolon on my not be irrelevant. It is from Paracelsus. He writes in one of his writings that the one thing that you reduced to ash in the crucible, whatever it is you do, that with anything right? Is raised again at that moment as an eidolon. So that thing of reducing, you know, finally consuming yourself, this self-self, the ego self, you can say if you want to be pedantic or something like that. She's consumed all of this experience. She's brought it all into this alchemical poem in this sense. And then at that moment, you raise the eidolon.

Waldman: In Buddhism, it's like om.

di Prima: He says that every, in one piece he says that everything's going to disappear, including God himself, but not everything will disappear because he says of man, the heart will remain of the universe. The flower is eternal. And that's an eidolon, an image of a flower.

Waldman: Or we winding up here? Well, no, I was just thinking of these bodies, bodies of form and bodies of light and also invoking energies and how you invite you know, you invite the deities. The way she's doing constantly is invocation, ritual, inviting these energies and deities in, which then have, I mean, they have the sheer miracle quality, but they're also totally real as existing before and throughout time or sort of pre-primordial. Primordial. And that's a kind of Buddhist view. I did have a couple of quick notes. But yeah, maybe should take orders sort of winding. You should wind up first. Especially reading.

Augustine: I think that I wanted to wind up with the idea of the pause in the infinite rhythm of the heart and of heaven as that mysterious gap between conceptualization and whatever the finite moment, which no infinite joy can disperse, is a way of actually bringing back the spiritual and tying it to the body so that there is that ultimate union, for what is finite is what belongs to us now, and so I believe that the finite moment belongs to the body and that there is a kind of ultimate statement of writing the body in the infinite rhythm of the heart and of heaven.

di Prima: We're going to end up with everybody reading.

Waldman: I was just going to say she's incredible, an incredible teacher as a writer and as a source and as a way to proceed and process one's experience, and a way to work with Eidolon and with Muse, and just through taking one, you might try this as a sort of experiment, just taking a deity or a goddess or a or something that you feel some real connection with and actually go into the etymology as well as the resonance in your own life in terms of dream or mythology. It's quite amazing as a study. I've been doing some work, which I feel is really influenced by her work in this process, and it can be very rich. Just, and I had some notes on the Hermes just, you know, tracking that through Hermes as originator, as Muse say for hers or something in all of us. You could say Coyote—you mentioned that the other day—but process of using this form, which Hermes does to contain a dynamic power of the psyche in order to work directly and skillfully with your own psychological processes. His name literally means, or her name because it's an androgynous figure, means the hastener. I think you said inventor of language, the inventor of the alphabet guide through the underworld, always guide, messenger, and so on. And it's great in this Jungian book actually talks about Hermes and Mercury as there's the Tantra—Shiva Shakti concept, which is also in Mercury and Hermes. There's the quote from an old text. Alchemical studies as the chapter, the spirit more curious. He talks about the circular nature of the Ourobóros, the circular snake eating its own tail is one image of it, and it's saying I am one and at the same time, many in myself. There's also the revealer of divine secrets in the form of gold, in alchemy is conceived to be the soul, the arcane substance. And the other word is Hermeneut. Hermeneut. Hermeneutics, the interpreter. So I mean actually to have so much richness and resonance in and of itself, just as a research for all of us. I think it's great teaching.

[Audience question, indistinguishable.] Well, Jane talked about this a little bit the other day.

di Prima: What's the relation between Hermes Trismegistus and Hermes?

Okay, Hermes Trismegistus was conceived to be the author of the hermetic texts. It is believed by Robert Duncan that the book *Thrice Greatest Hermes* by G. R. S. Mead, which came out around 1905, was seminal to H.D.'s work. It's a three-volume work. It's re-printed now. It was a translation of the hermetic texts, together with a book of commentary and a book of notes. A three-volume thing. Hermes Trismegistus was believed until the 17th century to be the author of these texts and that they were from Egypt and very, very ancient. In occult schools in some way, that's still believed, although we know the texts were written in 200 A.D. We also know that they're very ancient from Egypt and these aren't contradictions. So that Thrice greatest Hermes that came from Egypt would have been the equivalent of Thoth. Thoth is this a god of writing and magic and is the Egyptian forerunner of the Greek god, Hermes, so there is also the possibility that Jane and I were talking about that. Gertrude Levie talks about that in relation to the word Orpheus, that there were a series of Orpheus's or Orphei, that it was a lineage, that the mysteries were developed of. There are mysteries which developed over hundreds of years, and Orpheus meant something like teacher-bard, bard-slash-teacher. In this same way, you can think of Thrice Greatest Hermes as in fact three incarnations of Hermes in Egypt. You know, that were an oral tradition still in Greece. Something like that. And these figures relating in some way as emanations of the God principle Hermes, or the force Hermes. Right, okay. I mean, that doesn't answer you, but it sort of does. I wanted to... (Audience asks a question, indistinguishable.)

Waldman: We're all bisexual.

di Prima: Yes, absolutely. Absolutely. Absolutely. You all are too.

Waldman: What?

di Prima: All of them are too.

I think those are only given to people who are doing the same work. I could not give you any of my names. The name that I used until recently, I imparted to the people I was doing the deep visioning work with and the name that I received this last year I've only imparted to the person who's on the same level of work with me of that group of four now. And it's not because quote, "so you lose your power," exactly, it's more like what your intent is on that level should not be diffused.

Augustine: H.D. uses., in the novel *The Mystery,* the word acroamatic, which means self-secret at certain stages of development. What you're doing would only make sense to other people who are doing the same thing.

However, it's probably open secret that when you take refuge as a Buddhist, you get a new name. And when you take your boat aside for value, you get a new name. And when you go to, you do shake, and that there are many names for people in different kinds of spiritual functions. That's it. And those are spiritual names and they do carry a personal weight and express personal...

di Prima: I can tell you my name that I got from Suzuki Roshi. That's a good example of a name that isn't in charge in that way. He called me Ken Kai Man Tō, which means Ken—Inkstone, Kai—Ocean, Man—Ten thousand, Tō—Waves, Inkstone—Ocean—Ten Thousand Waves, but when you use Ocean and Wave in that way in Japanese, it also means Mother and Child. So Inkstone Mother, Ten Thousand Children. So it's meant multi-dimensionally. Do you have a name you want to tell?

Augustine: Oh my. Well actually, my Buddhist name was given to me by Rinpoche, as I think an inspiration, as they often are. My Buddhist name is Lodro Tsar Tso, which means Gold Lake of Intellect.

Waldman: My name was given to me by Chatral Rinpoche. And it's Dechen Chömtso, Ocean of Endless Dharma Bliss.

di Prima: I do have one last thing to say about H.D., a teacher, which was that for me, the biggest teaching was to stay with the truth of the feeling, even when it completely defied everything we've ever seen or defined as our feeling and went into areas that you simply felt... I mean, there was so far from the stereotype of what you thought you were supposed to feel, that you felt there was almost no way that this related to human experience, like the truth that she stays within hermetic definition of passionate, sexual love, age seventy-seven for men, forty-seven, which she only sees twice and many of—and who dies—and many of the critics reduced this to impose embarrassing situation for which, in fact, it's nothing like that. It's high tantra. It's amazing entry for her into like terms. I think she journeys all her life toward her body. And finally, in that poem, fully possesses her body. She keeps talking the reddest rose unfolds. They've got to take that into account.

Augustine: I think for me, H.D. is an unexpected teacher, although it's interesting that I first heard about her because I went to Bryn Mawr College, the college that she had gone to, so she was already haunting the halls, and I walked in as an undergraduate and aspiring poet, but for me, the transcendent element in H.D. is the way negative, difficult, painful, sometimes excruciatingly painful experience is transformed into her path. That truth comes not through necessarily what's beautiful or helpful or obvious, but through what is painful and difficult. That work can continue and it can continue in poetry has been very important to me.

Waldman: Well, let's read. Maybe we should read the select.

Augustine: What would you like?

Waldman: "The Invocation," "We've seen her."

This is *Trilogy*. Yes. You are welcome to stand.

Augustine: Yes, we should.

di Prima: Should we stand?

Augustine: I think so.

Here we are together. We'll just read the section...

Waldman: Section Twenty-nine.

Everyone: [6]

[Poem 29]

We have seen her
the world over,

Our Lady of the Goldfinch,
Our Lady of the Candelabra,

Our Lady of the Pomegranate,
Our Lady of the Chair;

we have seen her, an empress,
magnificent in pomp and grace,

and we have seen her
with a single flower

or a cluster of garden-pinks
in a glass beside her;

we have seen her snood
drawn over her hair,

or her face set in her profile
with the blue hood and stars;

we have seen her head bowed down
with a weight of a domed crown,

or we have seen her a wisp of a girl
trapped in a golden halo;

6 From *Trilogy*, "Tribute to the Angels"

we have seen her with arrow, with doves
and a heart like a valentine;

we have seen her in fine silks imported
from all over the Levant,

and hung with pearls brought
from the city of Constantine;

we have seen her sleeve
of every imaginable shade

of damask and figured brocade;
it is true

the painters did very well by her;
it is true they never missed a line

of the suave turn of the head
or subtle shade of lower eye-lid

or eye-lids half-raised; you find
her everywhere (or did find),

in cathedral, museum, cloister,
at the turn of the palace stair.

[Poem 30]

We see her hand in her lap,
smoothing the apple-green

or the apple russet silk;
we see her hand at her throat,

fingering a talisman
brought by a crusader from Jerusalem;

we see her hand unknot a Syrian veil
or lay down a venetian shawl

on a polished table that reflects
half a miniature broken column;

we see her stare past a mirror
through an open window,

where boat follows slow boat on the lagoon;
there are white flowers on the water.

[Poem 31]

But none of these, none of these
suggest her as I saw her,

though we approach possibly
something of her cool beneficence

in the gracious friendliness
of the marble sea maids in Venice,

who climbed the altar-stair
at *Santa Maria de Miracoli,*

or we acclaim her in the name
of another in Vienna,

Maria von dem Schee,
Our Lady of the Snow.

[Poem 32]

For I can say truthfully,
her veils were *white as snow,*

so as no fuller on earth
can white them; I can say

she looked beautiful, she looked lovely,
she was *clothed with a garment*

down to the foot, but it was not
girl about with a golden girdle,

there was no gold, no colour
there was no gleam in the stuff

nor a shadow of hem and seam,
as it fell to the floor; she bore

none of her usual attributes;
the Child was not with her.

Unto Herself

Interlude by Stephanie Michele

Rose, *a woody perennial flowering plant of the genus Rosa, in the family Rosaceae, or the flower it bears. There are over three hundred species and*[7]—*A table means more than a glass. A table means necessary places...it means there has been a stand, a stand where it did shake*[8]—It is possible to train roses to grow up and over walls, evading their presence. To climb. Escape. Be unruly. Language is the same sort of plant if nurtured. Organic and ravishing.

At the Portland International Rose Garden, the rain nurtured the colorful buds, the dead roses crunched together in a garbage bag behind the bathrooms was something I found beautiful, dark, the romance of their clipped heads. I thought I saw Gertrude Stein there, sunbathing in the rain, one of her hands in the garbage bag, grabbing at the dead flowers with her nude figure hunched under rose bushes penning odes with her other hand.

Words are like roses competing with weeds. They are things of the other and also things which are not words are words. Like the anti-word, word opposite. Opposite of the word, which is not a planet. It is and isn't alive, but is breathing.

The roseswordsroseswordsoserowds feed our desires and intentions. *Go red, go red, laugh white*—Gertrude Stein is so uncapsizable, so unaffected by a wave. Perhaps her legacy is as alive and feral as earthworms intimately mating into tunnels of compost, her language matriculated into a science, a syrup while remaining wholly an experimental tool for moving through the world. Diagramming, reframing, silvery repurpose of writing a book to tell a story but the story is a—*new cup and saucer.*

---

7 From *Wikipedia*

8 From *Tender Buttons*, This piece was written while listening to a recording of *Tender Buttons* while performing writing sprints. Lines from the book are dispersed throughout the rest of the piece.

And that winter Chris came to me with the phrase, *sudden spoon* after reading *Tender Buttons*. We forged our linguistic memory for a name, a title for our experimental literary magazine—*a sudden spoon is the wound in the decision*—was this just another surrealist word game to her? She didn't know how much it would change our lives.

Tiny Spoon.

We wanted to hold that presence, to also be women with the desire to alter the logic of the publishing community, the logic of logic of logic of—*Only a yellow, a green, a blue...a line distinguishes it...if red is in anything, is it unnecessary*—the beauty in opening a household for new worlds to build, a publication, out there, in a vast existence, we stick together like webs.

What is this? Why is that? I asked, searching my own archive of meaning to make sense of rampant and thrilling semantics, the tender meat of her somatic world for similarities, on a timeline of all beings. It hurt and confused and expanded.

Connection. Movement. *Water astonishing and difficult all together*—and she threaded herself into these moments in tight stitches, through absurdism, cracking the sentence into a billion spinning, fine-toothed shards.

And even in her life, she was magnetic. In her Salon a slew of artists knitted around her, like tails to a comet's body, a collection of minds at her disposal: painters, writers, queer radicals that flowed in through her doors—*A little calm is so ordinary a closet does not connect under the bed*—and of course, her fascination and devotion to Alice B. Toklas, her figurative dreaming with language deepening this beautiful attribute.

It contracted us all to Stein, a landing sight, a revelation, a planet. *Use heaviness in mourning*—

Supposing there is no change in appearance—A planet. Are all planets all knowing? She persisted into the unknown, foraging piles of language in the middle of her page, the surreal oceanic void of white space, arranged like a line of drowning houses—*if lilies...if they do this they need a catalogue*—the puncture of time and space with a misplaced word placed in the universe.

Our roots can be anywhere and we can survive because if you think about it, we take our roots with us. I know because you can go back to where they are, they can be less real to you than they were 3,300 miles away.[9]

Gertrude left us the tools for the experiment, the great unfailing, recklessly brave art of trying and turning which we now hold deeply in our cavernous chests as our world ricochets into a chaotic shuffle of unrest and rest—*In feeling anything is mounting, in feeling there is recognition*—and here in the rose garden is where we bathe and nurture our intellectual and creative curiosity in her legacy with her books. Our revolutionary heartbeats quickening, quietly preparing for action, for the loud chaos unfolding.

But perhaps more importantly, a sentence can never be complete. It is more and less than complete, or as Stein says, "A sentence must hold another. This is a sentence but not restful." A sentence is restless and multiple.[10]

A world holding another world, a nest, a mother, a book eternally worldful for future harvesting worlds—are all planets all knowing? are all planets all? *Collect more trembling and not even trembling... nothing quite flat and more round...nothing breaking the losing of no little piece*—are all planets? are all? are?

So, what is a world? I ask the search engine we call Google, the internet mind created to mimic the workings of the human brain. It is a virtually intensive planet all on its own. Google is something which Gertrude Stein never got to meet. I feel she'd find its invention hilarious and uncanny, most likely utilizing it in literary companionship as I do, as I am doing now in an effort to conjure her experimental heart into this space.

Her path to worldness came through persistent experimentation. Surrealist joy. Writing and art. Google replies, *The world is the Earth and all life on it,*

---

9 From the Naropa Archive, *American Women in the Experimental Tradition: Gertrude Stein* by Joanne Kyger

10 From *Tao's Journal of Poetry*, online archive.

including human civilization. In a philosophical context, the "world" is the whole of the physical Universe, or an ontological world (the "world" of an individual).

Gertrude Stein : an entire entity unto herself. A spirited beam of her radiates into the Silver Maple Tree in the yard. She comes back as a bird today, beak to the sky in exploration. Nibbling words like worms in savory delight.

A planet larger than my mouth, a button so tender that from afar, it appears as blue as the galaxy on which we spin into the night.

American Women in the Experimental Tradition: Gertrude Stein

Joanne Kyger
July 13, 1991

Transcription by Stephanie Michele

Joanne Kyger: As you can see, this is covering a lot of material in this class, so mostly what I'm giving you is some kind of biographical information where you can see the relationship of what's happening in the beginning of the [nineteenth] century and different forms of writing, and we won't have a lot of time to go over the work of the writer herself, so, certainly with Gertrude Stein, she has her re-investigation of what writing is all about. It's hard to call that poetry or prose.

(Student asks a question about the subject material.)

The subject material? How did I choose the women? Well, Anne Waldman called me up on the phone last fall and she said, I want you to teach women poets, and I said, women poets? And so we made a list up at the very beginning, and I just went back historically. Amy Lowell for me was the first person who makes this bridge from the kind of iambic writing at the turn of the century, and onto Gertrude Stein, so it's kind of an early historical picture of what goes on, and once we get started here, we'll figure out how they are all indeed related.

Okay, Gertrude Stein. Everybody knows who Gertrude Stein is—she's become a household word, a household world.

She also believed herself that, "Einstein was the creative philosophic mind of the century and I have been the creative literary mind of the century." She did not have a small estimation of herself. As late in her career at 1937, she said, "It always did bother me that the American public were more interested in me than in my work." (Pulled from the quote, "And after all there is no sense in it because if it were not for my work they would not be interested in me so why should they not be more interested in my work than in me. That is one of the things one has to worry about in America.")

And she was of course a flamboyant figure, somewhat like Amy Lowell was. The material I've got from this kind of synopsis biography from John Malcolm Brinnin's book called *The Third Rose: Gertrude Stein and Her World.*

She was born February 3, 1874, and died July 27, 1946, and she has a lot in common with Amy Lowell. Amy Lowell's biographer points out, whether you believe in astrology or not, there's a lot, there are similar parallels in their lives. (Presumably from Amy Lowell's biography *Amy Lowell, American Modern* by Melissa Bradshaw.)

Since they were born under the same sign and their family constellations were almost identical and they were both born late, of large families after... they came late in their mother's lives and their mothers were, at this point, kind of semi-invalids and older. They were both the last children and both of the families were well-to-do, which helped them a great deal, although the Lowells were a lot wealthier than the Steins. They were both exceptionally bright babies who learned to talk at an early age and they were physically plump children. They were the baby of their family, and Amy was called the postscript where Gertrude was called the after-thought. Both were stubborn, self-willed, quick to anger, and quickly restored to good nature although Gertrude Stein did carry grudges a little bit longer, vis-a-vis Hemmingway, who she never talked to again.

They both were sturdy children who tended to be tomboys and never played with dolls, and as they came of age it was apparent that neither one of them would marry. Both had grown from plump children following puberty into huge women with imposing, kind of intimidating figures looming over their territory. In Stein's case it was Cubism and the New Art. In Amy Lowell's case it was Imagism and the New Music, and they were both frequently compared to being a Roman Emperor since neither was over five feet tall and they both weighed around two-hundred-and-fifty pounds, as I said before. They were kind of square, imposing-looking women.

Both of these literary personalities took female companions as mates and the given names of their respective friends, both began with the letter, A—That's kind of pushing it. In both instances when they met their future companions they recognized each other at once and their companions filled these multiple needs of smoothing the paths of their career. In both cases these women, Gertrude and Amy, liked to stay up and write all night, and there was Alice and Ada in the morning picking up the type scripts and taking them off to get re-read and typed.

They never met. As some commentators said, it was however they differed in their intellectualism, they were so much alike that we should be grateful that they set up shop on different continents. Some people feel that Amy kind of surrounded herself with people of less genius, people that liked to flatter her, while Stein attracted geniuses like Picasso and Hemmingway, etc., but nonetheless, both in their separate ways contributed the freedom of Modern American Literature and by their lives, they led to the liberation of women, lesbian or otherwise, the world over.

The beginning of this *Third Rose* book starts out with a little joke; Gertrude Stein was always of course the butt of great comedian's great jokes. A guy named Fred Harmon who's a comic on the burlesque circuit says, "Well I can go along with those first two roses of hers, alright but when she gets to that third rose, she loses me." That's the name of her biography, *The Third Rose*.

In the middle of the biggest snow storm in thirty years, Gertrude Stein is born in Allegheny, Pennsylvania, the youngest child of Daniel and Amelia Keyser Stein. Her parents both of German-Jewish extraction had at the time of their marriage in 1864 agreed to have five children. They had a planned family with nice spacing they achieved that in seven years, but then two of the children died, so they had two more. They had Leo and two years later, they have Gertrude. Leo and Gertrude grow up as comrades together, Gertrude being the youngest of the family. Father Daniel worked in business in nearby Pittsburgh with his brother in wholesale wool, an uncomfortable thought to think of today, but they don't get along. Neither do the wives, so the business is broken up and Daniel moves his family to Austria, Vienna, where they live for three years and Gertrude has memories of horses and Vienna woods.

"She talks all day long," her mother says so plainly. "She outdoes them all—" even then. "She's such a round little pudding, toddles around the whole day and repeats everything that is said or done."

But Mother Amelia gets lonely there after her husband returns to the US on a business assignment and one day moves everyone to Paris where she leases a whole house. Gertrude has her first formal schooling there and talks baby-French and then they go back to Baltimore to the Father's family. She is five having learned Austrian, German, French-French, and then American-English, so she's had kind of a European, multicultural background up to the age of being ready to go to kindergarten.

Then her father moved the whole family to Oakland, California, which was a house on a rise on the center of ten acres, and at that point Oakland, California, was pretty much out in the sticks. And of course she's very famous, or people in Oakland certainly remember her for her famous phrase, saying, "There's no there, there."

It has a beautiful eucalyptus avenue, flower gardens, a hayfield. It's kind of a great bucolic country scene and nature is a wonderful and adventurous place for her there. Gertrude and her brother Leo stick together and take little walks and hikes and they share precocious intellectual interests. Her mother becomes sick with cancer and her father is very authoritarian making up strict new rules all the time. They come to resent him and Gertrude ends up calling him depressing. The father is Vice President in the street railway business and the older brother Michael, Michael Stein, joins him there. At this point, Gertrude loves to read. She reads the family library. She reads Shakespeare and writes plays. At this point she writes plays called *Snatched from The Death of the Sundered Sisters*, right into the style of the turn-of-the-century when she is eight years old.

She reads everything she can from home and the library; Swift, Defoe, Elizabethan literature, Wordsworth, Scott, Burns, Fielding, Smollett, and then Darwin's *Evolution*. Evolution was as exciting as the discovery of America. "It opened up the history of all"—this is her quote—"of all animals and vegetables and minerals and man." At fifteen she begins to understand boredom.

"You would spend all day intending to go somewhere and nothing happens and you wonder if you will be revenged."

Everything important seemed to be beginning all at once; the understanding of money, of possessions, the idea of eternity, the suspicion that some people were enemies. She writes down her feelings for clarity. Her mother dies when she is 14. Leo and Gertrude continue going to Oakland High School, even though it is very dull for them. They are part of a very few Jewish families in East Oakland, a minority. Their father died suddenly in 1891, two years later than his wife's death. He is found dead in bed by Leo and Gertrude, and so the oldest brother Michael heads the family and he invested the family money, and Gertrude has a share of a small fortune which gives her ample, dependable income throughout her earlier years. She's all kind of set up. She's bright, she has her own active intelligence, and she has a small monthly income. His job is then being in charge of the street railways in San Francisco. In 1892, the family disperses and Leo goes to Harvard after he goes to the University of California and Gertrude goes back to the Baltimore Stein family which is a very opulent, and clannish, warm family with many Victorian possessions representing good solid riches.

There she moves from her inner life to her outer life where everybody knows and accepts her. She is allowed to enter Radcliffe in 1893 when she was 18 years old. Leo is next door at Harvard, and she enters school there to do independent college work. She takes classes from George Santiana, the famous writer on philosophy and metaphysics, Josiah Royce, and she studies the morphology of animals, the embryology of vertebrates.

She's already into science and becomes social in the boarding house in which she lives, and this is young Gertrude of 19, 20 years old, and she becomes president of the philosophy club. This is her social life. A classmate at this time describes her as being heavyset and an ungainly young woman with hair cut short, when this was not the fashion, and always wore black and her ample figure was never corseted.

Although she has come to Cambridge because Leo was there, she has her own life. Going to museums, riding her bicycle, taking solitary walks, but she's not interested in clothes and she's not politically interested. She's not interested in suffrage like Amy. Or politics. She is a jolly, simple, natural, and once you knew her, charming. But her biggest interest is the mind and person of William James, brother of Henry, who was teaching there.

Gertrude is asking questions like, "Is life worth living?" She writes down. "Yes, a thousand times yes. When the world still holds such spirits as professor James,"—this is from her journal. "He is truly a man among men. A scientist of force and originality, embodying all the strongest and worthiest in the scientific spirit. A metaphysician skilled in abstract thought, clear and vigorous and yet too great to worship logic as his god. He stands firmly, nobly for the dignity of man. He fights, he suffers, he endures. His is a strong, sane, noble personality."

So she has a strong homage crush on William James at this point. William James who has written a variety of religious experiences and was a well-known thinking mind, living in the United States, where his brother, Henry is over writing his books in England.

Her acquaintance with him is long. She is allowed to join his graduate seminar. An honor. She meets Leon Solomons, who is working on problems of consciousness. Are you familiar with who William James is and his famous books of writings and religions and so forth? Working with problems of consciousness.

At this point she does experimental work with him that results in the report, "Normal Motor Automatism." These are the experimental works she makes with a fellow named Leon Solomons. This is published in the *Psychological Review* in 1869, her first published work. Then they do joint projects together, "The Place of Repetition and Memory and Fluctuations of Attention" and another piece called "The Saturation of Colors."

They were their own subjects, so they experimented on each other, and one experiment while the subject wrote the same word over and over again, he also was reading a story out loud. This resulted in involuntary recording of words, or parts of words from the story, and usually they were immediately noticed, but in repeated experiments they usually found that many words would be recorded with no break in the subject's attention.

So this is an experiment where you're writing down like *blue, blue, blue, blue* all the way, while also reading a detective story or something out loud. Then they try wholly spontaneous writing and they find evidence of logical thought is rare in wholly spontaneous writing.

In 1934, BF Skinner, the Behavioral Psychologist writes an article in *The Atlantic Monthly* saying, "This would be the easiest way to understand Gertrude's writing by understanding the fact that they had experimented with automatic handwriting." Kind of a dismissive way of looking at her writing.

Then she decides she's going to go to medical school at John Hopkins and become an MD in order to proceed with psychology, upon William James' recommendation, but before she does that, she joins Leo in Europe for the summer for her first adult trip which is a grand, cultural experience for her. She is abroad since the first time since she was five. When she comes back she passes Latin, finally passes Latin. She's not a great scholar at this point. Well, she's got a good mind, but she doesn't like to study too much. She's had a hard time with her Latin, struggling along and she finally passes that and graduates from Radcliff. She travels back to California and travels around a little bit and continues to travel with Leo each summer in Europe.

She sets up a household in Baltimore, finally with Leo, who brings his Japanese prints along and they have a household with a kitchen and a maid and etc. She's getting bored with school but she loves having her own household. She loves Baltimore's kind of easy, Southern style.

And at this point someone writes about her as being, "An extraordinary person, powerful, a beautiful head." We hear about her beautiful head constantly. "Something holy intense, a deep temperamental quality which was inspiring. A kind of almost unfeminine beauty, a deep academic past in which her ego was apparent. Her extraordinary life quality and her beauty were what struck the eye and the imagination."

One summer when they were abroad, they visited Bernard Berenson, the famous historian and art esthetician, outside of Florence. The Stein's were not Berenson's type, Gertrude offered the aesthetic sensibilities which Berenson had been defining for so many years, but he found Leo a tiresome bore, but he could not resist a man who lived in his mind, even when he considered the mind mediocre. So he was willing to rescue Leo from his intellectual funk. Leo, if you read about Leo Stein later on, he's got his own individual, relentless intellectual circling about subjects. Finally, she goes back and the final exams have come up, and she hasn't really prepared for the final exams, although warned about it, so she flunks.

And rather than make it up in summer school, she decides she's not going to lead a career in medicine and she returns to Europe to be with Leo and they travel over Italy, Assisi, to London, and they get a flat in Bloomsbury where Bernard Berenson is again and meets Bertrand Arthur William Russell and has an argument with him; what she writes about showing according to him, the American mind is closed to new political ideas, she's never really closed to new political thinker, not interested in the politics, let's put it that way. She's political in her own turf. In London she finds the British Reading Room and she reads and reads and reads. She's voracious. At this point she's finding what the English tone is about. She offers her experiments, offers science background and years of living continuously with the rhythms of the English language bring her taste to this kind of sophistication, and she records phrases that please her, and she likes the satisfaction of caressing words and phrases. She goes back to New York City, and she spends the winter there with three friends, three women, and begins a novel, a psychological study of young women which kind of was published posthumously; we're set in the '70s (1870s) somewhere. It is kind of an emotional romantic novel of the relationships of these three women in which she takes from every direction what they must be thinking emotionally with a kind of relentless detached, scientific manner that she's learned what their relationships are and this whole arrangement comes to an unsatisfactory end.

Leo was supposed to join her over there, but he doesn't because he has this great satori in Paris after he's been talking to Pablo Casals. He has this great awakening and he starts drawing himself in the nude in his own mirrored image—Leo's great character on his own right too—so he finds a place there in Paris because he's had this wonderful sense that now he's a drawer and he can draw himself nude in the mirror, and so he finds a place there through one of his cousins who is a sculptor, artistry runs in the Stein family, at the famous 21 Rue De Fleurs.

Gertrude arrives, comes back over, and they both settle there, and now we are up to 1903. There is an area where a few American and English painters have already settled, and it becomes a real and permanent home for them that is convenient for everything. She continues writing her novel about the relationship of these three women and she finishes it and puts it away and it's lost for thirty years, as I said, until it was printed after her death it is published under the title, *Things As They Were.*

It's kind of written as conventional fiction, Henry-Jamesian and relentless in its analysis. Anyway, Paris then becomes the place for her, quote, "That suited those of us who were to create the 20th century art and literature."

She believed the creative individual needed the experience of another civilization besides his own. Paris gave her the calm and peace necessary to mode her life and work, and she loved the French because they were cordial, yet not obtrusive, and Paris was elegant.

So they furnished their quarters, stuffed it really, with Renaissance pieces they had picked up in Italy, the style of the time, and Leo starts buying paintings. He buys Cézanne's, Renoir's, Gauguin's, and he starts to recognize this work where he can still buy it at reasonable prices, but it starts to be an investment, it starts to be a drain on their income, so their brother Michael comes from California, the guy who was running street cars on the streets of San Francisco, and he arrives with his family and he starts collecting and lends them money, so they're serious American collectors of art now, that is in museums these days.

So their flat starts to look like a very small and crowded museum. Gertrude is the curator, and Leo is the guide. People come from all over to see and Leo rattles on, the floor exclusively his, while Gertrude sits silently.

"By that time I was writing and arguing was no longer to me really interesting. Nothing needed defending and if it did, it was no use defending it."

She adopted a practice of writing only late at night and worked until daybreak, sleeping until late mornings. When she would review by daylight the results, few revisions occurred. The major part of her work was composed and final before it was set down. So here she is, she doesn't have to rewrite, doesn't have to rethink. She's already so in command and confident of her own mind and the way it works. *Three Lives,* a piece called *Three Lives* is her first piece of writing influenced by William James and Cézanne as an attempt to create a continuous present, and that's one of Gertrude Stein's philosophical, psychological, what you want, the continuous present, the continuous present.

She meets Matisse. She meets Picasso, and Picasso paints this famous portrait of her when she is only 24 years old which is now in the Museum of Modern Art in New York City, I guess. *The Portrait of Gertrude Stein.* They become friends, and he begins doing these word portraits using words and Picasso is the first. She finishes *Three Lives* and starts *The Making of Americans,* a book that is still in print. *The Making of Americans* has got this rolling and repeated cadence. It covers time like the Cubists as if it were a flat surface.

Marianne Moore says about it, "By this epic of ourselves we are reminded of certain, early German engravings in which Adam, Eve, Cane, and Able stand with every known animal, wild and domestic, under a large tree by a river. It is a kind of living genealogy, which is in its branching unified and vivid. A truly psychological exposition of American living."

She finishes it in 1908 by killing off her hero, "My hero, I've killed him."

"Why?" says her friend Mildred Audridge.

"I know all about him and about them and about everyone in that story, so that's it."

I don't know if you've ever had the experience of killing off a hero in your writing, you never really get to hear from them again after that. So she's writing away at this book, she still has to get *Three Lives* into print, and publishers turn it down, nobody is really interested in it. Has anyone read *Three Lives* or part of it? Yeah, it is a fairly accessible book, but for that day in age it was unreadable.

Publishers turn it down so she pays to have it printed herself. She has 1,000 copies printed at the price of $650 which I guess was a good sum in those days.

Now we'll have a flashback to Alice B. Toklas who was living in San Francisco. Gertrude was born in San Francisco too, but they never got to meet each other. She's living there taking care of her widowed father, she's a spinster also, and the earthquake of 1906 necessitated that Michael Stein, Gertrude's older brother, go back to check out some of his real estate holdings, and when he's back there, he meets Alice B.

She expresses an interest in travel so he and his wife say, okay, we will take you back to Paris with us. There she meets Gertrude Stein and hears the psychic ringing of bells that announce the presence of genius and heart too. Only two times does this happen again for Alice B, when she meets Picasso and when she meets Alfred Whitehead, the three geniuses. When she hears bells, it's like a cartoon strip. *Ding!*

So Alice is from a Polish-Jewish family settling in California during the Goldrush of 1849. She's from upper class gentility but a rather dull lifestyle, so when she gets to Paris she is released to the kind of life she's only known through hearsay and romantic novels. She soon shares the Stein's friends and becomes secretary. She has some skills, typing and correcting, and sending proofs for her, for *Three Lives*.

Three Lives soon becomes published by Grafton Press in New York, Vanity Press. Alice B. visits Italy and decides she likes Europe and decides she is going to stay. *Three Lives* arrives on bookshelves in New York City in 1910, and there are hardly any reviews. William James reads thirty pages and says, "I must go back and finish it someday." And then he dies.

But she doesn't really care if she has followers or not, she's really sure of her work. She goes into a Cubist style of writing from 1908-1912, writing a book called *A Long Gay Book, An Account of All Possible Relationships Between Two People: Many Many Women and Matisse, Picasso, and Gertrude Stein.*

She follows the pictorial Cubist moving around an object to get several successive appearances which infused in a single image, reconstitute it in time. She uses words as if they were unencumbered plastic entities of such and such texture, weight and resilience.

From *The Long Gay Book*, "Started fresh with Fanny and Helen and Business-women with earthy-type intellect, large on this and go back to flavor, pseudo-flavor, on Mildred's group and to the concentrated groups. From then on complicate and complete giving all kinds of pictures and start in again with the men. Here begin with Victor Herbert Group and ramify from that. Go on then to how one would love and be loved as a man or as a woman by each kind that could or would love anyone. And so on."

The Portraits of Matisse, Picasso, and Gertrude Stein comes to the attention of Alfred Stieglitz, the famous photographer, and he publishes these pieces in a special issue of his magazine *Camera Work* in August 1912, which I guess is the first time that she's published in the United States in a publication, yes, her first appearance in a periodical anywhere. It was her introduction to the American reading public. And to American literary life. Then next she writes *Tender Buttons,* which is concerned only with visible things and surfaces and appearances.

As Pierre Rivardee says, "It is only in that moment when words are freed from their literal meaning that they take on in the mind a poetic value. It is at that moment that they can be freely placed in poetic reality."

Soon after this, she meets a real mover and shaker called Mabel Dodge. Mabel Dodge, soon to be Mabel Dodge Luhan. Mabel Dodge at this point was from an affluent Hudson Valley family from Buffalo has moved over to Florence and started a salon. Here she meets Gertrude and Gertrude comes and stays there at the Villa Curonia and writes a piece called *Mabel Dodge at the Villa Curonia.*

This is a piece that then Mabel Dodge has it printed on Florentine paper, and then she distributes this at the famous Armory Show in New York City in 1913, that showed all the whirlpool of modern art. That had Duchamps' *Nude*

Descending the Staircase, that everybody remembers Brâncuşi is there for the first time, Picasso, Matisse, Van Gough, Gougan, Brach, Monet, Kandinsky, Picabia, and this is just a huge rival of visual art and a hundred-thousand people come and see this show.

Mabel Dodge distributes this piece of writing by Gertrude Stein and also writes a small article on Gertrude Stein that's published in an art magazine, explaining what she does with words and this gets a great deal of publicity and makes Gertrude Stein, for the first time the American public becomes aware of her, and of course, she is parodied almost immediately by the newspaper but she's able to live through this. At this point, she's gone through the way that Picasso and the rest of the Cubist painters were received in Paris with a great deal of public scorn at times.

At this point they're saying this is a big change for the American population who, where upon the walls of every wealthy home there hung two staple oil paintings; a still life for the dining room showing a dead fish on a plate and a pastoral for parlor showing a collection of cows drinking out of a pearling brook. So this great introduction of Modern Art, which of course is a very famous show, also presents Gertrude Stein. The piece that is written about Mabel Dodge when Gertrude Stein is visiting her there is a funny piece, but I don't know if I'll go into that now.

Actually, there is a funny piece that Mabel Dodge talks about in her memoirs about Gertrude Stein, she says, "Gertrude Stein was hardy. She had a laugh like a beefsteak. She loved beef, and I used to like to see her sit down in front of five pounds of rare meat, three inches thick and with strong wrists, wielding knife and fork, finish it with gusto, while Alice ate a little slice, daintily, like a cat."

This piece of *Mabel Dodge,* the little pieces of it, you can see how the American public perceived this writing, here are some excerpts from *The Portrait of Mabel Dodge:*

> Blankets are warmer in the summer and the winter is not so lonely.
> A bottle that has all the time to stand open is not so clearly shown when there is a green color there.

> Abandon the garden and the house is bigger...This is comfortable.
> There is the comforting of predilection.
> ...Although there was the best kind of sitting there could never be all the edging that the largest chair was having...
> There was not that velvet spread when there was a pleasant head...
> There is the use of stone and there is the place of the stuff...
> There is the room that is the largest place when there is all that is where there is space.

Mabel had a little flirtation with Gertrude, as well as having a torrid affair with her son's tutor. Gertrude is sitting next door, reaching into the depths of herself, reading these sentences out for Mabel, and meanwhile Mabel is having this kind of rustling next door, which Gertrude continues, "There is that desire and there is no pleasure. Praying has intention and reliving that situation is not solemn. There is not that perturbation. There is no action meant. The forgotten swelling is certainly attracting. It is not sinking to be growing. There cannot be sighing. This is this bliss."

Allusions there. So, about this time she meets Carl Van Vechten who then becomes a lifelong friend and writes introductions for her work and edits them and even arranges for publication. He eventually becomes her literary executor and only in 1958 gives up that job to Donald Gallup because of his advancing age. She's still trying to find a publisher. She's been writing, so she goes to London and she tries to meet the Bloomsbury group of thinkers, which really do not turn her on at all. She calls them The Young Men's Christian Society with Christ Left Out. And John Lanes decides to publish her, but *The English Review* returns her work curtly:

> "Dear Madam,
>
> I really cannot publish these curious studies.
>
> Yours Very Truly,
>
> Austin Harrison."

They continued to be original and curious studies. About this time Leo Stein and Gertrude Stein part ways and he leaves the household and they split up the painting collection. You can imagine what that was like. They just differ, and they go on their separate ways. Gertrude is on her own ground right now, and Leo is a relentless chatterer, and he's becoming more and more insecure around Gertrude's sense of her own authority and groundedness, so he goes to Florence, and she and Alice stay there and they put in electricity. At this point, Gertrude still regards Henry James as her most immediate literary ancestor.

Can you imagine from Henry James we get to Gertrude Stein? She really feels that is her... well there's nobody else doing anything like she really is, so she makes a trip to London at this point because they're refurnishing their place to get chairs, and the war breaks out but that is when Amy Lowell is there at the same point, but they never run into each other, and they never visit Alfred North Whitehead and when they return in August, October of 1914, they find that the city is half-empty and poor of goods and spirit and the war has started. So they put their shoulder to the effort and they outfit a Ford that her cousins have sent over from New York City, and they turn it into an ambulance and they deliver supplies to hospitals and they visit soldiers there and they, the soldiers, give her the latest slang from home.

But after the war, things aren't what they used to be and a spark is gone. But then the invasion of the American Ex-Patriots starts. Sylvia Beach starts her famous bookstore, Shakespeare and Company, and Gertrude meets James Joyce but doesn't want to be connected to him. I mean, it's just a little too close, she has her own territory, and it's just a little too close for her to involve herself in his form of writing.

This is the time of the Lost Generation and Sherwood Anderson visits and gives homage. He says, "Gee, I love you," and they hit it off and remain friends forever more. Ezra Pound and she don't hit it off. She finds him, this is a famous quote, "A village explainer, which meant that his talk was excellent if you were a villager, but if you were not, not." She finds him competitive and refuses him entrance to her salon at Number 327. He calls her an old tub of guts. So they part ways on that one.

She likes F. Scott Fitzgerald and his writing, *This Side of Paradise* and *The Great Gatsby,* but she usually stays insular about their writing. TS Eliot is met formally and dismissed. He says about her writing, kind of in her style, "It is not improving, it is not amusing, it is not interesting. It is not good for one's mind, but its rhythms have a peculiar, hypnotic power, not met with before. It is a kinship with a saxophone. If this is the future, then the future is, as it very likely is, of the barbarians. But this is a future in which we ought not be interested." So he's quite final on that.

A long relationship with Hemmingway ensues which eventually becomes quarrelsome. Ford Madox Ford starts *The Transatlantic Review* and serializes small parts of *The Making of Americans.* At this point there are many small literary magazines coming up and ceasing. This is the only way that this new writing can be published and once it is published, how is it distributed? Hemingway, at this point, hand-copies from her bound manuscript volumes, a copy to send to the publisher, to Ford. He hand-copies this out for her so from then on, she has a real indulgent weakness for him. Probably as he learns from copying this out by hand, he learns the value of this skillful repetition that she uses and the simple power of the declarative sentence and the necessity for saturation in an attitude. So Gertrude is talked about, listened to, made into a legend, but she isn't read much and she isn't published. Carefully bound, the completed works of more than twenty years stand on her shelves. (Audio recording skips.)

His wife Briar offers to do *Making of Americans.* The printing job was done in France, and it was a nightmare. Countless repetitions, minute inversions, infinitesimal variations, all the characteristic tricks and turns of the early Stein were quite beyond them. They make hundreds of barely discernible mistakes. Alice and Gertrude go practically blind during proofreading and Gertrude has a mixed pleasure in reading this book she wrote twenty years before. A bit profound but some pretty wonderful sentences in it. It is published in September 1925 more than 900 literally transparent and almost unreadable pages, paper-bound. Mcalman in his contact editions—he's a very a famous, does this series of books—also publishes Ernest Hemmingway, Ezra Pound, William Carlos Williams, H.D., Djuna Barnes, and Marsden Hartley.

She has a little difficulty with Robert Mcalmon's book *Being Geniuses Together* that he does with Kay Boyle. They have a falling out over this book. I'll just read a little shortly from this, "Let us now add Gertrude Stein to our list of megalomaniacs and add that on occasion she could be much of a mythomaniac as well. In her recent autobiography extolling herself she says that, Mcalmon wanted to publish her, *The Making of Americans* and she graciously allowed this. The fact is that she wrote to that individual asking him to tea and suggested he publish the book in a series of 4-6 volumes over a two-year period. Thinking it over, Mcalmon decided all or not at all, it's a unity, as Miss Stein assured him she was sure of about 50 people who would buy the book. He took it on. Months later when the book was in the process of being bound, he again had tea again with Miss Stein and assured her he would not allow the edition to be shipped to a New York publisher for distribution with a definite contract or the payment outright by those publishers covering publishing costs."

Well, to make a long story short, she goes right ahead and gets in touch with a printer and says that they should be shipped over. He's still got all these books; he has no way to recoup his money on them. After numerous wars with letters, Miss Stein had telephoned the printers on Mcalmon's instructions that the shipment should be made. As it was in direct contradiction with what he had said, Mcalmon was very angry. Miss Stein had explained in a letter that Miss Heap had assured her that Mcalmon would not object. Mcalmon's anger did not cool when Miss Stein involved Miss Heap in the matter. Miss Heap had never been Mcalmon's agent; she had no connection with his business, and he had not seen her while he was in Paris. Since Miss Stein so believed in her own genius, it occurred to Mcalmon that she might sell a painting from her collection for fifty times what she had paid for it and pay her own printing bill. She had not sold more than ten of the fifty copies she had counted on selling and the remaining forty she had given out as review copies or to friends, who at that time were her only substantial public, her friends. What happened to the rest of the edition is quite another story."

The book got few and mainly unfair reviews, and he writes a review of it. "Incidentally *The Making of Americans* is a beautiful bit of printing," this is Mcalmon writing about his contact edition book. "A beautiful bit of printing and makeup and binding, and Miss Stein complimented Monsieur on the job.

He did do a very fine job but the publisher chose the paper, the print, the binding, the design, the jacket, and the makeup of the book. Nevertheless, Miss Stein has qualities which command admiration. She has vitality and a deep belief in the healthiness of life, too great a belief for these rocky days." So she often got into trouble with this, and this book then, I don't know what eventually happened to the copies of it. They were held up at the American, getting books over, they were held up at the American customs.

So Gertrude is a leading figure in the expatriate world at this time. Her home at 327 assumes something between a court and a shrine, the dramatic persona changing from month to month, week to week. Gertrude said she liked to see people come just as much as she liked to see them go. In the spring of '26, Gertrude and Alice go to the county in the spring in the East of France and find a summer place in Bilignin, which they lease for many years and so the Salon has a summer location until 1945.

So Alice Toklas decides that she will be the publisher of Gertrude Stein's books, in which nobody wants to publish, so Gertrude sells one of her Picassos and gives the money to Alice and something called *Plain Editions* starts. And *Lucy Church Amiably* comes first, and then *Before the Flowers of Friendship Faded Friendship Faded,* and *How To Write* and *Operas and Plays* and *Matisse, Picasso & Gertrude Stein,* her three Cubist pieces. *How To Write* she publishes, which is concerned with equilibration and the technical aspects of grammar, narrative, and vocabulary. It is perhaps the most opaque of all of her books.

Quote, "Paragraphs are emotional. Sentences are not. To read *How To Write* is finally to learn what language sounds like when it is consciously divorced from sense, and the ordinary sense of sense."

In the summer of 1932 at Bilignin, she chooses a voice which to register on every page in the speaking voice of Alice Toklas and written from a point of view assumed to be Alice's. She puts down the anecdotal history of their long life together. She writes it in six weeks, destined to be her most popular and republished work, a spectacular bestseller, her only one, that finally gets her the American audience she wants. It turns her into a celebrity. It first appears in installments in *Atlantic Magazine*. It is published by Harcourt Brace in August 1933 and lead to a lecture tour in the United States which is enormously successful. However, in France her contemporaries, which she writes about, are enraged, and they publish something called *Testimony Against Gertrude Stein,* as a supplement to *Transition Magazine.* They have George Bracht, Matisse, Christian Sarr, among others each take an issue with her account of her relationships with them. Matisse states that, "*Autobiography* in its hollow, intensive, bohemianism, ego-centric deformations may very well become the signal of the decadence that hovers over contemporary literature." Tristan Tzara talks about, "Two maiden ladies greedy for fame and publicity. A clinical case of megalomania."

But this doesn't faze Gertrude a bit, as you can tell. She wouldn't be who she was if it did. She probably loves it. Because of her association with the young Virgil Thompson, he sets her play *Four Scenes and Three Acts* to music. It opens in New York City on February 20, 1934. It's brilliantly staged, and the audience has a good time while the opera is going on, a thing that does not very often happen to them at the theater. Though it is a plotless work, in which all the conventions of time, exposition, and crisis are dismissed, it is of an intensity that finally defies analysis. Defying analysis is pretty much where Gertrude Stein's work is a lot.

But getting back to her trip to the United States, which she arrives in October of 1934, the reporters are there when she arrives and the headlines on the tabloids say "Gerty! Gerty! Stein! Stein! is Back Home, Home Back!" And more than six months later she does her tour, she feels like she's wedded to America and you could look upon every evidence of being the lion she had hoped to become, and renews this love affair with her native land which remains passionate with her until the day of her death.

"All these people including the nice taxi drivers recognize and are careful of me."

She's a real celebrity. She crisscrosses the nation by ear from Massachusetts to California in a series of some forty appearances. Each of them surrounded by fanfare and adulation.

"Our roots can be anywhere and we can survive because if you think about it, we take our roots with us. I know because you can go back to where they are, they can be less real to you than they were 3,300 miles away."

Little of her past returns. She has tea at the White House with Eleanor Roosevelt and gets to meet and talk with Charlie Chaplin, so the most obscure writer of the century for a time becomes the most famous. She becomes a household word and the newspapers just can't get enough of her. America can't take her seriously, but they can't ignore her either, so they just decide to turn her into this kind of popular darling. At the outset of the tour, she decided to limit her audience to five-hundred, so this made everybody want to go. At Princeton, her first college lecture, the police had to check crowds, fighting, trying to fight their way in, like it was a big rock concert or something.

She's happy to return to a quiet summer and all this publicity puts her into another frame of mind and she begins to write *The Geographical History of America, Or the Relation of Human Nature to the Human Mind,* a work primarily of the idea of identity.

"To know what the human mind is, there is no knowing what the human mind is because as it is, it is."

So the history of her time in Paris comes to an end in 1937 when the landlord terminates their lease and they move and start a new salon dragging all their stuff with them, those masterpieces of paintings and turn it into an instant museum of Picasso's, but war soon comes along and although Gertrude never took the possibility seriously, considering Hitler a German Romanticist who could not stand real blood and fighting, she is quite shocked that this happens. They close up their Paris apartment taking only Picasso's portrait of her and the portrait of Madame Cezanne, and they don't return again until 1944. That's seven years they move out to the country during this time. In their country place, she becomes, as she says, rich in ways to say "How do you do?" When Paris is occupied she becomes scared, completely scared and makes plans to move to Spain, but then decides to stay put upon the advice of friends.

She and Alice are protected and the mayor of the town never gives away their identities. "You are too old for life in a concentration camp, and you would not survive it, so why should I tell them?" he says.

She is protected by the affection of her French neighbors and sticks it out there during the war. In 1945, they lose the lease on the house and move, and she writes a book called *Wars I Have Seen,* and it is a personal document, an intimate modest record of realities of life under the occupation and it ends when the American army arrives in August of 1944 and she makes a broadcast in the country there with Eric Sevareid. She says, "I am so happy to be talking to America today."

She loves the GI Joes, she really does, and they love her too. They return to Paris after seven years and she finds all their paintings intact, amazingly. Two groups of marauders had visited the flat but were unaware of the value of the paintings. Her new place becomes like it did in World War I, a place for the postwar visitors to come, a kind of shrine. All the GI's recognize her, and she is such a hit that on one occasion at least they walk her home, fifty strong, forcing automobiles into side streets and causing the puzzled police to investigate the nature of the procession.

In her own home she listens to the rhythms of American speech and writes, bruisy and willy, with the authentic GI flavor. She's asked to make an official tour of bases in occupied Germany. In June of 1945 her and Alice go off for five days and they visit Hitler's home.

"The visit to Hitler's home," she says, "was a lark. There we were in that big window where Hitler dominated the world, a bunch of GIs just gay and happy. It really was the first time I saw our boys all gay and careless, really forgetting their burdens and just being foolish kids climbing up around and on top. Miss Toklas and I sat comfortably and at home on garden chairs on Hitler's balcony."

Amazing, huh? She finishes the script of *The Mother of Us All* and sends it to Virgil Thompson, about the life of Susan B. Anthony. It's an opera, a discussion in song. About this time, a digestive disorder she had complained about is diagnosed as needing hospitalization, and she's received into the American hospital on July 19, 1946. She makes her will and leaves her manuscripts and correspondence to Yale and the bulk of her estate to Alice. She has an abdominal tumor in an advanced state of malignancy and although they operate, it is too far advanced.

As she comes out of the anesthetic, she says, "What is the question?"

No one answers.

She says, "What is the answer?"

And then she dies of cardiac arrest at 6:30.

An editorial in *The Nation Magazine* says, "Hearing that Gertrude Stein is dead is like learning that Paul Bunyan has been eaten by his ox, Babe."

(Kyger proceeds to play a tape of Stein reading, in her own voice for the audience. The tape is not played in the recording.)

A Handful of Clitoral Words

Interlude by Ada McCartney

When Lorna Smedman finally performs after building towards "A Wife has A Cow," ultimately launching with a laugh, she takes obvious (and somewhat self-conscious) pleasure in each word, lingering over phrases, tonguing 'and' and 'is' and 'how' as if they are the very clitoris of which the poem speaks. Finally, as the poem verges on climax, she invites the audience to speak the last stanza all together with her invoking a cacophonous, aural orgy. Like a good orgasm the cacophony expands and shudders beyond the last word, energy spurting and jittering and coming in waves.

Throughout the lecture Smedman is on the edge of voicelessness. It is hard to understand her through congestion at times. It reminds me of the last time I performed in front of a live audience. I was near delirious with respiratory illness and a high fever, but not doing it was not an option. *The show must go on*—or so I thought. There is also a surprising erotic quality to her hoarseness, it requires a leaning in and attentiveness to truly follow where she leads. Coughing belies enthusiasm and underscores the moments when passion overtakes her.

Lorna Smedman graduated from the Jack Kerouac School of Disembodied Poetics in 1980 and credits experiences there as emblazoning her with passion for modern poetry, "I had my mind blown open." She goes on to say that Naropa informed her understanding of poets as scholars. The charged atmosphere of the JKS instilled a notion of poets as legitimate, studious keepers; purveyors of hermetic wisdom; and most importantly for Smedman, activists experimenting with the boundaries of where language can go, what it can do through subverting its oppressive structures and co-opting grammar for erotic feminism.

Her first appearance in the Naropa archives is a reading from 1978. After a thick block of male poets, she takes the mic and in a clear mellow voice that flows like Boulder Creek in October recites a poem featuring lyrical repetition of the words *red, breakfast,* and *day*, "I finally heard birds at dawn/the sky was red, no paler than red ... breakfast flung like a brick ... come back here and finish your breakfast ... there should be no noise at breakfast ... I only go out for breakfast" In this experimental poem, she also evokes Stein's wordplay foreshadowing her work to come.

More than a decade before she lectured on Stein's unconventional reiteration of "small words," Smedman is employing them to experiment with capacities of language, testing its limits, and rendering it fresh through repetitive meditation on single words and phrases. Smedman's multi-decade relationship with Stein and her work reveals the profound depth of her scholarly activism and includes a dissertation called, "Gertrude Stein and the Politics of Grammar," and a tongue-in-cheek book called *The Dangers of Reading* (1983). In her works, Smedman often returns to the notion of grammatical terrorism offering it up as a tool of the marginalized. Grammar is a foundation of the endlessly colonizing English language. It can be used to oppress or liberate. It can be corrupted, used against its purpose, or restructured entirely. Gertrude Stein wields it with force against the perils of patriarchy, undoing grammar at its seams and resewing an entirely new garment of meaning. Smedman visits Naropa a few years after "A Wife has A Cow" to offer a 2-part lecture called "Primer on Grammatical Terrorism." To begin she asks, *Do women and men in patriarchal societies have different relationships to the language they speak and write?* Definitely yes, is her answer. Terrorism refers to experimentation, skewing or even queering the grammatical status quo. In "A Wife has A Cow," Smedman posits, Stein queers the act of marriage, writing as a man and skewing all the possible linguistic implications of the words "wife" and "cow."

Gertrude Stein relied on language that was unsuitable for what she intended to create and so she created something new from small pieces of language. The poem "A Wife Has A Cow" contains a mere seven nouns and is composed primarily of articles and prepositions. The word "and" is a desperate word, according to Smedman, because it joins and separates. The building blocks of "and," "a," etc. become what Smedman refers to as clitoral words—words that massage, that enliven, that effectively express female sexual enjoyment.

Lorna Smedman articulates the political importance of establishing language for and elaborating on the intricate intimacies of erotic femininity. The female orgasm has been labeled "elusive," often becoming a bit of a joke, an afterthought in heterosexual circles to the point where actual women that I've spoken with as recently as 2020 have admitted to being unsure if they've experienced an orgasm, let alone multiple, let alone ventured beyond missionary or maybe the occasionally doggy style into the taboo territory that is erotic, sensual female pleasure. Even within the space of her lecture Smedman is faced with a man usurping her space with phallic logic in the Q&A session to question the accessibility of Stein's small words and Smedman's readings of them, asserting that Stein, and Smedman are speaking in "coded language" that he is unable to connect with. Smedman, bless her, claps back, her tired voice embracing a deeper register as she cuts his off and puts his comment in its place.

According to Audre Lorde, Eroticism is what you're drawn to, what draws you in. And it's always political. For many women, attraction is shrouded in shame. In *Chronology of Water* Lidia Yuknavitch devotes an entire chapter to her first pussy spanking and the wellspring of healing that it undammed within her. Yuknavitch employs plain yet poignantly searing language with phrases like "gushing swollen twat" and "titty whipping."

Stein wrote before it was conceivable to utter such vibrantly, politically wet and graphic terms. In "A Wife has A Cow," the word "cow" becomes a stand in for orgasm. Use of the word "wife" signifies Stein's tendency to identify as a male in writing. Empty of their usual semantic context "cow," "wife," and the other five nouns in the poem rejoice in their conveyance of concealed lesbianism: terrorizing conventional grammar in a hermetics of subterfuge which engages language in an endlessly fluctuating, anti-authoritarian way. Static contemporary context shatters into experimental fragments. Smedman licks Stein until a trail of orgasmic juices emerge leading to the poetic reclamation of a sensual feminine erotic.

As A Wife Has A Cow A Love Story: Gertrude Stein and The Ways Words

Lorna Smedman
July 18, 1991

Transcription by Ada McCartney

Lorna Smedman: Good afternoon, everybody. This lecture is titled "As a Wife Has a Cow, A Love Story: Gertrude Stein, and the Ways Words." I hope my voice doesn't totally give out—I'm reading from a holey text, full of holes. The problem when you're computerized, and then you travel away from your computer back to some archaic textualization. "As a Wife Has a Cow, a Love Story: Gertrude Stein, and the Ways Words."

In her lecture "What is English literature?" Gertrude Stein made a distinction between writing indirectly, meaning writing the way it had been written, and the holier mission of writing directly where the relation between the thing done and the doer must be direct. While Stein certainly wrote against the grain of how literature had been written, perhaps more radically than anyone before and most since in English, her goal was not to make it new. As a writer who was marginal in many ways, whose culturally inscribed and self-inscribed identities, deviated wildly from an Anglo-American normative as a woman writing as a female genius, as a Jewish woman, an American, an expatriated American, as a lesbian, as a large woman, a fat woman—Stein came to writing, not so much to make it new, but to make what had never been before a different "it" altogether.

Her pursuit of the direct relation between herself and the thing done was in a sense the only relation possible, since writing the way it had been written would have meant silence, pseudonym, a notion Stein actually toyed with her first book *Three Lives* was almost by Jane Sands, who might've been fathered by the French woman writer, George Sands, or the ignominious E. S. S., one of the fates of women writers.

Of course, women had already pursued writing seriously for centuries before Stein, usually with not more but less success. Stein had been closely proceeded by another American writer who religiously tried for the direct relationship between doer and thing done: Emily Dickinson, "a word made flesh is seldom and tremblingly partook. And then nor then perhaps reported," she wrote in one poem. Dickinson did come back and report her linguistic transport. Like Susan Howe, I see Dickinson and Stein as pathfinders, who if we take them seriously, reveal whose order is shut inside the structure of a sentence and also ways to break through and escape is confining structure and order. When I began to see how explosive, how deconstructive their writing is to systems of meaning and expression and how it implicates other institutional systems of oppression as well: gender race, class, compulsory heterosexuality. I started calling Dickinson and Stein, grammatical terrorists. The grammatical terrorists, dangerous pet plastique is the word. And what gets blown out of the sky de-transcendentalized are genre syntax with its diagrammable rules and hierarchies semantics, the authoritative texts.

I'll just tell an anecdote. I was describing to Ron Padgett, my project of working with Dickinson and Stein, and he said, Oh, I have a great title for you—"Two weird chicks"—which is really how they've come down through the title of my dissertation.

But, I don't think they were two weird chicks, just working in isolation. I think there was a lot of interesting connections going on between them. "... only excreate, only excreate a no since." One line from Tender Buttons, which tailed by its shadow pun, excrete a nuisance could be one manifesto of the American grammatical terrorists lineage I'm interested in. X create, not just undo, but create outside of, "a no", any no, any interdiction, since. Since writing beyond what has been written cannot proceed without this preliminary step, which begins to make language available and thrilling again. Thrilling, one of Stein's words.

In this presentation, I will attempt a reading, one among not infinite, but many possible readings of parts of one terrorist text, Stein's "As a Wife Has a Cow, a Love Story." I want to pay rather microscopic attention to one stanza. One of the stanzas you have on your handout, particularly to Stein's use of little words and their terroristic potential. I also to talk about reading against the heterosexist bias that is so built into our reading and interpretive strategies and how this text both recognizes and resists this heterosexism. The assumption that heterosexuality is the natural against which all other sexualities are measured and judged.

Some questions: Where is the love story? Where is the sex in a poem which contains few verbs? Where is the body in a love poem with hardly any nouns? This is a long poem, but I want to try to do a reading of it. How many people are familiar with this poem? Anybody have it memorized? (laughter) Okay, Larry, you can recite along with me.

I remember Robert Duncan reading this poem, and then adamant saying, every third grader in the United States should be made to memorize this poem. You know, then I dunno what he thought that would accomplish. But yeah, brilliant writers everywhere. Change the world.

"As a wife has a cow, a love story."

Hey, wish me luck.

> Nearly all of it to be as a wife has a cow, a love story. All of it to be as a wife has a cow, all of it to be as a wife has a cow, a love story.
>
> As to be all of it as to be a wife as a wife has a cow, a love story, all of it as to be all of it as a wife all of it as to be as a wife has a cow a love story, all of it as a wife has a cow as a wife has a cow a love story.
>
> Has made, as it has made as it has made, has made has to be as a wife has a cow, a love story. Has made as to be as a wife has a cow a love story. As a wife has a cow, as a wife has a cow, a love story. Has to be as a wife has a cow a love story. Has made as to be as a wife has a cow a love story.
>
> When he can, and for that when he can, for that. When he can and for that when he can. For that. When he can. For that when he can. For that. And when he can and for that. Or that, and when he can. For that and when he can.

And to in six and another. And to and in and six and another. And to and in and six and another. And to in six and and to and in and six and another. And to and in and six and another. And to and six and in and another and and to and six and another and and to and in and six and and to and six and in and another.

In came in there, came in there come out of there. In came in come out of there. Come out there in came in there. Come out of there and in and come out of there. Came in there, come out of there.

Feeling or for it, as feeling or for it, came in or come in, or come out of there or feeling as feeling or feeling as for it.

As a wife has a cow.

Came in and come out.

As a wife has a cow a love story.

As a love story, as a wife has a cow, a love story.

Not and now, now and not, not and now, by and by not and now, as not, as soon as not not and now, now as soon now now as soon, now as soon as soon as now. Just as soon just now just now just as soon just as soon as now. Just as soon as now.

And in that, as and in that, in that and and in that, so that, so that and in that, and in that and so that and as for that and as for that and that. In that. In that and and for that as for that and in that. Just as soon and in that. In that as that and just as soon. Just as soon as that.

Even now, now and even now and now and even now. Not as even now, therefor, even now and therefor, therefor and even now and even now and therefor even now. So not to and moreover and even now and therefor and moreover and even now and so and even now and therefor even now.

Do they as they do so. And do they do so.

We feel we feel. We feel or if we feel if we feel or if we feel. We feel
or if we feel. As it is made made a day made a. day or two made a day,
as it is made a day or two, as it is made a day. Made a day. Made a day.
Not away a day. By day. As it is made a day.

On the fifteenth of October as they say, said anyway, what is it as
they expect, as they expect it or as they expected it, as they expect it and
as they expected it, expect it or for it, expected it and it is expected of
it. As they say said anyway. What is it as they expect for it, what is it
and it is as they expect of it. What is it. What is it the fifteenth of October
as they say as they expect or as they expected as they expect for it.
What is it as they say the fifteenth of October as they say and as expected
of it, the fifteenth of October as they say, what is it as expected
of it. What is it and the fifteenth of October as they say and expected
of it.

And prepare and prepare so prepare to prepare and prepare to prepare
and prepare so as to prepare, so to prepare and prepare to prepare
to prepare for and to prepare for it to prepare, to prepare for it, in preparation,
as preparation in preparation by preparation. They will be too
busy afterwards to prepare. As preparation prepare, to prepare, as to
preparation and to prepare. Out there.

Okay, now this is where you can all join in, for the last stanza. (Laughter, audience joins, their reading pacing increases gradually.)

Have it as having having it as happening, happening to have it as
having, having to have it as happening. Happening and have it as happening
and having it happen as happening and having to have it happen
as happening, and my wife has a cow as now, my wife having a cow
as now, my wife having a cow as now and having a cow as now and
having a cow and having a cow now, my wife has a cow and now.
My wife has a cow.

That was great! Okay. That's the end of my lecture. (laughter)

"But isn't the surest pleasure of all the pleasure of talking about love? What is more, in order to tell the truth?" It's a quote from Luce Irigaray, *The Sex Which is Not One.*

"As a Wife has a Cow, a Love Story," originally printed by Kahnweiler in 1926, with lithographs by Juan Gris. This is a facsimile of that. A Love story. Generic. We all love love stories. The sentence "a wife has a cow" is interesting enough, especially juxtaposed with the promise of a love story. "As a wife has a cow" is not done. The subordinate clause waits for something else to happen. An event occurring simultaneously, perhaps as a wife has a cow, I write this, or it waits for something to compare itself to. As a wife has a cow, a husband has a wife. There are seven nouns in the poem "As a Wife has a Cow, a Love Story": a wife, a cow, a love story, (actually, noun phrase) a day, the 15th of October, and the numbers two and six.

But this list of substantives hardly sums up what the poem is about. Wife, cow, and the unnamed husband, whose existence is implied by the word 'Wife' might be the coordinates of a bourgeois, rural love triangle, a study model of contentment that Stein appropriates, and then makes her own by emptying out the usual semantic content of these nouns, and then rejuicing them.

What does it mean when Stein writes about a wife? Standard literary lore figure Stein as a male identified self-proclaimed genius, the Butch member of that Butch-fem team of Stein and Toklas. Toklas not only sat with the wives of important and artistic men, but like a properly domestic wife, did everything she could to make Stein's writing life easier for her.

Stein's grammatical terrorism is often interpreted as a Hermetics of subterfuge, a densely encoded language, which she employed in order to conceal her lesbianism, the love that dare not speak its name. Whatever the actual terms of Stein's relationship with Toklas were, these terms are buried in Pére-Lachaise Cemetery. The remaining texts do not represent love stories shaped by a dominant-subordinate, masculine-feminine paradigm, but rather love stories concerned with the endless fluctuations of relation, anxious, moving towards separation and ecstatic closing of degrees toward reunion.

I don't think that these love stories and all Stein's writings are love stories, all concerned with exploration of relation. I don't think that these stories can be read or savored in all their complex jouissance, except by accepting that these texts are written out of a lesbian sensibility of pleasure, out of an anti-hierarchical, anti-authoritarian engagement with language. Stein's position on several margins, paradoxically left her with less investment in the traditional conventions and structures of English literature, and so more room to move outside of these conventions. But, she also had a critical vantage point that allowed her to critique the oppressive particulars of the culture that she was in many ways, excluded from.

Catherine Stimpson in an article called "Gertrude Stein and the Transposition of Gender" concludes that Stein's attitudes about gender are often self-contradictory and that things like Stein's frequent use of the term wife can be seen as either a repudiation and/or reconstitution of patriarchal values, an argument that was once convincing to me. About last week it was convincing to me, but now I'm not so sure. Though I admit that I am often disturbed by Stein's use of hetero terms to represent her own lesbian situation. For instance, there is this more autobiographical reference from "A Sonatina Followed by Another," Little Alice B is the wife for me. Little Alice B so tenderly is born so long as she can be born along by a husband strong who has not his hair shorn." Is this use of husband and wife giving into the system, or by claiming those terms to Stein aggressively confer legitimacy upon her relationship, radically defying denotations that make her relations illegal and invisible, unnamable? These are questions similar to those coming up around the issue of legalizing lesbian and gay marriage ceremonies. Is it a sellout or the quickest way to change a social-political-religious system that now refuses to recognize any of the multiplicity of relationships happening outside of the syntax of father plus mother plus kids.

The indefinite article "A" makes the wife and the title equivalent to any wife, a wife doesn't get particularized until the last stanza when a first-person narrative, voice claims possession, "My wife has a cow." The plot of this love story, if one can be so bold to call it that, transforms the generic heterosexual wife of the first stanzas into a different kind of wife. One who no longer goes on top of the wedding cake. She is transformed into a lesbian authored wife, and that is part of the magic of this poem.

I just want to go back and bring in my interest in Dickinson as well. There's an interesting parallel. A vis-a-vis using the word "wife."

This is from one Dickinson poem, "Title divine—is mine!/The Wife—without the Sign!" she exclaims in one poem, conferring upon herself, the status of a wife, a sexually mature adult woman status, which her society denied to unmarried girls. By expanding the word wife to include herself, Dickinson calls into question, the efficacy of the sign, the word itself, and its attendant, outer signs—gold ring, lost virginity, initiation into heterosexuality, Husband's name replacing father's name—to mark the change from girlhood to womanhood or from sexual emotional innocence to experience.

In another poem. Dickinson tries on several titles. "I'm 'wife'—.../I'm Czar—I'm 'Woman' now—" She finally chooses "I'm 'Wife'! Stop there!" As well as expanding the category wife to include herself. Dickinson returns the word to its more archaic meaning, which was simply, "woman," I mean wife, I guess old English, or even middle English simply meant a grown woman.

Dennis Baron in his study of etymologies of some gendered language reveals the blind spots in this science. Words for women are more likely to call up notions of physiology or social, particularly domestic functions in the minds of the invariably male etymologists. Just once in the history of this, of the language, a wife was a mature member of society and old English could speak of a housemistress. Now my old English is really bad. So, husbonde, or house master, husbonda—in old English, there were two terms and husband could be either a feminine or masculine meaning house housemistress, housemaster.

She [Stein] writes in white ink, a quote from Hélène Cixous' "Laugh of the Medusa." The word cow also has levels of gendered history that Stein excavates in her repeated use of the word. Cow, when not the gentle nourishing, mooing bulk in a field can be a derogatory word once referring to a clumsy obese, coarse, and otherwise unpleasant person. Then more specifically referring to women, a degraded woman, a prostitute, but in Stein's texts, no one is a cow. Someone has a cow, a cow comes out.

Again, this is from "A Sonatina":

> Can a cow keep sweet. Yes if it has a blessing. Can a cow keep its retreat. No not if it has a blessing. Can a cow have feet. Yes if it has a blessing. Can a cow be perfect? Yes if it has a blessing.

> I bless the cow. It is formed, it is pressed, it is large, it is crowded. It is out. Cow come out. Cow come out and shout.

Stein critics have generally accepted that "cow" is Stein's euphemism for female orgasm. In the midst of all Stein's wordplay, which is sexually explicit or suggestive. Another example, I'll give you, Stein, I'm saying there are certain lines that are not so hermetic, and this is another line from ... hermetic is that use of "cow" ... This is another line from "Sonatina." I love this line:

"Why is pussy like the great American army. Because she buds so many buddies."

In the midst of all Stein's wordplay, which is sexually explicit or suggestive, "cow" does seem hermetic, a private association, but also dazzlingly solid, complicated, crowded. Is "cow" a code word, which requires an initiation, such as the one I just gave, before Stein's texts are more fully comprehensible? Is Stein hiding her sexual expression behind the cow? It would be as easy to hide a cow in a treeless meadow in broad daylight. What is accomplished by the repeated substitution or association of cow with orgasm is it an escape from a noun, which is virtually meaningless for women's sexual pleasure. Since an orgasm is reductive, totalizing, mono, that some native Americans have numerous words to describe different kinds of snow, while we have only a handful in English reveal something about our cultures about different preoccupations and concerns.

Since there are not fifty words available to describe some of the variety of female sexual pleasure, Stein chose her own word "cow," because this word is semantically so far removed from our conception of coming, of orgasm, Stein leaves a large space open for multiplicity to happen. The meaning of cow depends on context. For instance, I find it difficult to plug in my primary static heterosexist image of as a wife has a cow, an image of a frowning

French farm woman in a blue kerchief into the last stanza. You know, I don't see how she fit in "...my wife having a cow/as now, and having a cow has now and having a cow and having a cow now..." Now the static is shattered into the experiential.

Okay. So, now we can imagine that when this kind of wife has this kind of cow, we are in a new love story. One that ends a little bit like Joyce's Ulysses with jouissance, women's pleasure, certainly an indeterminant closure, although very much from a very different point of view than Joyce, different gaze. Steins de-stabilizing semantic plays an attempt to find a more direct relation between doer—wife, writer—and thing done—having a cow, having a text—but the words, "wife" and "cow" virtually disappear between the opening and closing stanzas, and this is where I think the sex in the poem really happens along the syntactic axis of the poem when Stein jams small relational words together.

Now we're coming to the good part. The sex part.

Another quote, "Woman takes pleasure more from touching than from looking, " from Luce Irigaray, *The Sex Which is Not One.*

Let's look at "The Ways Words" in Stanza Thirteen reprinted in your handout. That's the first stanza. I'm not going to read it again over again. I'll read a little, "And in that, as and in that, in that and and in that, so that, so that/and in that, and in that and so that and as for that and as for that and/that," etc.

This is not a stanza where broken syntax can be reconstituted or word codes unlocked. We all know these words, conjunctions prepositions, relative pronouns. Those tricky, hard to define words, funny adjectives, soon, just. I can never remember, what kind of word is "just?" You have to look it up in the dictionary. Stein like little words a lot. About prepositions, she wrote, "Prepositions can live one long life being really being nothing but absolutely nothing but mistaken and that makes them irritating if you feel that way about mistakes but certainly something that you can be continuously using and everlastingly enjoying." It's from *Poetry and Grammar,* one of her lectures about conjunctions have made themselves live by their work.

William Gass has a delightful essay titled "And," a detailed meditation on the multiple meanings of six ands in a sentence from Gertrude Stein's story "Melanctha." He describes "and" in one instance as a desperate part of speech, precisely because it separates and joins at the same time. "As" and "in that" are in some kind of relation, simultaneously particular bounded, but also components of a larger entity. One and one equals a more complex one might be the romantic equation underlying some of these phrases, so I'm looking at the stanzas and sort of taking out phrases and seeing what's really happening in there.

Gass also mentioned another daring function of "and" when an "and" appears between two terms, a place where these two things belong together has been implied. I think this is true in this stanza, you know, you sort of read it. It's like, where are we? I mean, we're somewhere, though. There's something definitely created. To say there is an "in that," in this poem in this world is one thing, but when I say there is a "so that," and there is an "in that." I trace a line between these two particles of speech and "there" then points to a kind of ground instead of a single isolated dot. Beginning, the stanza with "and" places us in media res, very old literary convention, and so creates history as well as place. It is not difficult to maneuver in this abstract world of the poem, the additions to the original equation "and in that" are logical.

"So that," "for that," "as for that," between the commas, which are themselves implied "ands," Stein varies the number and order of the terms, testing the limits of what our attention can cognitively process. "...and in that and so that and as for that and as for that and/that..."

I think the mind can only hold something like seven to ten things, little things together, something Stein would be would know about from her, her studies at Harvard. Not content to just let "and" inscribe time and space, she forces it into positions where it can be mistaken, such as the double and in the phrase, "in that, and, and in that," where the function of each is ambiguous "and" as part of the larger term, "and in that," as well as the conjunction between the terms. The "ands" echo, waiver, create anxiety when they meet face to face, which is the conjunction? Does one and have to become subordinated to the other?

One seldom has the opportunity or the necessity to read these functional words with so much care, except if, when one is teaching a composition class and late at night in front of a stack of student essays, one sits pondering suddenly how to explain to a student why he or she should or should not use the word "that" in a particular sentence. In lieu of a noun "that" becomes the object. If we can even think of it that way. In stanza thirteen, just as Stein uses the indifferent indefinite article, "a" as a wife has a cow, she picks "that," the further removed, the less obvious partner of "this." The inaccessibility of that also produces tension. It is too far away on the level of word to word relation, "that" is the other that all the prepositions struggle to possess and remake, but "that" turns out to be promiscuous, shifty, indeterminant, and always in a way obscure and self-contained. "Just as soon as that" echoes the final line of stanza twelve, "just as soon as now that, and now," giving these two phrases different balances, one on the side of time that smugly solid. What does all this have to do with a love story? A wife and a cow? Stein is more interested in here in expressing her love of little words that could suggest so much and not get stopped by semantic sense.

This wordplay was also foreplay leading up to the ecstatic last stanza. The one we read together. Variations on "having," "happened," and "happening" accumulate, bunched up, take the breath away in the long first part of the second sentence, and then resolve into a litany of cows. Having to have it as "happening" with Stein's constant desire in her writing. Having to have it as happening, not happened, not will happen, "happening." Direct relation requires immediacy while happening expresses Stein's absorption in the present moment, "having" is a threat since it is so orally close to halving, H-A-L-V-E, to cut in half, being split or separated, cutoff from the sustaining relations. Okay, so if you think about that split in your mind, of having, happening, and also splitting, splitting in half, have it as having, having it as happening, happening to have it as having. So I'm saying that there's this immediate moment and then an anxiety about an immediate moment in a fusion and an anxiety about whatever's being in relation being cut in half again. Union ends up winning— "...and my wife has a cow as now, my wife having a cow/as now, my wife having a cow as now and having a cow as now and/having a cow and having a cow now, my wife has a cow and now./My wife has a cow." The indefinite article is replaced by the possessive "my" and they, we, everybody lives happily ever after.

"As a Wife Has A Cow, A Love Story" is a successful just as a sound poem, an incantation full of sex magic, a chant to ward off the evils of exile and war. The reference to the 15th of October is the date that Stein and Toklas returned to Paris. They ended up getting caught in England at the outbreak of the war and staying at Alfred Whitehead's house for, I don't know how long, a couple of weeks or a month and desperately wanting to return home, so that's another separation and reunion. It is a sustained investigation into the mysteries of how words, particularly little words, work. And originally that was the title of the paper, "Gertrude Stein and the Way Words Work," and then I realized this emphasis on working, so then I was going to change it to "Gertrude Stein and the Way Words Fuck." Again, you get into semantics again, somehow it just didn't ... So then I left it "Gertrude Stein and the Ways Words," but one thing it shows is how words shows, both how words work, how words do their thing, and it is a catalog of relations happening between lovers, between writer and word, between words, between legs. Stein certainly was not the first writer or thinker to discover how important small words were.

Nathaniel Hawthorne once jotted down this idea in a notebook to personify "if," "but," "and," "though," et cetera, a project never realized as far as we know. The last line of Wallace Stevens poem, "The Man on the Dump" ends dramatically with the double instance of the definite article, where was it one first heard of the truth? "The, the... The, the." And I think ... I haven't looked this up, but I think the last word of *Finnegan's Wake* is also "the" and then ellipsis.

"The" becomes the paradoxical place to start speaking when speech has failed. While Stevens foregrounds "the," the, for a moment, Stein's project entailed a more radical and permanent rearrangement of foreground and background, rejecting the language that had traditionally been charged with truth-telling, the language of literature, she adopted the back to basics approach to language that Stephen's only imagined. As a woman writer, she had less invested in the tradition, and so she could more easily afford to ignore these rules. As an American, she liked to champion the underdog and had a feeling, a democratic interest in feeling, in regular speech, not too fancy or elitist. She liked small words because they did a lot and went their own ways, which also seems to be very American, the appreciation of busy-ness and iconoclasm. She liked the science of grammar because it was science. And because understanding it let her make amazing discoveries and Mina Loy has a wonderful poem where she called Stein "Curie of the laboratory of vocabulary."

Little words were also important to her because they're important in intellectual or meditative writing, and in fact, act as the essential muscles in any written representation of thoughts or thinking. It is not the things we think about that are so important, but establishing the connections between things.

Stein's interest in relation and its problems, processes, and joys went way back. Her first literary projects, the novels *QED* and *The Making of Americans* were attempts in part to systematically describe and categorize every kind of character type and how each type might affect every other type, as if accomplishing this would make living in the world, foolproof. Her relationship with Alice B. Toklas gave her the security she needed to change course. The idea of relation became less threatening when Alice replaced her unsupportive brother Leo at 27 Rue de Fleurs. Even when Stein was not writing love poems to Alice or about Alice, she was associating the pleasures and struggles of composition with the struggles and pleasures of love. The lover, the other, was not a distant muse, and not really an absent inspiration to writing as Toklas transcribed Stein's notebooks every morning, so they had a very interesting collaborative... I mean, the composition and relationship, very, very complex. It wasn't as if she was helping her write the stuff, but her presence was very, very necessary for Stein's writing and her permission and her support. Boundaries shifted and overlapped. Her interest was in the small daily details of a shared life that never seemed to lose their miraculousness.

Finally, I would like to venture that Stein's interest in spotlighting small words is not just rooted in an abstract association between her own marginal status and the status of invisible utilitarian transitive words, as compared with substantives. Metonymy between a social reality and the politics of word classes within grammar, right? I mean, just as women have a certain marginal status, these small words have a very marginal status in the language, and I'm making this kind of crazy autonomy between that impulse to Stein's interest in, and also Dickinson's interest in, foregrounding that part of language. The small words' qualities of being easily mistaken of shifting of attaching endlessly, of being everlasting irritation, of going wild in the absence of the regulatory noun, suggest to me that Stein's little words also might be considered clitoral words, the grammatical terrorists, most potent tools.

And that's the end of the lecture.

So I know that's very cumbersome to sort of do that sort of microscopic stuff to an audience, but any questions, comments—?

Audience Member 1: I guess the first thing that strikes me about "my wife has a cow" is it's usually what men say to their wife. If their wife gets angry about something and they don't want to talk about it, "oh my wife has having a cow."

Smedman: Right, right. Yeah. The Bart Simpson t-shirt, you know...

Audience Member 1: Or don't have a cow or something of that sort. So I'm wondering that phrase was commonly used at that time, and also another interpretation I'd heard was a cow referred to a female sexual organ, if there was that sort of double play going on?

Smedman: Yeah. As far as I have, I haven't been able to find that having a cow that extremely popular phrase in California now that Stein would have used it that way, like having a fit or being angry, I haven't found it. And a cow as female genitalia, I don't know. I haven't found that reference either. Although there are the references to referring to prostitutes or sort of bad women is as cows.

Audience Member 2: I thought I had, after you explained the sexual undertones of it, if they were, if somebody were in bed and somebody said, well, wouldn't so-and-so have a cow if they, you know... wouldn't our parents have a cow, if they knew, so ...

Smedman: Well, what kind of Cow would they have? A Steinian cow or a Bart Simpson cow?

Audience Member 3 (Larry): I don't remember it, before the, maybe late fifties, that that phrase occurs. "Don't have a cow, don't have a cow man." So you don't notice that, "Don't have a cow, man." My question is, or query is, in your Steinian and studies, do you follow the lesbian shadow language as a precondition to the work? In other words, do you feel that she was, how much did, how much was she deliberating with that shadow language and is it endemic to her work in general? I know *Lifting Belly* is a good example of that shadow language, but...

Smedman: Wait, what do you mean by shadow language?

Audience Member 3 (Larry): Or code, lesbian code? I call it shadow language.

Smedman: So I want to go against the idea that there's a lesbian code. Cause I think you only, I mean, you can see it that way, if you're coming from as a more dominant... if you're looking from a heterosexual, literary stance and then you look and say, Oh, that's coded language, that's hermetic language. And I think the direction I want to work on now is especially French ideas of women's sexuality and sexual economies informing, writing, that she wasn't writing in code. She was writing the only way she could write. And it's not in comprehensible and it's... and if you read it, if you don't know what's going on, then you're really off, you're really not taking the text seriously.

Audience Member 3 (Larry): Okay, fine. That's good (laughter). Don't have a cow, man... But what I was really getting at, whether the intent of the meaning was, but in the composition, because I know earlier when she wrote, I mean, she would write overnight and bring stuff down in the morning to be transcribed. I mean, it was ready, and there had to be a certain amount of fluidity, of spontaneity involved in it. So the deliberate... I'm just interested in how deliberate she was as a composer and how fluid that got and whether anyone even knows that, because that's something I've never read anywhere is, you know, how does she does it? It's like Coolidge, how does he do it? How do you do it?

Smedman: Yeah, I'm very interested in her compositional methods also. One question at a time. (laughter, someone was approaching the mic to speak)

Multiplicity, let's be linear here. But some of the poems, if, when you look at them, you can tell, like you would do with Coolidge, what she's starting with. All right. She starts with a phrase or, maybe in this, in this case is really an exercise in [audio cuts out temporarily]... so that, I think she thought about that a lot. She, I don't think she sat down and did diagrams or stuff, but she was thinking about it. And part of the reason I think her stuff is, you know... that it's not coded is that she was very spontaneous. She really was bringing up stuff really right out front. I don't see it as being hidden and shadowed.

Audience Member 4: Is it my turn? I love this talk and I love this method, and particularly you're coming from Irigaray and the necessity of seeing everything that's happening in the text and in a Stein text as plural and elusive, impossible to pin down to one final authoritative meaning, and to say it means this and not that, because there's always a possibility of its meaning something else. I was thinking of several possibilities at several points, and I wonder what you would think of them. One that the wife having a cow is playing with the children's game. The farmer takes a wife, the wife takes a cow... And then. Which I think, I feel when it's done all the time allusions to children's play as a means of making us lighten up with literature and relax, fool around. So I, does that seem to you as if it would work with your sense of ...?

Smedman: I mean, I think that's good.

Audience Member 4: And it's a game, it's a way of saying this text is to remind you of a game. This text is a game.

Smedman: And Larry, this might be a sense where you could say that could be the seed, as you know, farmer takes a wife and a wife takes a cow as... Magic beans? (Larry is speaking back off mic.) Right? Yeah. And Stein, and there's other texts where you can find that your fairytales or stories like that.

Audience Member 4: Okay. Now, another angle I was thinking of the had, having, the have having, that repetition seemed to me to be an illusion to the Shakespeare sonnet on lust. Lust as the thing that is defiling, that is a big mistake, "Had, having, and in quest to have, extreme;/A bliss in proven and proved, a very woe;" And would you think that you could read this piece as an attempt to appropriate and rewrite the Shakespeare sonnet, such that lust, sexuality would be fine? A pleasure, no bad repercussions. The had, having, not a form of madness, not a form of sin.

Smedman: That's great, I love these allusions. She has another poem called, "Ode"... her parodies that she did, there's one, something like "Ode, to My Mistress's Eyebrows" as a title, and then she, does it her own way, so she's very conversant with all that literature and reworking it.

Audience Member 4: Right, and the piece on the husband and the wife in patriarchal poetry.

Smedman: Right. Terrorizing Shakespeare.

Audience Member 4: Now third, I wasn't sure that when you said the transformation of "a wife" to "my wife," I'm not disagreeing that that's a personalizing and an affirmation of the lesbian relationship, but can't it also be at the same time, an expression of possessiveness. Wife, a wife, can be an independent person on her own having her own cow, whereas my wife is attached to and close to me, and I think Stein was very conscious about the problems of possession and that this would also be part of the piece.

Smedman: Yeah. Well, when I was talking about all those "that's" being maybe chased and possessed by different conjunctions, I mean, it's not all happy utopia, like, Oh, now we're in the...nothing's wrong. It's all perfect. There's lots of tensions. But that whole thing of coming down to say, "my wife has a cow" at the end, I would read as not, you cannot read it in the same possessive way as a conventional, as we conventionally think as Shakespeare would be writing to my lover. Since there's been all that play that's gone on before it, where you know, where nothing is ever a possessable in the rest of the text, so when you get to the end, if you read it that way, it'd be a total contradiction of everything, all the wordplay that came before it. So I think she's also playing with it saying, I can say this, and it doesn't mean I'm a possessive person and I'm oppressing my wife.

Audience Member 5: Thank you for a really brilliant talk, and I really liked the fact that you put it under this sign of a libidinal economy, and for me, it's another *Tender Buttons*. I mean, it's a sex manual and there was vibration, excitation, and, you know, we need all that clitoral excitation. My question is not really a question, but I wonder if you could elaborate on the incredible tension that exists between having possession, who and what do we possess, and who are the people who have, the have and have nots, and so on the whole political economy right there. Since the having is to have something which is jouissance, jouissance being a dépense, the dépense as expenditure, I wonder if you could elaborate on this incredible tension between the necessities she says having to have. So there was an imperative here for women, wives, for people to have a wife who has an orgasm, so between having jouissance and dépense, something that is expenditure.

Smedman: Okay. And, you know, we get to the end of the poem it's sort of all calmed down. My wife has a cow, we go back to that tense, past tense, but by foregrounding all the words that are used all the time, I mean, I don't get a real definitive sense of closure. I just get sort of a little bit of resting and then everything will start over again. It's kind of like in the title "As a Wife has a Cow," sort of leaves it up in the air as this is going to be not a linear sentence, but a continual process of pleasure and having and not having, finished and starting again. That's what I would think, that's part of the reason for that title being put in that form. Is that, do you think that would be convincing...

Audience Member 5: It's good. We'll talk more.

Smedman: And the whole thing too about the cow, I mean, sort of the economy of a wife having a cow, you also think of dowries or what do people possess, in the sort of exchange of women in the same way as farm animals might be exchanged, especially in a rural economy where everything's very practical and you don't have a lot of choices, so I think she's also setting that up to really break that apart.

Audience Member 6: I was still thinking about the whole code, lesbian code thing, and it just struck me that the only decision I would assume she would make is that she, at some point she'd make the decision about her writing in general to be abstract as any artist might make that decision. Then at that point, being a lesbian, she would draw like a lesbian pallet, meaning P-A-L-E-T-T-E, though other one's great, too, so that she would naturally be drawn towards the...in the same way that…it's like the panel the other day, I mean, I used a mustache. Is that a mustache? Is that a code? Or is it a prop? You know, what's the prop that a lesbian would use? And it's, so what's the secret code, you know, I mean, there's no code. I think that the decision is to use a prop to be theatrical or in the case of Stein to be abstract, to have an intensely subjective language.

Smedman: Yeah. And I think her, the choice to be abstract is a political choice. That's how I'm seeing it more and more to say, if language has this structure and confinement, then it's a political choice to say, I'm going to write against that. And the whole thing, like with your mustache would be context, I mean you couldn't just have an abstract question, but you need context. You're sitting here or you're in a theater or whatever. I mean, you're alone, looking in the bathroom mirror, and I think that's part of what Stein really insists upon is that there's no… you can't take this and say, this is what this means. Even with a general sense of it, it's always fluctuating. And, and the only way you can know what it means is, is in context in the moment as it's happening,

Audience Member 3 (Larry): I have to say something about her relationship to Picasso, Juan Gris, Braque, those people from Cubist...not necessarily constructing a poem like a Cubist was, but to come at language from these many angles, from these many, you know, seeing languages as planes, angles, and vectors, which she definitely was aware of because of her relationship to these men who were mostly painting, certainly not Marie Laurencin, but these men. And that's one thing also, had you thought at all about the word "have" as a, to "have" a woman to, like to know in the biblical sense?

Smedman: That's certainly all there. I'm never sure about the relationship between Cubism and this kind of writing because it's not so easy to translate. I mean, we're looking at it from our perspective saying, Oh, of course, you know, they're doing this and they're doing that, but I mean, could you, look at a Guston and say, Oh, I'm going to do exactly that. I mean, you make an attempt, but it's difficult to…

Audience Member 3 (Larry): Yeah, not exactly that, but concurrent with Stein, or at least around World War I, there were people who were making a kind of attempt, Reverdy in France, Reverdy, and here Walter Arensberg, and people who were seeing language in terms of planes and angles and volume, actually seeing language whole that way. And I know that Stein's at least aware of Arensberg, actually and of Reverdy too, but if you look at their work at Reverdy's, particularly, the early work around the World War I, and Arensberg's, he was more obscure, but can be found, you'll see, echoes of that concern regardless of having nothing to do with content at all.

Audience Member 7: I just wanted to say that I agree that, it's kind of like in the moment, but also there's like the context of remembering that, "and" is always referring back to Stein. Anyways, I don't know if that makes any sense, but the "and and" thing, I think I was thinking in a way, it wasn't ambiguous. It was like in that, "and and for that as for that, and in that," I mean, "the and is in, the and is there" was like not ambiguous. But anyways, that's just...

Smedman: It's almost like making little nests. I mean, as these phrases they could either be nested or when you have, "and, and" something else, which side are you standing on? I mean, and if you're standing on and then you're very aware that this comes first and this comes second, so this must be doing more work. Or once you have that consciousness, you can sort of shift it around and say, well, maybe not, maybe, maybe the first "and" actually goes with the first phrase and it's the second "and" that's the conjunction, that's what I'm saying. See what I'm saying?

Audience Member 7: Right, but that's what "and" is. It's what she's saying. Yeah, I understand. The other things I was thinking about is like the had-have-having, that thing. I was thinking how, in a way it's like, if you have every...I mean, in order to have something, you have to have it to have it, so I was thinking maybe in the context of women, instead of women, like being like half the population, women being the whole population of women and having that, and having that would, would mean that our experience as women are, is shared, you know. Something like that. I don't know.

Smedman: Yeah. I mean, that's a good reading. I'm glad you could come up with a reading. I don't know if you have to have having, I mean, again, and you started thinking about these whole concepts. I mean, do you really have to have something, and as you know, to have it, do you have to have it to have it? I mean, she's got to have it. I mean, it sort of makes sense to me just in terms of women's sexuality where you can be... it can be less definite about you have something where you don't have it or it's happening. If it's happening, you have it, and it's not, you don't have it. Okay. Next question.

Audience Member 8: This is sort of in response to what Larry said. I think Larry's quite right to like contextualize her historically with what else was going on. I mean, it wasn't in a vacuum in that way, but I don't somehow I see her as like, as being really independent of all that too, and not like in the sense of being influenced by Picasso or anybody else. I mean, she strikes me as one of the few people who was really, had the sort of presence of mind and determination to go out on her own and do something really new that hadn't been done before. I think that something you said about her freedom from the tradition or from the Canon or whatever, I mean, that's sort of how I see her too, is she was totally outside of any type of Canon of influence from predecessors, and I think that's how she was. I see her as having been able to do it because of that, so I guess I disagree with Larry.

Smedman: (laughs) Ooh. You know, she's not isolated. She's not one weird chick, sort of springing out of nowhere like Emily Dickinson, where did... they just come from somewhere, doing their, this idiosyncratic thing. I think she was very, very aware of the conventions and deliberately sitting down a lot of times to say, I'm going to...all right, I'll write a love story. That's a genre, whatever that big genre, and I'm going to write it this new way, and she certainly had all those old love stories in her head, just like we all do. But I think she really was isolated. And also her, her isolation from the other lesbian communities in Paris had a lot to do with the fact that she was writing jouissance in a very, very different way than the experiments or the poetry that they were pursuing, and so there was those choices that I think made her not, join up, become part of that.

Audience Member 9: I had a couple of observations that may sound redundant, but that's in the spirit of this. So, if she's anti-hierarchical, which, well I'm positing that she's anti-hierarchical, and that long words are one means by which you can create a hierarchy of meaning, and then it's also structural. It kind of has a whole rhythm that determines the...everything I think. And by sticking to one syllable words, I mean, I'm just I'm just sort of supporting what you were saying about that, that I think it leaves a lot of space and motion in her work. Also if one thinks in terms of constants and variables and of nouns and verbs as possibly being the consonants, then you just end up with these variables sort of bumper car pavilion, the play of the conjunctions, the preposition...

Smedman: The transitive parts of language.

Audience Member 9: Right. The articles. That's it.

Audience Member 10: Just a point of information, please, if you could tell me. If you go to Pére Lachaise in Paris and look at the grave stone, you see the front of it is Gertrude Stein, and then on the back of it, there's a tiny little carved writing, which says Alice B. Toklas. Could you just tell me how that happened? I'd just be interested.

Smedman: Stein died several decades before Toklas and, I mean, this is, it's a good, it's an interesting story. She ended up leaving most of her money and property to her oldest nephew, so she sort of, at the very end, ended up perpetuating this system. I think part of her assumption was that the family would allow Toklas a lot of the stuff, but as soon as she died in the will was there, they came in and took everything and left Toklas with nothing, so Toklas was really poverty stricken the last decades of her life, had some paintings was selling them off slowly, but really got cut out by the family who just said, we have nothing to do with you. So it's interesting. I don't know why Stein did that. I mean... she ended up... So I'm saying when Stein died, there was the money there for whatever there was, I assume that when Toklas died, there was only money for a little chiseling on the back. I don't know if it was in the will that way.

Audience Member 11: Since, I mean, I'm going to take this as we're in an act of conjectural imagination here, and I would like to just hark to the thing that Stein said relative to herself, wanting to deal with words as the painters who were her friends dealt with paint, so that when I look at these words adjacent to each other, I am inclined think of them rather than as meaning, to think of them as individual brush strokes, and to think of the, "and" and the content of "and" being the significance of "that" and the "in that," and I feel that the refusal almost totally of explicit sentences is the refusal of the line of resolution that you hear in music, where you have the thing constantly not resolving until there is a moment when it resolves as allowing you to relax.

Smedman: Do you also see when you put those brush strokes next to each other, that they do so much, I mean, there's …?

Audience Member 11: And then I got into the brush strokes. In fact, even if you have brush strokes adjacent and they are the same color or variations on it, what then begins to happen is an accumulation of an atmosphere, and I tend to look into her work as that. I think that the quality then becomes the fact that these individual words isolated from each other are essentially atmospheric words or words that are involved with relating—"having," "happening," "have," "as," "and"—all of those feel very atmospheric to me. I have more problem with taking, having as sounding like halving and then moving into further conjecture off the halving.

Smedman: Well, but she plays with that in other...part of the reason I brought that up, is that she plays with it more explicitly, that punning between "have" and "halve" she plays with quite explicitly in other poems. So I have that information, coming into this as well.

Audience Member 12: When you were talking about, if you have to have it to have it, and if women have it, I was thinking about it, she's got to have it, and what she has to have, and she's got to have it is sex, but not, but male… sex with men, she's got to have a penis. And I started thinking about Freud's whole deal was that women have this huge problem because they don't have it. (laughter) So this is in this poem, they have it, you know, they don't need it because they have it.

Smedman: Terrorize Shakespeare. Terrorize Freud. Terrorize Spike Lee. (laughter) Are we done? Thank you.

Finding Jouissance:
Feminine Writing and the Dissolution of Ego

Interlude by Chloe Tsolakoglou

Having grown up in Greece, I nurtured my young mind with the stories of the Odyssey and Iliad. I was a voracious child and I consumed every book I could get my hands on. Naturally, it began with the phantasmagoric myths that were inextricable to my culture, and as I grew, I eventually ventured into more worldly literature. But, everything really did begin there; in the enclave of the myth and the war brought on by the severity of one woman, Helen. In elementary school we studied both texts diligently, and there seemed to be a consensus among the pupils as to the overarching themes of both epics. The rhetoric went like this—if Helen had been subservient to her husband, then the Trojan war would have never occurred, and Odysseus would've been able to live out the rest of his days on virile Ithaca. The onus of guilt was always placed on Helen, regardless of the variation in myth. And, admittedly, a part of me wanted to hate her for it. It didn't matter how she was abducted at a young age by Theseus, or how she was forced to marry young, or how she was seduced by Paris. My frustration with her blossomed from one very real fear that was mirrored in my own life. Helen was not an active agent. Things were always happening *to* her, and yet she remained the harbinger of despair and loss.

The question of female agency was fractured in the conditions of my upbringing. The outline of my existence was perpetually illuminated and constricted by a dominant male figure, namely my father. Oftentimes, I was labeled hysteric, or overly emotional, when I tried to confront the conditions of pain. My Baba, resting on a leopard print couch, would nonchalantly wave a heavy hand through the thickness of smoke and tell me to simmer down—"*It is not important.*" The walls of the room sagged with nicotine and I recoiled with every airy word that departed from his lips. In those moments I wish I could have killed Helen, or cradled her, or kept her in my breast pocket.

The fact remains; women are consistently sequestered in positions where they have no identity. In her lecture *L'Écriture Féminine,* Jane Augustine explores and contradicts the notions of Ego generation that exist in Lacanian and Freudian psychoanalysis. She argues that the formation of Ego manifests very differently in women and uses Helene Cixous' theory of *L'Écriture Féminine* as a conscientious rebuttal to how women are portrayed in literature, and goes on to say "...writing is dominated by a gendered situation which is skewed in favor of male dominance."

If women are beings devoid of identity, then they must also lack basic understandings of humanness, such as pleasure. How many times have we encountered women in pieces of literature who seem perfectly content to exist as the phantom rib of a man? Would it be too unorthodox to consider that Helen was an initiator in the seduction of Paris, or to realize that she was driven by the quest of pleasure? In French psychoanalytic theory, the word *jouissance* gestures to an all-encompassing pleasure of life; here, language and sexual pleasure exist as a unified one. Augustine uses the fundamentals of *L'Écriture Féminine,* which is really the crux of jouissance as it pertains to women, in order to unpack the literary prowess of Brazilian writer Clarice Lispector. The theory of *L'Écriture Féminine* could also be described as the pointed needle of the feminine imaginary—when women write, they are thrown into a perpetual state of imagination, and the way to enter the imaginary is to absolve the Ego. Hélène Cixous considered Clarice Lispector to be the ultimate perpetrator of the feminine imaginary in the sense that she did not write from the construct of Western dichotomy. For Clarice, writing was not a question of male vs. female, but rather a return to the ultimate root: passion. She rid herself of Ego in order to unveil the purity of Idea, of jouissance. When one is able to write from the perspective of a "not-me" (absolved of Ego), they are able to realize that life is both the progenitor and product of passion. And suddenly, it seems quite foolish to write from within dichotomies.

Of course, as my own literary tastes evolved, I found myself gravitating toward women writers who are traditionally considered inflected and hysteric. I say hysteric not because I believe that they were genuinely disturbed, but because they wrote from a state of repression and oppression. Perhaps a good example of such writing is *Ariel* by Sylvia Plath. As a teenager, I was completely engrossed in her mess. There was something unequivocally attractive about her pain; a pain that I desperately tried to articulate in my own life. Plath was suffocating under the thumb of every male figure in her life. In college, I began writing poems about my Baba and turned them in for workshop. Once, I had an older, male professor tell me, "We don't need any more poems about fathers. Plath already did it, and yours are unsuccessful," I burned red-hot with rage. Was I a failed hysteric? Plath's *Ariel* is indicative of the eccentricity and incomprehensibility that is paradigmatic of *L'Écriture Féminine,* and while I admit that my writing was still very young, and tangled up in the dichotomy of father/daughter, I felt that I was reaching for the door handle of jouissance. Plath and I were very much involved with our Egos, but it was liberatory to write about such matters. As I got older, I realized that my professor had said those things because feminine pain was illegible to him.

Later, I left the figures Plath and Helen behind for writing that sprung forth from the well of life. During my MFA, I was introduced to the work of Cixous and Lispector. I have this memory of reading Lispector's *The Hour of the Star* and tossing the book across the room as it overwhelmed me too much. How was it possible for an author to write from a place of unity with so much success? She was the perfect combination of feminine and masculine. Lispector sunk her fingers into passion and lapped the honeyed ingenuity that it offered her. In her lecture, Augustine remarks "Clarice gives us the example, it is a question of the lesson of things, if we know how to think in the direction of the thing, to let ourselves call to it, Thing leads us into a space composed of the Thing and of Ourselves. The lesson of Clarice is in letting the Thing recall to us something else—not to forget, not to disremember, but to bring back to ourselves that immense Other of life. Clarice teaches us to give ourselves time, not to forget, not to kill. To know how you see before the view, to know how to hear before understanding." Maybe the entrance into the feminine imaginary is through the act of perseverance.

Hélène Cixous, in her book *The Newly Born Woman,* describes how, historically, language "perfects itself to the detriment of the information that it carries and progressively separates itself from the wealth of the original meaning" (Cixous 28). Augustine touches on this issue by explaining that Lispector, having meshed philosophy and literature in her writing, was able to utilize language in an entirely different way. In her books *The Passion According to G.H.* and *Agua Viva,* it is almost impossible to recognize where Lispector, the author, ends and where the characters begin. Her writing is able to maintain a literary autonomy that dissolves all notions of fragmented being. Instead, readers are actually confronted with characters/speakers who are very much aware of what is happening *to* them. Passion bubbles up from the page and oozes between sentences, between words and letters.

In her book *The Stream of Life*, Lispector remarks, "I want to write the dimension of she." This linguistic indication not only reveals that the narrator a feminine capacity, it also uncovers the brevity of the feminine imaginary. The dimension of *she* is not planar, rather, it is electric, amorphous, and continual. It is s/he, feminine and masculine. The structure of her writing is perpetually modified in order to negate collective tradition and individual invention, and it is situated in direct opposition to the crude line of patriarchy. So much of feminine writing has built itself on the premise of "other," of being defined by a masculine lexicon. I would like to lean in to Cixous once more, specifically this passage from *The Newly Born Woman*: "The paradox of otherness is that, of course, at no moment in History is it tolerated or possible as such. The other is there only to be reappropriated, recaptured, and destroyed as other. Even the exclusion is not an exclusion." (Cixous 71) But, this is the key to Lispector's writing; the bearings of it are not adhered to the wheel of western understandings of gender. There is no exclusion, only unity. She never concerned herself with the feminine Ego, instead, everything became a quest for jouissance. She was the sorceress who conjured the Thing.

Clarice Lispector:

Brazilian-Ukrainian Avantgardist Before Her Time

Jane Augustine
July 17, 1990

Transcription by Chloe Tsolakoglou

Jane Augustine: ...On the handout is Clarice Lispector and L'Ecriture Feminine, French theorists meet a Brazilian internationalist writer.

I noticed that in the catalog the Spanish spelling was La Escritura Femi-nina—same thing. And in fact, it's an important part of both the theory of Hélène Cixous, the main critic that I want to mention, in connection with Lispector.

Cixous is very polylingual. She is the Director of the Center for Feminine Studies at the University of Paris 8, which is actually Vincennes, the place where the 1968 student revolt took place and what became a general strike in France and in Germany. It was a student rebellion, which is something that people have forgotten because it's more than twenty years, but it is a very important changing point for Europe and for the education system in France for general advancement of democratic goals. The University of Vincennes, where Hélène Cixous teaches... [indecipherable, talks while writing on chalkboard.]

The Sorbonne is the University of Paris 4, there are eight campuses of the University of Paris. This is the radical one, and so the theory of L'Ecriture Feminine has come out of French radicalism. What I want to talk about today really is radical Avant Garde writing and what it did, what the true Avant Garde means. What real invention of writing means in the context, particularly of the advancement—that may not be quite the right word—but I'll use it. The entry is a better word. The entry of the fact that women write into the French philosophical perspective. French philosophy and criticism have been male dominant for a long time, as if the province of ideas were solely restricted to men. As a result, women rebelled, particularly this Luce Irigaray, who also taught at Vincennes, the other writer.

Luce Irigaray is replying directly to Jacques Lacan. He was a psychoanalyst and the most prominent of psychoanalytic critics—he said women don't know anything about their own pleasure, because they have no identity. I'm still in shock that anybody in the 20th century could be saying women don't exist, but that is still a submerged but dominant attitude. Women are defined by men in many situations, and that is a problem for women writing.

So the term L'Ecriture Feminine, it does not mean feminine writing! It was invented to make it possible for women to have a philosophical handle to hold on to, in order to think about themselves in the face of massive or important figures of French philosophy, which is very psychoanalytically oriented following Freud, saying women are stuck in the pre-Oedipal phase. It's all sort of merging with the mother, they don't really have an identity, and that submerged but pervasive attitude is hard on women writers. How are women going to write if all of what they do is defined externally—if what you write meets someone else's criteria. The French have fancy language for that, the woman is a signifier who was always in opposite, always speaking to an opposing signifier, and what you want is to speak for frankly from the self, with your own significance. That's the philosophical background to the term L'Ecriture Feminine. I think it's fine to put it in the Spanish as well. Hélène Cixous, who is a Jew born in Algeria, a refugee. She is French, German, wrote a big dissertation on James Joyce and became very interested in the writing of Clarice Lispector who is Brazilian, who lived all her life, well no, she did not live all her life, but was born in Brazil and died there. Portuguese is her language. In the middle of her life she was married to a person in the foreign service, and lived in Italy, Switzerland, and for eight years in the United States, but her language is Portuguese, and she is talking about both language and experience in the books that I have given you excerpts of.

The fundamental thing in L'Ecriture Feminine elaborated over and over again is what I call the paradox of "empty self." This is a profound paradox because Lacan has said is that women don't exist, they don't know anything about their own pleasure. And, yeah, women writing have felt the problem is really the solidification of a masculine self, which is the consequence of dominant society. If you have any brush with [indecipherable, talking further away from mic at the chalkboard]... The society in which there is a general and pervasive and solidified masculine ego that Lacan justifies with Freud's psychoanalytic theory.

(In response to indecipherable student question.) I'm talking about the fact that ego in women forms in a very different way.

As an overall, social phenomenon this is not...ego generation happens in everyone, and that's not the problem. I'm really talking about the fact that in Lacan, in defining women follows Freud, who essentially has a view that the ego or identity in women is locked. Women can't undergo the Oedipus complex, the competition with the father to grow up, supplant him, and become civilized. That's a whole digression that I will not get into. But the premise of L'Ecriture Feminine is that writing is dominated by a gendered situation which is skewed in favor of male dominance. That is the view that generated L'Ecriture Feminine.

But, as you're beginning to see rightly, ego's a problem in everyone. But how do women inquire to solve this problem? That's the particular—and under the particular social circumstance, you're all here as writers and want to be writers. That presents a particular problem, which, in fact, is larger than L'Ecriture Feminine, but the theory of L'Ecriture Feminine is very important because of its notion that you do not solidify a feminine self in reply to the theory of solidified psychoanalytic, which actually Lacan has put it this way; the phallus is the supreme signifier. That means, if you don't have a penis you are driven biologically to do an ego formation or to some kind of problem.

Now the French feminists say that language itself is the supreme signifier—signifier is a word that means sign, okay, it's a fancy term—now French feminists say that language itself is... [Augustine writes on blackboard]. I'm not sure that this is true, but it's... [Augustine writes on blackboard]...

The phallus is a signifier and identifies with the word as a signifier, which is [indecipherable]. And so we have to invent a new language.

Now, that's really a metaphor. Words are neutral. They belong to everybody. They're here, but they come in a social context. They come floating—in conversation with Harry Smith last night he was saying "You know, it's very hard to write anything, language itself seem to get you into such gender problems." Harry was talking about cosmology—the highest, most cosmic stuff.

It's true. Every word arrives loaded and we have to unload it as writers, not just as people, but the theory of L'Ecriture Feminine is to point very carefully and powerfully to ways to do that.

Now on page one from the Hélène Cixous' book, the *Newly Born Woman*, she poses a question, and it refers to the "not me."

How could a woman, who has experienced the not-me within me, have a particular relationship to the written? To writing as giving itself away (cutting itself off) from the source?

There is a bond between woman's libidinal economy—her *jouissance*, the feminine Imaginary—and her way of self-constituting a subjectivity that splits apart without regret, and without this regretlessness being the equivalent of dying, of the exhaustion described by Valéry as the Young Fate—answering herself with anomalies, without the ceaseless summoning of authority called Ego.

I'm just going to stick to that right now. Okay, Key word in French... [tape cuts out temporarily].

In the theory of L'Ecriture Feminine this jouissance is related to Lacan's theory of pleasure. Jouissance is a term that—it actually, I think, used to be sort of casual enjoyment—what it means, though, really is sexual pleasure. In the broadest and most powerful sense, that is that the idea of jouissance, as is implied in this first quotation, jouissance means you should enjoy your world, the language, as much as you enjoy sexual pleasure. That is the complete, complete enjoyment of yourself, which is the non-self.

I suppose the idea, the ideal of absolute truth as completely empty. Emptiness in Buddhism means many things, but briefly, the simplest meaning is—and keep in mind all the time—is free from, empty of preconception. The word that is empty of overload. Now that's like absolute zero, theoretical situation, but empty of a separate self, our separate self is a projection—our ego is a projection. It is an idea. We all have ideas about ourselves and they are wrong. Insofar, as you are trying to think of yourself having an identity, you are probably being pushed around by a society, male or female, absolutely no distinction with that.

The ego is a mind construction that interferes with experience. It interferes with direct contact with your world, and when you have direct contact with your world, you have jouissance. It is because the images direct contact with the world has that same flaming passion, unity, completeness, that you feel really good during sex. Which is really transcendent. We have many stupid, degrading ideas about sex. They are terrible, and they get in everybody's way. True image—there is such a thing as ideal sex and it is an idea that you can have, that that union between self and other is complete transparent, transcendent, and happiness.

So behind L'Ecriture Feminine—here I am talking about this dry French theory—not at all, but the heart of the matter is jouissance, passion, and how you could actually get to that and write it.

That's what Hélène Cixous calls the feminine imaginary—when we're writing we are imagining.

How can we get language to do what we want it to do? How can it give itself away, empty out? Lose that ego baggage. So, simply, the "not me" is a key idea in L'Ecriture Feminine, in the same way that jouissance is a key.

Now, Hélène Cixous considered Clarice Lispector, this Brazilian writer, to be the paradigm of expression, of L'Ecriture Feminine. She is a writer concerned with spirituality and ideas, and lots of Western cultures have completely forgotten the fact that our world is dominated by ideas and ideas arouse our passions. So, Lispector is radical in her return to the roots of passion and human desire.

The Passion According to G.H. is a book about Being, and *The Stream of Life* is a book about writing and the intimate relations.

So, how can you be if you don't have a self? And what is writing if it isn't coming from the self?

Now, the sourcebook is something for you to take back and read, every underlined word is a kind of the key to an idea that I hope will return you to the beginning, the route to the real radical base of writing. When you really get down with language, your language will have the qualities that Cixous explains in Lispector, which I'll get to in a minute, because the language of Lispector, even in translation, is truly Avant Garde.

Now, the true Avant Garde has some qualities. First of all, nothing is cooked up. It's not something that you get—the traditional Avant Garde, the conventional Avant Garde, is a historical tradition. It has many interesting qualities to it and goes back from punk to surrealism to various kinds of formal experiments, but a real Avant Garde writing is not cooked up by thinking about any kind of form in advance, and that is to say, the form comes from what we have to do, and you have to do what you have to do by going deeply to the question. So there is a very powerful primal link between L'Ecriture Feminine as Cixous theorizes about it, and as Lispector practices it, and Buddhist principle. I think primal link because there is absolutely no historical or social connection. As far as I know, Hélène Cixous, who was very well read in European literature knows nothing about Buddhism, and I think the same thing is true of Lispector—though their international perspective and interest in many languages is a kind of openness that lays the ground for the kind of thinking that arises, and that is very similar to what happens when you sit in Buddhism and open up and things happen. In sitting practice, the very simple basic sitting practice, which is done by many, many non-Buddhists as well, you drop your ideas about your ego; there is the gap, and the world comes to you in a different way. You can drop your assumptions about your ideas, but they all come back, so we've still got to deal with ideas.

Briefly, Lispector was born in 1925. Only Cixous mentions the fact that her parents were Jewish. They were Russian cousins. Peter Wilson has just told me that there was a pogrom in the Ukraine where Lispector was born just before 1925. Her parents were peasant refugees persecuted by anti-Semitism, who left for Brazil to find a new life when Clarice was two months old. The family was poor. They lived in Recife. [Indecipherable, roughly about a particular bishop in the area.] I have forgotten his name, but the bishop of Recife was in defiance of the Vatican and European Catholicism and was an advocate. [Student interjects, asks if the name is Paulo Freire.] Freire was inspired by the bishop of Recife—who gave Freire, Paulo Freire, the great educator—actually licensed to travel in Recife and teach people how to read so that they could understand what their government was doing to them. As a result of this literacy program, peasants who had never seen a book learned to read in six weeks because they understood there was no other way to freedom other than to be educated, so that's the kind of general environment in this day. I don't think that Lispector had any interest in Judaism. In fact, her writing is very influenced by Christianity.

The professional critics, typically, their male, and they'll say that Lispector was influenced by the existentialism of Sartre and Camus. I don't think so. She was influenced by her own experience. She describes herself as a young girl—right after she graduated from law school in 1944—as supersensitive. She cried easily at all sorts of things, but she was also very [indecipherable], and so her being is permeated by a profound sensitivity and as a very small child, she thought that books were like plants—that they grew naturally. When she discovered that books were written by people, she decided that she had to be a writer. She was obviously very small. She published her first novel when she was 19, and after law school in 1944, married a fellow law student named Maury Gurgel Valente and he joined the Foreign Service. They return to Brazil, to Rio, in 1959. They have two sons, she later divorced him, and she died of cancer in 1977 at the age of 56. She wrote six novels and many short stories, but she valued her law school training and wrote with it. She wrote in Portuguese, and I think that it is helpful to look at—I've given you the whole introduction to *The Passion According to G.H.*, because of the very interesting headnote to potential readers.

This is a book just like any other book. But I would be happy if it were read only by people whose outlook is fully formed. People who know that an approach—to anything whatsoever—must be carried out gradually and laboriously, that it must traverse even the very opposite of what is being approached. They and they alone will, slowly, come to understand that this book exacts nothing of anyone. Over time, the character G.H. came to give *me*, for example, a very difficult pleasure; but it *is* called pleasure.

I think she is using the normal Portuguese word for pleasure, but there is an obvious link to jouissance. There are a couple of important ideas in this introduction—that is, that you must approach the very opposite of what you are. That is to say, only reach the not me though the me.

She's talking about very radical, deep, profound approach to your subject matter, and that's a paradox as well. When you write, you're going to be writing [indecipherable].

Now, the other idea is taking time. If you want to go back to the beginning, to the root, radical base, you have to take time, you can't jump over it. This idea is actually stated by Cixous in an untranslated essay—I'm translating it, because I'm fascinated by it, which is on page two of your handout. I didn't type it as I should have, write in over roman numeral two, that is by Hélène Cixous—it's from the previous page, but just in case you missed it, the approach of Clarice Lispector is in a book called *Entre L'Écriture* which is the same thing in French as it is in English—between writing. You can't say that between is a preposition that implies that you've got to have two things in opposition.

The approach of Clarice Lispector is a developed essay by Cixous and makes some remarkable assertions. At the same time that it emphasizes taking time, but this essay by Cixous points out the Lispector's approach is political. There's a famous slogan from the feminist movements' heyday of the early 70s, "The personal is political." That's particularly true for women who have been codified, not just straightjacketed, by male dominance and ideas.

[Indecipherable, roughly referencing Lacan] And they are a pervasive political atmosphere for which no particular man needs to or does feel responsible at this point, but the recognition of the atmosphere is something everyone needs to do. So, Cixous says of Clarice Lispector, her approach is political, the approach parentheses of Clarice is in the French—Cixous like Lispector does a great deal of play with language. Cixous wrote a long dissertation on James Joyce and has written several novels. One of the male critics thought that Lispector must also have been influenced by the language of Joyce. The idea sort of being that if you're a writer, somehow, you've got to have been influenced by some prior important male writer. Lispector said, no, I didn't read Joyce. She was an avid reader as a young girl. She read Katherine Mansfield and Virginia Woolf and Rosamond Lehmann, but she did not read Joyce. Her language does not come from imitating anyone—it comes from the radical depth of her childhood. She chose to work through investigation in her writing.

"Her approach is political"—the approach of Clarice— "it's living space, the intimate, which one must be careful to keep, to have humility, generosity, not jumping over anything, not avoiding... Precipitousness annihilates. We live in a period of the faux thought screen, the faux newspaper, which doesn't leave time to think of the smallest thing according to its living [indecipherable]. We must rescue the approach which opens and leaves this place for the Other underlined. We must rescue the approach which opens and leads a place for the Other. When you drop the self, what you're paying attention to is the Other and the distinction is not always clear. But we live mass media hurry under pressure, under blackmail. Speed is one of the disguises of intimidation."

Lots of women feel lots of pressure, lots of hurry, to not pay attention to what is immediately happening. Speed is one of the disguises of intimidation. When you're being hurried, somebody's intimidating you, something's intimidating you. Now, this is true for everyone, not just women. We rush, we throw ourselves on the ground. We no longer know how to receive—to receive is a science, to know how to receive is the best of gifts. [Indecipherable, roughly an addition about giving and receiving.]

Clarice gives us the example, it is a question of the lesson of things, if we know how to think in the direction of the thing, to let ourselves call to it, Thing leads us into a space composed of the Thing and of Ourselves. The lesson of Clarice is in letting the Thing recall to us something else—not to forget, not to disremember, but to bring back to ourselves that immense

Other of life. Clarice teaches us to give ourselves time, not to forget, not to kill. To know how you see before the view, to know how to hear before understanding. To keep open the days of waiting, and in her language to wait means to hope, to hope is given in the French, not in the French, it's given in the Portuguese.

And so there is a hopefulness in Lispector's mind. Let's look at it.

I was about to point out to you some phrases in Ronald Sousa's introduction to *The Passion According to G.H.* Lispector is a philosophical writer—once within a room, his title refers to the plot—which is very small. I'll get to it, *The Passion According to G.H.*

Her texts described, well, let's see, on the first page, the fact that the Ukraine-born Clarice Lispector became a literary celebrity in her adopted Brazil, but is viewed in France because of the very same text as an important contemporary philosopher dealing with the relationships between language and human, especially female subjecthood, says much about the genre problematic. Are we to take G.H.'s story as fiction or as speculation on philosophical problems? He goes on to point out they're not separate. Where does literature end and philosophy begin? Intellectually speaking, they both end in language, which for Lispector is the medium. The problem is that for her, language is also fallacious, unless it is pushed to its limits and thereby made to reveal what the structuring as a container it seeks to hide. This to say that it is paradoxical. It contradicts this theory—L'Ecriture Feminine is not a rational theory. That's why it's also said to be indefinable; Cixous said, "Defining a feminine practice of writing is impossible for this practice will never be able to be theorized."

So I have been trying to lay a ground of theory for something that can't be theorized. And that contradiction or impossibility is the heart of the matter. And that's the challenge to you as writers.

Because she is putting together philosophy and literature, she uses language nontraditionally, and Sousa also says traditional expectations have been violated. He apologizes for his translation and says, "I invite the reader to imagine a Portuguese text that transmits a much greater sense of potential language chaos than the translation."

But I'd like to go into the opening sentences, the paragraphs *of The Passion According to G.H.:*

> I keep looking, looking. Trying to understand. Trying to give what I have gone through to someone else, and I don't know who, but I don't want to be alone with that experience. I don't know what to do with it, I'm terrified of that profound disorganization. I'm not sure I even believe in what happened to me. Did something happen, and did I, because I didn't know how to experience it, end up experiencing something else instead? It's that something that I'd like to call disorganization, and then I'd have the confidence to venture forth because I would know where to come back to: to the prior organization. I prefer to call it disorganization because I don't want to ground myself in what I experienced—in that grounding I would lose the world as it was for me before, and I know that I don't have the capacity for another one.

This is a very bizarre way to open up—the problem is, however, it's dramatic and it's profound. This is not Lispector at all. This is a character, and the only definition of that character is that it's impossible for her—it becomes clear that she is—the speaker is aware, who has encountered something that has changed her vision and she continues to deal with that problem. The writing is very dense and there are a lot of important ideas that I'm skipping over. On page nine at the top of the page, I've underlined, "How do I explain that my greatest fear is precisely in relation to being?"

But the original problem is that people encounter fear in relation to the world. This idea in Shambala—is the parallel was developed into the idea of the original sin in Christianity, that is that there is some kind of the basic split, and people go in the wrong direction, and the whole Christian pile, the Judaistic pile of sin is from that.

But psychologically, everyone at some point or other has experienced the fear of being, the basic fear of being. And so there is a decision—are we going to address it or not?

Fear of being is tied in the fear of not being and the whole question of whether one has a self. At the bottom of the same page, it just says something like,

"Have I lost a third leg"—"The two walking feet minus that extra third one that holds a person down, and I want to be held down. I don't know what to do with the horrifying freedom that can destroy me. But while I was held down, was I happy? Or was there—and there was—an uncanny, restless something in my happy prison routine?"

Okay, prison routine is conventionalized. However, it exists in you, and that conventionalized thinking attaches to notions of self.

She goes on to say, "But I also don't know what form to give to what happened to me. And for me nothing exists unless I give it a form. And…and what if the reality is precisely that nothing has existed?!"

On page 11, she says, "I am the priestess of a secret that I no longer know" that gives us a good idea—skip over to page 11, because there are some important ideas on that page.

All sudden understanding is, in the last analysis, the revelation of a clear non-understanding. That's the difference between conceptualizing and preconceiving your experience rather than just encountering it.

She goes on to say that [this actually comes before the previous quote in the text]:

> Any comprehension on my part will never be equal to that understanding, for I can reach only the height of living—the only level on which I function is the level of living. Only now, now I know of a secret which I am already forgetting; oh I feel it already forgetting…
>
> To rediscover it now I would have to die all over again. And knowing it again could be the murder of my human soul. And I don't want to, I don't want to. What could still save me would be to deliver myself over to that new ignorance; that would be possible. For all the while that I'm struggling to know, my new ignorance, which is forgetting, has become sacred."

Okay, what I mean, nobody else in the world writes like this! Who can say these things? The passion is complete—"I don't want to. I don't want to, but

I've got to do it." This is the kind of emotionality that we experience, but it's always attached to something else, and this character is experiencing as much as possible without reattachment—of reference points, ego points, preconceptions about who you are, and it is the process of consciousness, but this language is wholly unlike the stream of consciousness that we know of in James Joyce or Virginia Woolf, because they're fixated on some level, but consciousness includes both fixation and non-fixation. This is an attempt to show—dramatize—through language, the continual breakdown and contradiction of our thinking, especially when we get involved in ideas, and yet we are always involved in ideas. And that's something that people don't say in writing schools very often. There is a kind of feeling that somehow it's all beyond the realm of ideas. But no, it isn't. It is involved all the time with the most profound questions of being—how shall we be? What kind of body do we have, what kind of speech do we have, what mind do we have, and how do they fit together and why do they break apart continually? And what happens then in terms of trying to give that to someone else, which was the initial statement that Cixous made.

Student: You just hear this relationship of not self coming in and undercutting in the writings of madness, where it is over the edge. This is not over the edge.

Augustine: This has nothing to do with madness. It's, in fact, madness. One piece of advice, just in a commonplace way that I often give to students writing is, don't write about people who are crazy. Their fixations aren't illuminating. You have to write about some other...a crazy central character won't get you anywhere. That's just a piece of practical advice. This is the very opposite of insanity. Insanity probably has terrible physical causes, chemical imbalances, one of repetitive pattern, without any seeing of that pattern.

This character in Lispector has realized that her struggle is a spiritual struggle, and that is why she says "for all the while that I am struggling to know my new ignorance, which is a forgetting, has become sacred. I am the priestess of a secret that I no longer know...I don't want in the least to have anything explained to me that would have to be made to go beyond itself, to be explained."

And at the bottom of that passage, I have underlined, she repeats that she saw something, "I don't understand it, worse yet, I don't like what I saw—it explodes my everyday life."

Now—this is, as a plot introduction, an introduction of the familiar formula for conflict of the central character, which you've heard about, but this is very different from all the kinds of conflicts, and yet to have something explode one's day-to-day life is both liberating and terrifying and a real problem. I've given you a brief summary of the plot of *The Passion According to G.H.* The central character who is never named, you don't know what G.H. stands for, it doesn't stand for anything—goes into the empty maid's room, her apartment in Rio, and the maid has left and the room is clear, and there is a wardrobe, the big old-fashioned portable closet, an armoire, and G.H. slams the door of this wardrobe on a large cockroach.

On page 12, you can see that one chapter ends. The numbers that I gave you referred to sourcebook numbers, not the Xerox pages. It shows that each chapter ends with a sentence that is repeated in the beginning of the next chapter—it is a kind of formal device that this book has.

She is looking at the crushed cockroach in extreme detail at the end of the prior chapter.

The narrator is addressing—well we actually need to build it up—because there is a "you," often, that is unnamed. In *The Stream of Life*, the "you" is the narrator's former lover, and the stream of consciousness is like letters.

But here, the "you" is undefined—someone to who she wants to give the experience. The word "passion" in the title has a double meaning, at least a double meaning. The translator says you could call this "Love According to G.H." but he properly says "The Passion According to G.H.," because of many suggestions in this novel of the passion of Christ, which passion has quite a different meaning—it means suffering. Passion is in one sense of the meaning of the word—go to the dictionary and start reading it. I read the dictionary a lot! So many meanings of words, and passion is the opposite of action. Passion is the state that you let happen to you, as distinct from what you do, and *The Passion According to G.H.* —even the phrase, "according to"—is one word in Portuguese, which is sort of like the French "selon," but it's also the term that's used in the Gospel according to St. Matthew—it's a New Testament, it has a New Testament sound, which is part of the multilingual polyvocal way.

Passion in this case means if you love, it means suffering, it means enduring, it means going to the bottom—the ultimate bottom of experience, which is real psychological and mythic meaning of the passion of Christ, the crucifixion, which has become so conventionalized that we have lost what it actually meant for that person, his spiritual exploration to have been crucified—put to death by a painful and degrading way of dying, and this novel plays on what it means to carry experience to that depth. The whole of what the narrator does—not all, but most of what she does—is it look at the cockroach.

I want to move on to *The Stream of Life,* just briefly, and then I would like to come back to do some actual writing.

The introduction to this volume of—to this translation, is a long essay by Cixous on the language of Lispector and I included it so you would have some technical sense of what Lispector's ideas require and what she is doing. I have underlined the verb demonstratives. There is a recourse to demonstratives. I'm on page 21 of the handout—"a recourse to demonstratives, to a deictic usage that points and undermines." Deictics are very interesting in terms of language because they point to something that actually is in the visible world, is outside of the language—not a cup but this. This and that are words which stand for some other, and even when Lispector addresses this vague "you," "you" has a deictic meaning of a specific person. Now in poetry, "you" is used as a synonym for one. But "you" is really deictic—you are different from you and you! And that deictics—I'm pointing out to you in very simple words—there's nothing complicated in the language per say. In fact, the words, the sentences are very simply written. There are no tricks here. If you are going to face basic being, you have to also get to the basic being of words, no overlay, no tricky double meanings where you might not be sure what's what. Deictics have the power of throwing the reader outside of the page—or unifying the writing with experience because of the continual paradox of dealing with not me and me and never being to come down on one place. That makes the language of Clarice Lispector the radical instrument that it is. Much of this introduction by Cixous deals with the work on objects—dropping the preoccupations with the self [indecipherable] of objects—and the cockroach in *The Passion According to G.H.* is one, and there are many in *The Stream of Life*.

On page 22 at the end of this essay, which I've excerpted, I have underlined Cixous' quotation of Lispector—"What I write you is a This." That's the deictic pronoun, demonstrative pronoun made into a noun, and of This, there's no other way to say it. Cixous asserts that it is the reader, it is at least the reader, but I think it is also a character implied in relation to the narrator of *The Stream of Life*. At the bottom, Cixous says, "the truth," let's say the first sentence, "is in the second look at yourself and love yourself. That is to say, you think you read me, but what you do is look at yourself and love yourself. Once again, there is a relay, a relay of You. It is caught in the general problematic of a not I, and there is no more humble way of saying I."

Now, "I" is an object of non-objects.

This is Cixous' introduction on writing on Lispector.

Água Viva, the title of *The Stream of Life*, I have said on page twenty-three, *The Stream of Life* does, as the translation convey the sense of stream of consciousness as the technique here. But Água Viva also means living water, which is quite a difference, it gives me a different kind of feel. But there is a gap—that double play in consciousness, perhaps only my consciousness.

"Let me tell you," says the narrator, "I'm trying to capture the fourth dimension of the now instant. I want to take possession of the thing's is." It becomes clear that this narrator is a painter.

"I want to write you completely whole and I feel a pleasure in being, and my pleasure of you is abstract like the instant, and it's with my entire body that I paint my pictures and, on the canvas, fix the incorporeal—me, body to body, with myself. One doesn't understand music. One hears it. Hear me, then, with your whole body."

One of Hélène Cixous primary statements, which I quoted here before in other lectures, is "Women must write the body."

> Woman must write her body, must make up the unimpeded tongue that bursts partitions, classes, and rhetorics, orders and codes must inundate, run through, go beyond the discourse with its last reserves, including the one of laughing off the word "silence" that has to be said, the one that, aiming for the impossible, stops dead before the word "impossible" and writes it as "end."

That is an essay called "Sorties" in this collaborative book. "Sorties" has two meanings. It's simply the word for exit in French, but of course in English, which is Cixous' double language, a sortie is an expedition of a bunch of people from the army off into the enemy territory. Reconnaissance. To make a sortie means to go out, do a quick raid and reconnaissance or, you know, a quick strike and come back.

So, Cixous loves double plays, and her language actually in her novels is very different from the language that she admires but her criticism sounds like Cixous. The whole essay that I'm beginning to translate and given you a little chunk of her prose in the approach of Clarice Lispector and in another essay on L'Ecriture, in between writing, is all about the relationship between the writer and the painter. A lot of its ideas are very parallel to the ideas of marriage in *The Stream of Life*.

One more thing I want to say, there are many objects in *The Stream of Life*, and many portions of this prose are like poems. Many of you here are writing poetry, and the passages contain many images, and in that way, we can see that *The Stream of Life* is profoundly different, kind of character, the central character is very different from the central character in *The Passion According to G.H.*

> I want to write you as one who is learning. I photograph each instant. I delve into words as if I were painting not just an object but its shadow. I don't want to ask why, one can eternally ask why and remain eternally without an answer…Even though I may guess that somewhere, sometime the great answer exists for me.

> And then I'll know how to paint and write, after the strange but intimate answer. Listen to me, listen to the silence. What I tell you is never what I tell you but something else… One instant takes me unthinkingly to the next, and the athematic theme keeps unfolding without a plan.
>
> …
>
> And if many times I paint caves it's because they are my submersion into the earth, dark but clouded with clarity, and I, nature's blood—extravagant and dangerous caves, Earth's talisman, where stalactites, fossils, and stones come together, and where creatures crazy through their own evil nature seek refuge. Caves are my hell. Caves, dreamlike, always with their mists, memory or longing. Frightening, frightening, esoteric, greenish with the ooze of time. Rats, with the cross-like wings bats, hang glimmering in the cavern. I see black, hairy spiders. Rats and mice run frightened on the ground along the walls. Among the stones the scorpion. Crabs, unchanged since prehistory, through countless births and deaths, would seem threatening beasts if they human-sized. Ancient cockroaches drag themselves along the half light. And all this, am I.

There are other passages similar to this in a symbolic kind of way. Lispector is deliberately avoiding, I believe, all conventional associations with symbolism or myth, but she does nevertheless work against them as she works against the Christian myth—in *The Passion According to G.H.*, here she's working against the psychoanalytic and symbolic and turning it into something new. The only plot in this novel is the effort to create, recreate, the now-instant. It's on page 26, "but the now-instant is a firefly that turns on and off." And the final word on page 27 is "what I write you continues on and I am bewitched."

The final passage at the end of the book is also the one referred to by Hélène Cixous—"What I write you is a this. It won't stop. It continues on. Look at me and love me. No, look at yourself and love yourself. That's what's right. What I write you continues on and I am bewitched."

But this writing is strange to us because it accomplishes that kind of breakdown in our assumptions about writing and that is valuable. We have about an hour left, and I would like to go back to some of the underlined words, ideas, and I would like to suggest that we take a few minutes to do some writing. It seems impossible to imitate this kind of writing, but I think that I can set up the [indecipherable].

(Augustine writes on blackboard.) Four themes which are central to the work of Lispector and these are all quotations from her. And then I'll tell you what I'd like us to do. (Indecipherable as she is writing on blackboard.)

She says in the beginning, the narrator in *The Stream of Life*, says, "I'm painting, and I'm painting how I'm writing." There are four phrases here—clear, non-understanding, the dimensions of she—which I think is in *The Passion According to G.H.* —and she says, "I want to write the dimension of she." That is again one of the places where we are more sure that the narrator is female. We've just seen the phrase "capture of now-instant," which is from *The Stream of Life*. To paint writing is related to "it's with my entire body that I paint my pictures."

What I would like you to do is look around this ordinary room and yourself in this room and pick a single object. Pick a single object and choose one of these phrases to dominate your writing about that object in whatever way that you want to do. Pick one of these to concentrate on—these are all abstract, these are all in the ideational realm. You must have an object, any object, which becomes the focus or expression or association or whatever, whichever phrase fragmentary that you choose, in whatever way you want to. Let's take seven minutes. First thought, best thought. That's the only way to do it. And then we'll see what happens. Any kind of paper. The teacher will not collect at the end of the hour!

Chickadee-dee-dee

Interlude by Marlie McGovern

Out my window, a black-capped chickadee nestles into a hollow knot on a hundred-year-old willow tree. A protective sanctuary not unlike my own during the Covid-19 pandemic. Mountain chickadees also rest and feed amidst the willow's branches. These two forms of chickadee, both small and plump with black heads and throats, gray wings and tails, white cheeks, and cream-colored bodies, are nearly identical, and yet they are distinct species. The mountain chickadee, *Poecile gambeli,* boasts a white stripe above each eye, a subtle visual difference from *Poecile atricapillus*, its fully black-capped sister.

My writing space, perched upstairs in the home my wife Erin and I fondly call our treehouse, is an alcove surrounded by windows facing west, north and east. Stately willow in the foreground, its branches now laden with February snow. Dakota Ridge in the near distance, its pine trees and rock crags crystalline with frost. It is from this tree-top vantage point that I listen to Jane Augustine's lecture "On Form and Function" from Naropa University's audio archive. Her words were recorded more than thirty years earlier in this same Boulder, Colorado landscape.

Accept the challenge things offer to language. Augustine, emphasizing the first line of Francis Ponge's poem, "The Carnation," extends his challenge to writers as vocation, creative impetus, and contribution to humanity. In accepting the challenge things offer to language, Augustine suggests, the writer moves beyond habitual and limiting ways of being in the world. *Routine thinking, conventionalized thinking is what impedes the world, it impedes us individually.* The writer, and the reader along with them, can together transcend generalized categories and imposed expectations of form, entering into a realm of openness and possibility.

In the willow, a pine squirrel meticulously preens its thick coat in a shaft of winter sun. Tufts of red fur warm its alert ears. *Every time you read a poem you get a new idea about poetry*, says Augustine. *We also have to break down our idea of what poetry in quotes with a capital 'P' is, in order to find a new form, in order really to say something new.* From delicate top-most branches, a trio of red-breasted nuthatches survey high-altitude desert. *One of the conventional categories of thinking about poetry is that it is different from science*, continues Augustine. *Not so. Break down that idea.*

Where in the writing body does poetry with a capital 'P' reside? Is it a self-imposed limit that restricts the shapes my tongue can make? Is it breath made shallow by cultural expectations of exclusively pleasing speech by women? Is it the narrow, downcast gaze of unconsciously repeating the world to myself as I already believe I know it to be? Ponge lists tools the writer may use to metabolize codified ideas and embodiments of poetry and develop language that brings us closer to reality: *the dictionary, the encyclopedia, the imagination, dream, the telescope, the microscope, both ends of the opera glasses, lenses for the myopic and the presbyopic, puns, rhyme, contemplation, forgetfulness, volubility, silence, sleep, etc.*

Accepting Ponge's and Augustine's challenge, I turn to indexes of flight. I begin to understand the descriptions of chickadees in the Audubon and Cornell Lab of Ornithology guides as windows into perceiving new forms in the world. Black-capped chickadees sing *fee-bee* and *chickadee-dee* as part of their complex vocabulary. The black-capped chickadees in this willow are part of a winter flock, including mating pairs, which will disperse before spring. Perhaps the songbird I see in the hollow is scouting nesting sites, which it will then line with moss or animal hair in preparation for a brood of chicks.

I add field binoculars to my list of writing tools. I learn that mountain chickadees frequently feed upside down, gathering insects and pupae from twigs, branches, and bark. They have been observed using splinters of wood as tools for procuring sustenance from in-between crevices. I begin to see the birds themselves—quick, sharp-witted, inventive—as poetic forms. Poems of staccato rhythm and sustained vowels. Poems written in the alphabet of chickadee: *Poecile gambeli, Poecile atricapillus.*

FEE-bee, FEE-bee. I emulate a chickadee call, the first note's high, piercing strength, and the second note's lower-pitched decrescendo. Pulse and buzz of unfamiliar tones. New forms of sound radiate in the space between my eyebrows, and then in the core of my abdomen. *FEE-bee.* Vibrations breaking down boundary and barrier in this writing body. Awareness of my own internal landscape expanding in resonance with the sonic landscape around me.

What relevance does such arboreal poetry offer? *To introduce to human thought those traits which are not beyond its capacity and which routine alone prevents it from adopting,* explains Ponge. Recognizing and articulating mountain chickadee and black-capped chickadee as distinct forms of life situates me intimately within this living world. I come into new relationship with willow and with words.

To perceive with a scientist's eye, to craft my writing toward clarity, helps me to understand myself as a part of the splendor and infinite variety of living forms just outside my treehouse windows.

Two stories below me, at the base of the willow tree, animal tracks mark the morning snow. Five-toed prints indicate a large raccoon, *Procyon lotor.* Perhaps it is the same female raccoon who raised three kits in the safety of the willow's branches last spring and summer. Only a few feet away, from behind glass, Erin and I delighted in their playful ascent to the upper tree limbs for sleep.

Gray-furred, with white bands above black-masked eyes, white muzzle and banded tail, *Procyon lotor* shares its coloration with the chickadee, and its name with *Procyon*, the Little Dog Star of Canis Minor, among the most luminous stars in the night sky. Locomotive racoon poetry has guided my curiosity from willow to heavens. I yearn for Ponge's telescope.

What could be more essential work for the writer than to develop awareness and openness to new forms, new ways of sensing and saying? *You can get closer and closer,* encourages Augustine. *People who get closer...to what is objectively real are helping their world...our world works much better the more truthful we are.* Embracing Ponge's understanding of scientific and artistic research as poetry, and Augustine's commitment to truthfulness, I've come closer to the reality of interconnection.

Through simple attention, as Ponge offered to garden carnations, I've come to marvel at forms of life that I'd previously overlooked. Naming, studying, and writing the natural poetry of *Poecile gambeli, Poecile atricapillus, Procyon lotor,* and *Procyon,* are acts of respect and stewardship, of inclusion and communion, bringing me closer to the significant challenges and precious opportunities of living with and within the myriad forms of a collective body.

On Form and Function

Jane Augustine
July 18, 1989

Transcription by Marlie McGovern

Jane Augustine: You know that my name is Jane Augustine, and I come to Naropa with several forms of credentials. I have a PhD in English Literature, with a specialization in women's writing of the 20th century, and I'm particularly interested in the French feminist critics who are writing right now. Particularly Hélène Cixous and Luce Irigaray.

French feminist criticism takes off from Jacques Lacan who is the greatest French psychoanalytic theoretician following in the footsteps of Freud. Jacques Lacan is a big problem because he continues in Freud's notion that the male, the penis actually, is the transcendental signifier, that maleness is a privileged state biologically. Remember, Freud's theory is that the whole genesis of our psychological states of mind comes from the fact that little boys discovered that they're born with penises and little girls discovered that they are born without them.

A whole social definition follows from that, that women lack something. It's a very strange, skewed view of the human situation, but it's very basic—too much philosophical, almost all philosophical and psychological and social theory in the 20th century. Luce Irigaray and Hélène Cixous, and others, Julia Kristeva, are women who are active philosophers in France who are pointing out that fifty-one percent of humanity is, after all, female and that there is indeed a necessity for another view of our gender arrangements. That's a term from Dorothy Dinnerstein, who's an American psychologist.

But one of the fundamental facts which we encounter in our life, I suppose I shall put it in terms that fit our situation here as writers. The basic writer's concerned with form and new forms. The fundamental form that we first encounter in our experience is the form of our body, whether it is female or male. So, I'm taking you very far back, which is actually the meaning of the word radical—back to the root. The root of our thinking and our socialization processes is based on this fundamental form of our body. Female or male.

From that, a whole body, a whole group, a lot of countries, let's say, a collection of social ideas has followed, and we are told almost from the moment of birth, different ways of behaving if we're female or male. That has, and Freud's observation reinforces, I don't know what's cause and what's effect, but Freud's thinking about sexuality has codified or canonized the idea that having a penis sort of makes you a privileged human being and not having one puts you in a disadvantageous position. I state all of that because of the theories of Jacques Lacan, which have continued to refine that idea.

So, we are born to highly genderized situation, which is controlling our way of thinking in very profound ways from the beginning, and yet it's an asymmetrical or skewed situation. There is a kind of privileging of the male point of view based on this psychoanalytic theory of observation of anatomy. In fact, it was Freud who said that anatomy was destiny, and that places us in a skewed language situation. Just from day to day, language is both given and received, continually. We're talking and listening simultaneously. And so, there was a tremendous intermix in all of our thinking of this kind of privileged male position and a privileged position in relation to language. So, when you study literary tradition, that's what the men have written and said that has been paid attention to, for all kinds of good reasons.

But there is a kind of corresponding sense that what women say or do is not quite as important, it is more private; it is more interpersonal than large, public, and social. So for the woman who wants to write, particularly, there's a kind of additional difficulty. All of us have difficulty making, bridging the gap between our own experience and the world, but since we live in a situation which does kind of privilege what men write and say and tends to diminish what women writers say, we have a problem mutually because at the same time that these differences have been taught to us, we have always from the very beginning had the recognition that we are all human beings, and human beings coming to two varieties, that the dichotomy between male and female is not absolutely fundamental. And therefore, access to language in some extremely profound way beneath our socialization process is absolutely equal. And that is of the basis on which we work.

These two women, Hélène Cixous and Luce Irigaray, are writers who have particularly struggled to explicitly make clear, through male techniques, so to speak—Luce Irigaray is a psychoanalyst, is working specifically with the psychoanalytic tradition to redress this balance—to make it as clear to everyone as it is clear to herself that women's experience is just as important as men's experience.

But, socially as writers, culturally as writers, we have slightly different problems in relation to form because of this basic, fundamental, primary experience of the body as male or female, and the problem for women is to articulate experience that has somehow been shunted aside. It's been called ahistorical. The 19th century is very fond the doctrine of separate spheres. Men have one sphere—it's public, open, governmental, business-like—women have another sphere—which is domestic, personal, psychological, and so on. That notion of separate spheres has really governed literary criticism in the 19th century. And so, there were critics who said things like, well, women's sphere is the domestic, it's very improper for a woman to write anything. Writing is a public activity—you take the words and you make them public—you publish them.

Then if a woman wrote something, the highest acclaim was that she was writing like a man. The great writers of the 19th century took men's names. Charlotte Brontë wrote first into the name of Currer Bell. Marion Evans wrote all her life under the name of George Eliot, and her novels were praised, and, as her companion Henry Lewes said later, the critics, having praised her work when they thought it was written by a man, cannot take back their praise. But George Eliot was viewed with suspicion because what she was doing was unfeminine. She was also viewed with suspicion because she lived with a man to whom she was not married, one of the most successful Victorian's marriages is not to be married. A separate topic to discuss (laughter).

There's a delightful book called *Parallel Lives* by Phyllis Rose which is a depiction of five Victorian marriages of famous writers. Well, Ruskin is one, John

Stuart Mill is another, Thomas Carlyle is another, in the pairing of George Eliot and George Henry Lewes, it is the woman who is the famous writer.

So the sense of imbalance has in the literary world, in the audience for which we write, to the people to whom we want to communicate, we have to recognize that that is a genderized world, and that makes it particularly difficult for the writer writing at this time. The woman writer has to find a form for experience which has been somewhat denigrated, somewhat neglected, and even when she speaks of it, and perhaps this has happened to some of you women personally, you will try to tell someone something that's happened to you and the person listening to you says, "Oh, you don't really think that. That's not really the way it was." Particularly if you are trying to express something that is socially unacceptable or is related to sexuality. Women's sexuality is a much touchier than men's, because of the kind of assumptions about the kind of necessity or ordinariness of male sexuality as the norm.

But the male writer has just as bad a problem in this asymmetrical situation because men's minds have been exposed to a whole series of indoctrinations, which complicate your personal experience. Men are also told in very, quite powerful ways what they may or may not do. While the great artists, this is a dispute that goes on in art as well as in writing, the great artists are men. Nevertheless, some men are often taught not to be emotional, not to be introspective. Not to do a lot of things that you absolutely must do if you are going to be a writer.

So, in the highly genderized society, there are two sets of imposed expectations for men and for women which interfere with your experience. There are a different set of interferences, if your body is female, or if your body is male, but there is interference.

What I want to do today is introduce you to some ways to break down that barrier. Break through that static. The white noise of conventional ideas vibrates in everybody's head. Some of those conventional ideas have to do with poetry and writing specifically. I have said, "form follows function," and that you should recognize as a statement from Frank Lloyd Wright, the architect, who was pointing out that the form of a building follows from, comes from, what kind of life you're going to live in that building.

Now, you could say that there is an analogy: form equals words; function is like content or perhaps it's more accurate to say thought. We've been trying to get down to the processes of consciousness, of form. This is consciousness, consciousness raising. Form consciousness is what I would like people to have, to expand and enlarge. Form and content are inseparable in any poem, any piece of writing, but they are distinguishable. You can think about them separately, and I think all of you by now have had the experience that, you get an idea. You get a poem idea. Something happens in your mind and emotions. Emotions are simply highly charged thoughts particularly in Buddhist psychology. In Western psychology emotions and thoughts can be separated. I think it's more useful to think in Buddhist terms. The poem idea is a powerful emotion, that's a highly charged thought. Thoughts in other words cover both what is logical and rational and what arises as illogical and irrational. So something comes up, and you want to find the form for it and the form wants to be…the form has to fit the thought in some way, but that is actually the problem.

This is where I want to look with you at the first three pages of the handout that I gave you. I picked a poem, if that is the word for it, by Francis Ponge. I'm strong on the French today. Ponge is a writer, born in 1899, died just last year, and the opening line to "The Carnation" is a kind of manifesto, for me at any rate, and it should be one of your passwords: accept the challenge. This is in the imperative. He's telling you to do this as a writer, person, thinker: "Accept the challenge things offer to language."

Now, this, again, I think is a kind of radical starting point. In our experience, I'm suggesting it's worth thinking about the starting point is the form of our plotting, and in relation to, as we start to think about our world, we encounter things and things are completely different from life. It's a different form of discourse.

A lot of people don't realize that they are very muddled on the difference between a thing and a word or a symbolic representation of it. That's why people are muddled about burning the American flag. We confuse the symbol with the reality behind it. That's confusing the form with the content in some way. They think when you destroyed the American flag, you've destroyed something importantly American, but it's just a thing, and it's in the realm of things, physical things like chairs and lights that we register and see with our eyes. Buddhist psychology speaks, especially in meditation, coordinating body, speech, and mind. These are the symbols, by the way. The body is symbolized by the head, speech by the mouth, but mind is here in the heart, which is an interesting symbolic correlation in itself.

But, body, speech, and mind are three separate realms of experience. Body is the physical, and mind is our thought that we recognize in ourselves, especially when we sit. I strongly recommend sitting. I am a student of Trungpa Rinpoche and have been for fifteen years. I sit every day, at least for a while, to touch my own mind, to recognize my own thought, and by doing that, I can be sure that I'm clear as to what is thought, what is body, what is speech, and what is mind. Separate, as distinguishable again, but inseparable all three are operating at all times, but it's important not to muddle them.

So Francis Ponge, as a poet, interests me very much for a number of reasons, and one of them is that he is extremely serious about things and the physicality of things. One of his most famous collection of poems, is called *Le parti pri des choses*—you can't even translate it into English, a lot of his stuff is tied in intimately with the French language. This is things taking sides, but actually, things don't take sides, and that's a puzzling title, but what he is doing all the time is taking things very seriously, the physicality of things. At the same time, investigating with great thoroughness the language by which we try to capture what a thing is. He states very clearly in "The Carnation," which is why I've given this poem to you, what he is doing—accept the challenge things offer to language. For instance, these carnations. The end of the section tells you he's actually sitting in someone's garden looking at the flower called in English the carnation, œillet French.

These carnations defy language. Now it's as if there is a serious obstacle here, and I think there is. We have to go back and back if we really want to find out something about form. We're talking about new forms. I've been pondering this for two months because of the puzzlement of new forms, new to whom? All forms are old in some way. They come from something else. What is form? I've come to realize that it's a very radical idea, and I found a reflection of what I was thinking, or an elucidation of what I was thinking, in Ponge.

"I won't give up," says Ponge, "until I have put together a few words that will make anyone reading or hearing them say: this has to do with something like a carnation." That's kind of tricky wording. He's saying, I can't capture it entirely. The carnation is a physical thing, and the words won't get it. That's the kind of subtext. But what I write will make anyone reading or hearing the words say this has to do with something like this. "Is that poetry? I have no idea, and it scarcely matters. For me it is need, a commitment, a rage, a matter of self-respect and that's all there is to it."

So, another reason that I like Ponge very much is because he also says, I don't know whether this fits into the conventional category of poetry, and one of the suggestions that I'm going to make to you is that we are constantly accruing our ideas of what poetry is. Every time you read a poem you get a new idea about poetry, but that we also have to break down our idea of what "Poetry" in quotes with a capital 'P' is, in order to find a new form in order really to say something new.

Ponge refuses to use, as you can see, the forms that we are used to, line length and overt rhythmic structure, certainly no end rhyme, and he puts his commitment to taking things seriously and taking language seriously as a human activity. Then he goes on to say, "I do not claim to be a poet. I believe that my views are quite common. Given an object, however ordinary, it seems to me that it invariably presents some truly individual traits, which if clearly and simply expressed would be unanimously and firmly received. These are the ones I am trying to bring out." He's saying that the act of writing something is a direct communication, and implicitly, I think he's saying that it actually helps the world. If you look at some object, however ordinary, and bring out its individual traits, state them simply, so that someone else can connect.

I'm saying it over and over again. "What is to be gained by this? To introduce to human thought those traits which are not beyond its capacity and which routine alone prevents it from adopting." Now, this is almost a statement of vocation, what the poet should be doing. "To introduce to human thought those traits which are not beyond its capacity, and which routine alone prevents it from adopting." Routine thinking, conventionalized thinking is what impedes the world; it impedes us individually. Conventionalized thinking about our body, male or female, is a problem. And conventionalized thinking is at this point very male dominant. Psychoanalysis is an attempt to reconstruct or really investigate human thought.

Ponge is hopeful. He says you should do this to gain something, and that seems to me to fit with the Buddhist notion of the bodhisattva vow. You do what you're doing primarily to benefit others. To prevent the world from being a worse mess.

Last night, the excerpt from Beckett, which was read by Clark Coolidge, which was actually one of Beckett's postcards to his friend, and he distinguished words from the mess. Now Beckett has a very dark view of the physicality of things. Ponge is much more hopeful. Ponge finds things intrinsically interesting in themselves. For me, there's a correlation between this sense of the importance of things in themselves—the traits, individual traits, that ought to be brought out and communicated, and the notion that this has been expressed by Trungpa Rinpoche which is a Mahamudra expression, things are symbolic of themselves. If you look at Allen Ginsberg's *Collected Poems*, the title page has the epigraph "Things are symbolic of themselves," and therefore, what we are doing with words when we put them into a poem is to bring out that quality that is inherent. Underneath it all, there is a belief that things are inherently interesting, rich, and we have not paid a lot of attention to that.

So, there are implications for our topic, new forms, and our effort to find new forms in our own writing. Not that you have to write like Ponge, but Ponge has done something very interesting in his attention to first the thing, and then the words that go with it. He says, "What training is needed for the success of this venture?" It's really an effort to find new forms, as new words for things as they are.

"What training is needed for the success of this venture? Certainly, scientific thought, but particularly a large measure of art. And that is why I think that one day such research might also legitimately be called *poetry*." One of the conventional categories of thinking about poetry is that it is different from science. Not so. Break down that idea.

He goes on to say, "In the following examples—*The Carnation* is just one of them—you will see what serious groundwork this assumes (or implies), what tools you may or must call upon, what procedures and rubrics: the dictionary, the encyclopedia, the imagination, dream, the telescope, the microscope, both ends of the opera glasses, lenses for the myopic and the presbyopic, puns, rhyme, contemplation, forgetfulness, volubility, silence, sleep, etc."

Okay, this is a wonderful category. In order to find new forms, you have to look in new places, places you think are unpoetic. The dictionary. I recommend reading the dictionary. You find out a lot of information about words, you become intimate with their parts, their derivations, an etymological dictionary is particularly good, it will take a word back through from modern English through middle English to old high French or high German, depending, to Latin or even to Sanskrit. You get a tremendous amount of information.

The alphabet is a basic and wonderful tool, which is completely arbitrary and which has many uses continually to organize our lives. Therefore, it seems to have something to do with poetry in this large sense that Ponge is giving us. He also said, you've got to look at the world via telescope. The telescope looks off into the distance and makes things that are very hard to see large and visible.

Why the microscope? Because it enlarges something that is extremely tiny and lets us see it. Lenses for the myopic and the presbyopic. Myopic people are nearsighted. Presbyopic people are far sighted. These are metaphors for sight, and that always has to do with the first encounter we have with objects is visual in our perceptual field, and, of course, the visual has large importance in imagery of poetry. On the other hand, our experience of our body as the primary form is totaled and beyond senses.

But then he also recommends, and goes immediately into considering language, puns, rhymes, and then categories that you think couldn't help you poetically at all—forgetfulness, silence. But I think that once you start thinking about silence, in let's say relationship to music, it is the gap between words, sounds, which is like the caesura, the gap between words. We are used to thinking about the words, the spacing of the words and the placement on page is something that we need to consider more radically.

He goes on to point out—he says, actually, that he can't quite do this himself—one of the functions of form in writing is that it takes you out of yourself. It enables you to place your ego behind you, so to speak. He says, "After all, what is so unusual about a simple program (viable for all authentic expression) solemnly laid out above?" He is kind of making fun of himself for being solemn, as a theoretician.

This is a poem which actually crosses genres, as I had advertised in the description of this course, because this is a statement of criticism, it's written in prose, and it is also full of kind of personal expression, such as you might find in a letter written directly between two individuals. "What is so unusual? Undoubtedly just this, that instead of feelings or human adventures, I choose as subject the most emotionless objects available. That for me, the guarantee of the need to express appears to reside in the object's habitual muteness." It's as if the very thing that he—The guarantee of the need to express—Usually we think it's our emotions that we want to express, the things that we are immediately feeling, those are tied up with our ego and our day to day self, but for Ponge, and I'm suggesting that this is a very useful technique, the guarantee of the need to express resides in the object's muteness. It's the very fact that the thing is different from the word that makes him want to go work as a writer.

Yes?

Student: You say this is a piece of criticism, written in prose, and then you define it as a poem. I'm interested in why.

Augustine: Well, he is making a poem do a lot of things that poetry doesn't usually do, and I'm suggesting that that actually comes as a new form. In order to say what he wants to say, he is bringing in science, philosophy. He's talking—this is a manifesto. This is a description of how to write poetry. Like Shelley's *The Defense of Poesy*, or Sidney. Sidney, I guess, wrote *The Defense of Poesy*, and Shelley wrote *A Defense of Poetry*.

What he is doing is not concentrating on sounding poetic, which would limit him. He's moving into philosophizing about language, and he's telling you how to write a poem that's describing how he writes one. He calls it a program, the simple program, and he goes on to express this contradiction, and to have something in a poem contradicting the poem, contradicting the very idea of poetry, is good. Guarantees both a need to express and an opposition to language. People are often puzzled, I've said this before, but what makes you want to write is the obstacle in the way of writing, and that's what makes the women writers like Hélène Cixous, whom I've also given you a quote from in this set of writings, makes her do an even a more extreme version of what I've just described.

When she writes literary criticism, it's half poetry, half political speech. Well, half is not right. She incorporates a whole number of genres. She'll tell you something about somebody else's work of art at the same time she's telling you how she feels. She makes it personal. She is driven to do that because of the obstacle that I've just spoken of—a kind of prevalent Freudian view that women do not really have language. Lacan is very extreme. He said women don't have an unconscious; that's complete baloney.

But he is so, so privileging, so categorizing the male, according to Freud's initial misperception, let's say, or social conditioning, which led him to speak of male privilege. This poem goes on to make a list which looks like a dictionary. "*Papillotes*, paper frills, *papillons,*" and he's playing with words here, *papillea*. These are all related group words. This is what Ponge gets from reading the dictionary. "*Déchirer* (to tear or rend): from a German word *skerran*." By the way, one of the, this multilingual, multi-language approach is also a conduit to new form. French doesn't sound like English, and when you mix the French words, *papillotes, déchirer,* [continues in French]. Even with my not very good French pronunciation, it's a whole new sound of words, and we know that words not only are configurations on the page, letters, black and white.

Letters black, on a background white, but they are sounds. He makes this list, which has no grammatical structure; it's just a set of equivalences. It's yanked out of the dictionary. You wouldn't think it could fit into a poem, and yet, poems work by simply setting ideas next to each other and words continually resonate, move out from the center. And so, these words are ones which are suggested to him by the carnation, but the passage opens with his extraordinary expression, "Opinionated: strongly attached to one's opinion." These are all kind of one-sided words associated with one another by sound, and he continues, éternuer, to sneeze. This is a statement of all of the themes which he then goes on to develop.

And he has short sections:

> Contrast it to calm, rounded flowers: arum, lilies, camellias, tuberoses.
>
> Not that it's crazy, but it is violent (though well compacted, put together within reasonable limits).
>
> At stem-tip, the luxurious marvels of its linen come unbuttoned from toggle, unbudded from a supple node of leaves.
>
> Carnations, those marvelous rags.
>
> How clean they are.

[Several seconds lapse in silence] ...and then gets dropped. *Se déboutonne*, unbuttoned, actually that tends to be sexual. "*Se déboutonner*, to unbutton or unburden oneself, to come unbuttoned,"—unbudded— "see *bouton*, button or bud." That's like Bernadette Mayer's wonderful index to love. Cross reference. What do you think it could be in a poem? You wouldn't think that way, unless somebody said to you: Here it is, and it is a poem, because of its intimacy with language and the confrontation of language with things. Accept the challenge things offer to language.

I won't go on with the whole analysis of this poem, but the beginning is very understated. Notice that the words are not extravagant. They are ordinary. His tone is awfully kind of off-hand, he even makes fun of himself for solemnly laying out a program. One should not be deceived by this off-hand tone, in fact, one should start listening very carefully to off-hand tones. Words have more power than we know. You don't have to overstate. If you start overstating, you actually undo your own passion for your subject, but if you are addressing the muteness of an object, out there, you are going to be led to find the form that really says what it is, and Ponge says use every tool in the book that you can.

So, I started with him in your source book. I then put in a whole set of various ways in which the genres have been crossed by the group of poets called, or, who we casually refer to for our convenience, as mixed media or international concrete artists.

Student: Jane?

Augustine: I will come back to that in a minute. Yes?

Student: Before you go on, since the first day of the workshop, the first workshop of this summer session, I've been struggling with this whole notion of how to language the objective world, which raises a whole lot of problems for me.

Augustine: Exactly! One should take that problem very seriously because that's what will make you find the way to work. [Student interjection]. We want to do it. He says it's a rage, and it is because if we realize that words are completely separate from objects, objects take on their own reality. There's a sense of taking that external world much more seriously, which means actually subduing our own projections, our own private [indecipherable, student begins speaking].

Student: But isn't it futile though, if it is in fact a separate world, that is, there is a gap forever unbridgeable between signified and signifier. Language is only a system of signifiers that have something symbolically to do with the objective world. Then isn't it a futile project to think you can get the object of world in language?

Augustine: I don't think so. [Student interjection]. Because the objective world is other people. We want to interact. We are, in fact, all part of an interactive system. We want to clarify that interaction.

Student: That's the point. To me, it's always interactive and interpretive. The thing is never representative in itself, it's interpretive.

Augustine: You can get closer and closer. People who get closer leave behind their own projections and get closer to what is objectively real are helping their world. We live in a relative situation. I am speaking personally. It's my own sense that, my own effort, to be very clear about what is out there and distinguish it from what is in my mind, in my own projections, is helpful to me and helpful to others. I consider it part of my bodhisattva vow. I would be nonfunctional. There are no absolutes. We continue to work on certain kinds of projects. There is no absolute truth. We'll never find absolute truth. But our world works much better the more truthful we are.

Student: So to keep in mind, keep conscious of the difference. Not to forget.

Augustine: Yes. Otherwise, we are in a muddle. If we mistake our inner projections for the outside world, we are in a lot of trouble. The extreme end of that spectrum means you are carted off to the looney bin. The Buddhist image is that you look at a stick on the ground and you think it's a snake. But for most of us in ordinary life, we catch ourselves in the middle of projecting some idea that we have in our mind onto something out there, mistakenly. We have to break that down, and that's because the other great Buddhist's statement [sounds of writing on chalkboard, likely the Buddhist statement "form is emptiness, emptiness is form"]. The apex of the Mahayana teachings is to be someone who continually looks at the forms and realizes that one is projecting the interpretation of them, and cut that, as—Not take that for absolute, not take that for final. Form is emptiness really means that we tend to come to our world with a lot of preconceptions. That's where I began this talk, that we are governed more by our preconceptions, particularly in relation to sexuality and gender. That there are continual projections that we make in our moment-to-moment behavior. About what, depending on how much we have taken into our system of the messages that male behaves one way and female behaves another way.

Actually, listening to Beckett, you would think perhaps despairingly, that's the effect of the end of Beckett's life, the writing is a continual struggle with words, but a continual statement that words are meaningless. The wordy-gurdy, which is a wonderful way of expressing what is actually tremendous, tremendous confusion. If you really listen to all that stuff that's said, let's say in presidential elections, you do indeed think you are in a wordy-gurdy. You are in the midst of a world in which words are abused and they are mistaken for things. That's why it's really our job as writers to taking writing seriously. We want to clean up that act.

I don't want to be part of the problem of the word mess. Beckett is right on in that respect. There is a word mess, and a lot of that has to do with sexuality, sexual behavior and gender roles, permeates our politics. The whole question of how politics enters into our poetry is one of the most difficult because of that misuse of words, which is engaged in by people in power to keep their power and lust and greed going. So, it's really important to break into that word mess and recognize what it is.

We really have to clean up our act on all levels. Physically in relation to body, and in relation to speech, and in relation to life. But those are interrelated.

I just wanted to say a few things about Hélène Cixous' writing. I have given you also an excerpt from Susan Howe, to show you how we cross genres, and what cross genre expectations will do.

Actually, let me deal briefly with the Howe. The section that I have titled, "Theory of New Forms." I've said a compilation of cross genre writing, poetry, philosophy, and criticism. This is from a wonderful small book in which the poet Susan Howe discusses Emily Dickinson's poem, "My Life had stood—a Loaded Gun." I won't go into that poem at this point, but Susan Howe's writing about it is by far the best thing that I have ever read, and the reason it's good is because it isn't just literary criticism. It is a poem, and a discussion, and a selection from scientific research about Emily Dickinson that can inspire you. In one way, just to read the letters of Emily Dickinson makes you realize that Dickinson herself crossed genres. These poems, these letters are poems. Hardly anybody—there's no writing like it anywhere. Dickinson is an absolutely marvelous poet. What is marvelous is that these day-to-day letters to her mentor Higginson are poems also.

So, at the bottom of my page thirteen:

Dear friend,

> I did not deem the planetary forces annulled—but suffered an exchange of Territory, or World—
> I should have liked to see you, before you became improbable.

Amazing use of language. So, you should read the Howe excerpt. I would recommend the whole book.

On my page 14. This is also in short sections, by the way, and that is a formal innovation, very similar to Ponge's. Very popular, very good for our fragmented way of thinking in the 20th century. And also, I use short sections for perfectly practical reasons. I've got to do half a dozen other things. I can write a short section in 15 minutes before I go to sleep, if I can't do anything else, and you can do that, too. You may not think that fragmentary thought is worth anything, but we are in a social world that fragments us. Therefore, use that form. Don't think that you have to be Milton and write...[indecipherable]... nobody can read anymore, and on and on and on. Seize the fragment. The fragment is your daily experience. You could get a hit of the true object that you're [indecipherable]. That helps.

So, Howe is writing criticism in that way. She says, on page 14:

> "My life had stood—a Loaded Gun—" peers voluptuously through its own chronology straight through our time. This austere form is the aggressive exploration by a single Yankee woman, of the unsaid words—slavery, emancipation, and eroticism. In the fifth and toughest verse, HIS foe's unnamed power to harm is emphatically erased. None even *stir*—the second time. The stoic Scout-Gun's Yellow-Bullet-Eye, is righteous, isolate, cyclopean, feminine. Kill-deer and Hawk-eye. Mary Rowlandson guarding God. In War's necessity, supplier and suppliant are one.

That's an amazing poem. I would relate to this is sort of the end of the book, and you have to really see the whole book to pull it together.

But Howe is not only writing a poem. She is herself, by the way, a single Yankee woman, and she's exploring the unsaid words. So, the project, Howe's project and Dickinson's project, are identified. You should not be afraid to look into some writer whom you love to find out why and what would you say. Then, on the next page, is a pair of poems by Susan Howe based on her previous analysis.

Gun in My Life
  My Life in Gun
    My in The Owner
      The Owner in My

Notice the grammatical shifting. My, the pronoun is used like a noun, as the object of a preposition. You can do that, too. That is also a new form.

Catherine in Heathcliff
  Heathcliff in Catherine
    Edgar in Tom
      Tom in Edgar
        Panther in Boone
          Boone in Panther
            Doe in Rebecca
              Rebecca in Doe
                Killdeer in Deer Slayer
                  Hawk-eye in Kill-deer
                    Serpent in Chingachgook
                      Chingachgook in Serpent
                        He in I
                          I in He
                            Child Roland blowing Edgar's mad song.

An amazing series of reversals, oxymorons, wordplay, Deer Slayer, Hawk-eye and references to Shakespeare, *King Lear*, Tom and Edgar, you should recognize that. *Wuthering Heights*, Catherine and Heathcliff. The interrelations of male and female, which are actually the subject of Emily Dickinson's correspondence with Higginson, her mentor.

Then, at the bottom, what looks like a diagram or a flow chart or one of those corporate things, which is actually a spatially paced, placed or visual concrete poem, and using, borrowing words, fragments from the poem "My Life has stood—a Loaded Gun." I just gave you the end of the section so that you could read these amazing poems that Dickinson incorporates into to her letters.

Student: Jane? It's really interesting to me how, not technically, but by implication, in the poem, "in" becomes a verb.

Augustine: Yes. It acts like a verb, and that is, we don't often need the forms of the verb to be, so tremendous condensation can go along with fragmentation and still contain meaning. You can trust the fact that everyone knows the basic structure of a sentence. When you fragment a sentence, you can drop out certain words provided you are still sure that the reader will get your underlying sentence. That takes a lot of skill. I spend a lot of time correcting sort of freshman compositions for people who can't put together sentences, but that's because they don't know what the sentence is in some way that they want. They don't know how to construct a sentence they want, and so it has the wrong pieces missing. A skilled writer leaves out what is unnecessary, but you have to be very clear yourself in order to know what is necessary.

That's where we come to the need for very close attention to the words, but I suggest that Ponge is right—the spur, the urgency to find the words. To find the right word, comes from the quality of attention that we pay to things. Outside of ourselves, wiping the blackboard of our interior stuff.

The Hélène Cixous essay that I've given you is titled "Sorties," and I should say that Hélène Cixous began as a James Joyce expert. She wrote a huge dissertation on James Joyce. She is Algerian, French, spent time in Germany, Jewish, and fluent in English.

[Class break.]

Just for a brief lead in, you may be wondering what all these things that I have been saying have to do with this grab bag of stuff that I asked people to round up, and I hinted at it just before the break, that, and its implicit in Ponge's opening statement—he would like someone reading, hearing, looking at his poem to understand that this has to do with something like a carnation. To get at an experience of a thing, you want to use words and forms, those are not quite synonyms, but I'm also suggesting that you want to get back to a very fundamental sense of a word as a form. You want to use words in a way that will most accurately say what something actually is. What the experience of it is, is a combination of body, speech, and mind.

On page five, at the end of Ponge's poem on the carnation, he is talking about pleasure. He, in section fourteen, on the left-hand side of the page, he is really talking about the word for carnation in French, œillet. "O rent into Œ. / O!" Œ is a modification of sound of O. And so he's really saying the letter O is rent, changed, split into the word, the sound œ.

"O! Bud vigorous stalk/split into ŒILLET/Plant with immobile kneecaps/ ELLE," —the word œillet contains the word *elle*, which is the French pronoun she—"she"—and then he puts the words in English, the translator—"with juvenile vigor / L the supple pointed olive / unfolded in Œ, I, two Ls, E, T".

The word olive contains some of the same letters as the œillet. And, olive, by the way, is the same word in French as in English but its pronounced œillet, but here he's really talking about the word, and this is where Ponge kind of switches ground from his attention to the thing to the word by which he tries to represent it most accurately. "Little tongues shredded/by the violence of their intentions/moist satin, raw satin, etc."

That etc. is kind of his change of tone to the language of business letters, or something kind of casual. Throwing et cetera in a poem this is to take away from its elegance and continuity. And then, parentheses, "*My carnation shouldn't amount to much; one ought to be able to hold it between the fingers.*" It's contradictory that he's kind of saying "my carnation," the word, the poem word, ought to be as much as one could hold in one's head. Well, one holds a piece of paper in one's hand as well as the actual flower. At the end, he's talking about word choice. A rhetoric found for the carnation. He's talking about pulling the root of the plant up. "For you soon notice that beneath it there is a sort of long horizontal root underlining the surface, a long and very tenacious will to resist, rather strong. It is a sort of very resistant cord that throws the extractor" —that's the person pulling it out— "the extractor off balance, forces him to change the thrust of his effort. It is much like the sentence through which I am trying to express it "right now," something that uncoils less than it rips up, that grips the soil with a thousand adventitious radicles—and is likely to break off (under the effort) before I have managed to extract the principle." He's written a long, unwinding sentence to describe how to pull out the root of the carnation—it is a long root.

And then he says:

> Enough of that, right? Let's drop the root of this carnation.
> Yes, we will drop it, and yet, we shouldn't let ourselves think that I have described this carnation behavior simply to raise problems.
> Perhaps there was a perceptible will in vegetal behavior a will to bind up the earth, to be its religion, its religious—and consequently its masters.
> But let's return to the style of the roots. Why a string rather than a tap root or a branching up like ordinary roots?
> Two reasons might, have been behind this choice, either of them valid according to whether you look at it as an aerial root or rampant stem.

He's not only talking—he's talking about word choice here. What's the right word for this long root? Of course, it's a pun on a group of root words.

The length of these paragraphs devoted purely to the root of my subject must correspond to an analogous concern...but here we reach the limit.
Let's come out of the ground of this chosen place."

The last sentence is straight metonymy. "Let's come out of the ground of this chosen place." First pulling the root of the flower out of the ground, for us, let's pull our thought out of the basic area with which it's concerned.

He's trying to bridge the gap between thing and word, and in some way, that's what the various artists that I have—I'm calling them artists, the writers and artists—have tried to do in the varying samples that I have given you, which are configurations of words on the page, but to echo the thing they are talking about.

So, Ian Hamilton Finlay, who is a sculptor who turns words into a three-dimensional objects and mounts them in places, takes the names off of boats and then lines them up in a typography, a kind of lettering, that makes them look as they looked as the names of boats, but also, he arranges them in stanzas, frames them with a frame, and has grouped them according to a metaphor of the sea in each one of them, so there is a multi-dimension to the physical arrangement of the words.

For our convenience, and the shortness of time, flip over to Al Hanson. Hanson's vocabulary and forms are limited to the words, numbers, and lines, straight, on chocolate and silver Hershey bar wrappers, which he transforms into dynamic visual poems. The form he has chosen is just what you can find on a Hershey bar wrapper. Nobody has ever taken a Hershey bar wrapper this seriously before. I'm suggesting that that represents a quality of attention. These, this is a sexist poem, and they're kind of comic. It's a limited form. If you only have a Hershey bar, a Hershey bar wrapper, you've got lots of limitations.

There is one final thing that I want to say about form, and particularly new forms. Forms exist to be broken. You can do more with a Hershey bar wrapper than Al Hanson did, if, after having done everything you can do with a Hershey bar wrapper, you discover that there's more for you. Forms exist to be broken. Maybe that's another way of saying form is emptiness, but I think it's true of aleatory art, for instance. Lots of cut-ups are done around here, it a famous Burroughs method, and aleatory art, art by chance, taking segments out of the newspaper or putting your finger on a page of the *I Ching*, or whatever. Aleatory art is only an initial process. If you really want to communicate with it, there is a point at which the aleatory or chance procedure becomes something you choose, and you choose something to add to it. Nobody says that around here—that somehow, it's the idea is you could just take the aleatory thing and present it, and let the reader finish the poem for you. Unfair. If you are doing something by aleatory methods, chance methods, that's fine. What you are doing is engaging in a process of discovery. At some point there will be a quantum leap. Or, I'm speaking from my own experience in relation to this kind of work. At some point, working arbitrarily with chance forms, with cut-ups, with wrappers, with tape, with pieces of paper, with whatever it is at hand. What I have discovered is that there is a point at which there is a tremendous sudden escalation of my interest in [indecipherable]. Some kind of connection.

This is the point at which the form follows the function. It may be the breakage of form. That quantum leap means that something has happened because I have encountered the form, really, and there's a zap. It begins to tap me, like the tap root, it goes right down into the middle of something that I care passionately about, and that I would not have been able to get at by direct access. Working with forms, Bernadette said yesterday, kind of casually, it's a way to learn about writing. I think that you can say something even more radical in addition to that—when you work with forms you discover. The form aids you in your discovery of what you want to say. It keeps you from drifting, and you can, you will be absolutely clear when one of two things will happen, when you are working with form, any kind of form, that appears to be external. In this situation, its where there's teachers and students and there's sharing of experience. I'm going to give you some ideas about forms to work with and that seems to come from outside you. One of two things will happen. By doing that, you will encounter what it is in yourself that the form arouses, and then you will extend or break the form, make it your own. Or, you will feel that the external form is much too external for what you want to say and you will discard it. But you can't—you have to enter that process, somehow, and the new form arises from that encounter.

So, I think it's time to have a little bit of discussion, but then I would encourage you to look at your materials, the stuff with I asked you to bring. Or, to think more about Ponge, write a prose poem like his, picking an object in a room. Or, try a poem letter. Or, try working with one word in the dictionary, in a kind of sequence like one of those sections of Ponge. In other words, you could also write a poem to be inscribed on a wall. Ian Hamilton Finlay. By the way, in some way these visual poems are also cross genre, the little comment is part of the poem. Sometimes I go to museums and wish that—and this happens—certain, certain—Anselm Keifer for instance, does write things that sit next to his gigantic paintings, those two genres intermix.

This is the word acrobats. Ian Hamilton Finlay says, "Isolated single letters are a pattern, but letters joined in words as these are, are direction." Difference between pattern and direction. That's something to think about. "Those in the 'Acrobats' poem are both behaving like the real circus acrobats who are now individual units, now seen together the angles and the tower. Properly, the poem should be constructed of cut out letters to occupy not a page, but an entire wall over a children's playground." And Finlay has done a number of his pieces, there's another one in the book that I have, which is a sheet, an enormous sheet of clear glass with waves in it. Actually, I think the waves are not in it, but just the word says waves and rocks, and a sheet of glass, Plexiglas, is placed on a shoreline in Scotland, so that you look through the glass at waves and rocks, but with words waves and rocks inscribed on the glass.

So, Ian Hamilton Finlay is so internationally famous as a mixed media artist, but his roots are literary, they are in the word, but he also wants to unite the word wave and rock with the actual waves and rocks on the shore, so he says, "If you are going to write the word acrobats in this way, acrobats have to be very precise." This is a very precise configuration of letters. Because acrobats function individually, but they also have to meet, if you watch them, aerialists, a group of aerialists, they have to choreograph—it's a dance, and they must meet at the same moment. There must be extreme elegance and precision of motion. This is an example of a word placed in a way to make a comment or a reflection on the actual thing that happens in life to coordinate body, speech and mind.

Okay. So actually, I asked you to bring stuff, to look at because things are symbolic of themselves, and also this is time for discussion and protest. Maybe you think that this is not going to work at all and you don't want to do it. Or, you have more things to say about making a visual poem.

I prefer the term visual poems to either the term concrete, which is the name of the artistic movement, or the term avant-garde, its sometimes called the avant-garde, but that's a little misleading because it's a whole tradition. It's like saying avant-garde Renaissance painting or something. Visual poetry is based on the idea that the fundamental thing that makes a poem is the configuration of words on a page. Black print on white paper, which is the democratic or commonplace everyday way we look at newspapers and magazines and so on. In other words, the emphasis in the column is on its visual appearance, but we should reflect on that a little bit because we also think of poems as oral, and one of the aspects of concrete or visual poetry is that the isolation of words heightens our sense of the way they sound in English or in whatever language they were written in. There is also a minimalist aspect, in that, which you can reflect on, that in some ways, the fewer words there are on the page, to more emphasis each one of them has.

So, there is a quality of attention to the words that is augmented by the visual displacement. You look at a page and it doesn't look like a poem. Acrobats, for instance, because you're used to seeing a poem in parallel lines, it reads from the top of the page to the bottom, in English that is. If Hebrew in which you read back to front, right to left. In Japanese, the characters go down the page instead of across the page. But, I think that to start you thinking about new forms, again to go back to a more radical aspects of form, is that the poem is formed by what's on the page.

In my course description, I promised you that we would work on alphabet, figure alphabets. Paper bag music I'm leaving out, but paper bags do make music and John Cage once made a whole musical composition in which the musicians were told to bring various ordinary objects to make sound out of. That's a very wonderful radical digression, which I'll only drop in your head right now, but when you pop a paper bag, it makes a sound, when you click your eyeglasses or your pencil on a hard surface it makes a sound, and John Cage says that's musical. Well, I love that sense of music, that sensibility for hearing—everything you hear is inherently musical. Same thing as saying every word that you read is inherently poetic.

It has its individual traits and belongs. It is what it is. It's not foreign or strange. It is inherently ready for you. So, if you've got pieces of tape, for instance—things are symbolic of themselves— electrician's tape is smooth.... [recording ends.]

Women at Play:

The feminine undercurrent of Surrealism and the unconscious

Interlude by C. M. Chady

In Surrealism, the alchemy of the mind and its imagistic creations is limitless. Reality is spun into a dreamscape. Figures are mythic, bodies distort, landscapes collide. We learn to expect the unexpected, to see the world beyond our usual perception, to reach enlightened possibilities. Here the subconscious is feminine. Multiplicity reigns, enabling all possibilities to coexist simultaneously. There is no rigid order, no singular way that the subconscious unfolds. Rather, it manifests in endless iterations, allows the internal to become external, blurring the boundary between reality and fantasy. It is beyond our reality, beyond our sight, beyond our senses that springs forth something entirely new.

In considering elements of Surrealism, it begins to feel ever more inextricably linked to feminine spaces, to maternal logic. It calls to mind Cixous's theories of female pleasure, how it is dispersed in its manifestation and welcomes expression in multiple forms. It holds the space to be more than a singular identity, to defy definition or strict logic. In Codrescu's lecture, he states that the subconscious *is* feminine. That even the renown male artists and writers embraced a female muse, their creations evolving from a constellating feminine energy that allow for the juxtapositions and absurd the arise within surrealism, as opposed to a rigid reality. There is something about the female form, the unknown of the female consciousness that they yearn for. Their interpretations of the feminine however, are limited at best. Their engagement was generally that with a gaze, portraying the female body as one to be dismembered and refigured. The spirit of the feminine's open potential was with them, but its full potential could not be reached with their vision focused on desire.

Surrealism is truly opened when exposed to the women's imaginary. When even traditions of Surrealism itself that has a male dominant lens are broken open in order to create a space where women must find new modes of expression where there are none for the female and feminine experiences. Their Surrealism is of necessity—to write the body, to make the unconscious embodied, to manifest the internal.

I have always been enamored by the fantastical world of the subconscious created by Surrealism and looked for more ways to engage with the tradition, yet I did not always know about the women who were vital in the movement despite my attempts to find them. I've spent time at museums dedicated to surrealist artists, which featured only men. When I was younger, being more familiar with its art than its literature, I did an internet search for surrealist writing which was highly dominated by Breton. There was an obvious lack of women Surrealists, but surely, they existed? Augustine even states in her following lecture, "So one reason that I'm at this particular Surrealist gathering is to remind people that there were women painters and writers." My dilemma is one that has been present ever since the emergence of Surrealism. As I continued to search, results remained elusive, and I could feel the massive void looming that called to be fulfilled.

It took until my MFA until I finally found Surrealist women writers with the guidance of my professor. I was first drawn into Leonora Carrington's writings which were clever, subversive, and innovative. The prose was fresh and flipped male centered narratives on their head. She creates a world that uses surrealism as a means to carve a space for women that has not been present, where a women's experience and subconscious reign. In her novel *The Hearing Trumpet* myth and history are re-written with a blending of occult and Christianity, that move women into position of agency and narrative. With this novel, I had finally unlocked a secret that had been silent for so long. I felt resonance with her narrative, her fantastical world able to weave a new world around common conceptions and imagine them new. I branched out to other writers, finally feeling like my own self was represented in a tradition that I had so long admired.

There are certainly other examples of this lack that perpetuate. Many women writers and artists who've created ripples in literature who are overshadowed by male counterparts. As will be elaborated upon further in this section, Mina Loy, for instance, began writing her poetry within punctuation—edgy, revolutionary stuff that we now take for granted. But "credit" for this is given to E. E. Cumming who did it *after* she did. How often we see the latter presented in classrooms compared to the former? I am not dismissing or passing judgement on E. E. Cumming's career, *however,* I am here to highlight the women to whom we should be giving equal attention. It is time for their work to be upheld and their contributions to be recognized.

Overall, the Surrealist space for women created a unique and desperately needed opportunity to become unburdened by societal pressures and express what lie within the self. In *Subversive Intent,* Susan Rubin Suleiman opens by discussing the importance of seeing the mother play. This comes at the contrast of seeing the mother fulfill solely dutiful or domestic roles; Suleiman draws attention to how girls are taught to play as a means to introduce them to gendered roles, while boys are encouraged play as a means to open up creativity. The mother taking this role of play breaks down the boundaries implemented between the genders and allows for the creative potential for women to pour forth.

A similar role can be seen of women Surrealists. Surrealism and play go hand-in-hand as a means unconscious to undo the rigid tethers of logic and enter the imagination and subconscious through an openness to creative potential similar to child play. By entering into this state of mind, one begins to turn off the filter and expectations of their work, and instead, opens it up to chance and surprise. There is no longer a strict logic that must be followed, and new materials can be forged from this. Surrealists were long interested in different modes to get around the editor or the filter, such as automatic writing or other games that encouraged fun and originality.

The role of the woman at play becomes more revolutionary as a result, and an absolute necessity to reach into the feminine subconscious to allow what needs to speak come forth. As previously mentioned in the anthology, women writers lacked a language for their experiences, and hence, had to create their own unburdened by patriarchal traditions. They created their own language, their own styles, their own traditions that fit into the feminine experience in ways that traditional literature and art would not allow. Play and chance within Surrealism allow the unconscious to come forth. Women within the anthology play with grammar and syntax; they experiment with linguistic juxtapositions. As a result, a new space is carved out that is uniquely feminine whose legacy and lineage continues to expand.

Women in the Surrealist Movement

Jane Augustine
July 4, 1988

Transcription by C. M. Chady

Jane Augustine: Treat this very much as a workshop situation, not lecturing on Surrealism. There has been a lot of talk of one sort or another about Surrealism in the past week and I want to summarize that a bit, lay out a few basic ideas, but really try to apply them to get some notion of something that you can use as a writer, and that's going to be my basic position.

I thought I would start out also by telling you a little bit about myself, because you don't know who I am. I came yesterday afternoon. I've been on the faculty of Naropa last year, but I'm not on the faculty that teaches here year-round, but anyway, my name is Jane Augustine and I'm glad to be in this tent out of doors. I grew up in California, and I spend my summers in a small cabin in the Sangre de Cristo Mountains about 180 miles south of here, and I like to be out of doors. I like to walk in the mountains by myself. I take long meditative hikes and in my own writing, I've been very much influenced by the Chinese and Japanese poets who also like to go to the mountains and meditate, contemplate their exile from civilization, which was a regular feature of the lives of the poets of the late Tang, Du Fu, and Li Bo. Those poets lived in a kind of tension between the mountains and their meditative quiet and civilization with its needs, demands, and its arts. The Chinese poet is also an inspiration to me because the Chinese poet was always a scholar and I am a poet scholar. I have a Ph.D. and my specialty is women and the 20th century, essentially, and questions relating to women and their relation to the movements of the early 20th century—Surrealism, Dada, Futurism—will be something that I will talk about in my lectures on Thursday and also there's an MFA lecture on Friday.

One reason that I'm at this particular Surrealist gathering is to remind people that there were women painters and writers. In fact, the women painters were often writers as well. Surrealism is a mixed media movement, and there are very important reasons, I believe, for that mixture, the activities of the unconscious, which the Surrealists stressed, often present themselves in visual forms, not just in verbal forms.

You know that from your dreams. In your dreams, you see something visual. It's very strange. It changes. It doesn't fit with the logic of that particular object image in your life, and sometimes a word will appear in your dream or a sound where it takes on a new kind of life like an icon. Historically, Surrealism moved back and forth between the urge to express something in a non-verbal form, a visual image on canvas, and a desire to change the context of the word and transform the word on the page because of the contact that both of those forms have in the depths of fundament of our unconscious mind.

I wanted to let you know where I'm coming from in terms of being here and what my stress is, my emphasis is, in relating to the whole delightful, goofy, shattering area of Surrealism, and its historical background is important because people did important groundbreaking things to change the form of poetry from the very conventional notions of the 19th century that a poem had to be written in forms. Even someone as wild as Baudelaire in the late, mid 19th century, *Les Fleurs du Mal, Flowers of Evil,* was written about 1855, although he kept changing it. Baudelaire had an extremely wild vision of the world, but he still wrote in the conventional rhyming forms, often sonnets that were the proper forms for poetry in the mid 19th century.

I mentioned Baudelaire because I think in some very early fundamental way, he was a revolutionary. He broke the bounds of convention in his life and his art and wrote poems about rotting carcass of a dog, which he sees teeming with maggots as he's on a walk with his beloved, his girlfriend, and people were terribly shocked, no, poetry must not contain the rotting corpse of an animal teeming with maggots, which he sees as shining and rich and flowing and unknotting, all those teeming, sick, slimy, revolting creatures were his kind of objective correlative for what you might—you might actually look at these and see this as an aesthetic object, not as a conventional mind would say, oh, it's revolting, we mustn't have anything to do with that. Especially we mustn't have anything to do with that if its high art.

So in the 20th century, early in the 20th century, the Dadaists and Surrealists were particularly fed up with the idea that you had to have a category "High Art" and you've got to keep a sort of special set of attitudes. It's as if you had to wear a tuxedo all the time, no matter what the weather was or where you were sitting. The early Dadaists and Surrealists really didn't, they didn't want art to be isolated from life, so the Futurists in Italy wrote manifestos and set them out in sort of strange typography to shock people.

The poem or statement on the page wasn't even typeset in the same way that we are used to seeing things properly typeset. You recognize a poem because of the way the type is set. It's a line and a line and a line and a line, and you know the difference between poetry and prose because the page is filled up when there's prose and you stop at the margins. Those are corny, old-fashioned, and handy definitions, but fundamentally they are conventions and forms. The Surrealists want to break down those forms in order to break down the superficial, conventional attitude that people have toward art. They wanted art not to be separate from life.

So this idea of breaking down the conventional forms of art was directly connected with the idea of breaking down our conventional ways of thinking, not just about art, but about the world. Now, I personally think that that idea has entered into society. It's really permeating it still, and that may be kind of a problem for us now, so much breakdown down that there's no reference point. But in fact, when you're starting as a writer or you're committed to writing as you are here, now, you want to break down your non-writing attitudes or your prosaic attitudes or your day-to-day way of looking at the world. The day-to-day world says, okay, get up in the morning, take your vitamins, shave, take a bath, put on clean socks, go out, and get somewhere on time. Get to your job. Get to your class. Do this. Do that. We are surrounded by these prison bars, essentially, of conventional thinking and the practice of meditation—sitting in the shrine hall early in the morning—is a way of helping you recognize how much of that machinery goes on. I sat for an hour this morning because I also have lots and lots of machinery going on and these wheels, according to the laws of momentum, turn faster and faster. It's necessary to break that open and clear space.

That's what the Surrealists wanted to do, and the Dadaists before them, even about the turn of the century. Dada began in Berlin and Zurich around 1905, '06. It's as if the 20th century dawned and people really got fed up with all their 19th century ideas. Surrealism is largely a French movement historically, although, as I said, it began in German-speaking countries and moved to Paris, which became the center of Surrealism from the early days, 19th. Gertrude Stein got to Paris around 1906, and she's the person who might be an embodiment of radical change in approach to writing. She's not usually considered a Surrealist. That's not an official label, but she certainly broke down the language, and she lived in that whole environment and brought a whole new way of looking at objects. She said she wanted to get rid of the noun, and she said the nouns get in the way of our conventional thinking. Well, that's a very radical idea. All of our communicative sentences depend upon nouns. Actually, the heart of a sentence is a verb, and Stein said, get rid of the nouns because that process of naming things—grass, microphone, yellow, well, yellow, an adjective actually, tent, chair—all of those are, every time you name something, you bring up a whole body of associations with it, most of which are conventional. We got to use this tent because we got to get the sun off of our heads, but in fact, it's an aesthetic object and quite an amazing one. If you think about our sky suddenly strike yellow and white.

I'm going to talk about forms in relation to the idea of breaking them, changing them. Historically, one of the ideas that was important in Surrealism, which we have completely absorbed, was the idea of free verse, that you could write a poem that had no rhyme, no preset form, no literary form. That's all part of our ongoing stuff. Now, that's no longer a radical idea.

Well, it probably began really late in the 19th century. The Surrealists, when they actually come to what they write, however, don't use forms. They invented their own forms. In fact, they frequently don't use punctuation. Part of the idea of free verse was that you also didn't have to signal the syntax. You could put in a fragment.

(Student question off mic.) I didn't want to go too far back and be to professorial about it, but Rimbaud although he's still used rhyming forms, was certainly a seminal person like Baudelaire. Rimbaud's famous poem, "Vowels" is one in which he says, "A is green and a whole other," but he associates a letter of the alphabet with something seen, something heard, and you probably know the name for that. That's synesthesia. You say that grass is a subtle waltz of, you compare a sound to a smell to a taste. The vowels A-E-I-O-U in Rimbaud's poem called "Vowels" are associated with colors, tastes, smells.

That idea was one that the Surrealists took up in their idea that in the unconscious and emerging from the unconscious are wild juxtapositions of dissonant, unassociated objects or ideas or sensory perceptions, and that sort of wild juxtaposition of things that don't fit was expressed by Lautrèamont, the accidental conjunction of an umbrella and a sewing machine table. That image is a very painterly one. The Surrealist painters paint a staircase with an enormous daisy growing in the middle of it or a famous collection of Surrealist works was called Soluble Fish. Basically, the Surrealists took up the idea that in the unconscious freely associated wild things that aren't fit, that don't fit together by the logic of everyday life, and we need to free up that unconscious. We need to let our dreams take over. The Surrealists who are also influenced by Freud and the interpretation of dreams, but Freud was busy making a system out of that, out of dream analysis, and the Surrealists and Dadaists would not subscribe to that at all.

The characteristic of a Surrealist work is the juxtaposition of wildly discordant elements in terms of content, of things seen, heard, and felt, but that has an exact language corollary. Adjectives will appear without nouns beside them. Sentences will not have verbs. They won't be sentences. A line on a page will not have any punctuation, no capitals, no commas, no end punctuation. Actually, I think I can assert that Mina Loy, who was a mixed media artist living in Paris and a poet, which I'll talk about on Thursday night, was the person who really first shocked people by not punctuating anything, except she punctuated, she capitalized certain nouns for purposes of her own. E. E. Cummings went on to do that later. It's now completely acceptable convention, but it represents a breakdown of what we usually do when we're writing according to the proper conventions of scholarship and letter writing and communication is to write in sentences—noun, verb, capital, period at the end.

The sentences themselves or the structure, grammatical syntax, is also broken in Surrealist practice, and a great deal of attention was paid to dreams, now that's interesting. The Surrealist painter, Frida Kahlo, who was a woman married to Diego Rivera, whose own work was not appreciated for a long time but whose paintings are very powerful, was asked if she used dreams in her paintings and she said, not the dream itself, but the mechanism of the dream, and I think that's an important point, because actually when we write, we're doing something with our consciousness, something is conscious. It isn't just a duplication of wholly mindless processes. We're not limited to just writing about our dreams. Although dreams are very suggestive, there are other ways of liberating the unconscious and one of them is to change the language, with which we address our ordinary world, blow that apart, and that's the part that really applies to us here as writers. So I like that phrase, the mechanism of the dream, not always the dream itself, because it's trying to get you to tune in on that.

Yes?

Student: One of my favorite aspects of Surrealism is that they're really funny. They had a really great sense of humor, and I was also thinking that there are some tribes of Native Americans in North America that ritualistically would have certain people in the tribes whose duty it was to go in and break down all the sacred objects, so maybe once a year they had their sacred objects break down or whatever, and those people were called clowns. I equate that with Surrealism in some way, just that they were really funny and trying to break things down.

Augustine: That's a nice point that you're making actually, that there is some kind of function and need within the whole society for the artist-clown, breaker-down of the serious social structures that everybody thinks have to stay in place. We don't collapse when things are broken down. We actually enter a new stage, a new level of consciousness. In all the talk about the unconscious among the Surrealists with automatic writing and the emphasis on dream and trance, there's an implied corollary, which the result is a heightened consciousness. That consciousness is our actual, not just our rational processes at getting things done, but our whole capacity to open up to our world, to let it enter us, permeate us, and actually enable us to do something, so in certain writers, particularly in Gertrude Stein, consciousness is very important. She wants enlarged consciousness. Now, I'm not talking about a higher consciousness in the mystical sense, because in certain Surrealists there is a mystical element and others none at all. And Stein, I would say, is one in which consciousness should be enlarged so that you can act, so you can do something, write better, write more penetratingly, write more shatteringly and challengingly to people. Yeah?

Student: I just wanted to point out, I always stated what Gertrude Stein is trying to do when she didn't like to use nouns was to get at all the stuff that is around whatever it is as it is and create more of a picture of what's really going on.

Augustine: You're absolutely right. You're using the term "negative space" as in painting. Remember that Stein was a great friend of Picasso and they talked a lot about art. There is, in *Tender Buttons* particularly, which is a series of prose poems, really, although Stein didn't... She wrote a lot that I would call poetry. She also wrote massive novels. She had studied with William James, the great, rather underrated, I think, American philosopher and psychologist whose principles of psychology are still worth reading. And Gertrude Stein's, one of her early literary passions was Henry James, the brother of William, and so for both of those writers, William James writing psychology, *The Principles of Psychology,* which came out the same year that Bergson wrote *Creative Evolution.*

The ideas of Bergson were important, too, but I'm stressing the influence of James and his notions of consciousness, stream of consciousness, were very important to Gertrude Stein. Much of her writing can be seen as a stream of consciousness around an object. The noun being eliminated because the name is too heavy, drags us down into too conventional a set of associations, so she will circle an object with all the ideas, all the responses to it, all the emotional suggestions of it, because for her, the stream of consciousness is a stream of emotions, sense perceptions, responses, and I think that that should be seen as a technique very close to the Surrealist technique and one that is usable for you.

Since I'm emphasizing form and I want to talk about women in relation to the Surrealist form, I've got a little comparison to make and texts to actually look at. The first is a very famous Surrealist poem, which you may have read called "Free Union," by André Breton. This has not got me the French with it. It's the translation. There are several translations. This is a translation taken from the general reference book that's being used in this Surrealist week, the Random House *Book of 20th Century French Poetry* edited by Paul Auster. It's a big kind of fat volume. There are several translations of this. Did everyone get "Free Union?" You too? Yes?

Student: What she mentions about the clown, it seems to be that after the Victorian period, a lot of people were really tired of having things be so set.

Augustine: Yes, I think that's true. The Victorian period really labels a lot of things in place in England. The French 19th century was...you couldn't call it Victorian, it wasn't ruled by Victoria, but there were certain heavy conventions and I think we could track those back to economic conditions that dictated quite heavily how people should act, what class they should belong to, how their speech and language behavior, which reflects their class, and all of that's very inhibiting and defeating to art.

There were, you know, dominant ideas in art and people you had to bow to. The French, particularly ever since the French Revolution, resent having to bow to authority, and so the anti-authority attitudes of the Surrealists and the Dadaists, are actually, I think, important to... (some students speak off mic for a moment). Anti-authority guys kept writing manifestos and the women didn't write manifestos. Mina Loy was influenced by Italian Futurism. She had an affair with Marinetti, who was the great manifesto writer of futurism, which is also an important strand that feeds into Surrealism.

Yes?

Student: Because she did write a feminist manifesto, that was considered a satire? As opposed to a manifesto?

Augustine: That manifesto was buried. It wasn't... She wrote it in 1915. I think she showed it to Mabel Dodge, her friend there. It was never published. It was published in 1982 when *The Lost Lunar Baedecker* was collected, in laid her papers in Meineke.

She never manifested her manifesto, which says something of an element in the practice of the of the women that I am interested in. Gertrude Stein, Djuna Barnes, and Mina Loy is to use the techniques in a very self-effacing way. There is no egotism, no proclamation of myself as the great artist in the actual work of those women. Stein herself was very interesting personally because she had, as one of the commentators on her, of a good natured will to power, and that was the power of realizing herself. She was very strong willed in that way and in some ways centered on herself, but she doesn't proclaim herself in her writing. In fact, her strategies are in some ways powerful strategies of concealment of her personal life and personality.

The language itself, I believe, other than *The Autobiography of Alice B. Toklas*, which is directly about her own life, although that's the trick of her writing to tell her own autobiography, but as if the pronoun "I" in the autobiography of Alice B. Toklas refers to Alice, her life companion, not to herself, so there's some very conscious distancing of trying to get away from—the style of proclamation, me the great artist, that women don't do that.

Student: That's a very important shift in terms of Surrealism that artists were getting away from the more blatant revelation of the self in terms of being identified directly with their imagery and that kind of thing or...?

Augustine: I think that it's important, for me looking at writing. I think the emphasis, women want the emphasis on their writing, not on developing a career as a great artist. Mina Loy kind of threw away her home. She thought she did that accidentally, that she was really an artist, a painter, but she didn't actually... She made lampshades. Well, she had to earn a living. She was very casual about her personal role, whereas Breton, as you pointed out, was a self-declared leader, is going to publicize a cause. He was going to get people to join his party and then to join the Communist Party and reform society and lead, lead at the same time that that he was proclaiming an anti-society attitude, that people had arguments. They broke up the Café des Lilas one evening because, I don't know, Sara said something that offended somebody else, and so that the Surrealists themselves had big arguments and public debates about who and what they should be and who should join which side, and the women just didn't engage in that kind of activity as much, and I believe that it has to do with the notion of being less invested, for better or worse, in the notion of becoming an Artist with a capital "A" and acting as an artist in society. Ezra Pound was the big publicist of Modernism and Imagism and Vorticism in England. He was also a writer, but he was very aware of himself as an important figure artistically, whereas H.D., who was really the person whose image, whose practice in poetry invented Imagism, who had been engaged to Pound, had a much greater struggle to think of herself as an artist and did not make statements about, as Pound did, which were sort of manifestoes, so that's partly a different sense of self and their function. Both functions are necessary and particularly became so in the 20th century to publicize, declare, make a manifesto isn't a very important function, but to, I also believe strongly in putting all of one's energy as an artist into the work, the poem. Focus, invite the reader into your poem and make that problem real to yourself and let the publicity take care of itself.

Student: How did the masses react to Surrealism? I mean, was it pretty radical?

Augustine: That's a good question. I think, I've actually been thinking about that because the Surrealists, Max Ernst and the painters, once Leonor Fini and Carrington and many others, they threw a big party. You were to come to this party nude from the shoulders to the top of your thighs and everything else was to be covered. And this party happened. I think the masses thought, well, there was safety in numbers. There were enough Surrealists. Oh, yes. Those guys, those people, both men and women, were... They could live that way in Paris in between the wars. That's why they were there. I think it was because it was it was odd, but it wasn't dangerous.

Student: So they had the same reaction to Surrealism they had to High Art, something a bunch of weird people do, and it doesn't really affect us.

Augustine: That's a very interesting observation, I think, though, that it was also a form of entertainment. It was fun for other people to watch. Yes, they were somehow, they had to be special cases somehow.

Okay, but let's look at "Free Union." Because in fact, I think this is a famous poem because I think it's quite accessible. It's a series of wild comparisons and it has the quality of automatic writing in the incantatory effect of the repeated line form.

Two things are going on in this poem. The comparisons themselves, "My wife whose hair is a brush fire/Whose thoughts are summer lightning/ Whose waist is an hourglass/Whose waist is the waist of an otter caught in the teeth of a tiger/Whose mouth is a bright cockade with the fragrance of a star of the first magnitude." The oldest poetic device, and it's still one of the best when used properly, is repetition. The chant, the magical incantation, the ritual. Repetition is something that not only rises from the unconscious, but it permeates the unconscious. It sinks into your whole being.

Formally this poem is very, very simple. Each line takes the same form as the line preceding it, not absolutely uniformly or monotonously, because there are breaks in it but it is "my wife whose..." and so there's a bedrock of a very simple form which is incantatory and repetitive. And in this case, it's all very simply a celebration. This is a love poem by a man who is in love with his wife's body and the way it's an erotic poem actually, if you want to think of it in that way, very subtly, by drawing every kind of aesthetic object into relation to her physical body, her arms, her armpits, her breasts, her eyes. And there is a very simple form, "my wife whose," and then playing against that, it's as if there were a slow, soft drum beat underneath, and playing against that whole musical motif, which is completely wild and invented, and which contains many synesthesias, many comparisons of, "whose tongue is made out of amber and polished glass." Well, the many qualities of amber and polished glass, which are completely unlike the actual physical softness of the tongue, but it's not, it's amber and polished glass that do things to him, remind him of things that her tongue reminds him of.

So one might also think of Gertrude Stein's titled *Tender Buttons*, buttons are not tender, the buttons you wear on your clothes, although somebody's pointed out that that's probably an erotic allusion to this. Like the tender buttons are the nipples, the clitoris, and that there is a whole kind of hidden suggestion there. But what it is, is a waking up of our consciousness and opening up by bringing into the field of our consciousness things which we wouldn't ordinarily permit to be there because we would have had our categories in place, things that are hard, things that are bright, things that function in certain ways, things that are mechanical, things that are organic, and so on. We have those categories and this poem breaks them down because it's not about anything that's useful or it's a celebration of, and I think an attempt to convey erotic sexual sensation that you feel about the body of the person you are with. That excitement is completely universal. It fills the cosmos when you are making love, and so this poem brings in every kind of strange element of that cosmos and makes it part of the erotic experience. The poem is long and the accumulative, the effects are cumulative, and all kinds of contrasts from line to line:

> My wife whose eyelashes are strokes in the handwriting of a child/ Whose eyebrows are nests of swallows/My wife whose shoulders are champagne/Are fountains that curl from the heads of dolphins over the ice/My wife whose wrists are matches/Whose fingers are raffles holding the ace of hearts/Whose fingers are fresh cut hay/My wife with the armpits of martins and beech fruit/And midsummer night/ That our hedges of privet and nesting places for sea snails/Whose arms are a sea foam and a landlocked sea/And a fusion of wheat and a mill/Whose legs are spindles/In the delicate movements of watches and despair/My wife whose calves are sweet with the sap of elders/ Whose feet are carved initials/Keyrings and the feet of steeplejacks/ My wife whose neck is fine milled barley/Whose throat contains the Valley of God/And encounters in the bed of the maelstrom/My wife whose breasts are of night/And are undersea molehills/And crucibles of rubies.

It reads aloud very well.

André Breton as a very good poet. The poem itself reads very well in French and translates easily because it's meant to be also like a song. Repetition is what happens in songs, and so there's yet another level of this poem. Yes.

Student: I just think it's interesting to notice that, I'm just thinking of a comparison of this and artistic visuals of Surrealism. Here the form is the metaphor.

Augustine: Essentially. The technical analysis of it, right?

Student: Yes. Everything is comparative, and I think it's different when you look at a painting, like see an apple core superimposed over a sky or something like that, that there is no direct correlation between the two as much.

Augustine: Well, there is actually, if you think of the page, which I do frequently, because I do mixed media work myself, think of the page as a frame and the way the words elicit objects you can frame in your mind a painting. Surrealism's poetry really is founded in painting. Apollinaire, who is, I think, one of the founders of Surrealism, partly because of his personal influence, but because he began poems which were called calligrams, and they're scattered on the page and they were handwritten, although a typesetter friend began to set type for them. There are some excerpts of a couple of famous ones in Alan's anthology of photographic poetry.

"My Heart, Like a Flame Turned Upside Down," was actually written on a page and a heart shaped form, so the page is a frame as a painting is framed and on the canvas are juxtaposed wildly discrepant objects. That's what Surrealist painting is doing. You can think of this poem as having some similarity in a line that brings together carved initials, key rings, feet of steeple jacks who drink, and the calves of feet, human feet. You might be able to make a painting out of the lines and objects in this poetry. But you were going to say something different?

Student: I think I agree with you on another level. It's a very self-conscious poem, surprisingly so for Surrealist. I mean, to construct a poem in which in which repetition and metaphor come together in such a predictable way so that by the time you get to the end of the poem, you could continue it yourself very easily.

Augustine: I think that's why it's popular. I think that that's part of the thread in Breton.

Student: It's sort of like et cetera.

Augustine: Et cetera. You can continue it yourself. And that's what I thought we would do, but I wanted to make a slight introduction comparatively, because, the simplicity of the structure, the simplicity of the concept and it is self-conscious. It's drawn very simply from our most powerful personal experience of making love.

Here's another poem written directly from the practice of Breton and "Free Union," and this is Anne Waldman's poem, "Queen."

And she turns it around and has her husband speaking of her, but she also speaks:

> My sandpiper husband who wears sackcloth when I don't behave, says, come sit on rattan, Woman. Your will is as brittle as glass. Your mad mouth is untamable and your heart is always in another country. Your ears are radar stocks, your eyes magnetize yardman. And when you sing, you shake the house. Ah, ah, ah! My wife is a burning house. My silkie husband, who tends the garden whose arms shake like branches in a storm, complains I'm a slug a bed on his time. He says, Wake up woman of sleep and cream. Wake up and sweep back your flickering night lids. Your hands are Lepidus, your shins are Cadillacs. Your thighs are palace of tears. When you weep, the house rises. My wife is the Indian Ocean rising. My husband is sacred vows, has October weather in his voice. He says Come to bed amorous woman your ancient desk is covered with leaves. Your tidy poem can't be coaxed, but we'll come to you like a queen.

Okay, some things that come out which I want to just mention in this poem, the Breton is a translation from French to English, but part of what is going on in this poem is alliteration, internal rhyme of sound. "My sand paper husband who wears sackcloth says, come sit on rattan, Woman." Okay, "rattan" and woman, there's the "aa" sound from "sackcloth" and "sand," and then there's a "woman" and "rattan." Okay, that musicality of sound interplay underlies the repetition, which is more varied here than in the Breton, but Anne told me that this poem comes specifically from working with Breton.

My original idea had been to go back to an earlier Anne Waldman poem, which I feel is strongly influenced by Breton because it is a simple repetition, and that's the poem "Fast Speaking Woman," but the introduction to this says "Fast Speaking Woman" is indebted to the Mazatec Indian shamanists in Mexico guiding persons in magic mushrooms ceremony and is a reworking and coincidence of the same for all wandering spirits.

I have read other Indian, American Indian, Native American chants that work on this same principle, and so we're drawing from another tradition completely, but you see that it has some profound root in the unconscious, which is worked with by Native Americans in chant and ritual.

So "Fast Speaking Woman" begins:

> because I don't have spit
> because I don't have rubbish
> because I don't have dust
> because I don't have that which is air
> because I am air
> let me try you with my magic power:

Same form, because:

> I'm a shouting woman
> I'm a speech woman
> I'm an atmosphere woman
> I'm an airtight woman
>
> I'm a flesh woman
> I'm a flexible woman
> I'm a high-yield woman
> I'm a high style woman
>
> I'm an automobile woman
> I'm a mobile woman
> I'm an elastic woman
> I'm a necklace woman
> I'm a silk scarf woman
> I'm a know nothing woman
> I'm a know at all woman

I'm a day woman
I'm a doll woman
I'm a sun woman
I'm a late afternoon woman
I'm a clock woman
I'm a wind woman
I'm a white woman

I'M A SILVER LIGHT WOMAN
I'M AN AMBER LIGHT WOMAN
I'M AN EMERALD LIGHT WOMAN

The repetitions, the form is exactly the same. It's intended to be magical and it doesn't change for that reason. The magic works by the repetition.

There are many alliterations—"shouting woman, speech woman, atmosphere woman, airtight tight woman, flesh woman, flexible woman, high heeled, high style." So that there are and there is a stream of free associations. Freud's principle of dream analysis was linked by him to the technique of free association in psychoanalysis, which was his way of getting the conscious patient to drop conscious boundaries of social communication and just say what was on his or her mind.

There is a sense in which the free associations of Freud and that technique fed into Surrealist practice. This is a translation into German, "Ich bin eine frau aus fleish/ich bin eine flexibel frau/ich bin eine frau mit hohem Entrag/ich bin eine Frau mit Stil." It's just as good in German, which happens. German and English translate rather readily back and forth.

We have a classic, so to speak, historical poem of Breton, which we've already said, you could go on doing it yourself, and a poem by Anne Waldman, with certain differences of strategy, partly because she's writing from her experience as a woman and partly because poetry has changed since the Surrealists introduced their ideas. Lots of people have capitalized on them.

(A student states something off mic, cannot distinguish.) You think Anne's poem is more self-effacing? It's not. Not at all. Given the form, this is very self-involved, yes. And in fact, this is a celebratory poem, too, and really is saying that the poem will rise like a queen and Anne herself will rise like a queen through the poem.

Student: The same with Stein doing *The Autobiography of Alice B. Toklas*, it's like she escapes into using, oh, this is what her husband is saying about her, she's not really making a proclamation.

Augustine: I think that that's true. She's celebrating what she knows to be his feeling for her and puts the words in her husband's mouth. That's a difference in strategy. You're going to hear me say a number of things about how women writers have different strategies, strategies of difference, because of the difference, and of course, each individual poet has a strategy of difference from what's been happening before, but I think that in general, as I study these Surrealist practitioners and teachers, practitioners, women practitioners of the past, I see differences in strategy from those which the men used, and that is not a problem, but a fact. Yes?

Student: Formally, her poem, the poem "Queen" is reactionary in the sense that it really, formally it's High Modernism. You know, it makes a nice little package. Now, the queen at the end is the same word as the title and it starts with a six-line stanza and ends with a six-line stanza, three five-line stanzas in the middle. It's very self-conscious in the way that it's...

Augustine: It's very formalized. Yeah. Well, like the forms of Marianne Moore, I would say yes. In some way you can say that's a Modernist poem, but it was written directly as inspired by Breton's and Surrealist practices.

Stevens, that first three lines would almost be a mirror of Bantams in Pinewoods, in which Stevens really pushes the sound to Surrealism.

Augustine: Oh yes. Yes. That's a wonderful... "King! As you can of Azcan in caftan..." [Text is: "Cheiftain Iffucan of Azcan in caftan"—she misspeaks in the recording when recollecting from memory.] Yes. Yes, but what Stevens was doing in that poem was imitating the way a chicken sort of pecks at the pebbles and the rocks, and so he makes the sounds that way but also, he's very philosophical and is punning on, "as you can."

There is no way of making categories strict, and that's probably come clear to you from the past week of people's talk about Surrealism. It can be a lot of things and there are contemporary applications which can develop in any kind of direction. Fundamentally, the Surrealist idea that we should tap the unconscious, break down the barriers of conventional thinking. Fundamentally, that is a search for truth. Now that's a very interesting idea, that you can, that if we could get the raw data out of our unconscious, if we could get rid of our inhibitions, we would be rid of our neuroses and rid of our social prejudices, and we would have a kind of purity, a naked reality that we could call that would be something like truth. I'm not sure whether that was a misplaced faith on the part of the Surrealists, I merely say that that was what was going on. The desire to liberate the unconscious was not to liberate Freud's libidinous chaos in the world. Freud said, you've got to watch out for that unconscious. It's a sea, a dark morass, a bog, a mess, murder and violence and rape and death and war all lie in your terrible subconscious, unconscious. Watch out for that stuff, said Freud. On the other hand, he thought you had to know what was there, that you had to know you wanted to murder your father and marry your mother, and before you could achieve any kind of minor stability at all.

The Surrealists, and certainly 20th Century Feminists, have rejected that idea of what happens when you wake up the unconscious. You heal self-division. If the unconscious emerges into consciousness, it becomes part of that stream, which is an open and active mind, which leads, as William James said, to the Manly Act—William James like to call acts manly, that annoys the hell out of me, frankly, because I'm always doing "manly" acts like carrying a backpack, 33 pounds over a mountain peak and writing my own poems and doing my own thinking and other kinds of things which are "manly" acts. All of us. He had some notion of the virile hero solely based on the assumptions of the 19th century and about male roles, and those were being broken down steadily by an insurrection going on among women since Seneca Falls in 1868 and through the writing of the Modernist women who didn't get the same kind of publicity, but who are beginning to be understood, but a widened, expanded consciousness of what is, of our world as it is its sensory data, its richness. That kind of consciousness is desirable and the unconscious is a creative source that feeds it. The Surrealists believed that H.D., as an Imagist and Post-Imagist Modernist writer, believed that you can tap the unconscious and bring it into consciousness and a page can hold it the way Breton's page holds the poem, in the way a frame holds the canvas, and in which wildly juxtaposed objects are given. Yes?

Student: I saw an exhibition of Frida Kahlo's work last summer and something that was interesting is that she painted on frame like the outside canvas.

Augustine: What could be a more obvious statement? Painting continues outside the canvas into our life, just as the poems leaves off the head, it becomes not only words that are read but are spoken, which become a chant, which permeates our being so it actually floats, the sounds float in space and in some way never ever end. I should refer you to a book that I think will be on the reserve in the library called *Women Artists in the Surrealist Movement.* It contains, it's a big book, *Women Artists and the Surrealist Movement* by Whitney Chadwick. It contains many prints, full color reproductions of paintings by women Surrealists, and also many photographs of the men and women of the Surrealist movement together, painters, writers. I brought that book with me, though actually, there's a copy here. I brought it with me because I thought that people might begin to get ideas from looking at some of the things that women did and there are some very beautiful reproductions of Frida Kahlo' work, which are very suggestive and symbolic and worth looking at.

So we have some time left, about half an hour, and my suggestion for writing today would be to continue either of these poems. On the back of your notebook or on the back of the page or whatever. Or just maybe this is really wild comparisons of the parts of the body to things that are wholly unrelated to parts of the body, play with that idea. You could actually choose several things, first, sort of enter Breton's vision and continue to "Free Union." Write your own poem of celebration. Or anti-celebration. It occurred to me that one very rich source of inspiration—you could express hatred, dislike, protest from the same kind of formal source with the same formal idea of comparing parts of somebody you don't like or whose done you a great deal of damage and whose damage has permeated your world, at least in some sense.

Form follows function, as Frank Lloyd Wright said, and the form and content are not ultimately dissoluble, but this form that is celebratory can also be used as... It celebrates erotic love and deepens it as a poem of anti-celebration might work just as well. In other words, I'm trying to say it don't limit yourself to celebration as a mode. Maybe you're not in a celebratory mood. Maybe there is something in you that really wants to denounce, tell off, proclaim, declare, exorcize, perhaps by writing wild comparisons, but I wanted to sort of play with that, to do that.

So, maybe we'll write for ten minutes, a list of wild comparisons, parts of the body to things. Might be your own body, you might like it or not like it, and then as an overnight assignment, so to speak. I don't want to block you with that word assignment, but take your list and the Breton and Waldman and write a celebratory or anti-celebratory poem. In this form, your choice, but simple line length. Concentrate on following your stream of consciousness or your stream of free associations to the wildest kind of association you can make in your poem.

Yes?

Student: Do you necessarily mean the repetition or basically just the list?

Augustine: I think I mean, the more free thing. This is, it's a very simple anchor, so to speak, I think what I mean is choose a simple anchor for yourself in forms and lists, catalogs, however you want to choose.

Okay, I wanted to take some writing time, but maybe people have got more things to say, ideas, questions.

(Student asks something about Gertrude Stein, too far off mic to hear.)

I was describing her starting point, which is important in *Making of Americans*, but that's really the groundwork for what became her radical change of strategy, which is...

Student: The way she conducted her evenings at home with the men sitting around her feet and the women go to the back of the room...

Augustine: We could talk biographically, but I was really talking about her... From another point of view, what she did was establish, completely and firmly without intrusion, the world of herself and Alice B. Toklas. Her own relation was not to be disturbed. We could argue whether that's a concession to whether she just simply sort of adopted the male role in order to do a "manly" act, but fundamentally, she was developing herself, I think.

Student: Those people sat at her feet (end of sentence hard to decipher).

Augustine: Well, that was it. That's right. If somebody dull or boring or stupid or conventional, she didn't monkey around with them. She let Alice serve cake to them, but that didn't mean that she found Alice dull or…

Student: Oh, no. I always figured the most interesting conversations was in the back of the room, and that up-front Gertrude Stein was pounding these big male egos into submission by forcing them to do what they were always forcing other people to do as writers.

Augustine: That's a nice way to put it, actually.

Student 2: It's very male perceptive.

Student: It is, but I'm just... (continues to discuss observation on Gertrude Stein, difficult to decipher).

Student 2: I mean, I think that, like, as Virginia Wolf said, that I think that women have had a really difficult time and still do with establishing some kind of lineage or linkage, so, you know, she was drawing upon ideas from a man. That's because there were no great women psychologists influencing her.

Student: Gertrude Stein was the first psychologist. I'm not objecting, but I think it's... [indecipherable]

Augustine: I don't think so, but I guess, it's really… there are a lot of ways to define and think about feminism, and I'm going to leave that as kind of tangential. There's no question that women artists get a lot from men artists, have to, because it's been a male-dominant tradition. The interesting thing is probably still in the works, when men will come to be more influenced by the women artists. Women do need help in establishing artistic identity and that drove them to the strategies of difference, which make their work special and make it especially good. Working through obstacle is very important to the artist. It is a Buddhist perception. You have to, you're not going to achieve enlightenment by trying to get away from your obstacle. In fact, you must study it and be with it thoroughly. So...

Student: Play with it?

Jane Augustine: Play with it, yes, yes. There is some interplay. Play and play with it. In any case, it's got you and until you have some consciousness. Consciousness is really what I was trying to emphasize in...(audio seems to cut off for a few seconds)...Because I think Surrealism is working toward a new form of consciousness which incorporates the unconscious, and that also means incorporating the experience of the women artists whose lives are different from the men, and historically, not much of that incorporation happened, I think, but we are still at that. History hasn't ended. We are in history, too. The strategies of difference help us understand what women were doing, why they were doing it, and enriches the whole notion of what we might now do with Surrealist ideas. And so, I wanted to pin that down, not to biography and theory, but actually to get people to start writing and maybe take a few minutes to write and then we'll read back. Maybe we can make a leap into a wild, a list of comparisons, essentially.

I think nowadays and if I were doing this myself, I wouldn't even have the verb "to be" in this. I'd probably say something like, "hair, brush fire, mouth, bright cockade with the fragrance of a star of the first magnitude. "

You could make your list that way, if you want, but I would like to take a few minutes to actually put something on a page.

(Students have time to work through Augustine's suggested writing exercises; remainder of the recording students share what they have written and Augustine offers her commentary.)

For One Night Only

Interlude by Kathy Tun

A glowing lamp shade beams at me from the corner of the stage. I keep glancing over at the solitary light as I stand off to the side, waiting for the show to begin. To steady myself, I read over the script for the thousandth time, which reminds me that I must head towards the light. As I fidget, my eyes wander once more from the words to the stage. This time, the light's warmth leaks through the fabric's pattern where tendrils dance like shadow puppets. The hypnotizing design calls out to me, and I feel the urge to run out and play.

For the past two months, I have watched both Mina Loy and Lorine Niedecker wait for their cue by the curtains. Their names topped the playbill as they took turns in the role of experimental poet and artist. In their own way, Mina and Lorine played the role with the ease of an adventurer who had no reservations. Mina's passion took her to Paris, Florence, and New York, where her artistry explored a boundless consciousness and a dance of language. Lorine, on the other hand, transcended the routine rhythms of a rural life to articulate the overlooked, natural beauty around her. As I read their lines, I tried to memorize where they paused on each word. I felt the pain of Mina's lost love cutting through the silence in my chest. And when I read Lorine's lines, I found myself daydreaming of a home that called me to stop and rest. On these nights, I donned the costume of an understudy to embody the power of an experimental poet. My role was to observe and listen. I held my breath every time Mina and Lorine sauntered towards the light, never believing that the mischievous flicker beyond the lampshade would be calling for me to share their stories.

The director called me before the morning light even crested over the horizon. Both Mina and Lorine called in sick and were unable to perform tonight. "It's a temporary thing," the director reassured me. "It'll be for one night only," she sighed. I paused, trying to imitate Mina or Lorine, but I could not remember what to do after saying "Yes, I'll be there." How did an experimental artist respond to the call? My memory slipped back to the opening nights when people packed into the plush velvet seats to marvel at our play *Embodied Unconscious.*

Mina first played the role as a soul-searching nomad who explored the breadth of her craft from all corners of the stage. She navigated the anguish of motherhood and lost love as delicately as a paintbrush dipping into oils, but the pain remained an indelible mark on her. Her sorrow poured out in words when it became too much to hold.

In the bustling first act, Mina immersed herself in the cafe scenes at Gertrude Stein's salons. She played alongside characters whose company lingered like honey on the tongue: these notable artists stuck together, letting their inspirations melt into each other's work. At this time, Mina experienced some of the most groundbreaking work of the 1920s in Paris. She listened to James Joyce read at Sylvia Beach's bookstore, she attended Ezra's Pound's opera "The Supper for Mr. and Mrs. Williams," and she continued to delve into her art while getting to know Peggy Guggenheim at the salon meetings. But just as quickly as she glistened in the light, Mina fell into the shadows and retreated inwards away from the crowd. She constructed sculptures out of trash and curated artwork that tapped into the curiosity she had for the world. After having worn the costumes of wife and mother, Mina then explored the movement of consciousness, the sexuality of a woman navigating the pressures of marriage, and the defiance she felt against the bondage of societal norms. Her time in the role lived on as a sort of *Lunar Baedeker*, or a guidebook that freed the female consciousness into new spaces.

A stagehand taps me on the shoulder, reminding me that the show starts in three minutes. I listen to the audience chatter like birds who have flocked nearby. I wonder who they expect to walk out onto the stage. Will it be Mina's mysterious, eclectic persona or Lorine's meditative, pragmatic essence embodied in an amateur like me? I close my eyes as I set the script down. The words evaporate from my lips while a fog creeps over my doubts. For a moment, I lose myself in an inner silence and drift to the island where Lorine found her peace.

During her time on stage as the experimental poet, Lorine captivated everyone with her love of the natural world. Around her, the sets reflected the simplicity of a pre-cottage existence, in which only the bare necessities surrounded Lorine. She knew how she wanted to deliver her lines and moved with purpose. If you watched closely, you could see that her performance followed a deliberate rhythm that cycled like the seasons. Gone was the three-act structure of the play for Lorine moved at her own speed, changing her role multiple times within the night. But what always stayed with her were the memories of everyday items that she encountered on her journey. Items such as the marsh mud and the clothesline featured in Lorine's words like a prized souvenir from a distant land. And without ever having to witness its beauty, I felt Lorine's admiration as if it was my own.

Lorine made me want to believe in the ethereal nature of the ordinary. She saw possibilities within arm's reach and captured it in clear, concise sound bites. When Lorine played the role, she explored what it meant to be self-sufficient and strong. She trudged her way out of poverty and out of her caretaker role. All the while, the light kept her warm as she gathered water from the pressure pump to survive.

One minute left till the show starts, and the light calls out to me once more. Try as I might, I still have no idea what went through Mina's or Lorine's mind before they took on this role of a lifetime. I saw them as artists crafting their own version of poetry. I held them up as revolutionaries attempting to speak louder than the critiques of their male contemporaries. I thought of them even as friends, who would want me to keep redefining what it means to be experimental and bold. But outside of this script, I had little knowledge of who Mina or Lorine actually were.

What little I saw would have to do. For one night only, I can share what I have learned as a student of Mina's and Lorine's work. I try to recall the words I memorized by heart, but suddenly something has replaced them. I feel my breath slowing down until my own thoughts beg me to try something new. In front of me is a wide-open stage where so many characters have played before, and it is up to me if I want to follow in their tradition. When I put on the costume of an experimental writer, I keep Mina's adventurous, soul-searching power close to my heart. Then I drape a coat over my shoulders to capture the warmth of Lorine's peaceful wonder. They have both given me inspiration, but now it is my turn to take the lead. What happens next will be my interpretation of Mina's and Lorine's artistry as it evolves from my own.

The light flickers, and I am ready to play.

American Women in the Experimental Tradition:

Mina Loy, Lorine Niedecker, and Gertrude Stein

Joanne Kyger
July 19, 1991

Transcription by Kathy Tun

Joanne Kyger: On the top of the sheet, you have the little review questionnaire, which in terms of its simplicity is kind of interesting. It's the last issue of their little review anthology. Remember I mentioned Margaret Anderson and Jane Heap before as being part of the avant-garde magazine publications in the... I don't know the exact dates, but I think they went on for about ten years. I'm not really quite sure. They moved around a lot. They published it from France at one point, and they've represented a lot of the revolution in arts that began before the war.

Anyway, we have somewhat simplistic questions: What would you like most to do, to know, to be? Why wouldn't you change places with any other human being? What do you look forward to? What do you fear most from the future? What has been the happiest moment of your life? The unhappiest? What do you consider your weakest characteristics? Your strongest? What do you like most about yourself?

Just like most, we have Gertrude Stein, who is just absolutely marvelously complacent about all of her answers. What is your attitude towards art today? And what is your worldview? And why do you go on living? Which Gertrude Stein says, "I am." And I put this little notation: "Marianne Moore very carefully answers. Mina Loy answers it with a certain passion that you see later in her life story that we will discuss. H.D., who is still calling herself Hilda Aldington in 1929, answers in terms of her cinematography that she's working in. We've talked about her being in the movies. And, so this is just for yourself to read through in terms of reflections of how these different women that we've been studying answered. The questionnaire went out to a lot of other people too: Ernest Hemingway, Bertrand Russell, Sherwood Anderson, so it was a large cross-section of answers.

I put the little piece in there about Ezra Pound, because he's kind of funny... he's starting to sound more and more like an old hot air balloon. He says, from Ezra: "Print what you've got on hand." He says, Ezra Pound: "Ezra refers to manuscripts of mine suppressed by you or Jane Heap when I last assisted you in preparing a number of *The Little Review* and never returned to the author. Suppressed by my dear Ezra and conscientiously thrown into the wastebasket. And a very good thing for you, such a collection of stale witticisms that has been rarely my lot to receive. We really couldn't have hoped to get away with him in a magazine published in New York City, USA, in the year 1926." Margaret Anderson. (laughter)

So I'm going to open with this which was printed in *The Little Review* as a matter of fact. A few paragraphs by Ezra Pound on Marianne Moore and Mina Loy. At this point, Ezra Pound seems to be under the slight misconception that Mina Loy is an American writer. I'll read some selections from this:

Marianne Moore and Mina Loy:

> In the verse of Marianne Moore, I detect traces of emotion. In that of Mina Loy, I detect no emotion whatever. It is possible as I have written, or intended to write elsewhere, to divide poetry into three sorts: Melopoeia, poetry, which moves by its music, whether it be music in the words or an aptitude for or suggestion of accompanying music. Two, Imagism or poetry wherein the feelings of painting and sculpture are predominant. And thirdly, iogopoiea (initially mispronounces logopoeia), or poetry that is akin to nothing but language, which is a dance of the intelligence among the words and ideas and modification of ideas and characters. These two contributors Marianne Moore and Mina Loy write logopoeia, which is a dance of language... as logopoeia not iogopoeia. It is in their case the utterance of clever people in despair, or hovering upon the brink of that precipice. It is a

> mind-cry, more than a heart cry. In the midst of this desolation, give me at least one intelligence to converse with. The point of my praise, for I intend this as praise, is that without any pretenses and without clamors about nationality, these 'girls' have written a distinctly national product. They have written something which could not have come out of any other country, and while I have before now seen a great deal of rubbish by both of them, they are interesting and readable by me, that is.
> (*The Little Review*).

This is meant to be an introduction and praise to the poetry and for these "girls," who are doing a good national product review there. It's a bit hard dealing with a Poundian voice. I'm going to read a short biography of Mina Loy, which is taken from her commentator Virginia Kouidis. It's called *Mina Loy: American Modernist Poet and the Last Lunar Baedeker* put out by Jargon Press, which is in the Naropa Library put out in 1982.

> Mina Loy, born Mina Gertrude Löwy, is born in London to Sigmund Löwy and Julia Bryan. She is the first of three daughters in a prosperous English middle-class family. Her father's family were Hungarian Jews. Her mother's family were English Protestant. Her father sends her off to art school in Munich when she is seventeen. (Kouidis).

She's already from a privileged background, so she can afford to be sent off to school, and because her directions are of that talent.

> Returning to London, she enrolls in a studio taught by Augustus John and meets her husband to be Stephen Haweis. His parents are prominent members of London society and authors. Her husband and she go to Paris and get married and have a daughter, who lives only a year. She sees Impressionist paintings and is turned on to Gauguin, Picasso, Manet, Monet, Renoir, and Degas, who she says frightened her for a year. (Kouidis).

Guess his technical skills were such that they put her off for a while.

> She has shortened her name by this point to Mina Loy and meets Leo and Gertrude Stein, who introduce her to Picasso and Apollinaire. As she is gifted in painting, she stays up all night painting the night her daughter dies. Mabel Dodge recalls: 'She made the extraordinary tempera painting called *The Wooden Madonna* that I still have. The foolish looking virgin mother holding her baby whose two small fingers are raised in an impotent blessing over the other anguished mother, who, on her knees, curses them both with great upraised, clenched fists, and her own baby sprawling dead with little arms and legs outstretched lifeless like faded flower petals'. (Kouidis).

I guess it was one of those crib deaths, which they don't know the reason for. I should put Mina Loy's dates up here first, so you can see that she's part of the women poets that were in the long (indecipherable). Same time as December 27, 1882 (writes on chalkboard) to...dies in Aspen, Colorado, September 25, 1966.

Okay, so she's gotten married at an early age to this English painter, and they move onto Florence where the artistic circle is around there that, where Mabel Dodge is at her Villa Curonia, where Gertrude Stein visits and does the *Portrait of Mabel Dodge*. Remember, we touched some of these places in the last biographies. She joins a circle of artists hanging around there. Carl Van Vechten writes of her at that time in 1913:

> She made an unforgettable figure with gray blue eyes, her patrician features, her waved black hair parted in the center. Tall and slender, her two large ankles were concealed by the tight hobble skirts she wore. Her dresses of soft dove colored shades, or a brilliant lemon with magenta flowers or pale green and blue were extremely lovely. Strange long earrings dangled from her artificially rosy ears. It is easy to recall her as she tramped along the dusty roads, enveloped in a brown cloak trimmed with variegated fur, scarcely able, thanks to her tight skirts, to move one smartly shod foot in front of the other. (Kouidis).

Gertrude Stein is there and she gives Mina the manuscript of *The Making of Americans* to read. She earned the appreciation from Ms. Stein that, "Mina

Loy was able to understand without the commas. She has always been able to understand." Mina Loy gets sick a lot about this time. She has got depression, and she's worried about her husband's infidelities. She describes herself as being full of "shilly, shally, and shyness, and of an utter inability to adjust myself to anything actual." She has a daughter Joella and a son Giles and becomes a Christian scientist.

> Conceptions of life have evolved while I have been stirring baby food on spirit lamps, and my best drawings behind a stove to the accompaniment of an alignment of children's clothing, hanging around it to dry. I have seen very little of what is going on with the exception of a few Picasso's, Wyndham Lewis, and Nijinsky dancing. (Kouidis).

So she paints the picture of herself as the housewife at home there with a spirit lamp and paintings behind the laundry. Of course, at that point she is really a lot better off than she is telling us, because she has help. She has a nursemaid and a cook. About this time, she hears Marinetti's readings of the Futurist poems. I won't go into it... The Futurists give her energy to turn some of her difficulties into art, waking her up with vitality. She has an affair with Marinetti. Her husband has gone off to Australia, and in the papers I gave you, at the very bottom, she has reduced the Futurist from aphorisms of Futurism. You can read that later.

> The mind is a magician bound by assimilation. Let him loose, and the smallest idea conceived in freedom will suffice to negate the wisdom of all forefathers. To your blushing we shout the obscenities, we scream the blasphemies that you, being weak, whisper alone in the dark. They are empty except of your shame. And so these sounds shall dissolve back to their innate senselessness. Thus, shall evolve the language of the future. (Kouidis).

A touch of Futurism there, which gives her some energy. She, at this point, exhibits paintings for the first time in London and decides that she wants a divorce from her philandering and absent husband Stephan Haweis, who you don't hear about too much from this biography. But if you read Mabel Dodge's intimate memoir, she paints another kind of, more of a sensitive picture of this kind of moody-looking man. She agitates for a divorce. Her first poems appear in print in Stieglitz's *Camera Work Magazine* in 1914. But war breaks out, and the American-English colony in Florence breaks up. Mina stays on there and takes a job as a nurse in an Italian surgical hospital. And she writes:

> "Strange," she wants to, quote, "get near a battlefield and hear a lovely noise." As somehow some of the Futurist insanities. "She is wildly happy among the blood and mess, and finds psychological inspiration in human shrieks and screams. (Kouidis).

Somehow this is expressing her inner turmoil. Her poetry shows an aggressive assertion of selfhood and is structurally experimental. Her affair with Marinetti ends, and she begins writing satires of Futurist attitudes towards women. She calls Marinetti "Raminetti." "Raminetti a stride up prismatic locomotive, ramping the tottering platform of the arts of which this conjuring commercial traveler imported some novelties from Paris in his pocket."

She goes on at this point, "I only have one idea in mind. Make money." Something that is familiar to all of us, and at this point she is supporting herself, I guess in some way. I don't know what her arrangements with her husband, who is off in Australia, is about, so she decides—

Student: Does she still have the children with her?

Kyger: She's got these children with her all the time with the nursemaid in Florence. In fact, that's the location where the children actually stay further on in this story. She has a reliable woman that takes care of these three children, so to make money, she decides that she will produce commercial art like magazine covers, dress designs, theater sets, and she decides to go to New York City to sell them, leaving the children with a nurse in Florence.

The Dadaists at this point have just arrived there in New York City. This is during the war. Picabia, Duchamp, and Man Ray...Her poems appear in Vogue and Alfred Kreymborg's *Others*. That's another of the important magazines at the time. She meets William Carlos Williams, Marsden Hartley, Marianne Moore, Georgia O'Keefe, and so on. Well, New York doesn't bring her a lot of money, but she meets many like-minded people and is chosen as the prototype of the modern woman and profiled in *New York Evening Sun*. This report says of her, the headlines say: "Painter, Poet, and Playwright: She can and does write free verse and hold the intuitional pause exactly the right length of time. She can and does paint lampshades and magazine covers." Now these lampshades—don't laugh about this—her lampshades were a beautiful artful form. In the *Lunar Baedeker*, there are some pictures that she invented this calla lily lamp, which is actually very beautiful. It's got these little lights that go out. And you have to remember electricity hasn't been around all that long, and lampshades are works of art that you can skillfully dim the lights with. I remember when Amy Lowell went to the first theater that didn't have gas lights.

> She can and does paint lampshades and magazine covers. She can and does act, design her own stage and social costumes, and wear them as if she had a whole regiment of customers. More, where she can tell why future isn't 'is' and where it came from. Mina Loy is of English birth and training, but she is particularly proud of the fact that like Columbus, she was discovered by America." She says, "If you are very frank with yourself and don't mind how ridiculous anything that comes to you may seem, you will have a chance of capturing the symbol of your direct reaction. Art always begins with a man quite simply being honest with himself. (Kouidis).

So she's put it right down to a simple level. At this point she plays the lead in one of Alfred Kreymborg's plays called, *Lima Beans*. Sort of sounds like a Ron Padgett play, doesn't it? She's a talented actress, and her husband in the play is William Carlos Williams, who gets quite a crush on her as they go through these rehearsals together. But Williams' wife Flossy sniffs, "I don't think you have enough money for Mina." So you can't afford her. But the play is a great success and they have sixteen curtain calls.

Then at this point, she meets one of the very central figures of her life, Fabian Avenarius Lloyd, alias Arthur Cravan. He is an Englishman, born to English parents in Switzerland, and he's the nephew of Oscar Wilde. She meets him in December 1916 when she is thirty-four years old and he is twenty-nine. Arthur had been to the United States before when he was sixteen, having been expelled from several schools because of his stormy nature. Running then in

New York, he made his way to California working as a lumberjack, chauffeur, orange picker, and butcher. He is six feet tall and well-built. He returns to Berlin for more low-life adventures...and Munich and then Paris. This guy is a real...not more than a character. He's very independent. He becomes a boxer and wins, finally, or becomes the amateur light heavyweight champion of France. He actually wins by default (laughter). He's part of the Dadaist movement. He would cite his titles and pedigrees before a fight. Shouting from his corner of the ring, ending with, "And a poet with the shortest hair in the world!" And he was a poet, publishing a violently polemical journal called *Maintenant*, which consisted entirely of his own writing in French. The distribution of this was done from a parked wheelbarrow outside the entrance to various racetracks, art galleries, and entertainment areas, where he hocked his publications.

The women painters and then men were the object of his insolent commentaries, which were all the more irritating as they were characterized by an irresistible verve and drollery:

"If I write, it is to infuriate my colleagues, to get myself talked about, and to make a name for myself. A bit of advice, take a few pills and purge your mind. Do a lot of fucking or go into rigorous training" (Loy). (laughter)

Right. "When you have nineteen inches around the arm, you'll be gifted." He is the beginning of the Dada movement. "Let me state once and for all, I do not wish to be civilized."

And there are other incidences. I believe he's said very churlish things about Marie Laurencin that got people out. The news always...He provoked people to the point where they wanted to hit him, and then he was very happy. A note in Mina Loy's unpublished papers talks about Cravan:

"Unique phenomena. A biological mystic, he traced his poetic sensibility to his power to think with any part of his body. Conscious in adolescence of his phenomenal strength alone, when later his intellectual faculties came into play the instinct of 'knockout' dominated his critique."

So it was a physical and mental knockout he was after. "His gesture of destiny was Sampson upsetting the temple," she says. So he's just arrived in New York City in December 1916, having earned his passage by fighting former world heavyweight champion Jack Johnson, going three rounds before he is knocked out, which might have been a setup. There was a big betting on this, so that might have been it. So anyway, the femme fatale and the homme fatale meet. The meeting of the immovable and the irresistible. This is a classic meeting. They sat, "Not only at night, but days and nights imperturbable on a bench in Central Park. It is love, but it is war too. And Cravan must leave the country to avoid the draft. And by November 1917, he is in Mexico City where he writes her, "I can't live without you."

Before this he's involved himself in...gone to some of those Armory shows, in which he comes clad only in bedspread and can't hardly wait to take it out (laughter), so he's causing a little scandal right away. You know, he wants to create scandal, so he writes to her and says, "Love, I can't live without you. Come to Mexico City. Tell me that you will come right away, and that we will spend the rest of our lives together. I want to marry you."

She joins him in January 1918, and they get married in Mexico City. Her divorce to her first husband having been finalized six months before. He's running a boxing school there, and in September announces a big fight. Boasting of his skills and an effort to increase the size of the gate. It's a disaster, and he is knocked out in the second round. The boxing school folds, and they bum around Mexico having a very hard time, nearly starving until they are rescued by a couple of English visitors in Veracruz.

At this point, they have a hard time. She finds that she's pregnant, and in November she takes the one available birth on a hospital ship, passing on its way to Buenos Aires where she'll wait for him until he can get there by his own means. Meanwhile, she would borrow off money to pay the passage, so that the two of them could cross the Atlantic together, collect her children in Florence, and begin a new life in Paris. They've known each other for barely two years. He never arrives. He totally disappears.

They never find his body, and there are many rumors. They find...an ex-girlfriend sends him a bloodied money belt. She chases down to the American embassy, prisons, and that's the end of Arthur Cravan. Although, she does later say that she feels that he was murdered than he kind of fled. You can imagine himself that kind of machismo meeting in Mexico and that he could have easily gotten into many difficulties, so you can read in *The Little Review* number here that—how she says her answers to "What is the happiest moment of your life? And what's the unhappiest?" Arthur Cravan, anyway, gave her something that no other friendship could provide, that one other intelligence to converse with. For the rest of her life whenever she longed for some contact with, "a mind extraneous to my own," she addressed herself to Cravan sometimes through medium mystic beings, sometimes by writing adonic verses. Oh here it is, the depth of her loss ten years later shows that in response to *The Little Review* questionnaire: "What has been the happiest moment of your life? Every moment I spent with Arthur Cravan. The unhappiest? The rest of the time." And she never marries again.

"The Widow's Jazz" 1931 by Mina Loy

> Cravan
> colossal absentee
> the substitute dark
> rolls to the incandescent memory
>
> of love's survivor
> on this rich suttee
>
> seared by the flames of sound
> the widowed urn
> holds impotently
> your murdered laughter
>
> Husband
> how secretly you cuckold me with death
>
> (*The Lost Lunar Baedeker*)

She's pregnant, remember, so their daughter is born in April when she goes back to London to kind of put her life back together. After two more years of this darkness time, she resumes painting and writing, and she eventually returns to Paris in 1923, where she stays for the next thirteen years. During this time, she's part of the cafe scene. Her ex-husband, at this point—she got a divorce—has stolen her son away, her thirteen-year-old son. The poor lad dies an early death, so she's lost two of her children. So she keeps her two beautiful daughters, who are beautiful daughters, very close to her. Takes them everywhere during these years in Paris.

The artistic community of Paris with its American ex-patriots and visitors put her center stage. Through her influence, Robert McAlmon gains access to Gertrude Stein's salon. Her friends are distinguished—Paul Valéry, Gertrude Stein and Alice, Peggy Guggenheim, Paulette, Ernest Hemingway, Sylvia Beach, James Joyce, Brâncuşi, Djuna Barnes, Eric Satie, Tristan Tzara. Harriet Monroe, a poetry magazine [editor] is there, meets her and writes:

> "I may never have fallen very hard for this lady's poetry, but her personality is quite irresistible. Beauty, ever young, which has survived four babies, and charm, which will survive a century if she lives that long are sustained by a gaiety that seems the worldly wise conquest of many despairs. All expressed in a voice, which is rich with all the sorrows of the world. Yes, poetry is in this lady, whether she writes it or not" (Monroe).

So this is a picture of her at that time. She is present at the decade's famous happenings: a reading of Joyce at Sylvia Beach's bookstore, a performance of Ezra Pound's opera *The Supper for Mr. and Mrs. Williams,* the Supper where H.D. thought that Flossy was trying to come on like a movie star and didn't really make it. Robert McAlmon writes in his memoir, *Being Geniuses Together* of the Paris bars and cafes enhanced by the company of his lovely friends Mina and Djuna Barnes:

> "Mina Loy and Jane Heap—remember she's the editor—were both talking brilliantly. Mina, her cerebral fantasy, Jane, her breezy traveling salesman of the world tosh, which was impossible to recall later, but neither of these ladies needed to make sense. Conversation is an art with them, something entirely unrelated to sense or reality or logic" (McAlmon).

That's probably after a few... (laughter) Will you pick up the bar tab?

McAlmon publishes Mina Loy in his Contact Edition books, so that's the *Lunar Baedeker*, which is her first book of poetry. But then on the other hand, she's in debt. "I'm supposed to be a fine artist and everybody thinks I'm mad because I have to make lampshades." McAlmon:

> She decided to open a shop off the Champs-Élysées. Mina was known for her beauty and wit. Slightly over cerebral, but she had a distinct talent for inventing fantasies. She made abstract paintings or designs by pasting colored papers of different shapes one upon the other. She transferred archaic pictures and maps upon glass globes and bottles and inserted lights inside them, and marketed these as table lamps. She invented the calla lily lights. Searched antique shops for medieval paintings and etchings, and having done all the work of painting and decorating the interior of her shop, she went into business. Fortunately, she had a degree of commercial success. Lawrence Vail had an exhibition of paintings in Mina's shop, and Isadora Duncan attended it.

This is a story of Isadora at this point:

> Isadora drank copiously of the punch that was furnished and went across the street to drink more at a bistro bar and returned to talk grandly of what paintings she would purchase. As she was then living more or less on charity, nobody took poor Isadora seriously. But the shop prospered. Orders came from England and America. She patented many of her designs. At one time, she employed a dozen French girls, and she worked along with them daily. Lawrence Vail's wife at that time, Peggy Guggenheim, has actually provided financial backing for this business and goes on to arrange exhibits of Mina's paper cutouts and painted flower arrangements in Madison Avenue windows and other fashion stores, including Macy's gallery. (McAlmon).

And [she] has a show of paintings called "Six Jaded Blossoms" so her artistic abilities are extensive.

Her daughter Joella, her oldest daughter, marries Julien Levy, who's a famous, well-known art gallery dealer, and they move to New York City. The lampshade business flounders, she has a fight with Peggy Guggenheim, and her new son-in-law has to help her out. She's publishing at this point in the *Dial Magazine* that Marianne Moore was a part of and *The Little Review*.

But when the twenties ended, Mina Loy kind of faded from public view. She bought an apartment in Paris in the same building as Djuna Barnes and Charles Henri Ford, but her business folds, so she works for her new son-in-law Julian Levy, and he appoints her as his Paris representative, and she does this for the next six years, monitoring the Paris paintings. She sends reports and recommendations to New York, handles commissions and shipments for artists, buys from dealers. It is a total absorption in the business of art. She performs agent functions for Cartier-Bresson, Braque, de Chirico, Salvador Dali, Max Ernst, Juan Gris, Giacometti, Gorky, Magritte, Toulouse-Lautrec, so she's very involved; she picks the paintings and sends them over. Only two poems are published in the thirties, and she writes a book, a novel, called *Insel*, which is going to be published this fall by Black Sparrow Press, which is her great Surrealist novel and a portrait of the German Surrealist Richard Oelze.

Student: What's it called?

Kyger: It's called *Insel*, and it's her great kind of autobiographical, Surrealist, narrative direction.

"Her sense of reality rapidly dematerializing in the face of the artist's chameleon-like ability to transform himself and his past as if it were the flesh and blood embodiment of one of his own surreal canvases"...*Colossus*.

Alright, so she has a show in New York City, and in 1936, she finally leaves Paris and returns to the United States where she lives for the last thirty years of her life. By the first seventeen years after she's back, she lives in Lower Manhattan and the Bowery, first with her daughter Fabi, her daughter by Arthur Cravan, then by herself. She's fifty-three years old at this point when she returns, and her personal history matters less to her. Her contact with friends lessens, and she gradually loses touch with the world she has known, the world of artists and sociability.

> She recedes from the messiness of the life traffic. She largely succeeded in living an unpublic existence and reducing her material claim to zero. Owning things and knowing people mean absolutely nothing. (Kouidis).

This is a very interesting phase that she goes through in her life. Throughout the 1940s, Mina is engaged in a metaphorical quest to find Christ in the Bowery. She actually lives in the Bowery at this point. She records intimate details of derelicts' lives on the Lower East Side. "Hot Cross Bum" is the name of the poem that she does during this time, which is finally printed in the *New Directions 12* in 1950. She meets during this time and becomes friends with Joseph Cornell, and she scavenges back alleys and abandoned lots for trash and assembles montages of street scenes and frames nativities of the Bowery into scenes of the divine grace.

If you look at the last *Lunar Baedeker*—that's the Jargon Press volume in there—there's some pictures of these trash collages, and they're incredibly adroitly done, paper-folded so these little sleeping bums look like crumpled figures, and they're not at all crude even though her materials are from the street. An art reviewer in *Arts Magazine* talks...she has a show in 1959 at the Bodley Gallery:

> Banana peels become licking flames around a trash can out of which rises a butterfly whose wings are a flattened, pleated paper cup and whose body spirals around a used vacuum can key. The common becomes triumphant through a spiritual effort. (*Arts Magazine*).

She has an opening night there in 1959, but she's not present, but artists and poets who have not been seen together for years come out. 1936 she moves to New York City. This is in 1959. This is more than twenty years later. She's been living a relatively unknown life. She's cut out all her social and artistic connections that she had in Paris during those years, and when they had this show in 1959, friends from the past come, which says it was one of the greater reunions of their generation. Marcel Duchamp, Peggy Guggenheim, Max

Ernst, Joseph Cornell, Djuna Barnes, Kay Boyle, but she's not there.

At this point, she's moved to Aspen, Colorado, and she's living near her two daughters, who still live there. Her contact with Aspen when she is there is slight, and she's looked upon by some as a town eccentric, by others as a cultural celebrity. The extravagance of her manners, conversation, and dress are pronounced. She may have begun a series of collages using scrap copper and construction refuse to portray Colorado bums, but reports on what her last experiments in junk actually were vary from witness to witness.

Jonathan Williams of Jargon Press visits her in Aspen and arranges to publish and does publish in 1958, the first *Lunar Baedeker* and *Time-Tables*, which is the first time she's been published since the late '20s. And eleven years later, Paul Blackburn and Robert Vas Dias interview her at her home in Aspen. That's in 1959. It's the only recording of her.

Paul Blackburn and Robert Vas Dias interview her, and that interview is probably with his tapes and interviews in San Diego and is not...Bobbie Louise Hawkins has a copy *somewhere* if she ever figured out how to de-file her filing (laughter). And that's the only recording of her voice, which I think would be intriguing to listen to. I think it would help a lot with some of the reading of her poems too. She dies in 1966 after a short illness. She also during this time... Jonathan Williams visits her. Her spirits are good. He has this kind of grim expression, and she writes back to him and says, "You've got to learn how to grin." And she writes a thing about how to reconstruct your face, so you have a little more pleasant experience on it. She's 84 years old when she dies.

Excerpt from "Letters of the Unliving" by Mina Loy

> Leave me
> my final illiteracy
> of memory's languor—
>
> my preference
> to drift in lenient coma
> an older Ophelia
> on Lethe.

> Mina Loy has always been considered an American Modernist poet, joining America's commitment to the rejuvenation of word and image, the search for new poetic terms derived from modern painting, and to depict the movement of consciousness. She's known for her structural innovations and her sexual subject matter. She analyzes a female self deformed by social morays that limit women to the role of wife and mistress. And her success in the marriage market depended on virginity and sexual ignorance. (Kouidis).

We will look at a piece of hers later. Her later poems are a series of vivid images unified by interplay of sounds, which are her trademark, that unite abstraction and images in flashes of vision. There's a long bibliography of her work. She does have a biographer now—just not a published book yet. Her name is Carolyn Burke. Let's look at page two of her *Lunar Baedeker*.

It's a lot of details about her life and those years would be, you know her biographer would be fond. And the variety of what she does in her life is amazing. Here's her little poem on page two—the Gertrude Stein poem that Lorna was talking about this afternoon:

"Mina Loy" by Gertrude Stein

Curie
of the laboratory
of vocabulary
  she crushed
the tonnage
of consciousness
congealed to phrases
  to extract
a radium of the word

"Brâncuși's Golden Bird" was a poem that was published in *Dial Magazine* along with the first printing of the... It was published along with T.S. Eliot's "The Waste Land." It was a very famous edition of *Dial*. It was a really classic number. A piece that she...I think there might have been a photograph in the magazine.

"Brâncuşi's Golden Bird" by Mina Loy

The toy
become the aesthetic archetype

As if
some patient peasant God
had rubbed and rubbed
the Alpha and Omega
of Form
into a lump of metal

A naked orientation
unwinged unplumed
the ultimate rhythm
has lopped the extremities
of crest and claw
from
the nucleus of flight

The absolute act
of art
conformed
to continent sculpture
—bare as the brow of Osiris—
this breast of revelation

an incandescent curve
licked by chromatic flames
in labyrinths of reflections

This gong
of polished hyperaesthesia
shrills with brass

as the aggressive light
strikes
its significance
The immaculate
conception
of the inaudible bird
occurs
in gorgeous reticence

(*Dial Magazine; The Lost Lunar Baedeker*)

You can see the sound play that goes through reading. It's almost a sound, which I assume that she must have had some kind of British accent if she was raised as such. It would maybe make some of those consonants a little more clipped. I'll let you read the *Lunar Baedeker* for yourself.

The love songs...I'm going to reflect, this was a long series that were variously put together as probably a composite of her various lovers, Marinetti, and husbands.

This is a numbered series; however, the *Lunar Baedeker* that Jonathan Williams published is in a different order. These were published in different places and times. At one point, Jerome Rothenberg talks about in his anthology, saying that if anybody could get these together you would get something comparable to Pound's *Cantos*, so there are thirty-four of these songs, and this particular order is not the one that eventually gets published. They were written from 1915-1917. Number one is one of her more familiar ones that's anthologized of love songs.

"Love Songs I" by Mina Loy

Spawn of fantasies
Sifting the appraisable
Pig Cupid his rosy snout
Rooting erotic garbage
"Once upon a time"
Pulls a weed white star-topped

Among wild oats sown in mucous membrane
I would   an eye in a Bengal light
Eternity in a sky-rocket
Constellations in an ocean
Whose rivers run no fresher
Than a trickle of saliva

These are suspect places

I must live in my lantern
Trimming subliminal flicker
Virginal   to the bellows
Of experience
Colored glass.

(*The Lost Lunar Baedeker,* also titled as "Song to Johannes" in 1923)

That's her later interest in lampshades (laughter).

And I'll let you read these to yourself. Try to see if we can actually talk to Lorine Niedecker her today, but that's going to push us all. "O Marcel—otherwise I Also Have Been to Louise's" is a piece…(audio cuts out)

...overtones of Carl Van Vechten's chattiness. "Yes, have a drink lady, teaspoon by teaspoon. No please take this. Do I..." So she captures—this is one of the only few pieces I know of hers that takes on that rambling monologue, social tone of many voices coming in. I think she does a good job of hitting the tone and the time. Notes on existence called "Ready Mades," which the editor Roger Conover takes pieces of her work. He finds in her writing unpublished pieces and puts them together in an order called "Ready Mades," which was Marcel Duchamp's kind of style of collaging materials. This is what the editor calls...he has some of her cynical and (indistinguishable).

Falling in love is the trick of magnifying one human being to such proportions that all comparisons vanish. Looking for love with all its catastrophes is a less risky experience than finding it. The longer it lasts, so much less can the habit of felicity when termed adrift

> will stand the onslaught of memory. Looking back on my life, I can observe one absolute law of physics that energy is always wasted. (Conover)

You know, she's got this density of intellect and this particular bitterness. The Feminist manifesto written in 1914 to Mabel Dodge, unpublished, has some of those newly harsh senses of oppressed woman that she was looking at. And certainly, she wasn't an oppressed woman at that point, but she does feel like it's down to...at one point she's professional and commercial.

> Woman is the equal of man. Professional and commercial careers are opening up for you. Is that all you want? If you honestly desire to find your level without prejudice, be brave and deny at the outset that pathetic claptrap war cry. Woman is the equal of man, she is not. (*The Lost Lunar Baedeker*)

She starts out with saying the Feminist movement as instituted at present is inadequate. We're looking at 1914. On the next page:

"...to obtain results you must make a sacrifice, and the first and the greatest sacrifice you have to make is of your virtue..." (*The Lost Lunar Baedeker*).

This is a post-Victorian sexual revolution.

> "The fictitious value of a woman is identified with her physical purity is too easy a stand-by. It renders her lethargic, and the acquisition of intrinsic merits of character by which she could obtain a concrete value. Therefore, the first enforced law for the female sex as protection against the manmade boogie of virtue, which is the principal instrument of her subjugation, as the unconditional surgical destruction of virginity throughout the female population at puberty—" extreme means. "The advantages of marriage are too ridiculously ample compared to all other traits. Under modern conditions, a woman can accept preposterously luxurious support from a man without returning anything, even offspring, as an offering of thanks for her virginity" (*The Lost Lunar Baedeker*)

Well, I'll let you read through that yourself. "Woman must destroy in herself the desire to be loved." I mean this is (indistinguishable). You know, and it's not really very workable, frankly, but this is her beginning attempts to take herself away from the bondage that she feels. "In defiance of superstition, I assert there is nothing impure in sex except the mental attitude towards it..." Well of course we've gone through some of that revolution hopefully enough... (audio cuts)

(Light discussion on class assignments.)

Okay, Lorine Niedecker. Lorine Niedecker is compared to some of the other women that we've been reading, is a completely American phenomenon. She doesn't travel in Europe. She doesn't have the worldly sense of what a cafe society is. She's born almost twenty years after some of the women that we've been reading. She's more in line with...she's in this century. She's born in Wisconsin, and she stays there her entire life, visiting New York City a few times. The source for a lot of this...there's not a biography of her work right now. There's one in the workings...I guess today it was mentioned by Michael Heller, by a woman named Glenna Breslin. Those of you who went to Michael Heller's lecture yesterday heard a little comparison of the two women.

The source of this biography is from a book called *Between Your House and Mine*, which is the letters of Lorine Niedecker to Cid Corman. These are ten years of letters. The other great correspondence that she had in her life is with Louis Zukofsky, which was a forty-year correspondence, and these are kind of the source of what her biographical material is about. She was never recognized as a writer where she lived. She lived in a small town. The inevitable comparisons with Emily Dickinson come up.

Lorine Niedecker was born on May 12, 1903. She lived all of her 67 years in Wisconsin, and most of these on Blackhawk Island, near the very small town of Fort Atkinson. It's an island that's surrounded by a river, and in her poems, you see that during the inevitable spring fog there's often a great deal of flooding. Her poetry is all located in the landscape of where she lives on Lake Koshkonong. She spent most of her childhood outdoors among redwing, blackbirds, willows, maples, oaks, fishing. She was the only child of a lovable, but philandering, hard-drinking father and a bitter, taciturn mother, who grew deaf shortly after the birth of her daughter. She went to Fort Atkinson high school and onto Beloit college in Beloit, Wisconsin, and she only stayed for a year.

That's her formal education—high school and a year at Beloit before returning home because of her mother's increasing deafness. Her mother has poor health, and Lorine, the only child, is needed.

Five years later after she's returned home. When she is twenty-five years old, she marries Frank Hartwig, but in two years they permanently separate, and she returns home to her parent's house. Then she gets a job working as a librarian's assistant in Dwight Foster Public Library at Fort Atkinson during the two years of her marriage and begins publishing poetry in little magazines. From her house on Blackhawk Island, she reads Louis Zukofsky's Objectivist issue of poetry in 1931. That was a famous issue that set forth... invented the term Objectivism, and put the writers who were then grouped under that Louis Zukofsky, Carl Rakosi... You know the rest of them. Who are the Objectivists? George Oppen, Basil Bunting...

She reads this issue, and she's absolutely caught by Louis Zukofsky and writes to him, and then ensues a forty-year correspondence. She finds similarities and initiates a correspondence with him. The Objectivist conception of poetry and of the ways a poem works believed in the particulars of a poem. Right here are the writers: Basil Bunting, George Oppen, Carl Rakosi, Charles Reznikoff, and Zukofsky. Lorine considers herself on the periphery, which she is indeed. She makes a few visits to visit Zukofsky in New York where she met the Oppens, Charles Reznikoff, but always returns home to her beloved Blackhawk Island. Her correspondence with Zukofsky is intense, nearly once a week. These are her peers in writing. She's part of no literary social circles. She's very local, but she leaves for four years at one point to Madison, Wisconsin, from 1938 to 1942, where she works as a writer-researcher for the Federal Writers Project, which was a famous Depression writing project. During this time, she also writes radio scripts. The book that was discussed yesterday, edited by George Bertholf (may mean Robert J. Bertholf), which has got some of her radio scripts in the back.

She returns to Blackhawk Island in 1942 and files for divorce from Frank Hartwig. Although, that was back in the early twenties, and what he's been doing all these years—we don't know what he's been doing. Her life story really lies in her poetry and her literary correspondence. By the 1940s, she was really a practicing poet. Her first book *New Goose* was published in 1946 in Prairie City, Illinois, by James Decker Press. Although another book doesn't appear for twenty years, she keeps on publishing in little magazines. She now has her own small house along the banks of the Rock River near her parents' home on the island. She earns a living for a while as a copyreader at Hoard's, publisher of the regionally known Hoard's Dairymen. She does this for six years until poor eyesight makes the work impossible. Six years. Hoard's Dairymen...so she does copyreading for the dairy industry. Her mother dies in 1951, and her father in 1954. He leaves her some land and two houses, and she rents these out over the years. She gets a small but sufficient income, but it's a pretty austere way of life that she has, so she gets during this time another job, which she holds for the next six years, cleaning kitchens and floors. You'll notice that six years. She seems to go in six-year cycles. Very interesting. So she does another job, which she holds for the next six years, cleaning kitchens and floors in a local hospital. When her mother died, her last words to Lorine are: "Wash the floors, Lorine. Wash clothes. Weed."

In 1963, she meets and marries Albert Millen, who has been renting one of her father's cabins while on holiday from his house painting job in Milwaukee, and for both, this is a second marriage. He has a daughter. He has children from a previous marriage. He's one-armed, having lost an arm as a young man in a machine accident.

They move to Milwaukee and use a house on Blackhawk Island on weekends and vacations until they retire there in 1969 six years later. Cid Corman, her other main correspondent in life, visits them there near the end of her life.

> Their tiny place was cozy and good, but they don't quite hit it off. But both had been through enough to give to each other even when impatient. They never could have made it at an earlier age. (Corman)

So this is a marriage of companionship and support. Like her father, Albert Millen was sociable, talkative, and sometimes drunk. Cid Corman sees him as having had a satisfaction in the manly formula. Gentle at heart, but clumsy. Cid Corman sees Lorine as bright and true, incapable of crudity. Others see her as quiet, gentle, unassertive. The marriage gives her a connection to life. Few in her community know she writes, and she has little companionship among the locals. Cid Corman living in Kyoto in the late '50s and '60s is publishing *Origin* magazine from there, featuring the latest, young, contemporary writing and publishes Lorine, bringing her into an awareness of a larger circle of writing.

She's already an established writer, but not very well known. Her correspondence begins with him in 1960 and continues until 1970, a few weeks before her death. Cid and his wife Shizumi come for a first and long-awaited visit on November 15th, and she dies a month and a half later. During this time, he makes a first and only recording of her poetry reading, which is the only one that's available, and I don't know where that is or what she actually sounds like. So the account we have of Lorine's life from 57-67 years is in her letters to Cid Corman. As her friendship with him grew, she became both a model for and a partner in the revitalization of the poetry in the '60s. Her work evolved so far beyond the Objectivist of her own generation that she rightly took her place with the young Gary Snyder, Denise Levertov, and Paul Carroll. It's interesting when she's published in this magazine, which at this point Cid is publishing Denise Levertov, Bob Creeley, Charles Olson, who is older, and Lorine Niedecker. She sends her work to him and is published in '61.

In 1961 when Jonathan Williams visits, she lives in a tiny greenhouse out on Black Hawk Island three miles from town. Right out back is the sparkling Rock River on its way to the lake. No phone, almost no neighbors, the river is a major fact in her life. Lying there sparkling and running, often flooding and worrying the people. He finds her reading some of Lawrence's letters—D.H. Lawrence's letters when he was (indistinguishable). She has a little book cupboard she calls her Immortal Cupboard—Louis Zukofsky, especially the short poems, Emily Dickinson, Thoreau, Lucretius, Marcus Aurelius, John Muir, (indistinguishable), W.C. Williams, and a book on haiku—the place where she keeps her favorite books. The house is small, one and a half rooms, and no indoor plumbing, but then after her marriage, a little, more solid house is built next to it, high on cement above the flood line of three rooms.

She reads Clayton Eshleman, Hamilton Finlay, Allen Ginsberg's poems. "Notably cuddish. It still moves me, but why must the show of vitality come by way of misery, dirt, sexiness?" This is a letter to Cid Corman. "Funny, I can't get the roaring, ranting, filthy, spiritual cuddish out of my mind." She essentially only really reads Zukofsky and some of her contemporaries, so the Cid from Allen Ginsberg takes her into New American Poetry, and she's heavily struck by it. She holds herself back from reading poetry aloud in front of an audience or even taping them. The only recording she makes is one with Cid Corman. She's never seen a cassette tape recorder before.

> I'm not sure my reading would be the best. Although, actually I say my verse to myself a million times. Sometimes whisper it aloud for 'moosic'. (Niedecker)

She's got that kind of Poundian sort of spelling, M-O-O-S-I-C. "What one hears as he reads to himself is the best, probably." So she's into that.

> I thought so much about poems read aloud and poems printed. With me a tendency to greater drama if spoken. To more words, to prose, but of a heightened kind, so compromise. But then you lose a tight, perfect kind of poetry. Poems are for one person to another. (Niedecker)

This is her poetics.

> Spoken thus, or read silently, how would that bird on the branch walking to the end of it, or the raindrop there be read to a hall filled with people? If your ear is acute, you sound your poem in silence. Silence is a wellspring of poetry. (Niedecker).

So she gets herself located down in this inner silence in which she hears her words, and this is how she wants her poems to be received. Basil Bunting comes on a surprise visit with his two daughters one day in July in 1967, and of course, the question came up of reading poems aloud.

> The world—this was in '67—is mad, mad on this subject. Would somebody start meditation rooms, please? Places of silence so silent you couldn't help but hear the sound of your page without opening your mouth. And reading books would come back. (Niedecker).

She writes to Jonathan Williams that the visit is a high point of her later life, so there's a handful of visits, a handful of things that happen to her in terms of what her everyday life is about in the literary world.

Soon after in *Southern Review* she sees an article on Mina Loy, and she says, "I never did know much about her, or see any of her poetry, so one lives and spends one's life not knowing, and then one autumn day one picks up a leaf of a dead poet." And that's her introduction to Mina Loy. She rarely discusses literary theory, much less her own poetic techniques:

> I abhor talking at length about one's own poetry. I write from notes, which seem to always stay notes. Grocery lists. I throw up my arms and scream, 'Write, cut it, and just write poems.' Why not arrest it at moments into quiet enduring love. Also, there is such a thing as silence and the great ever present possibility that our poems may not get read. Art is cooler than you think. (Niedecker).

This is in a letter during her correspondence with Clayton Eshleman, who was publishing in the *Caterpillar* magazine, which publishes her correspondences during the winter of '67 to '68 when a lot of anti-Vietnam War demonstrations were going on. She's aware of this political upheaval going on, because she reads the newspaper. She's kind of looking for a new form, and she expresses this in a letter to Clayton Eshleman. She's going through some intellectual struggle, and Clayton advises her to take 25mg of LSD (laughter). So there's this elderly woman at this point...she finally decides she doesn't really get along with him too well.

Her long-awaited book from Jonathan Williams Jargon Press was published in '69 with her book *My Life by Water* by Fulcrum Press in London. After her death, Jonathan Williams published epitaphs for Lorine, which are written by friends in her memory. I have a copy of it somewhere here. There was...

New Directions editor James Laughlin...she published a letter of her poems in the *New Directions* anthologies.

> She was always a delight to have in *New Directions* anthologies, because she was so completely original. The genuine US article. A person who knew exactly what she wanted to do and continued to do it, I believe, to the day of her death. Had she wished or troubled to play the games of poetry politics, she could probably have ended up as well-known as the ladies who are now wearing the establishment's official laurels. But that just wasn't her way. So it will be up to time to prove her merits, and I have no doubt what the book of judgement will be...Her words are like condensed, concise, clean-cut. Keen attention to nature, holding still to the Objectivist method of thinking with things as they exist. Reflective. The tone of a poem. A heat that is generated and takes in the whole of the poem. A heat. An awareness of everything influencing everything. Her description of the way poems work approximates the spirit of Olson's 'Projective Verse'. (Laughlin)

Early poems just the "folk" —she talks about the folk element "short." She moves later into extended forms and sequences. You can see those in some of her later works. She uses the 3-5 lines and builds up a lot of sequence story. There's no separation between the poem and the experience, and this continuity reflects the Post-Modern development in her poetry. No separation between the poem and the experience: that's the definition of Post-Modern.

She's always very sensitive to the page size, the cadence of speech, and the look of her words. She's content to have more trees for friends than people. The correspondence of Ezra Pound then Louis Zukofsky has a few comments in 1935 from which Louis Zukofsky is writing about Lorine Niedecker to Ezra Pound. Pound replies back, "I don't think your Niedecker is so hot. Thought he was a lady, anyhow. Lorine?" Pound's overtones at times are as dismissive as you could wish for.

And Zukofsky replies...at this point they're having an argument about E.E. Cummings. Pound is putting his money on E.E. Cummings. Zukofsky replies back, "Nor have I swallowed Ms. Niedecker's mental stubbornness; however, her output has some vitality, some spark of energy, which the solipsistic, daze maze of Mr. Cummings hath not."

So she has this differential sort of writing to Zukofsky who is her mentor, and he's sometimes in retrospect a bit dismissive. He does call her the best American poet after Marianne Moore, but the difference between Marianne Moore and Lorine Niedecker is in the fact that Lorine Niedecker is really living her life with her plants and animals in nature, whereas Marianne Moore gets her animals through books and her visits to the zoo. They are more of an intellectual, symbolic reality of animal and plant life, whereas Lorine's life is of the nature that she is living it in this rural place. She never does go to church, but she's very religious in the sense of what her estimation of nature is. She's a believer in the classic Bible.

She says, "Let each man hope and believe what he can."

I'll read one little section about what she's going around with this lady naturalist. The letters that are collected in *Sulfur* Magazine...I don't know what date it is...an excerpt from Zukofsky. Her letters from Zukofsky in this incredible forty-year correspondence are...unfortunately, she edits them. She clips them out and puts them on cardboard pages, and she takes everything that she thinks of as personal kind of out of them. So you have a real... (students indistinguishable) Some of his letters, but also some of her own editing. She just keeps this kind of critical notes intact. It kind of really reduces his letters to shreds. It might have been at his request. I'm not sure.

In 1946, she has this visit with Mrs. Maine, the bird woman. This is her letter writing style:

> Came one day this past week and took me with her down through the woods where we used to live to look at the birds. It was so beautiful. The small trees we left there three years ago already seemed big. The red dogwood and the other kind are so big and luxurious this spring. And now I know what kind of shrubbery I want around my place. Can get some roots from our own land where we now live. While looking at some white gulls along came a daddy long-legs—as her mother calls them the great blue heron they call them daddy long-

> legs—We just gasped. Nice was it again to be close to someone with some kind of enthusiasm, somebody with absolutely no kind of sophistication, or no 'pseudo' or 'super.' She had a little pad and pencil as she's preparing an article on birds at Blackhawk island. When we came to Indian arrowheads beside the path, she'd jot down 'arrowheads.' We saw a Purple Martin feeding its young about two weeks ahead of schedule, but on account of housing shortages they moved in fast and did their stuff I guess. She always had to see the birds to appreciate them, whereas I knew by their sound what they were and knowing what the colors were in my mind was happy enough. I showed her the willows at the point at what would be by August a cucumber. Wild cucumber vines, which would protect the pheasants at hunting season and provide them with seeds. I told her all about the banks swallows settling on the roofs last fall wanting to get inside from the storm. After that a thunder shower, the yellowhead blackbirds come onto the lawns and walk around among the dandelions. Looks like the dandelions were walking. She said, 'That's nice,' and put it down on her little pad (laughter). She'll begin to think I've got some talent with words, though I don't suppose she knows anything about my writing that I do. But I think it's best for her not to know and best for me. She has a lovely literary style: simple and so sincere.

So that's her observations and her connection to what's going on at her own privacy with who is in the village there. She also has a little note about hearing Marianne Moore on the radio and loving her relaxed and genuine style. I guess in those days poets hearing, actually hearing other poets was not so familiar, especially if you were in places where there were not any poetry readings. She says something interesting about Robert Creeley's poems, which she reads in...where does she read them? Louis Zukofsky sends them.

> I like the Robert Creeley poems you sent me. I'd be writing something like that if I weren't so form conscious. A heightened prose with a rather large rhythm, a slightly mystic abstract way of getting reality across. I have to be more concentrated. Though I am beginning to worry about the five-line haiku derived form that dogs me now. Doesn't fit everything. Maybe I'm not object-minded enough, nor minutely eye-seeing enough to fit a symbolism, because you have

> only a few words to use. When I read your—she's talking to Zukofsky—when I read your concise, bare but sharp lions—she says "lions." I think she's really into that kind of ear pun—I think both Creeley and I are on the wrong track, the wrong hill looking out and seeing everything and nothing. (Niedecker)

That's the only connection she makes. Let's go on and look at her work itself.

The more complete biography when it comes out will be something very wonderful to read. Her lines are very well, for me, expressed. It's very paired down, concise form. On page two...Let's look at page three first. That's got on the upper left hand, it's got that poem about her mother dying, which I love:

> Old Mother turns blue and from us,
>   "Don't let my head drop to the earth.
> I'm blind and deaf." Death from the heart,
>   a thimble in her purse.
>
> "It's a long day since last night.
>   Give me space. I need
> floors. Wash the floors, Lorine!—
>   wash clothes! Weed!"

A "Poet's Work", this is directly across from it:

> Grandfather
>   advised me:
>   Learn a trade
>
> I learned
>   to sit at desk
>   and condense
>
> No layoff
>   from this
>   condensery

I think there's a certain ear that if you could hear her, you could get some more of her inner vowel rhymes. The "Nursery Rhyme"...I love these.

As I nurse my pump

The greatest plumber
in all the town
from Montgomery Ward
rode a Cadillac carriage
by marriage
and visited my pump
A sensitive pump
said he
that has at times a proper
balance
of water, air
and poetry

She has to pump her own water all the time, and in the winter time it freezes up. She lives a very simple, kind of pre-cottage existence.

There's another poem,

"To my pres-
sure pump":

I've been free
with less
and clean.
I pumped for principles.

Now I'm jetbound
by faucet shower
heater valve
ring seal service
cost to my little

humming
water
bird

Little humming bird is her pressure pump. In the middle:

"Along the river
wild sunflowers
over my head
the dead
who gave me life
give me this
our relative the air
floods
our rich friend
silt"

And on the next page, there is "Remember my little granite pail."

Remember my little granite pail?
The handle of it was blue.
Think what's got away in my life—
Was enough to carry me thru.

And this beautiful one in the middle, which comes from going to a wedding, a rich wedding in which the bride has got all her silver out. "I rose from marsh mud"... so she's come from her river bank home.

I rose from marsh mud,
algae, equisetum, willows,
sweet green, noisy
birds and frogs

to see her wed in the rich
rich silence of the church,
the little white slave-girl
in her diamond fronds.

In aisle and arch
the satin secret collects.
United for life to serve
silver. Possessed.

Reads another poem:

Old man who seined
to educate his daughter
sees red Mars rise:
    What lies
behind it?
Cold water business
now starred in Fishes
of dipnet shape
    to ache
thru his arms.

A whole series of poems for Paul, who was Cecilia Zukofsky's son, was a famous and well-known concert violinist. "Paul" —and she wrote a series of poems for him:

Paul
    when the leaves

        fall

from their stems

    that lie thick

        on the walk

in the light

of the full note

the moon

playing

to leaves

when they leave

the little

thin things

Paul

Very pared down and concise. Little one...

My friend tree
I sawed you down
but I must attend
an older friend
the sun.

She gets a little light in her house...

The clothesline post is set
yet no totem-carvings distinguish the Niedecker tribe
from the rest; every seventh day they wash:
worship sun; fear rain, their neighbors' eyes;
raise their hands from ground to sky,
and hang or fall by the whiteness of their all.

You are my friend—
you bring me peaches
and the high bush cranberry
you carry

my fishpole
you water my worms
you patch my boot
with your mending kit
nothing in it

but my hand

And this one is at the end of the bibliography...

"That woman!—eyeing houses.
She's moved in on my poor guy.
She held his hand and told him where to sign.
He gives up costs on his tree covered shack—
insurance against wind, fire, falling aircraft, riots—
home itself was our break in the thick.
Because look! how can she keep it?—
to hold a house has to rent it out
and spend her life on the street."

So that kind of meagerness of near poverty life.

Student: Do you have the book with you?

Kyger: I don't have a book with her. There's one of her, *My Life by Water*, is one. Read that one. (Student indistinguishable.) No, I don't have that book. Do you have that book? *My Life by Water* is one of her—the name of one of her books. It's not printed in our little excerpt here. I mean these poems seem very simple at first, but they're so concise and so...stay there so much. There's such weight and substance inside them that their honed down to like bedrock. This is in her three-line couplets:

My life
    by water—
        Hear
spring's

first frog
  or board
out on the cold
  ground
    giving
Muskrats
  gnawing
    doors
to wild green
  arts and letters
    Rabbits
raided
  my lettuce
    One boat
two—
  pointed toward
    my shore
thru birdstart
  wingdrip
    weed-drift
of the soft
  and serious—
    Water

Any questions or discussions? (Student indistinguishable.)

Essentially, she's reading Creeley and saying that she likes Louis Zukofsky better than she likes Creeley, but there's a form of writing that interests her. She doesn't get particularized in that. It's in the letters to him. She'd be writing something like that if she wasn't so form conscious. I think she sees some similarities...although it seems like their form is kind of really similar in a lot of ways. I don't know what period her work was taken right at that point.

Trace

Interlude by Stephanie Michele

What is your secret name?
Can you trace it within the bounds of light?

Only once the cat is asleep by my knee can I contemplate these questions, which press inward on my Third Eye chakra, *Ajna*. An Indigo buzzing. A sporadic delight. Rows and rows of teeth chewing, chewing the process of language and life, and then suddenly, nothing.

Nothing. Nothing.

My mentor Sarah Richards-Graba told me I should track the light. It was the cusp of spring, winter slowly melting into the ground, the snowmelt nourishing the Rocky Mountain rivers. There was a pandemic then, as there is now, as there might still be always.

I noticed how the light swallowed, as any great revolutionary swallows, the tangles of ache. Light has that power.

Mina Loy was as revolutionary as light swallowing tangles of ache. Her work transcends time in its ability to dismantle the expectations of gender, the feminine spirit and her limitations. She nurtured a radically developed seed of intuition, allowing the raw spiral of motherhood, feminism, and the concealed identity of the female body and her public exposure.

In this transcription, Jane Augustine unfolds Loy's life with special care. A true Renaissance of the self, Loy delighted in many pleasures of her time as a playwright, poet, painter, lamp designer, Surrealist experiment, Mother, and Feminist. Sculpting of language-anatomy laid the groundwork for the relational spectrum to our human tongues.

In describing Mina Loy's collection *The Lost Lunar Baedeker,* published in 1923, Augustine details how Mina Loy broke through the conservative, male dominated space of her time. In her recorded history Loy was largely defined by the men around her and reduced to an artifact of her husbands and their fame, existing as a shadow of her true essence in the public eye, instead of the intellectual, sensational embodied presence she was. During her life the work she produced lacked the recognition it deserved.

Her work carves out her lambency. One of her most notable writings was *The Feminist Manifesto* which she crafted as an intellectual dialogue with Filippo Marinetti. This work documents and critically examines the society's view of women in tether to their relationship to motherhood and social expectation. Gravitational pull.

The glow through my window is warm. The lamp by my side has no shade, no covering. Raw light is given the permission to whisk itself hastily across the walls.

The soft fur of my cat's stomach rattles with a quick breath. His secret name crawls from this sound. Small ribs in motion, soundless inhale, soundless exhale. No light.

I met Mina Loy one night while fantasizing about moon phases. Our meshing of creative spirits under the offering of light in the sky. A Surrealist opening, a cave of radiance. Loy's lyric came from this space, like a metal passageway from a celestial body to a pen in a human woman's hand. Moon high, glazed light over a mountain's skin.

How lonesome are the crevices in your cheekbones? Nothing. Nothing.

Aspen, Colorado, is three hours from Denver, my home. Three hours exist between Mina Loy's last day and my current location and the embrace of her legacy. The tangible light between us is dazzling. I feel the purple buzzing of my third eye chakra conjuring the image of the Maroon Bells in summer, covered in a dappling of snow. Sky prohibited by cloud, a secret naming of a sacred reality. Jane Augustine presented her biography in Boulder, Colorado.

A point between us on a map. Scribing and unearthing the cryptonyms.

When reporters first heard of Loy's artistic contributions, they thought she was fictitious. A secret of the moon. A challenge, a brief shimmer of impact.

Humanity has always utilized code, a system of letters or numbers used to substitute, to skew.

What is your secret name? Can you trace it within the bounds of light?

Wide open. Gold flecks clustered of imagination hanging by silk threads. Trace.

Cryptonyms Under the Moon.

Mina Loy: Surrealist, Feminist, Poet, Artist

Jane Augustine
July 7, 1988

Transcription by Stephanie Michele

Jane Augustine: I'm Jane Augustine and my talk has a challenging title, challenging at least to the typist of the schedule. The proper title is *Cryptonyms Under the Moon, Mina Loy: Surrealist, Feminist, Poet, Artist*. She is not French, though she lived in France and was a participant in all the artistic movements of the late teens and twenties and thirties in Paris. My purpose today is to offer an antidote to the large quantities of theory which you have been doused with in the last few days.

I intend to introduce you to a writer who employs Surrealist techniques. My overall idea and message to you is that as writers, you do best to read the poets who labeled themselves Surrealist. Read their work rather than ponder excessively what that label might mean. Let their language and thought get to you. That's a very important part.

Surrealist techniques were used to support a long narrative poem, which is autobiographical. [Her poem] "Anglo-Mongrels and the Rose" is very, very long. I could only give you a chunk of it here. I think it's an extremely remarkable poem, how she is managing to do what she does with a short line and yet explain how she feels and really how she evolved as an artist.

She begins with her earliest impressions, she calls herself "Ova" which means egg of the female, eggs actually. Parodying her own name and in the passage illumination there is a kind of backdrop to *Lunar Baedeker*, which I think is interesting.

Ova is standing
alone in the garden

The high-skies
have come gently upon her
and all their
steadfast light is shining out of her

She is conscious

—Important word, "conscious" —

not through her body   but through space

This saint's prize
this   indissoluble bliss
to be carried like a forgetfulness
        into the long nightmare.

"She is conscious/not through her body but through space," is a kind of statement of the absence of egotism in the work of Mina Loy and the sense in which she wrote the poem about herself, which she puts in the third-person, again a distancing device, but she is conscious. Consciousness being extremely important not through her body but through space and the heavens which comes through *Lunar Baedeker,* but also this is indissoluble bliss, fundamental confidence almost in the Buddhist sense, which she carries into her life.

And paradoxically she calls it "like a forgetfulness" but what it is, is an intense memory. To carry an intense memory like a forgetfulness is to really pull the imagery apart but she has to carry it like a forgetfulness into the long nightmare. This is a strange way to talk about one's life and one's future. But if you are in a nightmare, what you want to do is forget it and return to something else. So, that's illumination. She calls that illumination, it's a mystical moment.

Even though she's a very down to earth person, she actually was a Christian Scientist religiously, but this is a high point of her... a mystical moment in which [she] herself is not present, and in the next contrasting section, she is growing up, and in this, she sees that an egg is smashed, and is disturbed by that.

She is contracting to the enveloping spasm of uneasiness with which she is involved with the big bodies. A little kid sees other people as big bodies. The garden, the child's first place of purity is becoming defiled.

> An egg is smashed
> a horrible
> aborted contour
> a yellow murder
> in a viscus pool
>
> She knows not Time yet
> It lies there
> for a thousand years
> of return   to puzzle
> over a defrauded race of chickens
> pecking the gravel in unconcern

The memory of seeing an egg smashed on the ground smashed on the side-walk...Liz? [calls on audience member].

Liz: I was just going to say the egg smashed is a referent to herself.

Augustine: Obviously it's a much larger metaphor. The egg smashed is everything that is aborted at birth, everything that is lost, everything...and she kind of sees it as a continual image in her eye for destruction, for the loss of the race, for no perpetuation, and it's an extremely painterly image, a yellow, smashed place. That fear of destruction, that hatred of the abortion, the lost race, the lost smashed egg is part of her human sympathy which is another very important aspect of Mina Loy and the one that I would like to stress by the end of this talk. Because Mina Loy came to America and settled in New York on the Bowery and began to look at the bums who live in the most degraded conditions. These are the people whom Harry Smith is recording, night and day, possibly from the same notion that there is some kind of archetypal terror for us as human beings when we see the degraded person and as Mina Loy developed and continued to write, she used her same techniques, short line, alliteration, wild leaps of connection to enlarge her subject matter so that she could write a poem of grief called "The Widow's Jazz" and speak of her husband.

> Cravan
> colossal absentee
> the substitute dark
> rolls to the incandescent memory
>
> of love's survivor
> on this rich suttee
>
> seared by the flames of sounds
> the widowed urn
> holds impotently
> your murdered laughter
>
> Husband
> how secretly you cuckold me with death.
>
> while this cajoling jazz
> blows with its tropic breath
>
> among the echoes of the flesh
> a synthesis
> of racial caress

I think that is an extremely moving poem, and the use to which the Surrealist techniques are put here is quite different from what I have seen before. So, in New York, the two poems, "Chiffon Velours" and "Hot Cross Bum"—"Hot Cross Bum" is also, you can tell there is a pun in the title, because hot cross bun is actually something that you eat, *"Hot Cross Bum"* was sort of inspired by her seeing the bums on the Bowery, sort of going to one of the soup kitchens and being given lots of buns to eat, and so she describes how these people look and "Chiffon Velours" is almost an Imagist poem of a woman lying rigid at rest against the cornerstone of a department store. Hers alone to model / the last creation. [There is] lots of punning on the word creation, creation means the fashionable dress that she's modeling, but she's a model of the last creation, the end, original design of destitution...

[Excerpt from "Chiffon Velours"]

> Clothed in memorial scraps
> skimpy even for a skeleton.
>
> Trimmed with one sudden burst
> of flowery cotton
> half her black skirt
> glows as a soiled mirror;
> reflects the gutter —
> a yard of chiffon velours.

The poem is metaphoric. (audio cuts temporarily) ...is halfway through the door into tomorrow. So, there was a time when Mina Loy was well-known and among artistic circles in New York, and that's no longer the case. I don't know why. In fact, I'm here to redress the balance. This writer is most interesting, she has influenced a number of writers today. Carl Rakosi, the Objectivist, talked to me about Mina Loy the other day. That's a very interesting connection.

Among other things, besides having a love affair with Arthur Craven, with Marinetti, she then met Arthur Craven who was a boxer and he was a Dada performer. He would go into a café and said that he would end his career as a lecturer by committing suicide in public. He announced that he would give his lecture in a jock strap and put his balls on the table. A number of people came to see him commit suicide. He then berated them for wanting to make a social event of death and delivered a dry lecture on Victor Hugo.

This Arthur Craven is a tall, young, clean shaven man who dressed in a torn flannel shirt, red belt, black pants and black pumps, talked, danced and boxed. Before speaking, he fired several pistol shots into the air, then half in jest, half seriously, made the most insane pronouncements against art and life. He praised athletes above artists, he praised homosexuals, by the way André Breton denounced homosexuals and thought that homosexuality had no place in the Surrealist movement, historically.

Arthur Craven praised athletes above artists. He praised homosexuals, those who robbed the Louvre, madmen, etc. He read standing, balancing first on one foot and then on the other, and from time to time he insulted the audience. His listeners seemed enthralled by this bizarre performer, things almost went too far, however, when Mr. Craven threw his briefcase into the audience, only by accident that no one was hit. Some friends of this dancer, boxer, and lecturer put the finishing touches on the evening by dancing, boxing, and declaiming as well. Arthur Craven did these things two years before the café the Cabaret Voltaire opened in Zurich.

He challenged Jack Johnson, the fighter. It was a much-publicized fight. There was a $50,000 prize. The fight went like last week's fight of Tyson versus Spinks [fight of 1998]. Craven was instantly knocked out, and the Barcelona papers took a dim view of it. "After a shameless and unworthy propaganda campaign, the fight, which was billed as 'The Great Johnson-Craven Fight,' which should have been dubbed 'The Great Swindle,' took place. Those who were aware of the shady events in Johnson's life or of his manager's lack of scruples, refuse to attend this event, which from the start, stank of pesetas. Those who knew that the duel with a nobody Craver were not surprised at Sunday's let down."

Arthur Craven and Mina Loy fell in love. She had been married before and had a child. They went from Florence and Paris to Mexico, and she became pregnant with their child. She separated from Arthur Craven in Vera Cruz and took a boat Buenos Aires; they were to meet later. Craven never arrived and nobody knows what became of him. This event devastated Mina Loy. The poem called *Widow's Jazz* is her expression of grief, a rare emotion in terms of Surrealist work and a very powerful one. She returned to Europe; she became increasingly seclusive. Her children grew up; she came to America in the 1930's where she lived on the Bowery and collected junk from the back alley of the lower-East side to make sculptures and art objects.

Even late in her life, as late as 1959, there was a large show in New York of her artwork. She went to live with her daughters in Aspen, Colorado, and died there in 1966. That's briefly who she is and her connection to Surrealism and Dada.

Audience member: The first daughter, Fabi, was from Craven. Where was the second daughter from?

Augustine: No, I'm sorry the first daughter Joella was the daughter of Stephen Haweis, who was an Englishman. Mabel Dodge said he was a very stuffy, repressed sort. There is a photo of him in *The Lost Lunar Baedeker.* The interesting thing about this book is that there aren't many photographs of Loy herself, her art of Craven, of her first husband, Stephen Haweis, whom she divorced in Italy. The marriage kind of dribbled away. Actually, she had two children...she had three children by Stephen Haweis, a son Giles, a daughter Joella, and an infant who died a year after birth, an experience which was absolutely crushing also to Loy, and is a kind of background to her poem, *Parturition,* and important in her art.

She painted a Madonna weeping over a dead infant on the night that her infant daughter died, which was on the eve of her first birthday. The son Giles died in 1923 after the disappearance of Arthur Craven, and after the birth of Fabian Loy, Arthur Craven's daughter in 1919. So actually, motherhood is important in her writing, and she writes a poem about parturition which couldn't possibly have been written by any of the male Surrealists. She incorporates one aspect of Dada, the aspect of radical doubt or she has an ironic, satiric eye continuously, and at the same time she embraces the positive idea. There is a positive idea behind Surrealism which I think I should summarize for you because it might not have come through in all the notions of revolution, that and freedom that Surrealism also espoused.

Surrealism had a positive view that if you liberated the unconscious mind, you would reveal real truth and what actually unifies all human beings. Loy had a profound interest in ordinary people, [like the] Bowery bums. That comes into her later writing, but is a note that she strikes from the beginning. She is like the Surrealists in that she is anti-patriotic, anti-traditionalist, anti-church, anti-sexual repression. I think that the Surrealists once carried a banner somewhere "HANDS OFF LOVE" in other words, don't repress sexual expression, and we will see that that comes into her writing.

Futurism is actually the source of this desire for freedom from the past, freedom from logic, freedom from the mystic ideal. In addition, Futurism celebrated speed and technology, and we'll see in Loy's poems a kind of technological imagery that is very interesting and provides a new note in her poems. Marinetti not only wrote a manifesto against Futurism, but he wrote one against love, against the tyranny of Amoré. "Sentimentality of lechery," he said. Though one observes quite noticeably that he was not free from lechery himself, but anyway. "Sentimental love is an invention of the poets," he said. "It is a romantic voluptuary obsession. It is unnatural."

He said, "There is nothing natural or important except coitus, whose purpose is the futurism of the species." And he even expressed the idea, or the hope, that science would find a way for a man to have a mechanical son by the fruit of pure will. Do away with women, and their wombs all together. Pretty misogynist stuff. I know why Mina Loy's love affair with Marinetti only lasted two months. I'm surprised it lasted that long.

But anyway, the anti-love theme is one that Loy takes up in her poem, "Songs to Joannes" which you have in front of you. Marinetti wrote a denunciation in prose of sentimental love, in effect this poem, "Songs to Joannes" says, *You futurists, you wanna be anti-love? I'll show you how to be anti-love. I'll give you anti-love in a form even you can't stomach.*

Excerpt from "Songs to Joannes":

> Pig Cupid
> His rosy snout
> Rooting erotic garbage

Sit down with Roman Mythology and sweet little Eros. In this poem she says, *You Italians, you're against love, but you don't know how to make love. That's the problem.* So, I'm starting with this poem because of the language and because of it takes the subject that is universal on common place and actually passionate and wonderful and still a source for everyone, rejection and love.

The poem is actually written after her affair with another Futurist whose name was Giovanni Papini which translates into German as Johannes, or Joannes, she disguised his name, it's really for him or after him, and yet it's for everybody who doesn't know how to make love and I mean sex, physical love. This is not a polite poem at all and shocked people because as you will see it refers to premature ejaculation, lovers who are indifferent and in a hurry, and other perennial problems for women.

> Spawn of Fantasies
> Silting the appraisable
> Pig Cupid   his rosy snout
> Rooting erotic garbage
> " Once upon a time "

—That is the cute fairytale, right? Once upon a time there were Romeo and Juliet, once upon a time there were nice people in fairy tales and they marry and get together and love and everything is perfect—

> Pig Cupid   his rosy snout
> Rooting erotic garbage
> " Once upon a time "
> Pulls a weed
> White star-topped
> Among wild oats
> Sown in mucous-membrane.

I don't think anybody would ever use the word *mucus membrane*. Especially referring to female genitals, in a poem before. And I don't think very many people have done it after either. I guess everything has been done. But I gave you the frontest piece to the title page from the magazine *Others*, 1917. I took this text rather than the one from her book because the great problem with this book is the texts are not always correct. Too bad, it is the only collection of Mina Loy we have but it's not quite right, but this is how the magazine *Others*, a radical magazine of 1917, published this poem and we should remember the date. The language is tight and mysterious.

I would
An eye in a Bengal light
Eternity in a skyrocket
Constellations in an ocean
Whose rivers run no fresher
Than a trickle of saliva.

I think that you should have an annotated copy. Nobody knows what a Bengal light is anymore. It's a kind of signal flare. This is actually a technological reference. I think Bengal lights were used on ships or they were set in pots like you see on airport landing strips or on roads being repaired, and so a brilliant blue gas flame. She's saying, *I'd like to see my lover's eyes light up like that.*

Eternity in a skyrocket
Constellations in an ocean

These are wild, Surrealist images for desire, what is wanted in a love affair? What's wanted in love all together? "These are suspect places" you have to figure out what *these* is. The crannies, the physical parts of the body, the desires themselves.

I must live in my lantern
Trimming subliminal flicker
Virginal to the bellows
Of experience
Colored glass

Tremendous associative leaps and yet saying, "My lantern is comparative of a Bengal light," but experience is a bellows and fans the flame of this, this virginal flame of, by the way that's a biblical reference. It's like the wise virgins who keep their oil in their lamps properly and do everything that is right. The bellows of experience blows all that away.

In part two, there references continue to be obscene.

The skin-sack
In which wanton duality
Packed
All the completions
Of my infructuous impulses

Part of the distancing technique and part of the fun and part of the range of Mina Loy's poetry consists of her vocabulary. Infructuous means not fruitful.

Something the shape of a man
[— the phallus—]
to the casual vulgarity of the merely observant
More of a clock-work mechanism
Running down against time
To which I am not paced

My fingertips are numb
From fretting your hair

His timing is not her timing and they're actually making love with the woman under the man. If you've ever done this, visualize yourself working your fingers through his hair. (laughter) My husband is bald, and she makes, "my fingers are *numb* from fretting your hair!" This is just absolutely devastating. I think this is hilarious.

A God's doormat
[—Thick, dark, probably dark, Italian, curly hair.]

A God's doormat
On the threshold of your mind.

For a poet who writes frankly about the physical body and physical love, Mina Loy is very interested in the mind. She actually was extremely intelligent and had a very fine mind and was aware that what is happening in the poetry of her time and the art of her time that effort to break forms is an effort to create a new mind.

That's why she said in the *Aphorisms on Futurisms*, "Today is the crisis in consciousness. Consciousness cannot spontaneously accept or reject new forms, as offered by creative genius, it is the new form." And so, we should see here a new form that is a feminist consciousness as well. That is the difference between Loy and her fellow practitioners.

You had a question? [Inaudible question from the audience pertaining to her reading Russian Futurism.]

I don't think so. I don't know how much was known of Russian Futurism at the time of Italian Futurism. One could say "Down with Love" from a number of points of view, I think that she's working much more profoundly from her own experience, and from her images, come from her consciousness of form and color in painting. Apollinaire was described as a poet founded in painting, poète fondé en peinture. That's very true of Mina Loy. It's very important that she is a mixed-media artist, so she is an exemplar of the mixed-media facet of Surrealism. Which I'm not sure...it has been talked about, Harry Smith mentioned it again last night the Surrealist painters also wrote. Some of them are great like Leonora Carrington, almost had dual careers in writing and painting.

That is not irrelevant. It is important to the way the images work in the poems. Mina Loy's poems can often be seen as Surrealist paintings with a blotch here and a blotch there. Her short line is like a zap of paint flung onto a canvas. At the same time, she is satiric and analytic of social situations, and the social situations of the self-involved men who is not a good lover is very wide spread and probably not yet solved. (laughter) So, why do I say probably?

So part three [of "Songs of Joannes"]:

> We might have coupled
> In the bedridden monopoly of a moment
> Or broken flesh with one another
> At the profane communion table
> Where wine is spillt on promiscuous lips

We might have given birth to a butterfly
With the daily news
Printed in blood on its wings

This kind of poetry defies explanation and... but also ridicules religion, as does the next section.

Once in a mezzanino
The starry ceiling
Vaulted an unimaginable family
Bird-like abortions
With human throats
And Wisdom's eyes
Who wore lamp shade red dresses
And woolen hair

One bore a baby
In a padded porte-enfant
Tied with a sarsenet ribbon
To her goose's wings [— *It's like Mother Goose.]*

But for the abominable shadows
I would have lived
Among their fearful furniture
To teach them to tell me their secrets
Before I guessed
— Sweeping the brood clean out.

I take this to be a statement of anti-family, anti-family ideal in the Italian sense. The Madonna's painted on all those churches. Skip over to section 9 and you'll see more imagery of night and love and an ironical view of it.

When we lifted
Our eyelids on Love
A cosmos
Of coloured voices
And laughing honey

"Coloured voices and laughing honey," is a technique of synesthesia, pulling all the senses together.

And spermatozoa
At the core of Nothing
In the milk of the Moon

Bizarre juxtaposition, it seems to me of semen and milk compared to moonlight. And number 10:

Shuttle-cock and battle-door
A little pink-love
And feathers are strewn

A mockery of, I don't know, quick sex? Yeah. And at the end of section 13:

Is it true
That I have set you apart
Inviolate in an utter crystalization
Of all the jolting of the crowd
Taught me willingly to live to share
[—That's her idealization of him.]

Or are you
Only the other half
Of an ego's necessity
Scourging pride with compassion
To the shallow sound of dissonance
And boom of escaping breath

Contrasting the ideal, a notion she had of her lover and getting the idea that it's just casual. He and she are only together because of ego's necessity. This is actually an analytic poem. Is that 12? Did I misread them? So in section 14, the momentariness of love and the idea of just a moment, "No love or the other thing." The other thing may be lust.

Only the impact of lighted bodies
Knocking sparks off each other
In chaos

There's no hope she thinks for love. It isn't even kind of honest lust; it is just chaos. A few sparks in chaos. Section 29. Actually, I should call your attention to the very end of section 20.

We sidle up
To Nature
— — — that irate pornographist

The whole poem is twenty-six.

Shedding our petty pruderies
From slit eyes
We sidle up
To Nature
that irate pornographist

This poem is developing—besides its critique of physical sex—is developing the idea that nature itself is the problem. The sex war between men and women goes back down to the cells. The next section begins:

Nucleus   Nothing
Inconceivable concept
Insentient repose
The hands of races
Drop off from
Immodifiable plastic

The contents
Of our ephemeral conjunction
In aloofness from Much
Flowed the approachment of — — —
NOTHING

Big capitals. And so, she says, it's really a permanent problem and that is what section 29 is getting at.

> Evolution — fall foul of
> Sexual equality

The problem of making love is a problem between the sexes. And...

> Evolution — fall foul of
> Sexual equality
> Prettily miscalculate
> Similitude
> Unnatural selection
> Breed such sons and daughters
> As shall jibber at each other
> Unintelligible cryptonyms
> Under the moon.
>
> Give them some way of braying brassily
> For caressive calling
> Or to homophonous hiccoughs
> Transpose the laugh
> Let them suppose that tears
> Are snowdrops or molasses
> Or anything
> Then human insufficiencies
> Begging dorsal vertebrae

[skips a stanza of poem]

> Let them clash together
> From their incognitoes
> In seismic orgasm
> For far further
> Differentiation
> Rather than watch
> Own-self distortion
> Wince in the alien ego

She continues with the idea that two egos are completely separate and the last page of this poem the last poem, section 30:

> Crucifixion
> Of an illegal ego's
> Eclosion
> On your equilibrium
> Caryatid of an idea
>
> Crucifixion
> Wracked arms
> Index extremities
> In vacuum
> To the unbroken fall

The crucifixion of ego is what happens when people can't get together. It is an unbroken fall, the quote unquote "fall" of man, of human beings. It is a religious reference.

> The moon is cold
> Joannes
> Where the Mediterranean — — — — —

She can't even go on. She starts another poem.

> The prig of passion — — — —
[—isn't it a terrible thing to be called a prig of passion?]
> To your professional paucity
[—she uses the alliteration ironically.]
> Protoplasm was raving mad
> Evolving us — — —

The idea that the animosity between men and women goes right back to the protoplasm. Nature isn't kind at all, she's an irate pornographifist. The situation is evolving to become worse and worse, most separate. And a one-line finish:

Love — — — the preeminent litterateur

"Litterateur" meaning man of letters, literary creation. I've gone into this in detail, which I will not do with all the others, to show you what she did in turning around a Futurist idea, anti-love, yes, but it means something quite different to her. Of using the short line, broken phrase, ambiguous suggestive image, and in order to express an idea that had not been previously expressed, and it is a woman's point of view, it is a strategy of difference. Though the subject is familiar, the treatment is not, at least not at this time.

Loy was also criticized for not using commas and punctuation. She punctuates with the pause at the end of the line and achieves her results with a very tight line which is different from other Surrealist poets who tend, like Breton's "Free Union," to use a long, flowing line. So, in addition to, it follows logically, that she wasn't so hot on the subject of marriage either. We might take a look at the poem on page 3...

Audience Member: Can I ask a question?

Augustine: Yes.

Audience Member: [off mic, cannot distinguish opening lines.] It doesn't seem like, though she doesn't say it literally, I get the feeling, and I like the feeling that I get about the notion of talking about cells.

Augustine: Scientific imagery, yeah.

Audience Member: And she never actually says anything about the one cell that everything comes from, which would lead one to question was it a feminine cell or a masculine cell? But she talks about nucleus, and that seems to imply one something.

Augustine: The question is really not whether she wanted to make a scientific definition of whether there was an original cell that was male or female; she is implying that the difference between male and female that has all these profound social consequences, and personal and emotional consequences, is so deep that we have to say it's in the protoplasm, it's in the nuclei. So, treat that not as a scientific statement but a poetic statement. The passion she is expressing in quite a tight line is so extreme and that is the only image she could find for it—it has to be cellular. And her mind is combining and her language combines in a very interesting way; the technical, the scientific, the intellectual with the extreme passion of devastated love, "Pig Cupid," and blowing away all that Roman mythology and sentimentality but certainly not blowing it away in the way that Futurists expected. The Futurists, they wanted women to go into politics. Marinetti said women should go into politics, that's fine. The parliamentary system is terrible anyway and if women get into it, they'll really break it down and ruin it. That's the way it ought to be and maybe the family even might be threatened that is really terrible, but we don't want the family threatened, particularly. That's the underlying subtext because marriage serves it purposes.

So in "The Effectual Marriage or the Insipid Narrative of Gina and Miovanni," Loy's discussing marriage, and again she is using extended vocab, unusual words, lots of alliteration, and you can see that Gina and Miovanni is a switch on Mina and Giovanni. Giovanni, besides being the name, John or Johannes also means youth, boy, so it's a generic guy. And these are satires, early, this is 1914 or so…

> The door was an absurd thing
> Yet it was passable
> They quotidienly passed through it
> It was this shape
> Gina and Miovanni   who they were God knows
>
> They were themselves
> Corporeally   transcendentally   consecutively
> conjunctively   and they were quite   complete
>
> *[—She cooks and she's in the kitchen. The third stanza says:]*
> So here we might dispense with her
> Gina being a female
> But she was more than that
> Being an incipience

So it's a devastating idea of what a woman is an incipience, something that is about to happen and this is her view of the Italian housewife. The interesting thing about this to me is that she writes this poem describing some people that she actually saw.

> Ding dong said the bell
> Miovanni Gina called
> Would it be fitting for you to tell
> the time for supper
> Pooh said Miovanni I am
> Outside time and space
>
> Patience said Gina is an attribute
> And she learned at any hour to offer
> The dish appropriately delectable

Obviously, it's sex that's being referred to as well as food. The dish appropriately delectable whenever he wants it. And Loy is making fun of the transcendent notion, the man who says, *I'm outside of time and space, I'm superior to the dinner, but it better be there when I want it. I am superior to my wife.*

> While Miovanni thought alone in the dark
> Gina supposed that peeping she might see
> A round light shining where his mind was

Light and vision are very important in continuing metaphor in Loy and is related to her painterliness. The light is what you want in a painting. So, "A round light shining where his mind was," the light and mind are identical.

> She never opened the door
> Fearing that this might blind her
> Or even
> That she should see Nothing at all
> So while he thought
> She hung out of the window

Watching for falling stars
And when a star fell
She wished that still
Miovanni would love her to-morrow
And as Miovanni
Never gave any heed to the matter
He did

There is more description of the woman in the kitchen.

She was Gina
Gina who lent monogamy
With her fluctuant aspirations
A changeant consistency
Unexpected intangibilities.

Miovanni remained
Monumentally the same
The same Miovanni
If he had become anything else
Gina's world would have been at an end
Gina with no axis to revolve on
Must have dwindled to a full stop

The poem goes on but actually doesn't end. It is broken off and there is just the footnote. "This narrative halted when I learned that the house which inspired it was the home of a mad woman."

Loy could not continue to treat this woman satirically when she discovered she had been driven mad by her circumstances. Romantic poets tended in the past to think about madness as a key to the unconscious as something glamorous but it is not, it is not helpful at all. André Breton's novel, *Nadja* because he was writing about a mad woman and in some way sentimentalizing her situation.

[Inaudible question from audience member.]

Yes, you're pointing out for Breton, Nadja, the woman is the subject of the novel, he is the preeminent Litterateur, man of letters. The woman is the subject of the novel, so as soon as she goes mad and disappears, he is not concerned about her, and that is a very serious problem within this whole period. That glamorization or indifference, treating the woman as an aesthetic object is like Marinetti's saying "Ah, I went to the battle field and saw the sun shining on the blue-black muzzle of the guns. A hundred thousand people writhing in pain and torture seemed trivial by comparison." I'm paraphrasing him, but in fact, he did say that. He aestheticized war and aggression; he made them into literary notions.

Audience Member: Your sense that the poem that she wrote, the anti-love poem, was apropos Marinetti? Ideal velocity?

Augustine: Yes, yes. I should have made clear that the specific occasion of "Songs for Joannes" and that specific name came after the collapse of her affair with Papini whose name was Giovanni, Joannes. John. But I think she was certainly touching on a larger subject than the failure of her affair with Marinetti and others possibly. She had a number of other lovers. Led to a meditation, satiric and observant, but also felt and internalized, and certainly a comment on the Futurist's general involvement with speed and technology. But they also were involved with flight, and took all of those things metaphorically, but the trouble with the Joannes is obviously he's in too much of a hurry.

And as you may know, that is a very bad thing in making love. And we are talking about physical love, you can't be in too much of a hurry to fall in love—psychologically, spiritually—that can happen instantaneously if you're lucky that will happen to you, but all the more reason then that you should take as much time as you possibly can to make love physically.

(Inaudible comment from Anne Waldman about gender repression. This grows into a conversation.)

Augustine: I think that is very clearly implied in this poem and that there is a clear connection with…

Waldman: Also, that time women were actually more repressed, enslaved.

Augustine: More repressed, more enslaved.

Waldman: There are statistics...

Augustine: More prone to madness. Therefore, the person who is in a mental hospital is more likely to be a woman and...

Mary: Well, and it was a way to incarcerate women who actually were not mad but...

Augustine: That further...Mary, thank you very much. Mary has pointed out that the incarceration of women in mental hospitals has always been a device to get rid of some women whose behavior is particularly unpleasing to the dominate people around her, and so there has actually been great abuse of putting people...Well, yes, Martha Mitchell and others that are mentioned in Phyllis Chesler's book of about fifteen years ago, *Women in Madness* actually offers the statistics. That's still an ongoing problem. What is rather normal rather and sane and possibly entertaining in a man is viewed as quite problematic in a woman. So, I suppose that's a way of saying that sometimes the male Surrealists got away with stuff that women might not have gotten away with.

(Audience question, indecipherable.) As I said in the very beginning, I'm calling her Surrealist because of what I see that she does in her poems and because she lived in this Surrealist milieu and was in communication with Stein. She didn't belong to the club, but she had what one might call a kind of ambivalent position because she was very beautiful and talked Surrealist, actually. She was sought after at parties and yet she herself was very private and I think that she drew back from becoming anybody's gorgeous muse. At the time that her poems were beginning to be published, I think it was Americans who were beginning to get the taste of Europe between the wars who first began to appreciate her poetry.

One of the scholars who has dealt a great deal with Mina Loy, Virginia Kouidis, says that Loy is really an America. She was not born in America but she copped to America. She liked America. She liked Broadway, New York. She liked Gertrude Stein. She liked Stein. Stein liked her. When Loy was criticized for not using commas, Stein said, "I understand perfectly well, you don't need commas. The sentence structure works in itself. Commas are not necessary." Some critics of the time actually did criticize Loy for not using commas, possibly they didn't even understand, but also using subject matter that was not quite right. Her denunciation, attack on sentimentality is also important in the poem *Lunar Baedeker.* Which is the title of the first book that was published, collection of her poems was called *Lunar Baedeker.*

And so, the final collection is called *The Lost Lunar Baedeker.* It is the opening poem. A Baedeker is a guide book. If you go to Europe nowadays you probably get, in Paris perhaps, a Micheline guide, or a guide bleu, blue guidebook. It is a small closely printed kind of thing you could put in your pocket and you could open it up and get a lot of information about the church on the corner and history of the artist and the works in it, so a Baedeker is a detailed guidebook. They were called Baedekers because the first compiler of such a guidebook was a German named Baedeker, and Baedekers were issued for all countries, you could get one for Switzerland, Italy, France, and so on. Just to juxtapose a brand name it is like throwing Campbells soup, like talking about Frigidaire's or Pepsi, Rand McNally. So it's a big contrast in the tone, *Lunar* the moon, that's an elegant Latinate word for talking about the moon and *Baedeker* is a brand name for a guide book. This [juxtaposition] also shocked people.

A silver Lucifer
serves
cocaine in cornucopia

To some somnambulists
of adolescent thighs
draped
in satirical draperies

Peris in livery

prepare
Lethe
for posthumous parvenues

I don't think this was an actual description of taking cocaine. It's a view of the moon and the sky which leads one into moon madness.

Delirious Avenues
lit
with the chandelier souls
of infusoria
from Pharoah's tombstones

"Infusoria" are tiny, microscopic creatures. Possibly the stars in the skies around the moon.

lead
to mercurial doomsdays
Odious oasis
in furrowed phosphorous

the eye-white sky-light
white-light district
of lunar lusts

Stellectric signs

"Stellectric" is a coinage. It is another thing she liked to used. Stella being the Latin word for star, the stars are electric. Stellectric.

"Wing shows on Starway"
"Zodiac carrousel"

This is very far flung, wild view of the moon, the stars, the heavens what they might actually mean.

Cyclones
of ecstatic dust
and ashes whirl
crusaders
from hallucinatory citadels
of shattered glass
into evacuate craters

A flock of dreams
browse on Necropolis

Very free associations with the moon and the sky.

From the shores
of oval oceans
in the oxidized Orient

Onyx-eyed Odalisques
and ornithologists
observe
the flight
of Eros obsolete

The musicality just goes off into a kind of wild view of "Onyx-eyed Odalisques and ornithologists" for all those O's, for the sound—

And "Immortality"
mildews ...
in the museums of the moon

Eros is obsolete, that theme and the idea of immortality is an old idea that mildews.

Nocturnal cyclops

—*One eye*

Crystal concubine

Pocked with personification
the fossil virgin of the skies
waxes and wanes

A commentary on romantic poetry and poets and their notions that the moon is a woman—she does or is this or that. She's pocked with personification. She has craters and things; she's been so literary that you're sick of it. She's cold and hard, the fossil virgin of the skies. There seems to be a very far-flung undercurrent of the wild imagination as the possible close to hallucination and moon madness, but this is a completely new look at the moon, and it's partly to contradict this dramatic idea of personification. Yes? Tell me your question.

Tim: (partially inaudible) This does seem to have a surreal quality. It is subtle but seems very unusual.

Augustine: I think this is wilder than a lot of Surrealist poems. This defies for me, transliteration. This is a poem that can't be paraphrased. Yes, it builds I think you're describing as a building or a focus is really how it works as a poem in poetic unity. I think you will find that many of the official Surrealists, though the Breton "Free Union" poem dribbles away. But in Éluard I think you find more. I don't know whether I care much if it gets categorized as Surrealist as long as you can see that it has qualities of wild imagination that you can use to focus on whatever you want to focus on. It's true that Loy has an element of satire, irony, social commentary that is not typical of later Surrealist poetry. But in terms of imagery and euphony and word play, I think that it shares a lot of common ground with Surrealists. You know, absolute Surrealism doesn't exist; it's an idea.

It is a term that we use. What I'm trying to get people to do is to look at and understand a woman writing in that milieu, in that context. Who has actually ideas of her own and they are anti-sentimental, anti-women's role, insisting that the moon has to be looked at freshly not pocked with personification, and yet I think this is a beautiful evocation of the moon and at the same time recognizing it is not the great symbol of love or immortality, all those ideas are gone. It is the white light district or lunar lust with the starry skies. The stars are "stellectric signs" that flash like somebody starring on Broadway, like a billboard of lights. The "zodiac carousel," that stars wheeling through there, the zodiac, but she sort of shouts those on the page like billboards, like signs, like technological phenomena. Or a fireworks show.

If you look up on a very clear night in Boulder, the stars cover the heavens. It is like all those sparks that we saw falling a few nights ago on the Fourth of July. One characteristic of women writing in this period all together, Modernist women, H.D. and others, is an anti-war attitude, particularly. I'd like you to look at the poem called "Der Blinde Junge." Because we see the Surrealist techniques put in an entirely different context. The wild associations are linked to an object scene. "Der Blinde Junge" means the blind young man, and it's in German, used for deliberate reasons. She sees a war veteran on the streets of Vienna and it starts out:

> The dam Bellona
> littered
> her eyeless offspring
> Kreigsopfer
> upon the pavements of Vienna

One way to expand your language is to have lots of words from different languages and this one gets in a Latin goddess, and a vulgar image of animals dropping their litter, and the German word and offering to war which refers to ancient sacrifice all in five short lines. The "dam," "dam" in this case is not something that holds water back. This is a mother of animals. But "Bellona" is the goddess of war, the equivalent of Mars, and "littered" means to drop a litter of small things, kids. So, the image is that on the streets of Vienna there are wounded war veterans and, in this case, a young soldier who has been blinded. The metaphor of blindness is that he also cannot see anything spiritually.

> this slow blind face
> pushing
> its virginal nonentity
> against the light

Virginal you can tell is a bad word for Mina Loy, and in the *Feminist Manifesto* she says that the purity of young girls, their virginity, has become a saleable commodity and in order to do away with that there should be a surgical divestment of every woman's virginity at the age of fourteen. Everyone should be surgically deflowered that would mean that you could not buy a virgin wife in the vulgar way that the commodification of women has always taken place. Last night there was a lot of talk about the commodification of the marvelous, or the commodification of the surreal, as the images were co-opted. No one talked seriously about the commodification of women as muses, as helpers. All that commodification is based on the notion that it is somehow better to possess a woman who is a virgin than to have someone who has been sexually involved with someone else, and that is the basis of property.

Actually, it was an ancient idea that a man had to marry a virgin so he was sure that the children were his and that the people who would inherit his property they were actually his flesh and blood and not somebody else's. Worship of the sperm is a secret and hidden religion which I'm afraid still exists.

There is a special sensitivity, however, on the part of women writing between the wars and in the generation that was born just before the turn of the century that lived through two wars. A particular sensitivity to war. It took interesting forms. Gertrude Stein spent a great deal of time during both wars driving ambulances, and the elegant parties in her salon held for artists and intellectuals like Picasso, Matisse, and all the Paris intellectuals who came were open at all times to veterans and soldiers who had known her as an ambulance driver during the war. That's very remarkable to me.

And so, the anti-war strain is important and has not really been investigated in that period between the two world wars. But this poem of Mina Loy's I find very powerful because she sees the blind veteran not only as the object of pity but as the object of terror. His face is a "virginal nonentity."

> Pure purposeless eremite
> of centripetal sentience

A hermit without purpose. His sentience, what he senses, is centripetal sentience, comes inside. You know centripetal is a technical movement for what whirls down in and centers on itself. Centrifuge, centrifugal is the motion that throws objects out. A centrifuge is actually a mechanical device for doing that. His sentience is all centered in himself.

> Upon the carnose horologe of the ego

— "Carnose" is the French word for clock. The clock of the ego.

> the vibrant tendon index moves not
>
> since the black lightning desecrated
> the retinal altar

A very terrific way to talk about someone being blinded. For Loy, sight and vision being extremely important and as an altar that is desecrated when someone is blinded.

> Void and extinct.
> this planet of the soul
> strains from the craving throat
> in static flight upslanting
> A downy youth's snout
> nozzling the sun
> drowned in dumbfounded instinct

Return of the animal imagery here, he doesn't have a nose he has a snout and he nuzzles the sun. He turns his face up to the sun, but it's like a creature, a pig or puppy, nuzzling its mother.

Listen!
illuminati of the coloured earth
How this expressionless "thing"
blows out damnation and concussive dark

Upon a mouth-organ

Notice that this is listed as an early poem. This is a poem that sees both wars coming, and expresses this extremely strong language, concussive and dark. The Surrealist techniques are here, but they are not at all light hearted. They are overwhelmingly dark and hurt. These are poems of act of protest and in that way, I think, are certainly in the Surrealist spirit. So we have the *Lunar Baedeker* against the romantic moon, the blind young man poem as an anti-war poem, the effectual marriage poem as an anti-marriage poem. "Songs to Joannes" is not so much an anti-love poem as an anti-bad sex poem, and so there is the theme which we can find, which is in this poem, the blind young man, and it is in the technique in "Songs to Joannes," and the sense of the woman's identity is concealed, hidden, lost, uncertain. Loy doesn't bring herself into her poems usually and the exception to that is "Anglo Mongrels and the Rose."

(Audio cuts out temporarily.)

Near death, one of those terrible old bag ladies that one sees in the streets of New York, nevertheless she has decorated her skirt. There is one flash, there is one hope, which is ironic or sad, but I think in Loy's eyes, admirable. And in the same way she has a double vision of the "Hot Crossed Bum."

Across a hell-vermillion
curtain of neon
lies the Bowery

a lurid lane
leading misfortune's monsters

the human...race
altered to irrhythmic stagger

Okay. "Race" is working both ways, as a noun, the human race, and as race, the verb. It's the way they work; they run to.

> along the alcoholic's
> exit to Ecstasia
>
> impersonal as wind astray
> confluent tides of swarm
> loiter
> in non-resistance calm
> through dialatory
> night and day
>
> crowds of the choicelessly corrupted
> disoriented
>
> the Bowery's sanctuary's
> invasion by the vanquished

[—a paradox]

> ...in lazy anguish

Masquerade of Inexpressionism

> inideate *[—that's coinage also, lacking ideas]* shutter
> halting the bon-fore of the soul
> from kindling eyes

There is still some faith, there is a bonfire in the soul, but the light can't reach the eyes. So, eyes, light, are the signals to consciousness, to elevated consciousness, to some new consciousness, and Loy's never sure whether that's going to be defeated or not. She uses the Surrealist techniques to present something that is a commentary on society and a hope for it, that not everyone will have to go on in complete non-communication, and yet finally, the only thing that saves this view of the world is the kind of language which is brilliant and strange and fresh and musical to describe what philosophically might be considered a pretty hopeless situation.

Actually, I wanted to end with a return to the idea of the cryptonym:

> Unnatural selection
> Breed such sons and daughters
> As shall jibber at each other
> Unintelligible cryptonyms
> Under the moon.

Do you think that people, do you think that you have a secret name that you can't tell to anyone?

Do you think that conversation with someone of the opposite sex is an attempt to tell your name, your secret name, which you can't tell? Anne says yes; Mary says yes. That's a way to open questions on Loy and commentary all together. Judy, what would you like to say?

Judy: I was just wondering, what seems to be an example of the particular phenomenon of women not being able to divorce their life, their art and their live, not being able to abstract human experience and turn it into a material of something? That seems to be something men can do.

Augustine: Judy thinks that Loy is an example of a woman writer having or being unable to divorce her life, the inability as positive, inability to divorce life and art. That she is turning her life into art in a particular way which is a contrast to what the men are doing sometimes. That is an interesting comment. Anyone else want to say something about that?

Audience member: Which men are these?

Augustine: Which men are these? It is probably hard to make such a generalization. The question is what kind of...I'm trying to make you conscious of the fact that there is a strategy by which a writer converts his or her experience, and that in the case of the poems I've shown you here is a strategy based on gender differences. That is not the only reason for a strategy or the only way it works. Liz?

Liz: Well there is Virginia Woolf's discussion of how women would draw upon their own experience and would write about their own experience because that was what they knew. An example of this is in *Pride and Prejudice*, this writing in the home.

Augustine: Yes, that is a kind of tradition or necessity that women writers have always drawn on their experience which is often circumscribed domestic experience because that is what they have lived in and that makes for a different kind of art. Virginia Woolf argued and it's still being argued, is such a thing as a woman's sentence? Is there such a thing as a woman's poetic line? Well, I don't think so but I think that the...

Bobbie-Louise Hawkins: Take someone like Edith Warton, who was certainly circumscribed, whose language, if one...I mean, you could take a passage out of Edith Warton and have absolutely no idea if it is a man or a woman. An incredible clarity of mind is apparently a human condition, and not sexed.

Augustine: I would say that I agree with you that the clarity of Mina Loy is not sexed. I think there is extreme clarity here that the short line commands the writer to find the right word, and it strips away what is blurry or unclear and when the right word doesn't exist, Loy is glad to invent it. The urge to compression seems to be Loy's own. There is no way to generalize from it. In some way, I don't want people to generalize from it. My purpose is still to introduce you to a writer who you can respond to, I hope like and understand, someone who hasn't been included as much as she should be in official histories and artistic movements in that period. Yes?

Audience member: Can we return to the question of can men and women talk to each other and express this secret name. For myself I think that to use the word man is too inclusive. I try to discover how many different languages I can understand.

Augustine: That is interesting. I think that I hit on the notion of secret names because of, and it is the relation of many languages, and you should have as many as possible and we should discuss what languages means, vocabularies for experience. The notion of a name, naming and the power to name one's experience has been much discussed among women writers because to give a name to something is to endow it with power. To have a name is to have power. To have the capacity to name your experience accurately is to have poetic magical incantatory power. That is why I wanted to leave you with the question which is implicit in Loy's passage. When you are talking to someone are you gibbering cryptonyms? Are you trying to say your secret name when you can't? Are you saying it when it can't be heard? Is that a situation in our present communicative life that we ought to pay attention to? Sometimes I think so. Sometimes I think I am gibbering cryptonyms. I am trying to say my secret name and it is not getting through. I do not; I'm willing to take that on myself as a possibly my private problem, but I have a hunch there is something larger involved.

Hawkins: That means you're up against an insensitive person. Whomever, male or female.

Augustine: Bobbie is as down to earth and as practical as Mina Loy. If you're talking to someone who can't hear you, get to someone...you sound like you're gibbering, get to someone who can hear you.

Speak your name, let your cryptonym be no longer crypto.

Arroyo del Alma

Interlude by A.M.B. Brennan

When considering how to write this introduction, the styles and structures available have been as myriad as the paths between trees along a creek, the branches overlapping and falling to change the landscape. Perhaps speaking to the historical elements of Heller's lecture, I could tell you that Marianne Moore was alive from 1887-1972 and that Lorine Niedecker was born in 1903 and lived most of her life in Southern Wisconsin until her death in 1970. Or, instead, how Heller describes Moore's and Niedecker's poetics relative to "gestures, movements, whatever else we might get into a poem... a more dynamic word, 'psyche'," with juxtapositions, interruptions, expressions formed from the strictures of history, cultural environs, natural environments, and the literary landscape of masculine Objectivist and Imagist evolution. I might describe how I listened and transcribed this piece within the solitary reaches, smoothed environs of the nocturnal world; handwriting words moved from object, tangible physicality, signifying word, spoken, remembered back to the page again, thought embodied, encircled, enlisted in list form as qualities of generative tactility. There is the question of whether the mythos surrounding the Greek Psyche, a butterfly with many metaphysical qualities alluded to in this lecture, has been inadvertently co-opted and rendered somewhat ironic; something which has remained curious to me every time I hear this name—Psyche as woman objectified? Psyche as made object into woman? and worse, are crystallized objects of the human soul rendered feminine become divorced from their name to describe this process of female poetics in a masculine voice?

These paths feel as blindingly apparent and immediately elusive, deer trails leading down to the water, tracks into deep burrows of small rustling rodents. Even now, I think of the landscape where family has grown and cared for the trees and the animals encompassed by a legality enforced still by pieces of paper agreeing that it is decreed and contracted to be this way.

These words are physical, or they are related to the physical, and they form one iteration or another into a topography that we navigate which erodes or collects sediment of human lives. Layli Long Soldier, in a 2018 interview about her debut *Whereas*, explained, "Language is a very physical thing. It affects you. We don't always remember that." Uprisings are formed of language, meanings manifest in actions, and it is through language, poems and the shapeshifting, revolutionary, new ideas which have so easily transitioned to the ancillary digital landscape we additionally live within, which might be our further undoing or the bridge to growth and healing. There is the land that we encounter, the land that we have created in overlay, boundaries and water rights that must be followed, because the water is allotted in this way—but the waters run down mountain, and in the spring it is understood your rights include the awareness that you really should stay away from that creek bank because the torrent will carry a body hundreds of miles away without question. Language echoes spring melt; poetics defines existence, and repression in culture, history blindly and subjectively reducing 'language' awash in a flood of 'fake news' and propagandic media stirring unrest. An awareness of a sequence coming to a head, where language and the power thereof is being discussed and judged. In 2020, this function of poetry has become potent and essential with the impacts of social and medical traumas and movements. We need to look clearly, each at our individual worlds, how our repressed and subjective topographies overwhelm the objective vantages of our landscapes and chart the course of the physical expression of our human condition.

In February 2020, poet and memoirist Safiya Sinclair was asked about the prominence of poets "at the forefront of political conversations, speaking for/about the people, inciting change and revolution." She said, "For me, poetry is quite visible and also indivisible from my understanding of natural, socio-economic, and geopolitical systems. Poetry by its nature shapeshifts and evolves like wildfire, pioneering ideas, revolutions, and language, and I think it is innately suited for digital formats, where it has been thriving much in the same way it thrived on paper, and the way it thrived before paper. Poetry, which began with singing, and existed before the novel or the essay, will continue to outlive us." We require this shapeshifting now, as well as the scientific processes and tools available to us as users of a language in constant flux, which is either hyper- or hypo- analyzed to frame certain politics as correct, factionalize and radicalize the social and thereby physical, landscape. A foray into isolated contemplation of the landscape might reveal in riddling contradictions new meaning to the words and deeds catered and presented to us. Poetry as wildfire, sounding different every time new sparks catch, leaves go up in sheets of heat and light, a sound that drowns the senses while familiarity is stripped away and something new emerges. Poetry, as language, is a force of nature.

To return to Heller's investigations of Niedecker and Moore, perhaps the approach of scientific condensation in their poetry is enough to serve as a template of sorts; one method of recontextualizing subconscious revelations into realized knowledge, changed states of being—as drastic as if we walked out of civilization and heard again the sound of leaves falling, the slither of snakes through the brush. The crystallizations of self-effacing observation, and transmutation of the natural and perceptive intuitions of these women in their times, are as movements in isolation that might aid a writer now in considering the intent and purpose of poetry. Heller has here condensed the works of Niedecker and Moore within a function of poetic expressions of the psyche through isolation and scientific inquiry being made in some manner tangible. Speaking on Niedecker externally to this talk, Michael Heller has observed that "[Niedecker's] gift . . . has been the courage to breach her reticence, to speak simply and accurately as few poets do today. Thus despite their often bitter quality, these poems are peculiarly consoling to the reader, for they offer, above all, the comfort of substance, of authentic possession." We require this authentic possession. It grounds us, reminds us of proportion.

So—how close does the psyche come to the natural force of these tellurian poetics? In McGovern's introduction to Jane Augustine on Form and Function, the embrace of traversing through "the threshold of body where it originates and into the world" resonates with Heller's observation of the raw, compressed analysis, constellated history and animal reaction which reveal a self-making and unmaking, the birth and shaping of poetic identity through the works of Moore and Niedecker. From these bitter consolations, as Heller describes these poems, is "the making of tradition" (Heller). Within the lecture, Heller describes Moore's poem 'about the sea,' and specifically how a line which is "based on an actual event when a man stood between Moore and her mother, blocking their view of the sea, is also a struggle over modes of interpretation. In this case, the making of tradition." This line struck me in context of both the week's focus on "Gender, Sexuality, and Marginalization," and how peculiar it is to have so many layers between myself, and ultimately, Moore's sea—ocean obscured by man, transferred to paper by a woman, contextualized and interpreted by a man, heard by a woman. I wonder anyway what Moore would have made of this concrete remainder, or Niedecker. What dynamics precipitate through language to be understood through scientific accuracy? Experienced through poetry, that "something known, that is experienced, but yet unknowable," repressed environs are revealed, and we see our individual profiles contoured in the gathered particulates. Sift through the sediments of sentiment left behind; is the shape of that "experience of the solidity of the vision of the mind which composed it" still evident?

Objectified Psyche

Michael Heller
July 18, 1991

Transcription by A.M.B. Brennan

Emcee: This is Michael Heller. Michael's latest book of poetry is *In The Builded Place* by Coffee House Press, 1989; it's in the bookstore. Also, he's published three other books of poetry, *Knowledge, Figures of Speaking and Accidental Center.* His poetry and criticism have appeared in *Harper's Magazine, the Paris Review, The Nation* and *The New York Times Book Review,* and one book that I'm particularly fond of is *Conviction's Net of Branches.* It won him the Di Castagnola Award from the Poetry Society of America and it's a wonderful critical look at the Objectivists. Michael Heller.

Michael Heller: Thank you, Rebecca. I'm always astonished to be at Naropa, and of course I'm especially astonished this week—Gender, Sexuality, Marginalization, all important topics. It's a delight and a surprise to be here.

Anyway, I hope the title of the talk is not misleading to you. "The Objectified Psyche," is actually a discussion of Marianne Moore and Lorine Niedecker. However, last night I suddenly got this flash that I hadn't really gotten into that particular term. So, in the wee hours, I scribbled out a bit of a coda to this paper, so I have, in effect, a paper and a coda to read to you, and then I hope we'll have some time for questions.

In speaking about these poets, I take a direction implicit in Wallace Stevens's comment, with respect to the poetry of Marianne Moore, that "the function of poetry is precisely this contact with reality as it impinges upon us from outside. The sense that we can touch, and feel a solid reality which does not wholly dissolve itself into the conceptions of our own minds."

This impingement, this solid reality is what I wish to suggest by the term "Objectified Psyche." That is, we can come away from a poem with an experience of the solidity of the vision of the mind which composed it, because in some sense, the unity of the poem expresses this solidity as an otherness. As a not-Ourselves. Moore, in writing about Emily Dickinson's work, referred to her poetry as "a notable secret." The poem was something known, that is, experienced, but yet unknowable.

If we concur, that both Niedecker's and Moore's poems are important as poetry, Stevens' formulation, as precise and useful today as it was forty years ago, obtrudes radically into any attempt to reduce or define these poets to some ideological spectrum of activity.

My method here will be to see what the notable secret, the residue of their poetry suggests. That is, rather than examine it from the point of view of conceptions or social conditions, some of which are feminist, if you like, I'll try to explore in what way the poetry presents itself as exemplary writing, as tutelary movement of consciousness. I want to chart in Niedecker and Moore a movement out from the various forms of their poesis, of their making-poems.

If from that activity certain ideological or political conclusions can be drawn, well and good, and I will try briefly to allude to them. My argument will move from how these poets work outward to the value such work has in terms of writing, a focus in keeping with this audience of writers, and possibly in its instruction to the writer's self.

My own faith in writing is in its open-endedness in the self-contract of writing, the possibilities of self-making or unmaking, in the dialectical relation of a work to a life or circumstance. Writing says nothing is foreclosed; writing and our reading of writers offers one unique discovery, for me. The promise of a consciousness's empowerment. So if we are concerned with strategies, for unraveling riddles, (that's Rachel Blau DuPlessis's term in her very interesting, new book, *The Pink Guitar: Writing as Feminist Practice,* which I urge everyone to read), if we are concerned with the riddles of psycho-sexual or cultural entrapment surely, we are also concerned with how one transforms the givens or mythologies of a culture into instruction. Both of these poets point by their praxis through and beyond the analysis of culture, to an unfinishable calculus of writing, which in the end, is one of culture's hopes.

Niedecker, who named this hope for herself as "reflectivism" and Moore's remark to Elizabeth Bishop that "a thing—a poem should make one feel after reading it that one's life has been altered or added to" propose the parameters I want to deal with here.

I begin with a sense of austerity, austerity as a kind of heroism. Part of the effect of the poetry of both these poets on its readers comes from a rigorous sense of stricture each has imposed on their poetics. In Moore's case this sense of stricture, an often-remarked scientific feel to the work, has been an explicit rejection of emotional sprawl. The poems exhibit, as Marilyn Brownstein suggests in her book, *The Gender of Modernism*, a constant tension between manners and their lack.

Niedecker, too, as evidenced in all her poetry and in her commentary in letters favors reticence over emotionalism. One thinks of a guiding notion of decorum; but if such exists either in Niedecker or Moore, it is by no means a conventional decorum. For both Moore and Niedecker, their borrowings or wrenching of texts, their modernist collaging of all sorts of material, constitutes an indecorous break with the linear patterning of history, with the inherited gestalts of imposing totality.

Such eruptive gestures are especially radical in Moore, whose juxtapositions articulate, as Pound does in the *Cantos*, something previously unsaid in the juncture between things. She'll offer one piece of information, another piece of information, and of course, it's their interplay that is most interesting to us.

Niedecker's borrowings, equally various, while mostly from male models, constitute as well a pantheon of—I'm going to use the word "doubled" in parentheses here—identifications. A longing on her part it seems for the autonomy and freedom which the male figure, poet, scientist, philosopher, has to pursue questions of meaning.

At the same time, Niedecker's technique of condensation, a paring away of what is not contingent to the structure of the poem, engenders a radicality of its own, one which is constantly searching for some sort of metaphysical high ground beyond the solipsism of the self or the self as victim. In Niedecker as in Moore, the impulse to condense, to be rigorous, can be likened to the scientist's quest for an efficient or necessary, if non-personal explanation.

Niedecker's way of planting her poems, as she puts it, "in deep silence," proposes a contemplative distancing activity, a form of isolation or separating out, similar to the scientist's experimental set-up. For both poets, the imposition of limitedness not only surrounds the poetic act but becomes the working dimension of being; a way not of inventing counter-roles against traditions but of out-foxing both the need for either role or counter-role.

In saying that, I just want to remind people that, of course, these poets are writing before a feminist movement exists, a feminist structure of criticism exists, and so they're more or less an example in my mind of, you know, Sartre's famous remark about genius, that it is, that it's a way out in desperate situations, and in this case, it's a very remarkable way out.

Now Moore's poetic disposition, the quiddity of her aesthetic concerns, is almost always toward the act of composition. At the same time, she is keenly aware of the existing state of affairs with respect to herself as a woman and as a writer. Moore clearly understood this distinction sociologically as it applied to her, in her refusal to play culture's assigned role or rebel by acting out its antithesis. Writing, for example, to Bishop about the double standards of her male colleagues, such as Williams and Cummings, she remarked, "They feel that they are avoiding a duty if they balk at anything like unprudishness. But I say to them, I can't care about all things equally. I have a major effect to produce. And the heroisms of abstinence are as great as the heroisms of courage, and so are the rewards."

Moore allows no one's expectations to interfere with her vision. Earlier in that same letter to Bishop she identifies her own heroic quest for poetry beyond other people's expectations, as a poetry in which there are significant values; one in which there is an essential baldness either of statement or effect.

Moore's poetry:

From almost the beginning of her career, two particular motions seem to describe Moore's poetics. I want to locate these in a number of poems to indicate how the poetic process in Moore is a move toward objectifying the psyche, of giving weight and materiality to a mode of relating to the world. The first of these, the more common of the two, I would call the motion of transposition; the act of recontextualizing or decontextualizing the materials of the poem. In effect, the poet making a new composition wrenches materials out of context or re-forms them, so they may fit into the composition she is making. The new context alters this meaning as well. Her model could be the German painter Dürer, mentioned in one of her earliest poems "The Steeple Jack," who, "emulating the seas different guises, according to the light and surroundings, changed the pine green of the tyrol to peacock blue and guinea gray." This modality is part of something in the modernist atmosphere in which Moore finds herself at the beginning of her writing career. This modality can be related to the culture's major assault on authority, on forms of what we call hypotaxis, that is, a kind of hierarchical ordering and a favoring of—I don't know if you've had any of this in any of your talks, a sort of paratactical thing, like Pound does, laying one, image, one time, one place, beside another and so on—this was the major thrust of his post-imagist practice, of the *Cantos*. We could relate this to Gertrude Stein's methods of composition as well; we could even relate it to the theory of relativity, for that matter, which debunked hierarchal-hierarchical orderings in classical science in favor of relative and local measurements.

At the same time as Jeredith, Merrin has pointed out, with respect to Moore's poem about the sea, "A Grave," there is in Moore an ambivalence, an ongoing opposition and revisioning of both the romantic and modernist traditions, the male dominated poetic legacy. Merrin discusses this in full, providing an interesting reading of the poem in terms of specific romantic identifications of woman with nature, the sea, fear by males of engulfment by female energies, or by women's presumed merciless, if unchecked, volition. Here I touch only on the symbolical working out of the conflict over tradition embedded in the poem. That is, I'm reading the poem metaphorically as a cautionary tale of the poets' relation—women poets' relation, if you like—to a cumulative tradition, resonant in the male, master metaphor of the all-encompassing sea, as grave to humankind, to tradition, and to history.

The first few lines of the poem read: "Man, looking into the sea,/taking the view from those who have as much right to it as you have to it yourself."

The announced struggle over a marine prospect, based on an actual event when a man stood between Moore and her mother, blocking their view of the sea, is also a struggle over modes of interpretation. In this case, the making of tradition. Vantage point, with respect to landscape or experience, is the determinant of articulation, and the battle over seeing is also the battle over saying.

Moore, who now and then treats the sea as beneficence itself, makes it in this poem something like the great abyss of history, from which traditions arise, then die, are threatened and overwhelmed. Moore ambivalently delineates this grave of poetic modalities. I quote from the poem, "The sea is a collector; quick to return a rapacious look./There are others beside you who have worn that look—/whose expression is no longer a protest. The fish no longer investigate them,/for their bones have not lasted:/men lower nets unconscious of the fact that they are desecrating a grave..."

The pronoun 'men,' by the way, in that last line was once originally 'people'; Moore went ahead and changed it to 'men' perhaps with an attempt to kind of sharpen or emphasize her point here.

Moore makes note of the tug-of-war in the predatory moves, 'men lower nets,' one makes toward tradition. To use or transcend the tradition, to seek with a rapacious look, is also to be aware of tradition's capacity to subvert and submerge, to co-opt. Anything less than this alertness, she warns, is to mistake the sea as if it were not that "ocean in which dropped things are bound to sink." As well, in this same Western tradition, the sea is feminine because of its identification with nature and with otherness. In that sense, the last line of the poem with its visions of things immersed in that sea, "turning and twisting neither with volition nor consciousness"—the way that line makes things clear, particularly to the woman writer, it is that this tradition, perhaps, all one has, threatens her also with oblivion. Moore's poem, then, a text simultaneously inscribed inside and outside the poetic legacy given to her, is meant to ironize her own desire to both dwell in, and to escape from its confines.

The other motion profoundly characteristic of Moore's work, and her thought is signaled in her poem "The Hero." I hesitate to talk too much about this poem since one of the best interpreters of this poem I've read, is in the room, Alicia Ostriker. She's given a very interesting reading of this poem in terms of the hero as having maternal qualities and notions of leniency not the usual male notion of 'the plunging ahead hero oblivious to things.' I'm going to deal with the hero here somewhat more traditionally, and that is, that heroism is a certain kind of self-denial, an abstaining from certain forms in order that a self-transcending goal can be achieved. The perspective of the hero as hero is always towards that goal, away from creaturely comforts and habits, from the self's acquisitiveness. An almost egoless condition, as Moore writes it out, beyond wanting, where "hope is not hope until all ground for hope has vanished." The poetic task as Moore sees it can be likened to this heroic act. A shearing away from subjectivity, from personal or even bodily needs, toward forms independent of personality. The gesture is in consonance with Imagist and Objectivist practice, in the sense that the work of art, the poem, or whatever, achieves a self-sufficiency apart from the author. "It's not what I eat that is/my natural meat,/says the hero./He's not out/seeing a sight but the rock/crystal thing to see—the startling El Greco/brimming with inner light—that/covets nothing that it has to let go!"

Humility before the matter of the poem, the refusal of the self-regarding demonstration; here, they're all functional poetics in Moore, somewhat at odds with her reputed shyness, or humbleness. This is made much clearer, I think, in the violence of a poem such as "Those Various Scalpels," a poem which can be correlated with both "The Steeple Jack" and "The Hero," as meditations on the artist's role with respect to tradition, and as an expression of that ambivalence similar to that found in "A Grave." The poem's first line fuses itself with the second line of the poem, so that we get "those various scalpels," "those various sounds consistently indistinct," and so on—'cutting tool' and 'cutting word' here seem to get juxtaposed. Certainly, a feminist reading of this poem with its couplings of scalpels and scimitars, with neo-baroque images of women throughout the poem—these are taken from other poetries. In fact, as I was reading this again I was reminded of, one of the most ambivalent images of women in poetry, which is Pater's paragraph on the Mona Lisa. These suggest a very ambiguous reading of literary inheritance. That inheritance as used by women must indeed cut both ways. The poem asks, are these images the defining and imposed image hoard the poet must work with? Are they weapons or scalpels "whetted to brilliance/by the hard majesty of that sophistication which is superior to opportunity"?

These things, Moore, says, are "rich instruments with which to experiment./ But why dissect destiny with instruments/more highly specialized than components of destiny itself?"

It's a tremendous irony in this—in these lines—which skillfully, to me, register the spiky terror attendant on an oppositional poetics. The heroics of cutting through the culture at the same time one is using the very instruments the culture has handed you. This ultimately requires, as Moore wrote of H.D.'s work, "a life denuded of subterfuge, the clean violence of truth."

How, given Moore's collaging poetics, could the clean violence of truth be realized?

"The Jerboa," a more typical poem of Moore's in some respects, shows intimations of her strategy, of her poetics. The poem is in two sections; one subtitled "Too Much," the other "Abundance." This contrast, by itself, is very instructive, the question being: what do we usually contrast with too much? Often, we say "enough." Moore's word "abundance" is significant, because it doesn't signal a poetics of poverty, of minimally reaching a standard, but instead indicates that objectivity might well produce greater richness of effect, a more penetrating look into, as she wrote above, "the rock crystal thing to see." The poem, though it overtly dwells on the desert jerboa, is a powerful demonstration of Moore's modernist poetics integrating her objectivist mode to the collage or montage, principle. In the poem, the "Too Much" section recapitulates the Roman Empire's conquests as a complex display of art, power, cruelty and conquest. Images of luxuriousness and extravagance are subtly, disturbingly yoked to the Roman Imperium. Let me read from this poem. I just want to read, more or less, the way—you're following Moore's poetry.

This is the beginning of the "Too Much" section.

"A Roman had an/artist, a freedman—" already you hear the word freedman and immediately what? A little... "freedman"... juxtaposed in this passage with slaves and so on; I'm just trying to get at the dynamics of this. Let me read further:

A Roman had an
artist, a freedman,
contrive a cone—pine cone
or fir cone—with holes for a fountain. Placed on
  the prison of St. Angelo, this cone
  of the Pompeys, which is known

now as the Pope's, passed
for art. A huge cast
bronze, dwarfing the peacock
statue, in the garden of the Vatican,
  it looks like a work of art made to give
  to a Pompey, or native

of Thebes. Others could
build, and understand
making colossi, and
how to use slaves, and keep crocodiles...

You see, I mean—the way that line about "a freedman" gets in there, sort of disturbing the simple message, the simple description of Roman Art. That disturbance then reinforced by the phrase "how to use slaves," the works of art compromised in the Roman system of oppression and slavery.

Mastery of nature, the Roman art most often displayed in this poem, is imitation. Let me just read one more passage here...just to give you a little sense of this.

Dwarfs here and there, lent
to an evident
poetry of frog grays,
duck-egg greens, and eggplant-blues, a fantasy

and a verisimilitude that were
right to those with, everywhere,

power over the poor.

"Everywhere, power over the poor." So you get that... that uncomfortable zippy zap... again in that last line of the passage.

Then, introduced as ironic contrast to the pomp and cruelty of Rome, is the jerboa, a small desert rat, a not-famous mythical animal, that lives without water. A number of elements are at work in this juxtaposition. First, there is the near-scientific principle by which Moore seeks for a relationship between form and function as a moral category. The anthropomorphized jerboa, who has happiness, "o rest and joy," and yet who lives in a cascade of absences, "no water, no palm trees, no ivory bed, tiny cactuses. But one would not be he,/who has nothing but plenty." The jerboa embodies for Moore the integration of form-function values. As depicted in the poem, "The Jerboa" is the moral spring of an attitude toward life, at odds with the malicious artificiality and plenty of corrupt Rome.

The "Abundance" section develops further this theme, positing the sparseness and uncluttered quality of the desert, the habitat of the jerboa, as the place of the imagination.

Abundance

Africanus meant
the conqueror sent
from Rome. It should mean the
untouched. The sand-browned jumping rat—freeborn;
and
the blacks, that choice race, with an elegance
ignored by one's ignorance.

Part terrestrial,
and part celestial,
Jacob saw, cudgels staff

in claw hand—steps of air and air angels; his
  friends were the stones. The translucent mistake
  of the desert does not make

hardship for one who
can rest, and then do
the opposite—launching
as if on wings, from its match-thin hind legs, in
  daytime or at night; with a tail as a weight,
  undulated out by speed, straight.

Here, the Jacob figure, as poet, envisions steps of air and air angels as friends with the stones. The desert, the open unconditioned ground, is enabling, a "translucent mistake which does not make/for hardship for one who can rest and then do the opposite."

The remainder of the section is a highly nuanced mimetic description of the jerboa; the concept of which moves between the poet's rendering and the poet's identification with the jerboa as symbolic artist. I'm quoting, "the Jerboa/honors the sand by assuming its color;/and in emulation of a composer, makes art of its own movements./By fifths and sevenths,/in leaps of two lines,/like the uneven notes of the Bedouin flute, it stops its gleaming/on little wheel casters and makes ferns seed/footprints in kangaroo speed."

The solid reality of the poem, the subtlety of its juxtapositions which is the enabling matter for the reader, is both comically and ethically apposite. Moore's radical poetic scalpel, excising the traditional, linear unfolding of history, and its corollary which is appropriate proportion, places side by side the miniscule jerboa and the Roman Empire. The critique is both social and moral. The artistic consciousness of Rome, mastery, imitative power, is contrasted with modernist sensibility searching for values in what will suffice.

These values are found or encountered dialectically, as oppositions between the overdetermined products of Rome, and the unprepared for intrusions, via Moore's reading in natural science, of the order, natural order as represented by the jerboa. Moore's language rather than mediating reality, attempts a return to physical relation. Moore writes in the manner of science but with a sense that the relation involved is a matter of language, a way of reaching objects not as physical entities, but as related or emblematic to a state of mind.

Let's consider this process of emblematizing further:

In considering Moore's menagerie of animals, we remind ourselves that these are products of her readings, they're not observed, they're not in the wilds, in the zoos, but they're mainly brought to her through texts and accompanying pictures. Thus, as Charles Molesworth has pointed out, they are already halfway toward being emblems, whose function—I don't know if you know much about the emblem, but to use a short cut, it is a figure that is both instructive and poetic at the same time.

In this respect, let's consider Moore's "The Pangolin." As with the jerboa, the pangolin in Moore's poem by that name is meant to provide an occasion for meditation on other things, among them grace, solitude, vulnerability, and artistic precision. As with the poeticized jerboa, a spiritual quest is under consideration. The textual representation of the pangolin in Moore's poetry, from its armor, to its fragile grace and ability to roll himself into a ball that has power to defy all effort to unroll it, constitutes a use of language both in agreement and at odds, with other Modernist uses such as found in Pound's Imagist "Do's and Don't's." That is, Moore's written out pangolin both is and is not the adequate symbol Pound sought in natural imagery. This is just another example to me of Moore going her own way. I don't know if you know this, but at one point, Pound wrote to Moore in one of his letters—"Obviously, your work stems from my work"—I'm quoting this very imprecisely—she just simply said, "Uh, no, no I'm sorry, it's not that way at all." And of course, this was just not some idle thing. She said this in the face of Pound accepting some of her work for publication.

Moore's lapse in this case from this new tradition comes out of her need to provide an exactness to the reader. In this she is closer to very deliberate artists such as Flaubert or Valèry—something decidedly un-American—than to Pound or Whitman. Within this intentionality, the emblem as a method of objectification serves her very well. For the emblem is always more and less than objectification. The emblematic designation in the medieval picture books stands for or projects qualities, the English lion rampant as courage, for example. In terms of the work emblems are meant to do, they provide Moore with a method that makes a bridge from psyche to expression, while at the same time bypassing anything overtly autobiographical or personal, anything which could register as "protest, or personal grievance."

Now, the emblem is almost always a simplified picture of an animal. The artist's purpose being not to accurately represent the beast, but to instill its particular virtue in the beholder. We get some idea of this from the poem. You can see certain analogues to Moore's poetics here, starting with the word "Pangolins, made/for moving quietly also are models of exactness,/on four legs; on hind feet plantigrade,/with certain postures of a man. Beneath sun and moon,/man." And then—then she kind of switches, and the poem is suddenly about man and beast as well. (I'm hurrying along here, a bit, because we haven't hit Niedecker yet.)

Molesworth, in his discussion of Moore's poem, notices that she carries the mode further, using the word "gryphons"—it's down here, a word deeply rooted in the medieval with respect not to the pangolin but to man, the self, the being we call human, writing master to this world. Moore's emblematizing expresses both the heraldic and hybrid—and in this case the hybrid is at least partially man and beast, and this is yet another strategy in Moore's repertoire for linking the aesthetic with the ethical.

The highly detailed portraiture, while maintaining that emblematizing function, rescues the particular out of which modernist universals arise without loss of the rich ambiguity of detail, so she's kind of having it both ways with that. Her objectifications, then, constitute neither a fictive nor a representative world, nor do they provide an objective co-relative expressive of her subjective state. Rather, their exemplary purpose, shrouded by the wealth of detail into riddle and ambiguity is meant to resolve the moral gesture with the artistic gesture.

Niedecker. There is an end to this talk!

Niedecker, in one of her letters to Cid Corman described herself as a "weak sister" of Marianne Moore. Like many of Moore's reading sources, her masters and influences were meditative men and women; Jefferson, Darwin, William Morris, the botanist Asa Gray, and more contemporary strategists of poetic silences, such as Cid Corman, Basil Bunting and her mentor, poet Louis Zukofsky.

From these latter, she learned to use contemplation and the absence of noise not as a defense against the world, nor as a form of withdrawal, but as a compositional element, a way of forcing the reader's attention toward the precision and subtlety of her verse. Trees, flowers, birds—in particular, those of her native Wisconsin—are among her favorite subjects, partly because they embody these qualities of growth and development which occur without auditory fanfare.

An implied poetics, remarkably similar to Moore's, can be read in her earliest poems. One of the most well-known is the poem below:

> There's a better shine
> on the pendulum
> than is on my hair
> and many times
>
> I've seen it there.

The poem is open to a number of readings. One possibility, as I've discussed in my own book on the Objectivists, is to see how the pause before the poem's last line holds two contradictory feelings: love of beauty and jealousy, in suspension, sort of allowing for the emotional fullness of both to be reached.

Another perspective, not contradictory at all, I think, suggests a kind of transference, a projection of meaning by Niedecker from herself to otherness, and this is a disposition found particularly in the early poems. They have all these vocabularies of endearment with natural objects, "friend tree," "older friend sun," "our relative the sun," "my pets the grasses," "our rich friend silt."

Powerful emotion for Niedecker is resident, for example, in objects, such as the "Little Granite Pail," or, "In Pa's Spitbox"—I don't know if you know that poem, but in it she wants this spitbox taken out of the house after her father's died and put in a museum, safely away from her, because it contains such power, negative power for her in some way.

In other poems, Niedecker's ambivalent relation with neighbors, "the folk from whom all poetry flows, and much worse," suggests yet another motive for the constant recurrence to natural things as poetic source.

The aim constantly in Niedecker is to disabuse herself of the sin of self-regard by maintaining an open, embracing attitude toward the world.

This is part of the Objectivist honor code, where external things seem to have more objective truth value than internal things. As with Moore's constant collaging of her readings into poems, Niedecker's poetry, as Corman pointed out, appropriates voices more than history. She favors the individual account over history's tendency to drown out the single voice; but even more what she loves about the historical figures who populate her poems, is how silence both enshrouds and energizes their perceptions. She cites Audubon, writing home from England to his wife, "Dear Lucy, the servants here move quick and quiet"—pardon me— "Move quiet as kildeer." She writes about Jefferson who hoped to establish an absolute power of silence over himself.

This silence provides one more dimension to Niedecker's contemplative figures. With them, as with Moore, she is part of a tradition in which the scientist, for example, masters phenomena by observation. But in Niedecker's poetry, close observation and silence moves the contemplated object from the controlling discourse of science and history into a realm approaching the spiritual and the mystical, a realm in which mastery of the object has been lost because it has instead become the focus for intense, nearly uncontrollable feelings.

Again, this is—to me, this is a radical variant from the usual scientific approach, the hinted at 'science of Objectivist poetics.' Niedecker's intense condensations to proto-scientific first causes, then, are constant calls to put her entire life into question. Stevens' impingements from outside, his sense of poetry as 'solid reality' transformed into uncertainty.

I'm going to move on, for purposes of speed here. I want to just focus, briefly, in closing, on the later poems of Niedecker, where I think interest in the future will focus on her work. These are her master poems to us.

Let me look at "Lake Superior" where the themes of this mystical so-called relationship with the world, or spiritual relation—perhaps a much better term—are announced right in the first few lines.

> In every part of every living thing,
> is stuff that once was rock.
>
> In blood, the minerals
> of the rock.

In these dense compactions of noun and verb, one of the poem's major figures, the priest-explorer, Marquette is seen as having,

> grazed
> azoic rock, hornblende granite
> basalt the common dark
> in all the Earth

Notice how "common," the word "common," there, rhymes semantically with stuff that once was rock in every part and so on. As in Moore, Niedecker's language of science is made to perform visionary duty. In fact, it prefigures the poet's own mimetic act:

> Ruby of corundum
> lapis lazuli
> from changing limestone
> glow-apricot red-brown
> carnelian sard
>
> Greek named
> Exodus-antique
> kicked up in America's
> Northwest

you have been in my mind
between my toes
agate

The absence of punctuation, a very common device in Niedecker, creates a verbal enjambment, a concatenation of material signs which compress identity between the head, mind, and toes.

"The stuff that once was rock" is now suffused with personhood, as sensation, physical object, historical idea, linguistic pun, and by virtue of a sense of closure, as poem. Niedecker's noun packed lines, as with Moore's near-seamless collage of her readings, are only partly in the service of rendering a physical object out there. Rather, they represent a fairly complex and contradictory state of feelings. Rooted though they are in Imagist practice, they more closely approach the spiritual iconography of H.D.'s early poems, such as 'Sea-garden,' with its mystic projections of the world of classical Greece."

In Niedecker's poem "Paean to Place," autobiography is constructed as a series of analogues to the rural lakeshore area where she grew up. Her mother's life and hers are both:

born
in swale and swamp and sworn
to water

the father,
...netted
loneliness

Geography, the natural world and its inhabitants are self-signatures for Niedecker, as in one of her most beautiful and telling passages:

...the solitary plover
a pencil
for a wing-bone
From the secret notes
I must tilt

upon the pressure
execute and adjust
    In us sea-air rhythm
"We live by the urgent wave
of the verse"

It strikes me that Niedecker here realizes that her poetics, her executions and adjustments, are dependent on the very pressures in both joy and pain which constitute her life, but that it is only in the totality of the environment in which those pressures occur that she can find the language to render them. The psyche is large, encompassing, and in the deepest sense, there nothing to escape. The urge to make poetry, the poesis of sea air rhythm, objectify the marks of her pencil wing.

In her last long lines, the material of her life, much of it as with Moore, in the form of close readings, come back to her as though constituting a sacred text.

Looking over this work, we can see that her formula is at one with Moore's usage in "The Jerboa" and "The Pangolin," the objectified psyche is self-scripted; marked, as in her Darwin poem, as

...holy
slowly
mulled over
matter

It is in this earned effacement of the late work, then, that Niedecker, as with Moore, comes as close as possible to a completely integrated psychic objectification, to a remarkable indivisibility between word, representation, and poet. That's my talk, thank you.

(Applause.)

I have a little coda, if I just can have a few minutes. Because I thought I was leaving something out. Let me just tell you a little bit of a story how the title to the talk came about. When Anne [Waldman] spoke to me about lecturing on Moore and Niedecker, she said, "Can you give me something over the phone for the catalogue?" I had just been reading Montale's little book, which I recommend, called *The Poet in the World.* In it, he talks about the Objectivist poem, the Modernist poem as the objectification of thought, and I said, hm, that sounds, pretty good to me, but I wanted a stronger word than "thought," because I wanted to also include not just thoughts, but poetic gestures, movements, whatever else we might get into a poem, and so what struck me as a more dynamic word, "psyche." I wanted to include those strategies and resistances in my talk. And then when I was at home last night, I said to myself, I really should say something a little more about this objectified psyche, because it is something I've thought about, it's something that is a subtext of my Objectivist book, for instance; and so I began thinking of a crude metaphor or model...not for real, not something you're going to take home and bank, but perhaps just something to reflect upon a little bit. And, that was the psycho-analytical or psychological model of the psyche.

Again this is something you can use or just throw away, to imagine the psyche as a show or display of the mind in terms of word and deed. In the subjective or perhaps troubled psyche, it is undergirded by repressed or unarticulated areas of psychic life, buried memories, traumas, fears, so on. This I would call a subjectified psyche; it's a psyche that's still attached to things it cannot itself see or articulate or understand. The subjectified psyche, the kind of response we have to it when we run into ourselves or into a highly crazy or very neurotic person, is a confusion and we're not quite sure what it is—this is the psyche we individually experience in ourselves.

The objectified psyche, on the other hand, is one in which its motions, its operations, its word, and deed are clear to itself and hence to us. The objectified psyche, we feel more comfortable with, at least in terms of knowing it. So I do a segway, from person to poem, saying that certain poems might represent this objectified psyche, because we feel this completeness about them once we look at them and examine them and study.

And by the way, there is a continuous tradition throughout the history of poetics of identifying poems with people, with psyche, and so on, I don't know, going all the way back from early Greeks on up. Anyway, this objectified psyche is something we are drawn to, we may even be made uncomfortable by, because it is like a person, that is, we may care deeply about it or hate it, but there's always something mysterious about it as well. And so, I would suggest in my own reading of poems that, I experience this objectified psyche, as a reader, in three ways, sometimes all together, or maybe just partially.

One...it reminds me when I encounter this, as I do in the works of the two poets I've talked about today, of my own aloneness or solitude. Because it's Other. It's definitely Other. And in this sense, it's very creative. It has a moment of, or a distance, of self-realization to it. Because it's a gap you have to cross somehow. You're not with it, in a way you are normally with yourself. And so we make discoveries that way.

Second of all, the poem will tell you something you didn't know, it doesn't necessarily mean information, but it could be stylistically—it will—the one thing it won't be is a demonstration of what you already know, because that's already redundant to you. It's too comfortable. So the objectified poem successfully for yourself, and I'm talking about an individual take on a poem here, will not have that redundancy. (Remember William Carlos Williams' famous remark that, "a poem is a machine," and he said that's because it doesn't have any redundant parts to it.)

Finally, this...objectified psyche may possibly transport you; that is, it will put you into a state you had previously not been in—hatred, love, ecstasy, or that state we often use by the word "sublime" and so on, and so it is mysterious, in that sense. For me, these are the serious tests of a poem. For myself. And of course this brings us back directly to the very beginning of the talk, into what Stevens said, which I will quote again and leave you with, and that is that "the function of poetry is that, as it impinges upon us from outside, it gives us that sense that we can touch and feel a solid reality, which does not wholly dissolve itself into the conceptions of our own mind."

Thank you.

(Applause.)

If there are questions, I have been asked to please say, you must use the microphone or you are lost to posterity. We have time for a few if there are any.

By the way, the books—Marianne Moore, two books of Niedecker's, *The Granite Pail*, very good selection, *From This Condensary*, a troubled full collection, and I mean very difficult to read, if you're very interested in Moore, one of the little bibles I got is this book which just came out, *Marianne Moore: Woman and Poet* from National Poetry Foundation; and the book which invented my thinking was, and I urge every poet to read this, Wallace Stevens, *The Necessary Angel*, probably the most elegant essays on poetry written in our time almost.

Questions?

Audience Member 1: Very simple question

Heller: Yeah?

Audience Member 1: Is there any move to do a better edition of Niedecker's complete works?

Heller: Well, there has been talk about it, yes there is. Because everybody is so infuriated with this one.

[Different audience member speaks inaudibly.]

Jane Augustine: Okay, I have another. *From This Condensary*, is complete, and those of you who are interested in Niedecker should have it and read it, it is all that we have.

But there are editorial difficulties in it: no dates, strange notes, hard to work with. Strange repetitions of poems that she revised. Don't let this worry you, read her for true content. The book that Mike has just showed you, *Marianne Moore: Women and Poet*, is one of a series, put out by the National Poetry Foundation, at the University of Maine at Orono. Jenny Penberthy, an excellent critic and commentator will be editing for the same people, *Lorine Niedecker: Woman and Poet*, which will contain an account of the difficulties that present the reader of *From This Condensary*, other problems, in relating to Niedecker's habit of revising many, many poems. It will also have essays in it by me and other women interested in Niedecker, and I think a version of the talk you have just heard by Mike Heller. So, read *From This Condensary*, for content, and write letters to Jenny Penberthy in Vancouver if you need—or to me—if you need help to follow up on precise dates and publishing history. We hope eventually that some of these mistakes will be cleared up. It seems that there was hasty editing in an effort to get the collection present to the public, so. We've fallen between two difficulties there. But. Read on.

Heller: Chuck?

Chuck: What else would you recommend reading on Niedecker? Any other articles, or studies or anything?

Heller: Well, there's an issue of *Truck* if you can get hold of it, old issue of *Truck*—There isn't really very much. Glenna Breslin in CA is doing a biography of her, isn't she?

Audience Member: Yes.

Heller: Yes, and there are things scattered around but I think a great many of them will be collected in this *Women and Poet* book.

Jane Augustine: I was just going to say, there are also her letters to Cid Corman.

Heller: Yes, her letters are out.

Jane Augustine: And forty pages of her letters to Zukofsky in *Sulfur 16* I think.

Heller: Yes... And these are— the letters that Duke-published, Lisa Faranda, are interesting in some ways. They're not sufficient, though, to really get an idea of what's going on in her life or work, I think, so she requires critics. By the way, in the same series, I'm editing—one on a poet who's been here a number of times, Carl Rakosi. So, if anybody's interested, in him at some point, well, talk to me.

Any other questions? If not, thank you very much.

[Applause.]

Where the Unconscious Monsters Are:

A Feminine Surrealist Guide to Andrei Codrescu's Outside

Interlude by Kendra Noelle Richard

"The Surrealist idea of the unconscious was female.
The Unconscious was a She..."
Andrei Codrescu

The dark powers have been getting more clever, as Andrei Codrescu elucidates in his lecture at what was then the Naropa Institute in 1988, titled *Surrealism and the Suggestion of the Unconscious.* Codrescu illuminates his concept of the diminishing 'Outside' as both a literal, ecological dimension and also a figurative or metaphorical space. Beginning his lecture by quoting André Breton, "Experience itself has found itself increasingly circumscribed. It paces back and forth in a cage from which it is more and more difficult to make it emerge." What is this cage today? We are both inside and outside of this cage. The borders so blurred between them that we can no longer differentiate ourselves from our unconscious.

Were there parallels between Dada or Surrealism—and Feminism? When thinking about the 'inside' and the 'outside,' I was elliptically brought back to this continuous parallel to the female body. I find the intrinsic dynamic between Surrealism and the feminine almost inescapable. How much of Dali's artwork consisted of the nude female body? This brings the inside to the surface, the innermost part of the body of a woman revealed and rendered outward. The feminine only permitted to be truly seen through a man's artistic and visionary lens. And yet, while working on a project translating 19th Century French Surrealist poetry, I found it immensely difficult to find female French Surrealist poets in that time period. In *The Posthuman Dada*

Guide: Tzara and Lenin Play Chess published in 2009, Codrescu talks about 'The American Woman' and historical female literary figures such as Peggy Guggenheim, Nancy Cunard, Gertrude Stein, Mina Loy, Baroness Elsa Von Frey-tag-loringhoven, Margaret Anderson, Jane Heap, Berenice Abbott, and Djuna Barnes. "European dadas admired the American Woman, that new fiercely independent (often rich) figure who ranged atop a horse with a gun in the West (Annie Oakley) and fashionably flaunted convention in New York (Peggy Guggenheim)." I reached out to Andrei Codrescu about the unconscious, and if in his research and writings on this, had he found any parallels within Dada or Surrealism—and Feminism? I wondered if he could speak to Surrealism's connection or relationship to feminism. He responded with:

"The Surrealist idea of the unconscious was female. The Unconscious was a She... In fact, by opposing official culture (military uniforms, war, duels, women as prizes, muses, or slaves) the Surrealists were on the side of women... so you can say that the "unconscious" of Freud and Breton & co was indeed female but one they treated badly and were afraid of." (Andrei Codrescu, 2021)

In reference to Dada, he echoed with:

"Dada was another story—the most interesting figures of the movement were women, Emmy Hennings, Hannah Hoch, Mina Loy, the Baroness, the publishers of the Little Review, and more. The Dada were literal radicals, radicalism in a straight line to communists Dolores Ibarruri, Rosa Luxembourg, and anarchist Emma Goldman... scholarship (where you can definitely see the erasure of women in history) should start to re-evaluate all the official stories, including those of the avant-gardes." (Andrei Codrescu, 2021)

I found these responses wildly comforting. I have always been drawn to Surrealism, but I have been disappointed by the lack of the feminine within its space beyond a muse, a sexual desire, monetary support, or scandalous affair. But as Codrescu described, Surrealism's unconscious itself *was* the feminine space. Surrealist art and poetry breathe differently in my mind, and I've always romanticized European cafés filled with intellectuals enhanced by each other's art and passions and poetry running through their veins and lungs like their psychotropic drugs. It was the call of the "outside" and refusing to only believe what can be seen with the eyes; allowing the imagination to completely take the reins. What is lost when we can longer reach the 'Outside' thinking of Dada, Surrealism, or Feminism or even the imaginary, and we're stuck in a virtual inside endlessly trying to become a more exact replica of what was once real in the Outside?

In his lecture, Codrescu reads his chapter entitled, "The Shipwreck of Dada and Surrealism" from his book *The Disappearance of the Outside* first published in 1990. In his *Preface to the New Edition* in a later edition of *The Disappearance of the Outside* in 2001, he revisits these concepts in a more contemporary context. In this preface, Codrescu—an almost soothsayer—forecasts what the next twenty years will morph into with the following eerie poignancy, "Daydreaming has already been replaced to a large extent by programming. Television has effectively turned daydreamers into screenwriters... We may have to resign ourselves to becoming "textual aids" to an interactive, virtual world." Later, Codrescu augurs this coming to fruition with, "There are also young people who like to use technology to an opposite means...To imagine as little as possible... The existence of the outside world scared them." This is already horrifyingly accurate, and we haven't even begun to reach the science fiction levels of AI and other technologies in our futuristic midst ahead.

Where does that leave the unconscious? Or the Surrealist spirit of insurgence? Or the imagination? Or feminine space within literary experimentation? Or our fertile connection with nature? We are now seeing the beginning of this answer. We are watching the outside world around us unravel, and the powers that control it continue to prosper off its destruction. Our current world mirroring the dark powers of the past. As Codrescu reads in his lecture, "Absurdity is the chief demon of Capitalism." Codrescu compares the

European 'Outside' to the American 'Outside' which helps to chronicle the trajectory that would result in the current 'Posthuman,' as Codrescu refers to our existentially virtual and bionic human existence. He also intuitively foreshadows a dystopian future reality and painted what had become of the 'wilderness' of the 18th Century, "The wilderness of the eighteenth century had pretty much become a park by the twentieth." This alludes me back to the question, is there an 'Outside' today? Or has it completely disintegrated within and around us? I wanted an answer to this question, so in our conversation, I asked Andrei Codrescu to consider the 'Outside' today, given that in his preface from 2001, he brings technology as it was then into his discussion; I wondered what his thoughts were on today's 'Outside' given our current climate (that he predicted with the virtuality and text and image concepts) and how social media is at the center of technology and today's interactions. I asked him, is there still an outside? He responded with,

"There is an outside that could be reclaimed through technology by 2050. I call it Ontological Engineering... All of it must proceed from Gaia awareness: humans thinking with animals, plants, and rocks. This isn't the romantic "outside" I had in mind when I saw it disappearing in 1999. That "outside" has in fact disappeared..." (Andrei Codrescu, 2021)

Codrescu's 'prophecies' both in his current responses to my questions, and throughout his works and this lecture, are precisely the type of thinking required to survive the Posthuman world. What happens when the inside completely eradicates the outside? In *The Posthuman Dada Guide,* he forecasts, "If you have any doubt as to whether you are posthuman or merely human, take a look at the following parts of your body: the city, the house, the car, the iPhone, the laptop, the iPod, the pillbox, the nonflesh surround." I find myself typing on a laptop, while simultaneously looking at my iPhone and amidst our addictions and vices so many of them have become digital. We are the bionic posthumans that he references. Codrescu eloquently particularizes this with, "The fog of history swirls about the thick forest where purely imaginary animals howl pitifully, not for blood, but for the pain of trying to escape from metaphors." I long for the imaginary animals and I've also murdered them—through my human greed and capitalist devouring of nature. He investigates where we have lost the Outside, we have lost nature. So, what does it mean to lose nature? In response to this in our dialogue, I implored Codrescu about the 'outside' from an ecological perspective in our current climate crisis. He responded with the following, "Precisely. Europe itself, colonized for millennia, had little wilderness by the end of the 19th century—but a lot more than it does now. European expansion outside Europe brought the rest of its malignancies to the planet..." (Andrei Codrescu, 2021).

In this posthuman world, with its disappearing outside and virtual inside, free of imagination and subconscious demons, where does this leave the unconscious or the surreal? Looking back in history, these embodied, birthed, or transfused themselves in art, poetry, manifestos, and rebellious renaissance periods of creative expression, experimentation, explorations of sexuality and psychology, as well as utopian bohemias of sexual and artistic freedom and radical political movements and feminist revolutionaries. Not only in Europe, but also in America in the 60s and 70s. In *The Posthuman Dada Guide*, Codrescu illustrates this with, "Among the Dada first principles was Collaboration... and reached its second peak after Dada in the works of the New York School poets of the 1960s and 1970s." In his lecture, Codrescu connects this with William S. Burroughs and the "cut-up," "Take, for instance, cut-up, the American version of a Dada poem... They believed that secrets lay hidden below the surface meanings held in place by grammar." He continues to describe how they wanted to see something work in a different way. To take language apart and strip it of its bourgeois systems, traditional forms, and meanings.

Surrealism can be traced to modern experiments in writing, art, and culture. Even though Surrealists *hated* art. As it once had in Surrealist cafés, poetry became a vessel for the unconscious, as Codrescu describes in *The Posthuman Dada Guide*, "Poetry pointed the way to something else, to an elsewhere, to a sense of the marvelous, to magic, to otherness." In his lecture, he continues to reveal a deeper look into Surrealist thinking and ideals, "If logic is the language of the machine, dream is the language of humans. The Surrealists advocated the rending of the veils of reason." The lifting of these veils, also becomes *the lifting of the skirt* and the *tearing of the skirt* in which Codrescu describes these phrases as, "potential erotica-linguistic displacements." The feminine is again revealed to be embroidered and woven into every seam of artistic revolutionary history, even without proper credit, historic preservation, or acknowledgement, especially at this particular time of the unveiling of the collective unconscious and Surrealism as a mode of unconscious rebellion—the release of repressed sexuality, imagination, and unrestricted explosions of experimental creative work. Language was freed and *returned to its natural state* as Codrescu quotes Tristan Tzara. The unconscious was accessible to everyone.

In his lecture he asks, "Where is the unconscious today?" He later answers his own question, with, "The fact is that the unconscious is gone." He then continues like a salve to the sighs of despair in the room, "There is no point in regretting the passing of the unconscious. We are a kind of new being now: we don't need an unconscious, we are unconscious." He delves into the creation and demise of the Surrealist psychoanalyst torrid love affair, *Surrealism creates chaos, psychoanalysis creates order.* Poetry and art revealing our dreams, our secrets, and our disappearing unconscious monsters. In *The Posthuman Dada Guide*, Codrescu contextualizes this idea of the link between the unconscious and art and poetry with, "Artists were struck simultaneously by the urge to rethink everything... revealing an elsewhere, a multidimensional beyond... a vast invisible world called by Freud 'the unconscious.'" Codrescu also examined the Surrealists using the unconscious as a tool. In his Preface to *The Disappearance of the Outside* in 2001, he referred to artistic hope as *the cry of the canary in the mine.* Is that true now? And can anyone hear cries from the Outside if it no longer exists? Are we able to create the *Gaia awareness, ontological machine*, or *textual aides* needed to germinate and flourish, to foster and sustain a new Outside or arouse and enkindle a newly awakened collective unconscious?

In his lecture, Codrescu describes Surrealists' "seeing" as an art unlike sight—the importance of 'seeing' beyond sight with, "The eyes became suspect, seeing was doubted, and a new adventure of the human spirit began…." Codrescu also labyrinths this Surrealist 'seeing' through the lifting of our gossamer cloaked language with, "Art began to depict a world unlike the one received by our eyes… Surrealist Wonder would create a new human being in the community based on inspiration, not ideology." I find myself digging further into this 'Surrealist wonder' and wonder where there is a place for it now, and if there isn't one, how can we create it? How can the veils be lifted again, but rather than the lifting of the skirt, we all lift the veils from our eyes, yet only to reveal the sight beyond the seeing? Where the imaginary animals and demons might show us something deeper, a beyond once thought of as our unconscious, taking hold of the process. If the unconscious is female, then maybe this is our super bloom. Where the conditions are just right and perfect for this opening from dormancy. As I look around at the present and future-looming destruction, the global climate in disarray, and the news haunting us all daily with continuously unfathomable atrocities, there is hope in a Surrealist insurgence. A creative influx and revolution, all with 'Gaia awareness.' Gaia, the feminine earth we all rest upon. Our creative minds released and untethered from our technological sarcophagus, genetically modified toxins, and systemic greed flowing like the rivers once did before we ravaged their paths.

Codrescu's lecture gives a timelessly relevant, eye-opening, and alluringly evocative scope inside the intentions and actualities of Surrealism through a lens of both its historical roots in Dadaism and Romanticism, and as it branched out through modern and contemporary experimental poetry and art. In his lecture, Codrescu surmises this with, "The surrealists demanded the taking down of the corral fences of the imagination, the opening of the borders between the human and the nonhuman, the monstrous and the domestic." The Surrealist unconscious was female—her, this She—this unconscious realm, as powerful as Mother Earth, as the American pioneer woman, and the poetess artisans who were their own muses and monsters. Maybe She'll save us all.

SURREALISM AND THE SUGGESTION OF THE UNCONSCIOUS

Andrei Codrescu
July 4, 1988

Transcription by Kendra Noelle Richard

Andrei Codrescu: Okay, this will be a sitting down talk. I usually stand and ponder. [Anselm] and I were at the radio station just a few minutes ago where somebody else said, what is Surrealism? Good question. I'm not going to give a historical introduction to Surrealism since that's easily available, anybody can find out about all that. I'm going to talk a bit about what the implications of this business are—particularly since Surrealists are not—I mean, the best of what Surrealism is doesn't have much to do with art or with writing, but it has to do with say insurgent spirit.

The Surrealists were, well, Surrealists. The wonderful Surrealist work called André Breton's *Manifestos* is a work that truly takes on the word and it takes on the world every which way and art is a particular strategy in this business, but no more than that, and if anybody hated art it was the Surrealists. Surrealists had an absolute—ah well, they attacked it—they didn't have an allergy to it because they produced it, so you can't really produce it and have an allergy to it, but Surrealists were against art and Breton's *Manifestos* are a terrific work because it is about a new strategy of being in the world at a certain point. Most of the Surrealists' look has dated. There is stuff in museums and there is stuff that has been incorporated in our culture that is pure Surrealism. MTV can deliver Surrealism in 15 seconds. More in 15 seconds, actually, than most of Andre Breton's poems do. That doesn't matter. Those are the formal aspects of a certain time and period, but the insurgent spirit continues.

The Surrealists called it the Surrealist revolution and for good reasons because they meant that—that it is a revolution. It is something that engages the world completely. So the little piece that I wrote and I'm going to read parts of it and go in and out of it is about this contribution of Surrealists of that Surrealism spirit, to the insurgent spirit in general, and what the Surrealist revolution means and can still possibly mean. It's a chapter from a book I wrote called, *The Disappearance of the Outside*, and you can hear reference in it to this business of the disappearance of the outside—it's a metaphor—and what the book does is it traces, what I call the disappearance of the outside through the last twenty years of American culture and through the writings of Eastern European writers who are also very much interested in this question. The outside in its most literal sense is the outside, which is to say not inside, not in here, out there. It has a serious ecological dimension or an environmental dimension in that the outside, this so we knew it, for a long time is being taken away in various ways. The inside and the outside have been changing places. Very quickly too. And one thing that is the outside at the moment will become an inside in the next. Again, it's a question of this migration of forms. So the question of what is outside, what is potential and what is possible, what is possible in the sense of being pure potential and the sense of what it is to be free, to be in the outside, is a sense that is getting crowded in by all sorts of things. This is what the whole book is about and this particular bit about the Surrealists is just about how particularly the Surrealists mode of thinking operates in this particular business, so I'll just read here and there.

Audience Member: How do you know the outside isn't coming from the inside—the energy— freedom's on the outside, but how do you know that the freedom isn't on the inside?

Codrescu: No, you're right, absolutely, there is such a thing. There is such a thing as an inside outsidedness you know, and it's a sense—it's an absolute sense of psychic freedom if your inner sense of freedom is an outside. It doesn't mean inside you actually is something inside you know because the sense of possibilities that you have is an actual outside. What I call inside is what is prescribed, what is regulated and in fact diminished every minute. And I think there is a real sense in which the outside has been diminished. Literally and metaphorically and it's a real thing. Which means only that the dark powers have been getting more clever, and one of the aspects of that cleverness is the ability to mimic the outside, to mimic some of the figures, the formal look of the outside and that's where the problems start.

This begins by talking a bit—it has two quotes from André Breton. This one from the first Surrealist manifesto which I think is the best one in many ways because then Breton himself became embroiled in a kind of bureaucratic structure of Surrealism, which Surrealism was. I mean to a large extent, Breton became the pope of Surrealism and everybody was enlisted and there were some kind clerics who went around and did that, but to the point where he actually excommunicated people as some of you may know, the famous Salvador Dali story where Dali's begging on his knees to be taken back into the Surrealist movement, and he has a thermometer in his ass which is how the story's described and Dali himself says that the reason for that is he had a fever so the only way he could actually keep his thermometer in was to be on all fours, but these are disputed anecdotes from a sort of a silly time.

These are the two quotes from Breton: "What is admirable about the fantastic is that there is no longer anything fantastic: there is only the real."

And the other one: "Experience itself has found itself increasingly circumscribed. It paces back and forth in a cage from which it is more and more difficult to make it emerge."

My sentiments exactly, and more so now. He begins with a prophecy which is a traditional mode of inspired speaking for poets and other people struck by the prophetic mode, and it describes the fact that prophecy in some sense is no longer viable right now.

Vindicated prophets are not happy people. The hells that they describe in order to project a utopic future swallow them. The major problem of prophecy has always been the circumvention of hell in order to arrive at the good future quickly. In the past, so-called prophets of doom from Isaiah to Allen Ginsberg—that I'm talking about—have tarried unseemingly long in the pits of darkness before surrendering to the inevitable light. I have always suspected prophets of enjoying the things they abhor and abjure because it is only in them that they can rise to heights sufficient for loosening their rhetorical lightning.

Today the problem of the prophet has been solved—eliminating, alas, the prophet. No sooner does the vision make its tingling appearance that the end comes quickly in sight before even a proper taste of doom. This is the fate of prophets in today's global village. They are right, no matter what they prophesy. Things and their opposites lie together in the beam of the projector we dust motes dance in. Who solved the prophet's problem while depriving him of the pleasure of hell? Who had the nerve to be convinced before the proper harangue even began? What kind of world is this where utopia's there for the taking, whether it be a microwave heaven or holy death by Iraqi gas? (Which is apparently what you know convinced Iranian warrior things because they're going to heaven.)

Surrealists have some of the answers. They foresaw in the '20s and '30s the growing importance of Seeing. Not "sight," that immobile noun pinned the lapel of high culture, but the active act of "seeing," the axis about which Western Civilization revolves at increasing speeds. Since involuntarily blind Homer, and willfully blind Oedipus, the eyes have been looming larger and larger in the stone forehead of the West. During Enlightenment, "seeing" became synonymous with knowledge and conquest. To see the unknown was to possess it. From the microscope to the telescope, the microcosm to the macrocosm, our effort has been to encompass the unseen by the seen. Voyeurism and rape are the dominant forces of the age of reason. That which was seen was destroyed by the dissecting gaze before it could return it. The unknown, pinned by the gaze of the knower, shriveled under the taxonomic light of marching sight. Prophecy, the art of seeing the future, became just one more extension of visual conquest. Human organizations as old as the species were overthrown one by one by the giddiness that accompanied the tearing of the veils. Even their memory, belonging as it did to the "ages of darkness," was obscured by the marching light.

But then, a "then" culminating in World War I, something paradoxical began to occur with alarming frequency. There were tremendous lapses in the steady progress of light. War irrupted ferociously in the newly lit world of reason, more destructive and apocalyptic than ever prophesied. (Sirens in background.) The quality of the darkness tearing the fabric of the enlightened world was of impenetrable density. A malignant darkness, infinitely more potent than the benign terrors of the ancient night or of "the primitive soul," in quotes began to make its appearance. Agents.

(Laughter at his comment about the sirens.)

After World War I our faith in reason was never restored. Artists flocked to the irrational. This would be an interesting movement actually, visually, artists flocking to the irrational.

The eyes became suspect, seeing was doubted, and a new adventure of the human spirit began. The Dadaists composed with their eyes closed, listening only for the discordant signals which alone seemed to hold an understanding. Logic, rhetoric, reason, closure, beauty, harmony, were put on trial. They belonged to the blithe ages of mindless sight. The various monsters awakened when the protective darkness had been removed by science now stood at attention. They had shapes other than classical and they were gazing at us. They were gazing back. At that point it occurred to quite a few startled souls that our orgy of voyeurism had stirred the last of whatever it is just behind the mirror and it was looking back!

Reason became a desperate and hasty campaign to shrink the Outside, at this point or that point, by definitively ridding the world of myth, religion, the supernatural—in short, whatever was not us. Quickly, psychoanalysis pointed inside and located all the monsters in the unconscious. Why, they were nothing but repressed sexual desires. Marxism found the demons hidden in the forces of production, veritable supervisor-devils in the factory of history. Art began to depict a world unlike the one received by our eyes. The new things it showed us had been ours all along residing in the imagination of course. The imagination, while roomier than the unconscious, it contained things that didn't exist as well as repressed ones, and less regimented in the factory of history, was the best corral yet: monsters could roam there in all their dimensions!

Grammarians discovered the self-referentiality of language. All those scary words! They had only been playing with each other since the beginning of time, meaning nothing by it. Language became both immanent and material, an infinite maze where the wandering monsters would be lost. Following the cue of grammarians, the sciences fell in love with their grammars as well, each one an autonomous world, with or without referent practical or theoretical, good forever. Structuralism transformed all the little rooms of knowledge into traps for the monsters of the Outside. Thus, a new world came into being: one in which humans contain monsters because they are neurotic, imagine the unimaginable because they are artists, are oppressed because of their class, use language because it gives them more language. This rapid deployment of defenses, it was hoped, would spare us from the Outside, which anyway and most probably, did not exist. And even if it did, at least we might contain it, making it the Formally Outside by marrying it. The Formally Outside would be smaller and once we got it all inside we could control it. The shrunken monsters would soon resign themselves to being mere appendages of our fancy. These ostrich-like tactics must have mightily amused the recently aroused demons. You can hear them laughing today in Iran, Baton Rouge, Israel, Beirut, India, and Africa. There's some water here. (Pours water into glass to drink.) This is a narrative poem of the monsters. (Laughter.)

André Breton was an optimist. So am I. I believe I have matches. Hoping very much, I have matches. Thanks. (Lights lighter.)

André Breton was an optimist. So were most of the Surrealists, though many of them committed suicide. Surrealist optimism was based on that possibility of a complete transformation of human beings. A complete transformation of human beings through radical "conservation" and through the return of the repressed. The overthrow of the acquiescent human being was an intoxicating proposition. The Surrealists proposed to do this through a thorough critique of reason, installing in its place the discarded or suppressed discourses of dream and fantasy. If logic is the language of the machine, dream is the language of humans. The Surrealists advocated the rending of the veils of reason.

(Laughter.)

That's one of them—going right there.
Before reason. (Laughs.) Before reason.
I remember so many things. I remember before reason.

Before reason had both stripped and obscured it, the unknown had been the true home of human beings. The tearing of the veils, the lifting of the curtain, the shifting of the gears, the tearing of the skin, the lifting of the skirt, the shifting of the eyes, the tearing of the skirt from the shifting of the eyes to the lifting of the curtain, all these and all their potential erotico-linguistic displacements constituted a kind of marvel of anti-engineering perfectly feasible in the great mechanical workshop of the West, which had so far produced only the destroying gaze. The Surrealist anti-machine produced two antidotes to the march of—I think I just lost my place.

Audience Member: Formulas.

Codrescu: Formulas! Where are those formulas, okay, formulas. Terrific. No actually these are the Surrealists, this is the historical part.

To this march of formulas: The marvelous and its companion, laughter, solidarity—building laughter, laughter that cut the Gordian knot, paradox-solving and paradox-making laughter. The Marvelous was the chief substance, though, and its producers were those discarded by the official production machine. Marginal beings, peripheral souls, dream operators, poets, but eventually everyone. Surrealist Humor would cause a liberating rippling of the Scale of Mirth, from the slight grin of Huysmans' Des Esseintes to the rippling proletarian guffaws of Fantomas, and Surrealist Wonder would create a new human being in the community based on inspiration, not ideology. Property relations would certainly be affected as well as the demons of production. The Surrealists separated the images of things from the things themselves and intended these images to be more than mere things, to be inspirational chariots. How to liberate it was the question in modern society. The Surrealists demanded the taking down of the corral fences of the imagination, the opening of the borders between the human and the nonhuman, the monstrous and the domestic.

"It was a tall order in the world where"—this is a quotes from Breton: "It was a tall order in the world where the imagination which knows no bounds is... allowed to be exercised only in strict accordance with the laws of an arbitrary utility; it is incapable of assuming this inferior role very long and, in the vicinity of the twentieth year, generally prefers to abandon man to his lusterless fate."

Man without imagination was a plaything of forces indeed. Madness was one solution, others were dreams, écriture automatique, hypnosis, exploration of the psyche, the study of magic, psychotropic drugs. Antonin Artaud was both mad and a taker of drugs. Henri Michaux took mescaline. The Surrealists differed from the Romantics, their predecessors, only by the texture of the world they lived in. The modern world's machine had put Nature, which the Romantics still had nearly unmediated access to, out of reach. The wilderness of the eighteenth century had pretty much become a park by the twentieth. Consequently, both Imagination and Nature has become more difficult to come by. The way to both our inner and our outer Outside was piled high with the debris of civilization.

The Surrealists investigated our inner wilderness with the help of Dr. Freud's unconscious. This unconscious was something which has been found by Dr. Freud not so long before Breton became a baby, under old photos of the Biedermeier trunk of old Vienna. All the reject of history and the flora and fauna of bourgeois dreams inhabited this place. It was as rich a place as anyone had dared to imagine, and it was there for the taking, at the beck and call of a linguistic mechanism called écriture automatique, automatic writing. Free association. The Surrealist écriture automatique differed from "free association" only in the order that analysis imposed on the things brought to light. Analysis deemed order necessary to reintegrate the individual into society. The Surrealists deemed disorder equally necessary in order to critique society. Nonetheless, the apparent complexity of both operations led to complicity between Surrealism and psychoanalysis to create and legitimize the psychoanalytic profession. The compact must have originally contained an equal clause for the creation of a professional Surrealist—something that didn't come to pass until much later, until now, that is.

Automatic writing is anti-verbal: it uses words to bring out images. Free association, on the other hand is anti-image. It is an organizer of images into words. The images resulting from automatic writing destroy the orderly subduing of consciousness to the rules of society. The images subsumed by the words of the sentence give up their ghost to the syntax. Surrealism creates chaos—psychoanalysis creates order. For all that, the Surrealists were intimately connected to bourgeois Europe, both as thinkers and as Parisians: they were city bohemians, adversaries of art in a world of art, outsiders by vocation, insiders in actuality. Psychoanalysis, born out of Central Europe also, proclaimed its allegiance to civilization: it was an intentional insider but its activity was international, possibly supranational.

Both Surrealism and psychoanalysis helped internationalize and eventually delocalize human beings, but each did so in spite of their professed aims. By supporting each other's aspirations, the two methods also wrote each other's death warrants. Psychoanalysis, the religion of the word, was absorbed by Surrealism, the religion of the image, but not until the word played itself out in modern Europe. There was a kind of politesse in their transaction, an opening-of-the-doors ritual: first psychoanalysis, which was allowed to close the close the modern era, then Surrealism, which took the end of verbal discourse out the same door. Then they parted ways. Psychoanalysis went off to dissolve in the inflation of the world and Surrealism disappeared in the proliferation of moving icons. The mall politeness of succession was all that was left of the old European contract between the words and images. After the manners were played out, the signs took over, leaving their old meanings behind like empty insect cases. Where is the unconscious today?

Freud invented it. Jung populated it with weird Germanic phantoms he called archetypes. The Surrealists made it a place for poets, like a cafe in the shadow of Tour St. Jacques. Criminals used it in court. Worst of all, men with pointy beards made money out of it, and filled a vacuum left by the death of the catholic confession. It also gave Jews a taste of Catholicism like pork that didn't come from a pig.

The unconscious was a boon to the barely educated, too. By having it there, at the bottom or behind of everything—who can say where?—one could always console oneself with the knowledge that if something emotionally strong was ever needed, it could be opened up—with qualified help—to have a "long draught of darkness," a psychic whiskey, as it were. For three-quarters of a century it was a populous place. A gold mine, a bottomless pit, a chunk of language attached to something many experts could attest to. Where did it go? The fact is that the unconscious is gone. According to a psychoanalyst of my acquaintance, every attempt to penetrate below the surface these days produces nothing but television jingles.

To his request to say anything that comes to mind, his patients now say: "It's not nice to fool Mother Nature." Asked how he is feeling, the patient replies: "The more you look the more you like." The earliest thing he remembers? "Reach out and touch someone." Identity crisis? "You're in the Pepsi generation." What does he want from life? "Double your pleasure, double your fun." Questioning the primal things, he gets: "GE brings good things to life."

It isn't just that the history of television populates the ontological pipeline. It is as if there are no more individual secrets: they seem to have all melted into one huge secret, now in the keeping of the military-industrial-entertainment complex, instead of the Oedipal one. There is no point in regretting the passing of the unconscious. We are a kind of new being now: we don't need an unconscious, we are unconscious.

(Laugher.) Yeah, great. It gets boring again actually. America is de facto Surrealist. There is no need to upset "reality" here. "Reality" is manufactured continually. The incongruous meeting of different realities is a routine matter. People inhabit the landscape at angles so odd they would surely fall if a continually evolving projection machinery weren't constantly correcting the perspective. It was only natural that the European unconscious, so structurally well furnished, would meet its demise here where the huddled masses of the nineteenth century came to eat. America was the projection of European utopias, a heaven on earth very much like that of Charles Fourier, who believed that the pear was the most noble fruit and whom the Surrealists adopted as an adequate counterweight to Christian Futurism and Fatalism. America was the last hope of European revolutionaries, the Outside par excellence. The Victorian upper class did not like America. They found it rude, awesome, and unmanageable. By its very presence it denied the miniaturized order of the Old World. In England, the interior went outside; in America, the outside came in. The English lawn was a carpet, the American table a tree stump. To British writer Frances Trollope, Niagara Falls was "an accompaniment to conversation." Or it was a marvel of technical efficiency: "So much over so sheer a drop," and "power of eye control is necessary for full enjoyment of the scenery." Oscar Wilde said about Niagara [Falls]: "The sight of the stupendous waterfall must be one of the first, if not the keenest, disappointments in American married life."

In the process of observing America, many writers concluded that tradition writing forms were made obsolete by the new social and psychological configurations of the New World. Having decided on the "novel's irrelevance to America," many of them looked for alternative forms: Kipling's epic, Stevenson's chivalric romance, Wells's and Huxley's science fiction were invented specifically to accommodate the new. It is curious, then, that American literature until Whitman and long after him stayed so closely and timidly in the shadow of the Queen's English. Even in the 1920s, when Surrealism seduced many Americans in Paris, the echoes of that revolution were only faint in America. It is even more curious when one considers that Surrealism was in the main an optimistic movement, both in its conservative and its subversive modes, and America is the only place in the world where optimism has been legislated, by making the "pursuit of happiness" a right. All utopians were avant-Americans, and if Columbus hadn't found the place, all these utopians would have had to go to the moon with Jules Verne. Isn't that a story? Small utopian communities functioned in America since its founding. This is more of a...the problem is sort of, this is a book. There are a few informational sentences but not too many.

Small utopian communities functioned in America since its founding. The utopian enterprise of the 1960's was in the suppressed tradition of countless utopian experiments of the nineteenth century. These communities were pressured out of existence but not before giving America the forms of its future. Their ecological concerns, their belief in crafts, in human-scale industry, became the legacy on which the anti-technological revolt of our time is founded. There are those who argue, like Jackson Lears in *No Place of Grace: Antimodernism and the Transformation of American Culture, 1880-1920*, that what began as an antimodern revolt ended up revitalizing the modern. This is true, but only in a formal sense. The contentless images changed the "look," just as the hippie "look" fed yuppie commerce and Surrealism feeds MTV. Forms are forever migrating out of that which has created them to become used against it. Isn't the old peace symbol the Volkswagen emblem? Aren't the rebellious anthems of the 1960s now used to sell soap on TV? On the other hand, the revelation of seams between images, caught the moment of leaving one content to be captured by another, and they increasing speed in which these decantings take place, make America sense in the kind of everyday working way. Far from being provoked to fits of deliberate intellectual eccentricity, the average TV watcher here could go straight from Carmen Miranda's hat or a cameo appearance by Sigmund Freud on *Fantasy Island* to a bathtub filled with strangers in the middle of the city and then go to work making cobalt bombs.

Does he realize the contradictions as Dada and therefore inevitably absurd, or Surrealist and therefore holding great occult and utopian meaning? Both. The continued existence, and relevance, of Dada is a religious phenomenon. Absurdity is the chief demon of capitalism, the material of endless "situation comedies." The absurd and the occult star side-by-side in every debate. For those unable to digest them in the abstract, there are supermarket tabloids. Aliens land continuously. We are both in awe of the industrial Moloch and in dread of what, if anything, it stands for, or in the way of. Thus, both one's quote "situation" unquote, comic and episodic, and one's fate after death, "the soul," quote, unquote, are constantly under consideration. Most electronic signals beamed at the mass carry "situational" and "metaphysical" messages. Can one participate in this kind of discussion? No. It is conducted through us. Which leaves the "real" again, quote, un-quote, "world," the will to the Outside, in the hands of *agents provocateurs*. The Dadaist perception can thus become the stimulus for a wicked, terminal kind of fun, techno-sense intended, yielding of poetic explosions and sensual derangement grander than geography. But, alas, it still delivers the amnesiac practitioner directly into the arms of the commodity.

(Sirens in background.)

They're coming.

The religious, great B-movie-inspired science of perversity and meticulous investigation that Surrealism demands is forgotten in Dada. Dada holds on to the thing, even in the simulacra: it suspects that the body's in the truck, while Surrealism holds on to the image, whose job is to assist the simulacra in disposing of the body. What is left of the romantic nineteenth century in people struggles between these poles of Surrealist production, "fun," quote, unquote and Dada consumption, "lifestyle," quote, unquote.

As Surrealist images become the signature of our *fin-de-siècle*, Surrealist writings sink into oblivion. Postmodernists are embarrassed by the revolutionary roots of Surrealism. The Surrealist spirit of insurgency is still active but it had had to be purged from the literature of the inside that succeeded it. Écriture automatique is still a threat because it assumes the unlimited potential of the imagination against the given facts of modern life. There is no doubt that many of the images liberated by early Surrealist écriture automatique are now mere advertising emblems. But the Surrealists themselves never put much store in the finished products of their insurgent methods. The familiar Surrealist forms became an archival enterprise, but not the deliberate pursuit.

(Loud booming sound/laughter.)

Recorded dreams became a bore but dreams remain interesting to the dreamer.

The object is not to become involuntary analysts or recorders but active dreamers. There is a quaint remnant of orthodox Surrealism today that labors under the illusion that the politics of the world of the 1930s are internal. This leftover ideology goes against the Surrealist spirit and accomplishes precisely what Surrealists hoped would never happen, namely, their becoming "literature," their "revolution of the world" no more than another historical thingamajig in the long succession of "isms"—realism, impressionism, expressionism, etc. Surrealist techniques of investigation and weapons are perfectly ambiguous in today's world: they can be read and used in diametrically opposed ways. Collage, for instance, is both a literary or painterly technique that shifts context to reveal something new and the dominant mode of visual control in the language of advertising and the media. Likewise Dada. When [Tristan] Tzara proposed making a poem from a newspaper randomly cut up, he was offering an alternative to the literature of reason. He freed the words: he returned language to its potential state. Tzara de-bourgeoisified—(laughter)—language by taking it out of the hands of perspective-makers. It was a revolution executed through the simple erasure of grammar and its tricks of meaning, the possibility that once words were detached from their grammatical jobs policing bourgeois interests the world might once again become visible has not lost its appeal.

A similar intention animated the painters who had begun dismantling realism even before Dada, but unbeknownst to them, the revolutionary Dadaists were also enriching the store of art where the future was already shopping. They were multiplying the materials. Tzara opened a hole in the hull of literature; he was the iceberg, hoping that reality would leak in. Instead, everything came to help itself to the new stuff. Nonetheless, the hastily patched boat is more vulnerable today at the mercy in fact of any passing Dadaist. The method works even if the patched holes have been neutralized by having them pass for art. Museums, to extend the metaphor, is where the patched holes can be viewed.

If we face a new situation today, it is the speed with which everything is copied, co-opted, and turned against itself. The original, if anything, whether it be a poem or an assassination still preserves something of the freshness of the intent. No such freshness will be found in the copy. And the copy of the copy will have long turned its energy against the freshness that spawned its ancestor. The simulacrum hatches in our lack of attention. It feeds in the dark of this lack from the relative rigidity of ideas until it disposes of the substance, which is everything but the resemblance to the original. Are there simulacra, one wonders, that have disposed even of the resemblance? Proudly original copies? Robots that have designed themselves? The disposed-of substance undergoes a reprimalization—one of those great words—reprimalization. It becomes primal again, becomes primary again, and escapes into the Outside, whose substance it is and where it awaits the formalizing forays of the next explorers.

Images do not have ideology, nor do they have a definite place of origin. Their *materia prima*, the Outside, is, however, always ready to send its projections along the lines of ideas and images. What activates the Outside is power. The Greeks, who authored our civilization—well, our Western civilization—did so by harnessing the Outside.

Here is a quote from Deleuze: "What the Greeks did, is not to reveal Being or unfold the Open in a world historical gesture. According to Foucault, they did a great deal less, or more. They bent the Outside, through a series of practical exercises. Force is what belongs to the Outside since it is essentially a relation between other forces: it is inseparable in itself from the power to affect other forces, spontaneity, and to be affected by others, receptivity. But what comes about as a result is a relation which force has with itself, a power to affect itself, an affect of self on self."

Thus the Greeks, unlike the showy nomads of the sweeping gesture, achieved the mastery of the Outside through repetition. Which does not mean that they then trapped the Outside inside their grammar, availing themselves of its force. The structures contain only models, traps, techniques, which have been getting better and better, culminating in the relentless ability for repetition of the machine. Machines repeat. It is their Greek job.

There is no conflict in the apparent inside world between Fordism and Surrealism. The assembly line is capable of producing infinite quantities of things, including Surrealists, and viding enough Dadaists to shadow them. It is not even a matter of demand. The market is the lifetime of the machine, which is practically eternal. The market is always the exact size of the production. As long as the machine churns, the market supports it. In the process, what used to be known as a human being stretches to make room in itself for the products. After stretching, it splits and each schizo-fragment walks away with its new load of production. And so on.

Assembly line artists are at work, quote, "on themselves," unquote, cultivating the increasing appetites of divided self which is itself in great demand for the market. Their job is to produce an infinitely reproducible self-capable of consuming all the simulacra spewing out of the repetitions of the machine. Surely, the Surrealist eye is pleased, even as the Surrealist spirit recoils. The horror of art, that Surrealist art conveyed way was the horror of the Surrealist vision coming through in an everyday sort of way. Surrealist art now hangs in museums, safely jailed from its own vision. Its escaped "images" issue nonstop from the electronic center. The Surrealist explorer of the unconscious has been replaced by the unconscious Surrealists.

Americans are horrified by the arbitrary—no matter that if they really looked around them they would find little that is not. Which is why Surrealism never took hold here. Surrealist techniques are modified so that they would seem "useful," in the manner of garage projects. Take, for instance, cut-up, the American version of a Dada poem. William Burroughs and Brion Gysin, who began cutting up texts in the 1950s, were not interested in completely dismantling "meaning," as had been Tzara's suggestion. They wanted to enlarge both the area of use and the area of sense. They believed that secrets lay hidden below the surface meanings held in place by grammar: suppressed heresies, conspiracies, webs of control. Their Anglo-American steadfastness refused to believe in the obviousness of the first control level as evidenced by bourgeois writing. In the area of use they wanted a large compost heap, a huge available store made up of all the words and sounds in popular and arcane use, including slang, newspapers, tape-recorded conversation, other languages: convertible capital for future works. In fact, while some of their cut-ups remain just that, many were mined by Burroughs for his later novels.

In the area of sense, cut-up had an experimental, mechanical intention. Mr. Burroughs from Kansas, an heir of the adding machine, took language apart in his garage not because it was the same apart as it was whole and not because it was better dismantled, and not because the dismantling act was joyous in itself, though certainly there was plenty of fun in it, but because he wanted to see if by rearranging the parts he could not somehow make the thing work differently. His intentions were not philosophical: they were experimental. Unlike those easily transcendent Europeans always ready to take their case Outside, Americans are practical: "No ideas but in things."

What did Gysin and Burroughs discover? Well, on the immediate level they saw that if you cut up the Bible, Shakespeare, and Rimbaud, they were still the Bible, Shakespeare, and Rimbaud. But in every case, there was a little left over. What? A new sentence here and there, full of odd sense. A prophetic sentence, for instance, I'm quoting Burroughs here, "It is a bad thing to sue your own father";

(Laughter.)

"And there is a horrid air conditioner." These things, says Burroughs, have nothing to do with the text being cut up. They are about the person doing the cut-up.

(Recording ends before the entirety of the lecture is completed.)

Surrealism & Humaneness

Interlude by Diana Lizette Rodiguez

Listening to Bernadette Mayer's work the last few months has created a presence, a sensation, and a liveliness that alters my space to feel as if she also has been living here. How in the near regards of the bedroom, bookshelves, closets, writing desk, and working pieces of art, Bernadette existed momentarily murmuring those words in the lecture. How there without knowing, I was creating under her influence. From the soundscapes of her voice, times of sculpting words, and numerous laughs, Mayer's audio recordings illustrate an artist who does not have a separation from her humanness. An authenticity easily listened to and displayed for the audience to know that here in the world of creativity one does not need authority, but the connection to feel relation.

Bernadette Mayer was born in Brooklyn, New York, in 1945 where she grew up and attended The New School for Social Research. A school that Mayer ended up teaching at after graduating in 1967, as she also taught numerous workshops at the Poetry Project at St. Mark's Church in New York. Writers like Kathy Archer, Charles Bernstein, Anne Waldman, and others had been ones who attended Berdanette's workshops. Mayer's work *Memory* from 1971 is a collection of 1200 film photographs and 31 recorded narratives. She recalls each moment captured in the photographs only to use those memories as points to fill the empty spaces of transition. Memory has become a continuously extracted imprint for me as an artist that works within Text and Image. I first encountered Mayer's work at the beginning of my writing career while taking a Creative Nonfiction class at Naropa University. I had just begun to shoot with my film camera and explore the spontaneous narrative images can arrange and dislocate when I realized how Mayer had done exactly what I was wanting to explore. And how much guidance she was able to give during that time.

I am able to return to those beginning stages of encountering Mayer's work. As there are days like this one in which rain creates its musical influence onto pavement. Where you remember those exact words that were used to describe Memory, as "an emotional science project." I process the need for replication as I shoot a roll of film and remember the walls of my old apartment being filled with prints. The considered printed timelines existed on their own and remained voiceless until a pacing process of its permanence, and impermanence began. I fall still in the idea that Photographs carry another setting, and into the deliberated question of "What could be?" if we just listen, question, and allow another world to become related away from the real moment. Mayer's work challenged poetic ability within autobiographical work as it conceptualized the working world of Visual Art. From here she cultivated a diaristic writing practice that sustained cycles through stream-of-consciousness. Her innovative writing and textual-art visuals are insightful foundations of experimental inclinations that have influenced and continue to influence many contemporary artists. The poetic conventions in which she survived throughout her life are small glimpses to others such as the Dadaist writers and Gertrude Stein.

These audio recordings of Bernadette Mayer June 22, 1978 [Part 1 & Part 2] highlight and show a full expedition of writers within the Dada movement. "What is Dada?" a question that throughout Dada history has to circulate and remind those who try to answer it that there is no answer, and yet somehow there is a formation who says that Dada is everything. Bernadette speaks of writers and artists such as Tristan Tzara, Antonin Artaud, Eric Satie, Marcel Duchamp, André Breton, and others. Shares glimpses of their work, world, and purpose of what they were trying to do. It is the broadening of our conceptions of the definition of art and creation. Mayer brings awareness to the important structures the Dadaists did with experimentation itself. A form of experimentation that hadn't been explored in the literary world as much as the Dadaists did. Diving into, opening to the creative subconscious occurring within absurdity, chance, dreams, and a developing to what we know today as automatic writing. The Dadaists refused existing structures only to have people like Tristian Tzara transform the idea of charming away from vigorous definition, as Mayer shares his work "How I Became Charming, Delightful." They disputed social spaces to form disorientation, disruption only to have artists such as Marcel Duchamp breakthrough the walking world to question "What is Art?" And such a question expands and follows the questioning of every other medium.

Mayer reminds us of the relevant work of Gertrude Stein, the cut-ups, specific sentence structures, and removal of punctuation. Stein's specific identity as a writer is brought in by Mayer. She reads and admires the relationship Stein had with punctuation to be the ability to manipulate grammar configurations. Showing the willingness to recalibrate words and form to fill meaning with uses of imagery and voice. Gertrude Stein, who in college studied with William James, brings creative writing a step closer to what we know as psychology. Creating an extension to study internal and external parts of the mind of the artists. Such as the Dadaists did Stein worked between the two worlds of consciousness and subconscious. Bernadette mentions Gertrude's specific studies from stream-of-consciousness, a term coined by William James himself, which later altered into a narrative technique Stein would practice. One that Mayer engages in her work, but adds that Stein confesses that her work within this specific study was all made up. Once again, we listen to a parallel to the Dadaists as they also focused their work on jokes and funny gestures. An emphasis on fluidity, chance, and openness to that reality presented in front of us and how it does not need to be stuck with seriousness. Although a relationship between Stein and the Dadaists has never been clear and direct, one does wonder the specificity of what these writers artists were trying to carve out.

As Mayer quotes, Stein says, "I like writing; it is so pleasant to have the ink write it down on the paper as it goes on doing." And with these words in mind, there is a certain simplicity to this carving out of these specific artists and writers. We listen to the time landscape bring these ideas of "new" throughout this lecture.

The numerous unpredictabilities Mayer speaks of is a significant lens, zooming in to those details that make this art important to remember and always learn from. Duchamp, Breton, Stein, Artaud, and even Mayer herself will remain outside the boundaries of what could be. Small phrases such as, "Artaud makes these statements like he wants to give words the importance that they have in dreams," as Mayer mentions are phrases that one cannot help but come back to and listen to over and over again. How a thin line between reality and the unconscious world is always available for us to seek, to reach for as artists. How we must not only create from the idea of what is "new" but also from what is directly already within our reach. A depth that the mind is capable of. A certain gift to glimpses that a microscope does in a lab or telescope does to those light-years away.

I know those glimpses, recognize them deeply to the profoundness of my work. And listening to Mayers audio recordings, searching through her countless interviews, and close study to her exhibition Memory reminds me of the word lineage. The involving lines, extraction that becomes a combination to creative influence. A giving to know how we can relate, unrelate, orient, disorient to what is given, and taken away to be closer to what is a human experience. I will always remember these audio recordings and lectures as the reasons why we writers, musicians, photographers, workers, artists come into existence. And why the line of descent easily follows us.

On Experimental Techniques in Writing

Bernadette Mayer
June 22, 1978

Transcription by Diana Lizette Rodiguez and C. M. Chady

Bernadette Mayer: I want to start out today talking about the Dadaists a little bit, just to tell you about them if you don't know about them. Are you all familiar with the Dadaists? And who they were and what they did? I wanted to talk about it in relation to what they were doing with experiments. We were talking last week about what is "new." In fact, I was having a conversation about the idea that at certain points in time everybody sits around saying we have to do something new, we can't choose to do any of the old forms. Did any of you read *Spring and All*?

The Dadaists were against Naturalism. Well, it started off being against Naturalism. Let's say that is in art and literature too. This is going to sound a little general, and they were against the bourgeoisie, against psychology, against academicism, and against art. They thought art was a swindle and pretentious thing to do. The things they were for—life, naivete. Of course, this my version of the whole story, and maybe we have a few for absurdity, jokes, chance, coincidence, abstraction, which is a tricky thing to say, maybe abstraction in literature as it occurs in dreams. And sacrilege.

I have a list here of who the Dadaists were: André Breton, Paul Éluard, do you know these names? Phillipe Soupalt, Jean Arp, Marcel Duchamp, Max Ernst, Hans Richter, Francis Picabia, Tristan Tzara, Erik Satie, Antonin Artaud, and also Guillaume Apollinaire and Kurt Schwitters. That book that is on the reading list, *Dada: Painter and Poets* edited by Robert Motherwell, did anybody see it? Is it around? [Student speaks indecipherably.] It's not in the library or anything? Well, am I going over stuff that you already know? Like if I were to tell you a few things that Marcel Duchamp did would you already know that?

Okay, well like you walk in the door to Marcel Duchamp's house and his floor is screwed with close pins. And there is a shovel in the corner and it's inscribed with the words AHEAD OF THE BROKEN ARM (from research the words inscribed are truly "In Advance of the Broken Arm"), which is also the name of the book by Ron Padgett. There's a birdcage filled with bits of marble, clumps to resemble sugar; there are anemic cinema spirals which are these things that go around and make patterns. Everything is covered with puns, among which this is translated into English as I dodge the ecchymoses of the eloquent Eskimos.

And Rose Selavy—I don't know how to explain Rose Selavy, do you all?

(Student speaks, indecipherable, mentioning "c'est la vie.")

I'm going to read you this work by Tristan Tzara... Rose Selavy is Marcel Duchamp's other name. This is a book by Tristan Tzara called *How I Became Charming, Delightful and Delicious*. Tristan Tzara was maybe the founder of the Dada's movement depending on whose version of the story you get.

> I sleep very late. I commit suicide 65%. My life is very cheap, for me it's only 30% of life. My life contains 30% of life. It lacks arms strings and a few buttons. 5% is consecrated to a state of semi-lucid stupor accompanied by anemic râles. This 5% is called Dada. So you see that life is cheap. Death is a little bit more expensive. But life is charming and death is charming too.
>
> A few days ago I attended a gathering of imbeciles. They were lots of people. Everybody was charming. Tristan Tzara, a small, idiotic and insignificant individual delivered a lecture on the art of becoming charming. And incidentally, he was charming. And witty. Isn't that delicious? Incidentally, everybody is delicious. 9 below zero. Isn't that charming? No, it's not charming. God can't make the grade. He isn't even in the phone book. But he's charming just the same.
>
> Ambassadors, poets, counts, princes, musicians, journalists, actors, writers, diplomats, directors, dressmakers, socialists, princess-

> es, and baronesses—all charming. All of you are charming, utterly subtle, witty, and delicious.
>
> Tristan Tzara says to you: he will be quite willing to do something else, but he prefers to remain an idiot, a clown and a faker.
> Be sincere for an instance: is that what I just told you charming or idiotic?
>
> There are people (journalists, lawyers, dilettantes, philosophers) who even regard the other forms—business, marriages, visits, wars, various congresses, joint stock companies, politics, accidents, dance halls, economic crises, emotional crises—as variations of Dada. Since I am not an imperialist, I do not share their opinion—I prefer to believe that Dada is only a divinity of the secondary order, which must simply be placed inside the other forms of the new mechanisms for interregnum religions.
>
> Is simplicity simple or Dada?
>
> I consider myself quite charming.

This is another Tristan Tzara where he is explaining what is Dada:

> I know you have come here today to hear explanations. Well, don't expect to hear any explanations about Dada. You explain to me why you exist. You will never be able to tell me why you exist, but you will always be ready to maintain a serious attitude about life. You will never understand that life is a pun, for you will never be alone enough to reject hatred, judgments, all these things that require such an effort, in favor of a calm and level state of mind that makes everything equal and without importance. Try to be empty and fill your brain cells with petty happiness. Always destroy what you have in you. On random walks. Then you will be able to understand many things. Intelligence is an organization like any other. It serves to create order and clarity where there is none. Perhaps you will understand me better when I tell you that Dada is a virgin microbe that penetrates with the insistence of air into all the spaces that reason has not been able to fill with words or conventions.

Actually, as I read that it sounds very eloquent, and it shouldn't, you know? I mean it should sound more funny than eloquent. I mean it should sound more horrible or something. I guess the trouble with a lot of the Dadaist writers is that they were very good writers when they didn't want to be. Apollinaire said this thing, which I thought was a good example of a Dada remark. He said, "My father was a doorman in the Vatican."

Schwitters in the beginning did this reading of this poem in the place where the Dadaists used to gather which was called Cabaret Voltaire. The poem was just the letter W, and he made his voice go down the line of the W and up to the middle and down, along reading. I guess that was at the beginning of the whole scene. Also, Duchamp has this great glass sculpture, have any of you seen it? It's called *The Bride Stripped Bare by Her Bachelors, Even.* Have you seen it? It's in Philadelphia. Well, the interesting thing about this sculpture is that it got dropped and it's all cracked. It's big pieces of glass and their cracks are just all throughout. The idea somehow is being that the cracks are something to be accepted and used as part of the art form. And that brings in chance, as in chance has given you the opportunity not only to have created this work but to have to crack. One might if one were in another culture then America takes those cracks and fills them with gold or something. Anyway, just to put those ideas in your head. (Student speaks, indecipherable.)

Yes, he has to think of these cracks as wonderful because that was his job to have that stance in relation to reality. I mean it was his duty. Okay here's this work by Erik Satie, called *The Day of a Musician.* Maybe I should show you actually how these things are written. Tristan Tzara's work looks like this, more or less what you would call prose, and this work by Erik Satie is in lines. Long lines sort of Allen Ginsberg lines. "The Day of a Musician":

> An Artist ought to regulate his life.
>
> Here is the exact time-table of my daily life:
>
> Get up: at 7:18 a.m.; inspired: from 10:23 to 11:47. I lunch at 12:11 p.m. and leave the table at 12:14.
>
> A healthy turn on the horse to the end of my grounds: from 1:19 to 2:53. More inspiration from: 3:12 to 4:07.
>
> Various occupations (fencing, reflections, napping, visits, contemplations, dexterity, swimming, etc....): from 4:21 to 6:47.
>
> Dinner is served at 7:16 and ends at 7:20. Then symphonic readings (out loud): from 8:09 to 9:59.

Going to bed takes place regularly at 10:37. Once a week I awake with a start at 3:19 a.m. (Tuesdays)

I eat only white foods: eggs, sugar, minced bones; the fat from dead animals; veal, salt, coconuts, chicken cooked in white water, the mould from fruit, rice, turnips, camphor sausages, pâtes, cheese (white), cotton salad, and certain fishes (without the skin).

I boil my wine, which I drink cold with fuchsia juice. I have a good appetite, but I never talk while eating, for fear of choking to death.

I breathe with care (a little at a time). I dance very rarely. While walking I hold my sides and stare fixedly straight ahead.

Having a serious expression, if I laugh is without meaning to. I apologize afterward, affably.

I sleep with only one eye closed; my sleep is deep. My bed is round, with a hole to put my head through. Hourly a servant takes my temperature and gives me another.

For a long time, I have subscribed to a fashion magazine. I wear a white cap, white socks, and a white vest.

My doctor has always told me to smoke. To this advice, he adds "Smoke, my friend: if it weren't for that another would be smoking in your place."

The word Dada is said to have fifteen different versions of how the word was coined. The most common one seems to be that it was chosen at random from the dictionary. From, I guess it was a French dictionary, and it means hobby horse. Anyway, the reason I am sort of throwing all of this at you is that the Dadaist's writers were the source of a lot of experiments that followed, that took place during that time, that followed in literature. Experiments with a chance, experiments with dream writing, one of them I believe was Phillipe Soupalt used to fall asleep and write his words while he was asleep. He would dictate. The source of work, the idea of simultaneously in music and also in writing like in the works of Jackson Mclaurin and other people. Do you know what that is? You know when you got a lot of different voices going on at the same time. The way the Dadaists first did it was that they would recite the same poem in a lot of different languages, simultaneously. Simultaneity in music may turn out to be a more serious affair.

Okay, experiments with nonsense, working with the unconscious. I'll read you this thing about trusting, the idea of trusting the unconscious over the conscious mind in terms of what you could use in writing. Also, experiments with cut-outs were introduced, like Tzara wrote this poem that goes like something like, "It's very easy to write a poem just take your favorite book and cut it up, and rearrange it to something new." Also, in the beginning, I hope I am being historically correct in this, the idea of publishing little magazines, independent magazines.

Now, this is a real serious work called the *Magnetic Fields,* which I don't know if I am going to read to you, but maybe you would want to look at it later. It's a long prose thing with collaboration between André Breton and Phillipe Soupalt. This is a section of it and it has a very dream-like nature. I'll read you a little part.

> Everybody loves a fire; when the color of the sky changes it's somebody dying. What can we hope for that would be better? Another man standing in front of the perfume shop was listening to the rolling of a distant drum. The night that was gliding over his head came to rest on his shoulders. Ordinary fans were for sale; they bore no more fruit. People were running without knowing why in the direction of the estuaries of the sea. Clocks, in despair, were fingering their rosaries. The cliques of the virtuous were being formed. No one went near the great avenues that are the strength of the city.

The interesting thing about this work is that it is so formal. Do you know what I mean? For this sort of, what is iconoclasm, is that these guys ultimately wrote in sentences and there is a great beauty. Apollinaire wrote great, beautiful poems. Are you familiar with his rhymes? I didn't want to read those because nowadays they sound too much like real poems. So, it's just like this idea, this state of mind, this idea not necessarily the word rebellious, but what's the word? It's not revolutionary either, but it's to change things or to find new forms or to turn everything upside down but they were doing it not only in art but in life. And then when I say that I realize that the whole point was they were saying that there was no distinction between the two, so then the Dadaist was beginning to think about that idea which nowadays we accept as being a totally natural state of affairs. Right? Do you agree?

(Student response, indecipherable.)

Also, pacifist to a great extent. Well, not speaking for everyone, but very against art because it was involved with money and selling paintings and that sort of thing. Against...well later, a little bit against the poem itself. I wanted to know though, do you agree with me when I say that nowadays we can sort of accept the idea that there isn't any distinction between life and art, the way that people at the turn of the century were having to deal with that issue?

(Student answers, indecipherable.)

I mean, ultimately, I suppose if we carry this through logically, like when I plan to lecture I always get very involved in logic, then I realize at this stage of my notes that the logical conclusion is that you have demanded that everybody rip up all their poems and stuff. I'll show you why. Why write at all? This is a little question, a little Dada questionnaire. Valerie said, "I write out of weakness." Then this guy Raoul Hausmann, do you know this one? He said, "I write to kill time." Now that's is the Dadaist consciousness. I mean easily I say imitated too, in a way. I can't think of any living writers who do that.

Student: Is this a put-on?

Mayer: Well it's a put on, but at the same time it's a put on to make a political point, right? And then again it is not entirely a put-on because one does write to kill time and one does write out of weakness.

(Sound of a pencil sharpening occurs; everyone laughs.)

Well, that is a little Dada gesture—pencil sharpener.

How many of you are familiar with the writings of Antonin Artaud? Okay, I really want to race through this part. Okay, he says "All writing is rubbish." (Giggles.) Oh, here's another Tzara thing:

> Dada; abolition of logic, which is the dance of those impotent to create: Dada; of every social hierarchy and equation set up for the sake of values by our valets: Dada; every object, all objects, sentiments, weapons for the fight: Dada; abolition of memory (that is the most interesting part) Dada; abolition of archaeology: Dada; abolition of prophets. Abolition of the future... To respect all individuals in their folly of the moment. Freedom: Dada Dada Dada, a roaring of tense colors, and interlacing of opposites and of all contradictions, grotesques, inconsistencies: LIFE

Tzara said a very interesting thing in the course of one of his numerous manifestos. He said, "Meaning is just another element in literature." Among the elements that literature is made up of like letters and syllables and words.

Okay here is the part of art being forgery. This is my favorite part. This is my favorite Dada. I think this is Valerie talking but it's being quoted by somebody else.

> A work of art is always a forgery. It is the product of the collaboration of very different states of mind. The slightest erasure is a violation of spontaneity. The striving for a rhythmical measured line, illiterate language comes up against conditions. Entirely aliened to the pattern of thought. If every work of art is a forgery it is not only because the man who composes it cannot possibly be sincere. In addition to the constraints of art, ordinary languages, 'the worst of conventions' because it opposes upon us the use of formulas and verbal associations which do not belong to us, which embody next to nothing to our true natures; the very meaning in words is fixed and unchangeable only because of abusive power by the collectively; 'one might very well know the word 'hello' and yet say 'good-bye' to the woman one meets again after a year's absence.'

That last is a quote from André Breton. Did you read *Nadja*? Anybody?

> So here's, now this is the part about only the unconscious doesn't lie. Think of this as a history, I mean this is sort of some of particular history of those ideas.

> 'The hypocrisy inherent in consciousness,' the general tendency that drives us 'to camouflage ourselves,' to seek justification of our words and acts, to cheat at all times in order to make ourselves look more beautiful or at least 'adjust' ourselves...
>
> Only the unconscious does not lie, it alone is worth bringing to life. All deliberate conscious efforts, composition, logic are feudal... At best the 'poet' can prepare traps (as a physician might do in treating a patient) with which to catch the unconscious by surprise and to prevent it from cheating...
>
> [excerpts from Marcel Raymond's *From Baudelaire to Surrealism*]

What do you think? I remember doing this actually once in a workshop and then all the people in the workshop thought that I was trying to say, to take this literally.

Gertrude Stein says, now we get to the interesting part which is really becoming the type of psychology.

(Student speaks, indecipherable.)

Oh, to prevent it [the subconscious] from cheating. I suppose what he means is the kind of thing that dreams are so difficult to unravel, and I think he is talking about the kind of things of self-glorification that would occur.

(Student speaks, indecipherable, roughly about Freud.)

Yeah, Freud didn't think much of these guys. I mean they were always quoting Freud and thinking that he would sort of join forces with them and somehow being on their side. I mean Freud's favorite bookstore is very different from the Dadaists.

(Student asks a question, indecipherable.)

Well, I think the distinction to be made is that Freud was doing what he considered to be a scientific endeavor, and since he was being harassed by on all sides from other scientists for his theories about sex, the last people he would want ally himself would be the Dadaists. But, then that all happens in history somehow, that the artist and the scientists would cross.

(Student speaks, indecipherable.)

Now the award is conscious as opposed to unconsciousness. But, I am taking off the lecture in a different direction which has to do more specifically with writing, and the process of writing, which is obviously is involved with the unconscious mind, whether we choose to use that word or not. Gertrude Stein says, "I like writing; it is so pleasant to have the ink write it down on the paper as it goes on doing." And that brings up that whole thing that we were talking about last week, the idea that someone else is writing your works for you.

Artaud makes these statements like he wants to give words the importance that they have in dreams. That's a pretty loaded idea. Okay, here is the worst thing that he says, "If there is still one hellish, truly accursed thing in our time, it is our artistic dallying with forms, instead of being like victims burnt at the stake, signaling through the flames." He's saying like no more forms, one of his works is called *No More Masterpieces.* This is all in relation to the theater too, like his idea about the theater, theater of cruelty. Do you know about that? I can't get into that. Here's another one though, which is sort of about studying.

"Not so much to defend a culture whose cultural existence has never kept a man from going hungry, as to extract, from what is called culture, ideas whose compelling force is identical with that of hunger. Not to waste in the soul concern for eating our simple power of being hungry."

Artaud is always saying we have to throw away all of our writings. Have some kind of art that is totally immediate and momentary, and lasts, the way theater is, it only happens once, and also happens to change the world.

We must get rid of our superstitious valuation text and *written* poetry. Written poetry is worth reading once, and then should be destroyed. Let the dead poets make way for others. Then we might even come to see that it is our veneration for what already has been created, however beautiful and valid it may be, that petrifies us, deadens our responses, and prevents us from making contact with that underlying power, call it thought-energy, or anything you like. Beneath the poetry of the text, there is the actual poetry without form and without text.

As I go through these things I don't know how much, well I don't know what I think about this anymore. *No More Masterpieces,* okay, we go on from there to Gertrude Stein's work *What Are Masterpieces, and Why Are There So Few of Them?* Do you have any questions? Does anybody have any questions? Any thoughts? How much of that for a lot of you were just a review in the sense that you are familiar with all those stories and everything? How many of you have you thrown away your masterpieces?

(Student speaks, indecipherable.)

I don't know about that. How many people have thrown away their masterpieces? I don't think so. I am not saying that the Dadaist should run the government or anything. There's still the idea, there's always the idea that what a writer writes is precious. I mean there is a tape recorder out here. There's always the idea that you type out a poem, and then say, the poets that have had all of their works destroyed in a fire or something. A totally traumatic situation, right? But, I think it's more interesting not in relation to that so much and whether it is bourgeois or whatever those words are, but in relation to the act of writing. I mean that is sort of what I am to talk about more. Here is a state of mind, you know?

What I was trying to say about the Dadaists is that there is a group of people who were the origins of all these ideas that supposedly new forms, like the way Williams talks about new forms. The ideas of chance and cutups, doing your own magazine, experimenting with dreams, all these things. So, it is a historical thing. Probably worthwhile to read their writings too for that reason.

(Student speaks, indecipherable.)

So nobody digs the Dadaists, huh? (Laughs.) Well, let's see what this turns into later. Let me ask you this, what do you think about the idea of looking for new forms and the making of experiments? I mean most of you have had the chance to read the list of experiments I gave you, right? What do you think about that idea in writing?

(Student speaks, indecipherable.)

Okay well, you are all being very laid back about that. What about the incredible drive and ambition to do something new. I am talking about something new. (Laughs.)

(Student asks a question, indecipherable.)

I guess I do, but my opinion is nothing of value. The point is...I mean even as an exercise or an experiment in itself, how about just to try to throw out all the old stuff that is known in one's mind. Just to see what happens. I mean it seems to me that as a writer you have to do that at least once, even if later on you end up writing totally traditional poems, as I myself do now.

What I mean is what we were talking about last week, like for each writer there's conceivably a new form, and until you can actually find it and be honest in that particular way then maybe you are just writing to pass the time.

(Student speaks, indecipherable, laugher.)

I guess what I am saying is that I'm trying to make some points about writing, the state of mind or the attitude in which one approaches writing and being a long-term thing. Like you don't say, here's the situation where I have this choice of writing a sonnet or piece of gibberish prose. You say, in some very long-term way, how am I approaching the page? Am I saying I'm going to put these words on the page? And then put them in a safety deposit box? You know? Or are you saying I'm going to throw them all around until I find some new order for these pages I have accumulated the way William's did when he was writing *Kora in Hell*? You know what I mean?

It always seems to me that if you can approach the word and the letter, and the meaning too, from every possible direction then that's what you do. The way an athlete gets ready. I mean you have to—it's a workout—and in the course of that isn't there a possibility of discovering something. Aren't there things to be discovered that are yet not known? I guess I hate to talk that way, but...

(Student speaks, indecipherable.)

I don't care if it is Avant-Garde. I mean that is a funny word. All the writers now that are called avant-gardes are sort of stuck in a morass.

I mean it is a question of energy, but then these words are so vague I hate to hear myself say them. Maybe we should go on. Does anybody have anything else to say?

Gertrude Stein says this thing that writers are always making the mistake of thinking they have to be excited instead of being exciting, and they have to be lively instead of being alive. Sort of like the idea that you have to be some analogy between being drunk and being ecstatic. She actually makes this analogy between being a saint and being a hysteric.

(Laughs and Student responses.)

Contempt? I guess that is where she is getting at, because of the way—she always likes to gerund in that way. Exciting or any gerund used to change the verb. But, it is also the idea of the present that, exciting is the present, exciting to hear is like we will get into this later. But, like an adjective, this dead old word, but the word that includes the present in it the state of the verb that has the present tense in it, and that's her favorite to do. So, it does include that as you said.

Let me go to this other experiment which I wanted you to add to your list. Which it would be to take a piece of writing and change it, first change it to the present tense and then change it to all the different tenses, one by one.

(Audio fades for some time.)

I'm going to run through it pretty closely. I don't want it to take too long. In the beginning of it she says something that has a lot to do with teaching, she says, "Talking essentially has nothing to do with creation." But, take that also to mean in relation to writing. And here's the great Gertrude Stein poem:

> The thing one gradually comes to find out is that one has no identity that is when one is in the act of doing anything. Identity is recognition, you know who you are because you and others remember anything about yourself but essentially you are not that when you are doing anything. I am I because my little dog knows me but, creatively speaking the little dog knowing that you are you and you're recognizing that he knows, is what destroys creation. That is what makes school. Picasso once remarked I do not care who it is that has or does influence me as long as it is not myself.

Should we stop for questions? I knew we had a few Gertrude Stein fans. Do you understand that? Okay, I'll go on.

> At any moment when you are you you are you without the memory of yourself because if you remember yourself while you are you you are not for purposes of creating you. This is so important because it has so much to do with the question of a writer to his audience.
>
> A masterpiece has essentially not to be necessary, it has to be that is it has to exist but it does not have to be necessary.

Now Gertrude Stein talks a lot to talk about in relation to writing the differences between identity and entity. Identity being the "I am I because my little dog knows me" and then the entity would oppose to the business of living, okay which is relation and necessity. The thing in itself as a masterpiece and not in relation to anything.

> ...Nowadays everybody all day long knows what is happening and so what is happening is not really interesting, one knows it by radios cinemas newspapers biographies autobiographies until what

is happening does not really thrill any one, it excites them a little but it does not really thrill them.

She has this great theory of why detective stories are interesting.

Well, in relation to writing—against it.

It is very curious but the detective story which is you might say the only really modern novel form that has come into existence gets rid of human nature by having the man dead to begin with, the hero is dead to begin with, and so you have so to speak got rid of the event before the book begins. There is another curious thing about detective stories. In real life people are interested in the crime more than they are in detection, it is the crime that is the thing the shock the thrill the horror but in the story it is the detection that holds the interest and that is natural enough because the necessity as far as action is concerned is the dead man, it is another function that has very little to do with human nature that makes the detection interesting. And so always it is true that the masterpiece has nothing to do with human nature or with identity, it has to do with the human mind and the entity that is in the thing in itself and not in relation.

I keep thinking that we should have some questions. The reason I'm doing this is because this essay and other essays called *Poetry and Grammar* seem like the few viable pieces of writing without writing. In the sense that I am trying to talk about it, which has to do with one's state of mind, what one is writing. So if anything isn't clear, if you want me to read anything over again, tell me. Okay, so now this is against memory. Remember we dealt with this last week like writing without remembering and that idea.

This is what makes secondary writing, it is remembering, it is very curious you begin to write something and suddenly you remember something and if you continue to remember your writing gets very confused. If you do not remember why you are writing, it may seem confused to others but actually it is clear and eventually that clarity would be clear, that is what a masterpiece is... I once said what is the use of being a boy if you're going to grow up to be a man, the boy and the man have nothing to do with each other, except in respect to memory and identity.

(Student asks a question about Marcel Proust.)

She says funny things about Proust. But, I don't know if she actually talks about Proust, does anybody know? I know Donald Sutherland talks about Proust in his book about Stein, and he says like Stein was trying to do this thing in *The Making of Americans* where she was cataloging all these people. She had charts and all the different kinds of people, and she was making them be all present people. I'm sort of using her words now to describe it, in the sense that everything would repeat. The way a character becomes a character in the making of Americans is to repeat everything that they do over and over again. Which is the way that people do exist in real life. They have no real histories in that sense they are only existing in the present moment. Then Donald Sutherland says that Proust in terms of the size of these books there is some comparison to be made. Also the time, that part of the century with what was going on. What Proust was doing just the opposite then, he was taking everything from behind, you know? But, then again, he elaborates it so completely that it turns actually into the same thing. Do you know what I mean?

(Students speaks indecipherable, roughly about Proust's approach to writing.)

Yeah, but it's such a large constellation, everything in Proust. Just somehow it all gets equalized because of the largeness. See Proust's reference was always himself and Stein reference, well I shouldn't use that word, that word has a different meaning now. Well, okay everything refers back to Proust in *Remembrance of Things Past* and Stein is all the outside.

It's his memory; it's him remembering everything and also his life. What she does is *The Making of Americans* is the comparable book of Stein's. What she's trying to do is make the whole entire rest of the world—I mean in relation to people and their personalities, I mean she is trying to include everything. And Proust was of course doing the same thing but only for himself, or through himself. Does that make sense?

(Student speaks, indecipherable.)

What does entity mean actually? We should have a dictionary. Being, right? Being and everything that is not in relation to anything else. Existing somehow on its own. I suppose what we were just talking about in a way?

She is saying that identity and entity. Human nature which would be identity, and the human mind which would be the entity.

(Student speaks, indecipherable.)

Creation. Talking about creation, creation in writing.

Maybe this will help. "*Why are there so few of them*?" —This is from *Masterpieces*.

> ...Why there are so few of them. Everything is against them. Everything that makes life go on makes identity and everything that makes identity is of necessity a necessity...And yet time and identity are what you tell about as you create only while you create they do not exist... so you write anybody does write to confirm what any one is and the more one does the more one looks like what one once was and in being so identity is made more so and that identity is not one any one can have as a thing to be but as a thing to see.

And this last thing from that essay in relation to the audience. How the audience creates the writer.

> When you are writing before there is an audience anything written is as important as any other thing and you cherish anything and everything that you have written. After the audience begins, naturally they create something that is they create you, and so not everything is so important, something is more important than another thing, which was not true when you were you that is when you are not you as your little dog knows you.

What she's saying is that once you have an audience like she did after she wrote *The Autobiography of Alice B. Toklas*, was that then she had a bit more of a struggle to get back in the state of mind where she could be as she describes herself, "Not you, the little dog knows you," which would be the stage referred to as an entity, or the human mind. It's all that old idea of the audience is what she brings up. Where's that supposed to be a crime, sort of.

I am not trying to relate her to the Dadaist. The only relation I mean in my mind, in some logical ways like the Dadaist are trying to do something new and make a total upheaval and then somebody like Gertrude Stein comes along who doesn't believe in any of same things that the Dadas believe, and then she really does it. So, logically in terms of writing it makes sense to be interested in say both those kinds of writing. Just because she was the one that carried out all these experiments. I don't think she is influenced by any of these guys. Was she? Gertrude Stein? Interested in any of those guys? Yeah, they came over for dinner or something.

I guess she knew Apollainaire. I mean they were all living there [Paris] for a time together. Gertrude Stein, when she was in college, she studied with William James, you know the philosopher? She did these experiments with what is called automatic writing. She became a doctor, she studied philosophy, and then she became a medical doctor. Then later on Donald Sutherland writes about this in his book that her experiments were not automatic writing, she just pretended that she was doing it. Everybody tries to make a case that because she did these experiments she was doing a stream of consciousness or such thing, but she said that she made up all the examples.

(Student speaks, indecipherable, talking about how to do automatic writing properly.)

She was so systematic about everything that she was doing in her writing, that it would be hard for her to accept any label like that.

If you do also read *Principles of Philosophy* by William James that it's hard, well, it isn't hard work actually, it is a loosely written book. In fact, Sutherland in the book on Stein that I was talking about keeps constantly bringing up William James and connections to William James.

I'm trying to remember something about what William James said about memory. He describes memory, you know, this was before psychology as we know it was really there. I think he describes it as—memory as looking at a piece of theater and like you see the people who are in front of the scenery, and then the scenery is there and painted there and it is fading away, and it implies everything. He's making some analogy like in a big backdrop, but there are actually objects on the stage and people. He was the person that made up the phrase stream of consciousness I think, I mean it came from him. And he does actually talk about it as being a stream, not a stream that is a river, but a stream, you know?

You know I was just talking about...Were you here last week? Others of you remember that I read this quote from Neal Cassady where he was saying that he sits down to write and starts to write a few words and tries to remember what the next words are going to be, and then so many words come flooding into his mind that he sits there for three hours and can't remember what he was supposed to say next because so many other things have come to his mind. He writes a few words and realizes that those are the wrong words and he has to go back and review everything that he forgot because he just remembered it but he's too busy and forgot it because he paid attention to the typewriter for a minute. Then he says, ends the quote by saying, like, "My mind is rotting in hell." Or something, by the end of all this. I mean it was a total description about that problem in writing and that's what the issue is, and that's what Stein's talking about too. She's also saying something else I suppose, the way the words wind up being in the paper has to be as close to the way the mind is working, otherwise then you are going to get stuck in the morass of trying to remember what you were saying next. Just like with 19th-century writers, if you sit down and say even in conversation if you know that you can't put a preposition at the end of the sentence. For example, "She was the person I came with." I can't say that so I have to plan ahead and say, "She was the person with whom I came." So then I'm remembering as soon as I said she was the person, I have to remember to say with whom then because I can't say it at the end. You know what I mean? So now how does your mind say it, how does it come out? She was the person I came with, right?

Okay, listen to this. This is from *Spring and All*:

> Though I have felt "free "and only in the presence of works of the imagination, knowing the quickening of the sense which came of it, and though this experience has held me firm as such times, yet being of the slow and accurate understanding, I have not always been able to complete the intellectual steps which would make firm in this position."

I mean he's saying something else there. But, in the beginning, he's saying the same thing Stein is talking about. He wrote a good essay on Stein actually, he was a fan.

I'm going to go on to this *Poetry and Grammar* like this essay she goes through each part of speech. Grammar might be boring to you. She has these little sort of romances with, or some of them are battles with, certain types of words. It begins by saying:

> What is poetry? And if you know what poetry is then what is prose? A noun is the name of anything. Why after a thing is named why write about it? People if you'd like to believe it can be made by their names. Call anybody Paul and they get to be Paul. Call anybody Alice and they get to be Alice.

When she wrote this essay she was totally down on nouns. Hated them. Later on, that changed like passing the time and the writing of *Tender Buttons*, and those works.

> Adjectives are not really or truly interesting. The thing that affects a not truly interesting thing of necessity not interesting.

What she is saying is that the adjective which is the thing that affects a not too interesting thing, which is the noun, then of course is not interesting either.

> Verbs and adverbs are more interesting. Nouns and adjectives can never make mistakes. Never to be mistaken, but verbs can be so aimlessly. Verbs can change to look like themselves or to look like some-

> thing else. They aren't so to speak on the move. Prepositions. I like prepositions best of all. The thing of all things that can be mistaken.

And do you all know what it means when she says mistaken? Like taken two ways or many different ways. Articles.

> Articles, please. They are a delicate and varied something.

Do you all know what articles are? A, an, the...

> Conjunctions have made themselves live by their work."

Pronouns.

> "Pronouns are not as bad as nouns.

Okay, now this is about punctuation.

> The completely uninteresting one is the question mark. It is alright when it is alone and when it used as a brand on cattle. Anybody who can read at all knows when a question is a question. It does not in its form go with ordinary printing. It is positively revolting.

See how this problem with what interrupts the look of the page. She could not stand the idea of a question mark sitting there with the letters. Because it interrupted the whole look of everything. Then we will get to commas later.

> Exclamation marks are ugly. They spoil the line of the writing and the same thing is true of quotation marks. The apostrophe for possession I can see and I do see that for many, that for some the possessive case apostrophe has gentle, tender insulation that makes it very difficult to definitely decide to do without it.

I want to show you something that is a big problem in my own writing these days. I have to constantly use this word.

(Writes on the board.) How about that? I mean isn't that awful looking? Let me print it again. I mean that is correct form, right? Do you also find it unaesthetic?

(Students speak, indecipherable, speaks intermingled with Mayer for a time.)

It is the correct form. Sorry to relate... Not singular. It's a proper name... This is the possessive form, not plural. "Lewis's Desk..." Not if it's a proper name...Can't say it ruins the sounds...Sometimes you can say it, but if you need that sound of Lewis's, you need that sound. And then have to look at this word all the time...Lew? Oh man, that's worse. LEW. Horrible. I think for writing, I always think it's good to fall in love with someone who has a one-syllable name. Really it is so much easier to deal with it. Especially in English where then it becomes the Anglo-Saxon part of the writing. Where there are a lot of one-syllable names. Okay, we go on.

Student: Did Gertrude Stein ever write anything on puns?

Mayer: Puns? She makes them all the time, but I don't know if she ever said anything about them. Not that I know of, but probably I am sure she has somewhere. Okay, here go with colons and semicolons.

> If writing should go on, what have colons and semicolons do to do with it? What have commas done to do with it? What have periods to do with it? What have small letters and capitals to do with it? With writing going on? Periods have to exist. One had to, again and again, stop sometime.

She loves periods, secretly, later in her life.

> Periods commence to break up things in arbitrary ways.

What she means there is like she would write these things, wait a second. (Flips through pages and does not find it.) Okay well, I'll make it up. She'll write these things like, "They do that. Period. In that. And then she'll say, And. Period. That. Period." You know just break up the whole sentence word by word, sometimes put a period after each word.

> Periods. They have a life of their own and did not serve you in any servile way as commas, colons, and semicolons do.

It's interesting that when she talks about periods, she talks about them in the past tense, which is a pointed thing to do. I always used to think that when I was writing this book named *Memory* that periods had to do with private property somehow, like it seemed that every time I got to a period which is not something I was using so frequently in that writing, that it was a question of somebody's private property. I don't know why though.

> You can think of colons and semicolons as commas and as such they are purely servile or you can think of periods and using them can make feel adventurous. I have finally come to be indifferent to them. Commas are servile and they have no life of their own. A comma by helping you along holding your coat for you and putting on your shoes keeps you from living your life as actively as you should need it. Commas are positively degrading.

That's actually true. What a comma does is it interrupts the clauses like if you are writing a whole string of sentences and you put commas in between the clauses then what do commas are doing, saying, *I am going to help you to read this,* and prevent any of the two clauses from interacting with each other and overlapping in a way that there would be two meanings or something. That's what she means.

> Complications make way for simplicity and therefore I have always liked dependent and arboreal clauses. You can see how loving the intensity of complication of these things that commas would be degrading and feebling them by putting in a comma. One does do pretty well by one pleases with capitals and small letters.

Okay, so we are getting close to time here now and there is something else I want to do. Then she goes on to talk about sentences and paragraphs.

> Sentences are not emotional but paragraphs are.

That's a pretty famous quote from Gertrude Stein. Well, here is a nice example of she's trying to write a sentence that is an entire paragraph on its own, and here are some examples of when she thought she had succeeded in doing that. "Once when they were nearly ready they had ordered it to close." And another one would be. "Battles are named because there have been hills which have made a hill in battle."

Just let me tell you she goes on saying about the emotional balance in prose. She said she figured this out by listening to her dog drinking water. She said that's when she realized that sentences aren't emotional, but paragraphs were. I mean, somehow that makes a lot of sense. Okay then to go through systematically with poetry, poetry has to do with a vocabulary based on the noun.

> Poetry is concerned with using, abusing, with losing, wanting, denying, with avoiding, adoring, replacing the noun, with caressing nouns. A rose is a rose, a rose is a rose, a rose is a rose, completely caressed and addressed as a noun. Poetry is essentially the discovery of the love and passion for anything.

Are they any questions about that? I was going to do a sentence diagram, but I don't if we have time. Is anyone interested in seeing a sentence diagram? No.

Student: Yeah.

Mayer: I know some people hate it. How many people would like to see a sentence diagram? (Student responds, indecipherable.) Okay well, I am going to do it real fast though. The sentence is, this is from Hawthorne, "Some authors, indeed, do far more than this, and indulge themselves in such confidential depths of revelation as could fittingly be addressed only and exclusively to the one heart and mind of perfect sympathy."

Should we really do this?

(Everyone laughs.)

Now I'll try to tell you what the parts of speech are. (Writes on the chalkboard—diagraming a sentence on the chalkboard and discussion of placements.)

That's a relatively simple sentence, right? In terms of keeping it in your mind as a structure, and that it exists that way. (Student asks question referring back to the diagrammed sentence) You break up the sentence. If I read along the bottom line here, this is going to sound like Clark Coolidge. And, indeed, for, and this, right? Now this is a more loaded word down here.

(Continued discussion around diagramming, much is indecipherable as students are off mic.)

Well, reading them backward is another really simple way to do it. You can lay them out anyway. But taking them all apart, this tends to be a nostalgic form with a lot of lines in it that makes it have some other, I mean it makes in fun in a way. But I do like to see, I mean it really inspires me, that authors are the subject of indulge. She does that like you don't notice when you're reading.

(Student question, debating the placement of words within the diagram.)

Maybe I'll do the rest of my notes here, talking about what is American more or less in structure or grammar. You know what I mean? But maybe I'll do that next time.

I want to read you these three works. Three one pages works. One by Clark Coolidge, one by Gertrude Stein, and one by Shakespeare. Then I'd be interested to see what you make of the connections.

This is a page from Clark Coolidge from *Polaroid*, which is a ninety-nine-page book that does not happen to be in the Naropa library.

> in itself is not because just
> just in stand in point
> that at which doing standing in tend
> that act back into either kind
> not as at last as about one

the long as a kind of in itself too
the just opened both kind of stand point
is left to part out really a single match
both itself in seeming and one in the open
an amid such the stand then wills apart
itself and come as same
in doing abide the last tending
around such then along one
in kind itself to them along a match bend
stand and point itself both open on and aside
have in thing during itself an aside
the last rite via a gotten apart
such itself gotten in to pass
itself between ever and often
in act here hence since there
in another itself points just lasts
itself seeming thence in itself
a standing itself during a past in back
off near two points in itself

This is "Stanza 53" from Gertrude Stein's book *Stanzas in Meditation*:

By which I know
Can they like me
Not only which they know
But they will wish
They will wish which they know
And now and ours not at all
Can they be once with which they will declare
And place and ours know
They can with better which they even will declare
That they can change or is it in a union
They can be finally to find that they
Can see and since as one can come.
Come one as one can add to come
Come which they have
Once more to add feeling to feeling.

This is "Sonnet 105" by Shakespeare:

> Let not my love be called idolatry,
> Nor my beloved as an idol show,
> Since all alike my songs and praises be
> To one, of one, still such, and ever so.
> Kind is my love to-day, to-morrow kind,
> Still constant in a wondrous excellence;
> Therefore my verse to constancy confined,
> One thing expressing, leaves out difference.
> Fair, kind, and true, is all my argument,
> Fair, kind, and true, varying to other words;
> And in this change is my invention spent,
> Three themes in one, which wondrous scope affords.
> Fair, kind, and true, have often lived alone,
> Which three till now, never kept seat in one.

Well, pretty great, aye? Here's some interesting connection for me among those three works. We can either, I don't know if I could articulate it, so perhaps we could leave it at that.

If I read you random lines from these three works, it would be interesting. I'm going to read you three lines, just single lines, one from each work.

"To one, of one, still such, and ever so."

"Itself in come as same.

"And now and ours not at all."

Now that I read Shakespeare, Coolidge, Stein. We'll do it again.

"Once more to add feeling to feeling"

"Off near two points in itself"

"One thing expressing, leaves out difference."

Then I read Stein, Coolidge, Shakespeare.

Okay, now we have a quiz:

"In doing abide the last tending"—whose line is that?

Students: Coolidge

Mayer: I know it. I guess we shouldn't have a quiz it's not fair.

The only thing I have to say about it I guess, is that it certainly does relate to what I was saying about stealing, but that isn't the point I'm trying to make. That it's useful as an exercise. I don't mean that kind of stealing.

I would say easily that those are three lyric poems, you could say that. Two of them are American.

> Why am I if I am uncertain reasons may inclose.
> Remain remain propose repose chose.
> I call carelessly that the door is open
> Which if they may refuse to open
> No one can rush to close.
> Let them be mine therefor.
> Everybody knows that I chose.
> Therefor if therefore before I close.
> I will therefore offer therefore I offer this.
> Which if I refuse to miss may be miss is mine.
> I will be well welcome when I come.
> Because I am coming.
> Certainly I come having come.
> These stanzas are done.

That's the last stanza [Stanza 83] from *Stanzas in Meditations* [by Gertrude Stein]. I couldn't decide whether to read that one or the one that I read you, so what do you think?

(Opens to discussion with students, indecipherable off mic, roughly about searching for meaning and comprehending the poems.)

Well, the meaning. The meaning is there in the words, right? I mean if you do the exercise of taking each word and looking it up in the dictionary, then you realize that each word has a meaning, apart from you and apart from the writer, apart from the reader. So that's unavoidable. It's there. Now if you say, if you open Gertrude Stein and say what does this mean? It's frustrating. Donald Sutherland says, with books like that, I assume you're talking about books like that, are you? I mean works that are dense and don't give their meaning easily?

Student: Clark Coolidge, for instance. When I know you read a landscape poem in your other class which was very accessible because I knew it was going to be a landscape poem.

Mayer: Well, in terms of reading, I mean just in terms of reading, the advice that I'm giving is just to read in it and find what interests you. If you take a book like *Polaroid,* which is ninety-nine pages long and don't start it at the beginning, or *Stanzas and Meditation,* which is a large volume, open to a random page and see if you don't start getting involved in it. The meaning kind of rides along with you. You have to give it a little room in terms of meaning in the sense that you would then be able to say, what does this mean, and say that. You can take it apart.

There's a funny thing too, actually, that Donald Sutherland did in the book (writes on chalkboard). He was trying to explain how she wrote, I mean, not how she wrote, but more like how you read her works.

Okay, so you're looking at this theoretical poem, right? And one says, what does it mean? He uses this example to say that the writer, conceivably, is sitting in a field and sees six sheep and twenty trees and an incredibly lurid sunset. There's something else about that too...

(Student speaks, indecipherable.)

Well, you take pleasure in it. You take pleasure in it.

How about John Ashbery There's a good example. He says, in the beginning three poems, the question is whether to leave all out or include all, do you remember that? Isn't that the issue that we're talking about?

(Student speaks, indecipherable.)

You mean to get rid of your own assumptions? Yeah. I heard someone say to read it aloud. That's a good thing to do.

(Student speaks, indecipherable, roughly about Clark Coolidge's work.)

I think the question is enough of an answer. It's a very interesting thing to say about Clark's work. The only thing that I can add to that, is that I always have a sense that Clark is using, handling, the words as if they were objects, putting them together in arrangements in an instinctive way to some extent, in a way that creates a structure that he considers to be appropriate...how do I say it...a structure that he has set for the words somehow that fulfills itself. And then it might be elucidating to know, to hear this poet describes Clark as a Yankee tinkerer, with words, always sort of poking at them and fooling around with them, and not being able to leave them alone really.

Clark has this phase of new poems which are lyric and melancholic. Now, very often, he and I will get into discussions about the idea of if you're doing something that everybody else thinks is programmed for some new kind of invention, or something like that. Then it always gets back to the thing I quoted you from Burroughs last week, "You don't want to be like the man who's involved in the sweet potato controversy the rest of his life. You have to do something else."

Ultimately if you're experimenting with writing, and if you're doing something like what Clark is doing, you're doing that almost compulsively, I could feel free to say, in order to get yourself so familiar with words and to find out everything there is to know about sentences and about punctuation and paragraphs and everything that's involved in writing, and then you're learning. And to some extent, I could feel free to say that I think it's boring to be writing if you're not doing things like that all the time, even if those works are, a lot of them are throw-away's, or they're done too fast or they're done some moment where maybe you are just practicing. Maybe you aren't really writing, as Gertrude Stein would say. Maybe you are just doing a little exercise or something like that. Then again, later, something else happens and then you find out what you've learned from doing that. And then Burroughs is saying like he's going back to those traditional narrative after fooling around with cut-ups and his book as we know them.

My writing has come very close to traditional poetry for a while, you know. It's very interesting to wonder what would happen next then, but I never could write poetry before, really write it. Clark is trying to teach himself how to write a sentence. I'm quite serious about this! In order to do that, he's reading proofs because he wants his writing to sort of lengthen out. At the moment they're short sentences. I mean you could talk about the histories of the basketball players like this, you know. I always like sports analogies because of the athleticism of the event, of writing, and the idea that one's state of mind is so important, one could even say one's health.

Stein says this funny thing, which might be interesting to throw in here. Among that reading that I did of Clark Coolidge and Shakespeare and Gertrude Stein, I was going to put in a section from John Ashbery's *Three Poems*, but then it's in prose, so that would have really screwed me up. But I think it's appropriate.

"Here, I tell all the young"—This is Gertrude Stein—"I tell all the young ones now to write essays, after all, since characters are of no importance, why not just write meditations, meditations are always interesting, neither character nor identity are necessary to him who meditates."

I think one could certainly look at the three works that I've read you plus John Ashbery's book *Three Poems*, and consider them to be meditations of a sort. I think the sonnets, Shakespeare's sonnets, can be looked at in that way, and you know, *Stanzas in Meditation*, and *Polaroid*, and *Three Poems*. So are there any questions, more questions? Does that seem to come together? Does anything come together from this class?

I was interested in asking you before we go, to tell me who the writers are that have influenced you. Just one or two, one is enough.

Writing Invitations

As the anthology is a celebration of the creative thought and writing springing from the Jack Kerouac School's Summer Writing Program, we have compiled prompts emerging from the previous lectures and classes to inspire the experimental application of their ideas.

Identity and Language

Our sense of self and identity is inextricably linked to our names, their history, their gendering. Conduct research into your namesake including its lineage and etymology. You might also consider any personal history as to how you were named. How might you reflect or reject its essence? To expand—in what ways, both in relation to name and language and without, have you felt marginalized or not felt marginalized? In what ways might these intersect?

Dislocating Gender

How can we recognize social locations while working against gender essentialism?

For this exercise, write a narrative or a poem, and describe an encounter between two people without using figures of speech. Also, try to avoid using the "to be" verb: *am, is are*; *was, were*; and *been, being*. Think about the process of disorientation, and how by omitting the "to be" verb you are also omitting identifying markers within the English language. Think of the writing as an instant that is suspended in emotion, or memory, or both.

Unveiling Cryptonyms

As Augustine states in "Cryptonyms Under the Moon," "To have a name is to have power. To have the capacity to name your experience accurately is to have poetic magical incantatory power. That is why I wanted to leave you with the question which is implicit in Loy's passage. When you are talking to someone are you gibbering cryptonyms? Are you trying to say your secret name when you can't? Are you saying it when it can't be heard?" Write into your cryptonyms. What is your secret name, your secret truth, your secret language? Foster your power through exploring the cryptic and known, what it means to discover and name experience and self.

Crafting Persona

The modern *persona* coined by Freud's student Jung came to mean "a kind of mask, designed on the one hand to make a definite impression upon others, and on the other to conceal the true nature of the individual." Craft or borrow a mask and enter a piece of writing with a personal other than your own. Perhaps this is a shift in class, gender, or even moving from human to other-worldly creature. How does perspective change? What confines and liberates you through a persona?

Personal Myth

Helen in Egypt is considered H.D.'s "personal myth." Consider a timeless tale, myth, or lore that deeply resonates with you. Now adapt it into your language of your personal myth. What does it tell you about the way you walk in the world? The way you perceive and perhaps the way you are perceived?

Origin and Myth

Anne Waldman was particularly inspired by H.D.'s mode of working with mythology and etymology. As an experimental writing study, she suggests, "As a source and as a way to proceed and process one's experience, and a way to work with Eidolon and with Muse...take a deity or a goddess or a or something that you feel some real connection with and actually go into the etymology as well as the resonance in your own life in terms of dream or mythology." Allow constellations across the depth of linguistic origin and personal introspection.

Dreams as Muse

Use your dreams as your inspiration and guide. Take their symbols and felt sense as the foundation for your work. Allow for associations to arise naturally. Follow where your subconscious takes you. Defy linearity.

Sound Linking

A large part of H.D.'s work plays with the origins and sonics of words, their opening potential through word play, mirroring, and mimicking. Choose a particular word or set of words to begin your writing experiment. Find commonality across the origins and allow linguistic links to form through the sonics and aesthetics of the words. What new meanings arise when words that look and sound similar are joined in the same space?

Dissonant Repetition

The first lecture on Gertrude Stein describes her play with automatic writing experiments. As she did, choose a word in which you will write repeatedly. In the lecture, the example is *blue blue blue blue*. While writing by hand, read aloud an addition text of your choice. Notice how and where the aloud reading enters your writing, what chance encounters might arise. Even more, upon finishing the section obverse the places where you did not notice the disruption to your repeated phrase. What comes from this experiment?

Language of Pleasure

Smedman notes that Gertrude Stein chose "cow" as a euphemism for "female orgasm" due in part to a lack of vocabulary available to describe the nuanced variables of female sexual pleasure. Consider the conventional words and/or re-invent your own, branch beyond words to create a language for feminine jouissance.

Sans Verbs

Write without verbs. In their place, utilize nouns, pronouns, or prepositions to add connectivity and action. What energy arises from this constraint?

Paint with Words

In the conversation following Smedman's lecture on Stein, a participant mentions that Stein said of herself that she liked to employ words like her fine arts contemporaries employed paint. How might you construct a 'painting of words'? That is, if each word, or even letter is an individual brushstroke, what might you compose? How do the words become atmospheric? Relational?

Object as Symbol

An object is consumed by its symbolic nature. Augustine states, "This is a very useful technique, the guarantee of the need to express resides in the object's muteness. It's the very fact that the thing is different from the word that makes him want to go work as a writer." As Ponge writes "The Carnation" or how Gertrude Stein writes *Tender Buttons*, choose an object and write into its symbolic state, allowing personal reflection, intuition, and significance to give definition within the abstraction of language. Circle the object with language without precisely naming it.

Performative Dimension

For this exercise, conjure a poem or a story that is not restricted to the printed page. Consider what it means to write or create in the dimension of *she*. If you'd like, you can inform your process by observing Martha Rosler's *Semiotics of the Kitchen*, or Gabrielle Civil's work on performance. When you are ready, expel the poem into the air—use your body or other material to express what is deeply felt. You might also feel inclined to film this moment.

Aesthetic Letters

In Augustine's lecture on Form and Function, she emphasizes how form follows function, how a piece of writing calls to unfold. Often, this is tethered to how a piece is experienced aesthetically on the page. Experiment with the spacing of words and the overall presentation of the page. How does this shape meaning and encounter? Embrace visual poetry where the physical appearance of letters and words hold equal value and relationship to their collective meaning.

Surreal Body

As inspired by Breton and Waldman's poem in Jane Augustine's class "Women in the Surrealism Movement," consider a body—be it your own body, a body of a beloved, a body of a detested, or otherwise. This might be a celebration or anti-celebration. In your writing, move to each part of the body and allow for wild comparisons to arise. Embrace juxtapositions, synesthesia, and mechanisms of the dream to navigate a pathway toward a revealed unconscious associations and surprising language.

Automatic Writing

Complete a session of automatic writing or stream of consciousness writing. This is best done in long hand. Allow yourself to write without interruption, without leaving the page. Record everywhere your thoughts go, its associations and tangents, its imagery and impressions. Try to sink into a flow so you are writing without conscious awareness, without trying to place the subsequent words; allow the process to take you.

Fragmented Experience

"The fragment is your daily experience," says Jane Augustine. "[W]e are in a social world that fragments us. Therefore, use that form." Write a ten-minute prose poem of made of fragments: begin with describing your own embodied experience in this moment, then allow all aspects of your mind to enter the poem, including fragments of memory, daydream, observation, and free association.

Recon(text)ualizing Collage

As Michael Heller states in "Objectified Psyche," "For both Moore and Niedecker, their borrowings or wrenching of texts, their modernist collaging of all sorts of material, constitutes an indecorous break with the linear patterning of history, with the inherited gestalt of imposing totality." In your writing pull from other sources and ideas, but break them from their usual context and patterns. Experiment with ways to decontextualize and recontextualize the familiar through combination and juxtaposition to forge new modes of connectivity and thought.

Cut-up Poems

In the spirit of Dadaists, create a cut-up poem. You might do this in a couple different ways. 1) Search around you for sources of text, be in magazines, cards, books, ads, etc., and cut apart text that calls to you. Rearrange it to form a new work. 2) Take a piece of writing that is your own. Cut it apart by word, phrase, sentence, or whatever form calls to you. Reorder and replace. 3) Combine 1 and 2 to create a work that is a hybrid of found and original text to cultivate new meaning through serendipity.

Recording the Landscape

Go to the nearest natural landscape; look for a space with minimal markings of civilization or human presence; find a comfortable place to sit. Return to this location as often as you can for at least a month, ideally return as often as possible for a year. Visit this exact location during different times and days, with a different notebook or writing implement. Record the daily changes to this 'unchanging' landscape with all of your senses. Regardless of repetitive natural cycles, each visit will be unique. Remember to see where you are, not what your mind imagines. Try for as little external interaction as possible; strive for isolation. Do not bring your phone or anything which interrupts the isolation. Note what fears or anxieties you brought with you without dwelling on them and return to your location. At the end of the exercise, bring someone with you to your site. Share with them what you've witnessed, concisely and without adding your emotions in the descriptions—you are showing them the location, not your presence in it.

Meditations in Writing

Gertrude Stein said, "I tell all the young ones now to write essays, after all, since characters are of no importance, why not just write meditations, meditations are always interesting, neither character nor identity are necessary to him who meditates." In the spirit of her suggestion, allow your interiority to open. What are your contemplations? Observations?

Reflection

In Joanne Kyger's lecture on Mina Loy, Gertrude Stein, and Lorine Niedecker, she opens by introducing a review anthology compiled by Margaret Anderson and Jane Heap that multiple writers of the time answered. Respond to these same questions: What would you like most to do, to know, to be? Why wouldn't you change places with any other human being? What do you look forward to? What do you fear most from the future? What has been the happiest moment of your life? The unhappiest? What do you consider your weakest characteristics? Your strongest? What do you like most about yourself?"

Homage through Experimentation

The anthology is full of women experimenting with the use of language. Create a poem in the style of or paying homage to a writer from within the anthology. How does this challenge or open your usual writing habits?

Works Cited

Introduction by C. M. Chady

(no citations)

What is in a name?
Linguistically ingrained gender and sexuality by C. M. Chady

(no citations)

Gender/Self Contradiction by Jane Augustine

Augustine, Jane. *Gender / Self Contradiction [1/2],* Jack Kerouac School of Disembodied Poetics Audio Archive, 1991, https://cdm16621.contentdm.oclc.org/digital/collection/p16621coll1/id/720/rec/2.

—. *Gender / Self Contradiction [2/2],* Jack Kerouac School of Disembodied Poetics Audio Archive, 1991, https://cdm16621.contentdm.oclc.org/digital/collection/p16621coll1/id/1737/rec/1.

Cixous, Hélène and Catherine Clément. *The Newly Born Woman.* University of Minnesota Press, 1975.

Irigaray, Luce. *Speculum of the Other (Woman).* Cornell University Press, 1985.

Rich, Adrienne. *Of Woman Born: Motherhood as Institution and Experience.* W. W. Norton & Company, 1976.

A Spiral Across Space and Time: The Life of H.D. by Emily Trenholm

Blackie, Sharon. "The Holy Longing," The Bone Cave, 27 February, 2021.

Campbell, Joseph. *The Power of Myth.* Doubleday, 1988.

Duncan, Robert. *The H.D. Book.* Frontier Press, 1984.

H.D. *Trilogy.* Edited by Aliki Barnstone, New Directions, 1998.

Jarnot, Lisa. Naropa University. Summer Writing Program, Boulder, CO, 18 June, 2020.

American Women in the Experimental Tradition: H.D. by Joanne Kyger

Kyger, Joanne. *American Women in the Experimental Tradition: H.D.,* Jack Kerouac School of Disembodied Poetics Audio Archive, 1991, https://cdm16621.contentdm.oclc.org/digital/collection/p16621coll1/id/1736/rec/1

Guest, Barbara. *Herself Defined: the Poet H D and Her World.* Collins, 1985.

H. D. *Red Roses for Bronze.* New York: AMS Press, 1970.

A Rose is a Rose Unless it is a Sea Rose by Amy Bobeda

Duncan, Robert, Michael Boughn, and Victor Coleman. *The H.D. Book.* Berkeley, Calif: University of California Press, 2012. Print. Pg. 449

Stein, Gertrude. "Sacred Emily" *Geography and Plays.* 1922

Imagism, Objectivism, and Feminism by Jane Augustine

Augustine, Jane. *Imagism, Objectivism, and Feminism,* Jack Kerouac School of Disembodied Poetics Audio Archive, 1987, https://archive.org/details/Jane_Augustine_class_Imagism_objectivism_and_feminism_July_1987_87P068

H. D. *Hedylus.* Shakespeare Head Press, 1928.

—. *Helen in Egypt.* New Directions, 1974.

—. "Hermes of the Ways," *Poetry,* 1913.

—. *Palimpsest. Carbondale: Southern Illinois University Press, 1968.*

—. *Sea Garden. Boston: Houghton Mifflin, 1916.*

—. *The Gift: the Complete Text.* Jane Augustine, ed. Gainesville : University Press of Florida, 1988.

—. "The Mystery," "Sea Rose." *Collected Poems, 1912-1944.* Edited by Louis L. Martz, 1983.

—. *Tribute to Freud.* Boston: D.R. Godine, 1974.

—. *Trilogy.* New Directions, 1973.

H.D. and Perdita Schaffner. *HERmione. New Directions Publishing, 1981.*

Niedecker, Lorine. *From this Condensery: The Complete Work of Lorine Niedecker.* Edited by Robert J. Bertholf. Jargon Society, 1985.

Zukofsky, Louis. "Program: 'Objectivists'." *Poetry,* February 1931.

Conjuring the Infinite Imaginary by C. M. Chady

Cixous, Hélène and Catherine Clément. *The Newly Born Woman*. University of Minnesota Press, 1975.

H. D. *Helen in Egypt*. New Directions, 1974.

—. *Trilogy*. New Directions, 1973.

H. D.: Mysticism and Language by Jane Augustine

Augustine, Jane. *H. D.: Mysticism and Language,* Jack Kerouac School of Disembodied Poetics Audio Archive, 1987, https://cdm16621.contentdm.oclc.org/digital/collection/p16621coll1/id/2647

Cixous, Hélène. "Laugh of the Medusa." Translated by Keith Cohen and Paula Cohen. *Signs,* Vol. 1, No. 4 (Summer, 1976), pp. 875-893, The University of Chicago Press, 1976.

Cixous, Hélène and Catherine Clément. "Sorties," *The Newly Born Woman*. University of Minnesota Press, 1975.

H. D. *Helen in Egypt*. New Directions, 1974.

—. *Palimpsest. Carbondale: Southern Illinois University Press, 1968.*

—. "The Mystery," "Sea Rose." *Collected Poems, 1912-1944*. Edited by Louis L. Martz, 1983.

—. *Trilogy*. New Directions, 1973.

Irigaray, Luce. *The Sex Which is Not One*. Cornell University Press, 1985.

Unto Herself by Stephanie Michele

Stein, Gertrude. *Tender Buttons*. New York: New York: Claire Marie, 1914; City Lights Books, 2014.

American Women in the Experimental Tradition: Gertrude Stein by Joanne Kyger

Kyger, Joanne. *American Women in the Experimental Tradition: Gertrude Stein,* Jack Kerouac School of Disembodied Poetics Audio Archive, 1991, https://cdm16621.contentdm.oclc.org/digital/collection/p16621coll1/id/719/rec/29

Brinnin, John M, and John Ashbery. *The Third Rose: Gertrude Stein and Her World*, 1987. Print.

Picasso, Matisse and Gertrude Stein. *The Long Gay Book. 1909-1912; The Project Gutenberg, 2015, eBook.*

Stein, Gertrude.

—. *Three Lives.* New York: Grafton Press, 1909; Bartleby.com, 2000.

—. *The Making of Americans.* Contact Press, 1925; Something Else Press, 1966.

—. *The Portrait of Mabel Dodge.* Florence : Privately Printed, 1912.

—. *How To Write.* 1931; Dover Publications, 1975.

—. *The Geographical History of America Or the Relation of Human Nature to the Human Mind.* 1936; Random House, 2013.

Stein, Gertrude, and Richard Kostelanetz. *The Yale Gertrude Stein: Selections.* New Haven: Yale University Press, 1980. Print.

Stein, Gertrude and Virgil Thomson. *The Mother of Us All. 1947.*

A Handful of Clitoral Words by Ada McCartney

Audre Lorde: dream of europe SELECTED SEMINARS AND INTERVIEWS 1984-1992. Edited by Mayra Rodriguez Castro. Kenning. 2021.

Smedman, Lorna. "Primer for the Making for Grammatical Terrorism", Lecture series at Naropa University. https://cdm16621.contentdm.oclc.org/digital/collection/p16621coll1/id/1740

Student Reading, Naropa University 1978. https://cdm16621.contentdm.oclc.org/digital/collection/p16621coll1/id/1853/rec/6

Yuknavitch, Lidia. *Chronology of Water.* Hawthorne Books. 2010.

As A Wife Has A Cow A Love Story:
Gertrude Stein and The Ways Words by Lorna Smedman

Smedman, Lorna. *As A Wife Has A Cow A Love Story: Gertrude Stein and The Ways Words,* Jack Kerouac School of Disembodied Poetics Audio Archive, 1991, https://cdm16621.contentdm.oclc.org/digital/collection/p16621coll1/id/2807/rec/26.

Cixous, Hélène. "Laugh of the Medusa." Translated by Keith Cohen and

Paula Cohen. *Signs,* Vol. 1, No. 4 (Summer, 1976), pp. 875-893, The University of Chicago Press, 1976.
Gass. William. "And." Essay on Gertrude Stein's *Three Lives* Melanctha.
Irigaray, Luce. *The Sex Which is Not One*. Cornell University Press, 1985.
Stein, Gertrude.
—. *Lectures In America*: "What Is English Literature." 1935.
—. *Lectures In America*: "Poetry and Grammar." 1935.
—. *Tender Buttons*. New York: New York: Claire Marie, 1914; City Lights Books, 2014.
—. *A Book Concluding With As a Wife Has a Cow: A Love Story*. Something Else Press, 1973.
Stein, Gertrude, and Richard Kostelanetz. "A Sonatina Followed by Another." *The Yale Gertrude Stein: Selections*. New Haven: Yale University Press, 1980. Print.
Stimpson, Catherine. "Gertrude Stein and the Transposition of Gender." *The Poetics of Gender*. Ed. Nancy K. Miller. New York: Columbia UP, 1986.
Dickinson, Emily. *Final Harvest: Emily Dickinson's Poems 1830-1886*. Boston: Little, Brown & Co., 1961.
Dickinson, Emily, and Thomas H. Johnson. *The Complete Poems of Emily Dickinson*, 1960. Print.

Finding Jouissance: Feminine Writing and the Dissolution of Ego by Chloe Tsolakoglou

Cixous, Hélène and Catherine Clément. *The Newly Born Woman*. University of Minnesota Press, 1975.

Clarice Lispector: Brazilian-Ukrainian Avantgardist Before Her Time by Jane Augustine

Augustine, Jane. *L'Ecriture Feminine [1/2]*, Jack Kerouac School of Disembodied Poetics Audio Archive, 1990, https://cdm16621.contentdm.oclc.org/digital/collection/p16621coll1/id/24
Cixous, Hélène. E*ntre l'écriture*. Editions des femmes, 1986.
Cixous, Hélène and Catherine Clément. *The Newly Born Woman*. University of Minnesota Press, 1975.

Lispector, Clarice. *The Passion According to G.H.* Minneapolis: University of Minnesota Press, 1988.
—. *The Stream of Life*. Minneapolis: University of Minnesota Press, 1989.

Chickadee-dee-dee by Marlie McGovern

"All About Birds: Mountain Chickadee." Cornell Lab of Ornithology, 2019. https://www.allaboutbirds.org/guide/Mountain_Chickadee/
"All About Birds: Black-capped Chickadee." Cornell Lab of Ornithology, 2019. .https://www.allaboutbirds.org/guide/Black-capped_Chickadee
Kaufman, Ken. "Black-capped Chickadee." *Guide to North American Birds: Audubon Field Guide*. National Audubon Society. https://www.audubon.org/field-guide/bird/black-capped-chickadee
—. "Mountain Chickadee." *Guide to North American Birds: Audubon Field Guide*. National Audubon Society. https://www.audubon.org/field-guide/bird/mountain-chickadee

On Form and Function by Jane Augustine

Augustine, Jane. *On Form and Function*, , Jack Kerouac School of Disembodied Poetics Audio Archive, 1989, https://cdm16621.contentdm.oclc.org/digital/collection/p16621coll1/id/2750
Cixous, Hélène and Catherine Clément. "Sorties," *The Newly Born Woman*. University of Minnesota Press, 1975.
Finlay, Ian Hamilton. *"Ian Hamilton Finlay (1964)." An Anthology of Concrete Poetry. Ed. Emmett Williams. New York: Something Else Press, 1967. N.pag. Print.*
Howe, Susan. *My Emily Dickinson*. New Directions, 1985.
Ponge, Francis. *Vegetation*. Translated by Lee Fahnestock. Red Dust, 1988.
—.*Le Parti Pris des Choses*. Gallimard, 1942.

Women at Play: The feminine undercurrent of Surrealism and the unconscious by C. M. Chady

Carrington, Leonora. *The Hearing Trumpet.* Editions Flammarion, 1974. Penguin Books, 2005.

Cixous, Hélène. "Laugh of the Medusa." Translated by Keith Cohen and Paula Cohen. *Signs,* Vol. 1, No. 4 (Summer, 1976), pp. 875-893, The University of Chicago Press, 1976.

Cixous, Hélène and Catherine Clément. "Sorties," *The Newly Born Woman.* University of Minnesota Press, 1975.

Codrescu, Andrei. *Surrealism and the Suggestion of the Unconscious,* Jack Kerouac School of Disembodied Poetics Audio Archive, 1988, https://archive.org/details/Andrei_Codrescu_lecture_Surrealism_unconsciousness_July_19 88_88P028

Kyger, Joanne. *American Women in the Experimental Tradition: Mina Loy, Lorine Niedecker, and Gertrude Stein,* Jack Kerouac School of Disembodied Poetics Audio Archive, 1991,https://cdm16621.contentdm.oclc.org/digital/collection/p16621coll1/id/726/rec/67

Suleiman, Susan. *Subversive Intent: Gender, Politics, and the Avant-Garde.* Harvard University Press, 1990.

Women in the Surrealist Movement by Jane Augustine

Augustine, Jane. *Women in the Surrealist Movement,* , Jack Kerouac School of Disembodied Poetics Audio Archive, 1988, https://cdm16621.contentdm.oclc.org/digital/collection/p16621coll1/id/2689

Auster, Paul. *Book of 20th Century French Poetry.* Random House, 1984.

Breton, André. "Free Union," *Book of 20th Century French Poetry.* Edited by Paul Auster. Random House, 1984.

Chadwick, Whitney. *Women Artists and the Surrealist Movement.* Thames & Hudson, 1985.

Loy, Mina. *The Lost Lunar Baedeker,* 1923. Edited by Roger L. Conover, Carcanet Press Limited, 1996.

Rimbaud, Arthur. "Voyelles/Vowels." 1871.

Stein, Gertrude. *The Autobiography of Alice B. Toklas,* New York, Harcourt, Brace and Company, 1933.

Stevens, Wallace. "Bantams in Pine-woods." *The Dial*, 1922. Poetry Foundation, 2021.

Waldman, Anne. "Fast Speaking Woman," *Fast Speaking Woman*. Pocket Poets 33, San Francisco: City Lights, 1978.

—. "Queen." Naropa University and Personal Archive.

For One Night Only by Kathy Tun

(No citations)

American Women in the Experimental Tradition: Mina Loy, Lorine Niedecker, and Gertrude Stein by Joanne Kyger

Kyger, Joanne. *American Women in the Experimental Tradition: Mina Loy, Lorine Niedecker, and Gertrude Stein*, Jack Kerouac School of Disembodied Poetics Audio Archive, 1991,https://cdm16621.contentdm.oclc.org/digital/collection/p16621coll1/id/726/rec/67

Kouidis, Virginia. *Mina Loy: American Modernist Poet and the Last Lunar Baedeker.* Louisiana State University Press, 1980.

Loy, Mina. *The Lost Lunar Baedeker,* 1923. Edited by Roger L. Conover, Carcanet Press Limited, 1996.

—. "Brâncuşi's Golden Bird." *The Lost Lunar Baedeker,* 1923. Edited by Roger L. Conover, Carcanet Press Limited, 1996.

—. "Gertrude Stein." *The Lost Lunar Baedeker,* 1923. Edited by Roger L. Conover, Carcanet Press Limited, 1996.

—. "Feminist Manifesto." *The Lost Lunar Baedeker,* 1923. Edited by Roger L. Conover, Carcanet Press Limited, 1996.

—. "Letters of the Unliving." *The Lost Lunar Baedeker,* 1923. Edited by Roger L. Conover, Carcanet Press Limited, 1996.

—. "Love Songs I/Song to Johannes [title changed in 1931]" *The Lost Lunar Baedeker,* 1923. Edited by Roger L. Conover, Carcanet Press Limited, 1996.

—. "The Widow's Jazz." *The Lost Lunar Baedeker,* 1923. Edited by Roger L. Conover, Carcanet Press Limited, 1996.

McAlmon, Robert *Being Genuises Together.* 1938. Edited by Kay Boyle. North

Point Press, 1984.
Monroe, Harriet. "Comment: The Editor in France," *Poetry: Magazine of Verse*. Vol. XXIII, Oct-March 1923-24, pp. 95.
Niedecker, Lorine. *Between Your House and Mine: The Letters of Lorine Niedecker to Cid Corman, 1960-1970.* Duke University Press, 1986.
—. "I rose from marsh mud" *Collected Works*. Edited by Jenny Penberthy, University of California Press, 2002.
—. "My friend tree" *Collected Works*. Edited by Jenny Penberthy, University of California Press, 2002.
—. *My Life by Water: Collected Poems 1936-1968*. Fulcrum P., 1970.
—. "My life by water" *Collected Works*. Edited by Jenny Penberthy, University of California Press, 2002.
—. "Nursery Rhyme" *Collected Works*. Edited by Jenny Penberthy, University of California Press, 2002.
—. "Old Mother turns blue and from us" *Collected Works*. Edited by Jenny Penberthy, University of California Press, 2002.
—. "Paul" *Collected Works*. Edited by Jenny Penberthy, University of California Press, 2002.
—. "Poet's Work" *Collected Works*. Edited by Jenny Penberthy, University of California Press, 2002.
—. "Remember my little granite pail" *Collected Works*. Edited by Jenny Penberthy, University of California Press, 2002.
—. "The clothesline post is set," *Collected Works*. Edited by Jenny Penberthy, University of California Press, 2002.
—. "To my pressure pump," *Collected Works*. Edited by Jenny Penberthy, University of California Press, 2002.
—. "You are my friend" *Collected Works*. Edited by Jenny Penberthy, University of California Press, 2002.
Pound, Ezra, "A List of Books," *Little Review*, March 1918; rpt. in Ezra Pound, Selected Prose 1909-1965, ed William Cookson (New York: New Directions, 1973), pp. 424-25.

Trace by Stephanie Michele

(no citations)

Cryptonyms Under the Moon. Mina Loy: Surrealist, Feminist, Poet, Artist by Jane Augustine

Augustine, Jane. *Cryptonyms Under the Moon. Mina Loy: Surrealist, Feminist, Poet, Artist,* Jack Kerouac School of Disembodied Poetics Audio Archive, 1988, https://cdm16621.contentdm.oclc.org/digital/collection/p16621coll1/id/2690

Loy, Mina. *The Lost Lunar Baedeker,* 1923. Edited by Roger L. Conover, Carcanet Press Limited, 1996.

—. "Anglo-Mongrels and the Rose." *The Lost Lunar Baedeker,* 1923. Edited by Roger L. Conover, Carcanet Press Limited, 1996.

—. "Aphorisms on Futurism." *The Lost Lunar Baedeker,* 1923. Edited by Roger L. Conover, Carcanet Press Limited, 1996.

—. "Chiffon Velours." *The Lost Lunar Baedeker,* 1923. Edited by Roger L. Conover, Carcanet Press Limited, 1996.

—. "Hot Cross Bum." *The Lost Lunar Baedeker,* 1923. Edited by Roger L. Conover, Carcanet Press Limited, 1996.

—. "Songs to Joannes." *The Lost Lunar Baedeker,* 1923. Edited by Roger L. Conover, Carcanet Press Limited, 1996.

—. "Songs to Joannes." *The Other,* 1917.

—. "The Effectual Marriage." *The Lost Lunar Baedeker,* 1923. Edited by Roger L. Conover, Carcanet Press Limited, 1996.

—. "The Widow's Jazz." *The Lost Lunar Baedeker,* 1923. Edited by Roger L. Conover, Carcanet Press Limited, 1996.

Chesler, Phyllis. *Women in Madness,* Doubleday, 1972.

Arroyo del Alma by A. M. B. Brennan

Baker, Jennifer. "Black Women Poets Will Start the Revolution." Electric Literature, 27 Feb. 2020, https://electricliterature.com/black-women-poets-will-start-the-revolution/.

"Lorine Niedecker." Poetry Foundation, Poetry Foundation, https://www.poetryfoundation.org/poets/lorine-niedecker.

McGovern, Marlie. "Chickadee-dee-dee," *Embodied Unconscious: the feminine space of sexuality, surrealism, and experimentation in literature.* Spuyten Duyvil, 2022.

Odelle, Melanie. "NBCC Poetry Finalist Interviews - 2018." Creative Writing at The New School, The New School Creative Writing, 15 May 2018, https://newschoolwriting.org/category/2018-nbcc-finalist-interviews/nbcc-poetry-finalist-interviews-2018/.

Objectified Psyche by Michael Heller

Heller, Michael. Objectified Psyche, Jack Kerouac School of Disembodied Poetics Audio Archive, 1991, https://cdm16621.contentdm.oclc.org/digital/collection/p16621coll1/id/2801/rec/5.

Breslin, Glenna. "Lorine Niedecker and Louis Zukofsky." Pacific Coast Philology, vol. 20, no. 1/2, Penn State University Press, 1985, pp. 25–32, https://doi.org/10.2307/1316512.

Brownstein, Marilyn. *The Gender of Modernism: A Critical Anthology*. Edited by Bonnie Kime Scott, Indiana Univ. Press, 1995.

—. "Marianne Moore." In Scott, ed., The Gender of Modernism, 323-32.

DuPlessis, Rachel Blau. *The Pink Guitar: Writing as Feminist Practice*. University of Alabama Press, 2006.

Faranda, Lisa Pater, ed., "Between Your House and Mine": The Letters of Lorine Niedecker to Cid Corman, 1960 to 1970 (Durham: Duke University Press, 1986), 185, 46.

Grossman, Allen R., and Halliday, Mark. The sighted singer : two works on poetry for readers and writers. United Kingdom, Johns Hopkins University Press, 1992.

Heller, Michael. *Conviction's Net of Branches: Essays on the Objectivist Poets and Poetry*. Southern Illinois University Press, 1985.

—. *Carl Rakosi: Man and Poet*. National Poetry Foundation, University of Maine, 1993.

—. In the Builded Place: Poems. Coffee House Press, 1989.

Moore, Marianne. "'Hymen' By H. D. (Reviewed By Marianne Moore)." Broom: An International Magazine Of The Arts, vol. 4, no. 2, Jan. 1923, p. 133., https://doi.org/http://libserv14.princeton.edu/bluemtn/?a=d&d=b-mtnaap192301-01.2.27&e=———-en-20--1--txt-txIN———.

— . Letter to Elizabeth Bishop. 16 October 1940. Found p 137. https://moorearchive.org/custom/claire/costello_mm_and_bishop.pdf.

—. Letter to Elizabeth Bishop. 07 March 1937. Goodridge, Celeste, et al. Selected Letters. United Kingdom, Penguin Books, 1998.

—. *Marianne Moore: Woman and Poet*, edited by Patricia C. Willis, National Poetry Foundation, Orono, ME, 1990.

—. "Moore's Masterpiece: The Pangolin's Alternating Blaze." Marianne Moore: Woman and Poet, edited by Patricia C. Willis, National Poetry Foundation, Orono, ME, 1990.

—. "Part of a Novel, Part of a Poem, Part of a Play: The Hero." Poetry: A Magazine of Verse, Edited by Harriet Monroe, XL, no. 3, June 1932, pp. 126–128.

—. The Complete Poems of Marianne Moore. 1st ed., Macmillan, 1967.

Niedecker, Lorine. *From this Condensery: The Complete Work of Lorine Niedecker.* Edited by Robert J. Bertholf. Jargon Society, 1985.

—. Truck 16: Lorine Niedecker. Truck Press, 1975.

Niedecker, Lorine, and Cid Corman. *The Granite Pail: The Selected Poems of Lorine Niedecker.* Gnomon, 1996.

—. *Between Your House and Mine: The Letters of Lorine Niedecker to Cid Corman, 1960-1970.* Duke University Press, 1986.

Niedecker, Lorine, and Jenny Lynn Penberthy. *Collected Works.* University of California Press, 2002.

—. "In Pa's Spitbox". Lorine Niedecker: Collected Works. University of California Press, 2004.

—. *Lorine Niedecker: Woman and Poet.* Orono, Me: National Poetry Foundation, University of Maine, 1996. Print.

Niedecker, Lorine, et al. *Lake Superior: Lorine Niedecker's Poem and Journal, along with Other Sources, Documents, and Readings.* Wave Books, 2013.

Penberthy, Jenny, ed., "Lorine Niedecker: 'Knee-Deck Her Daisies': Selections from Her Letters to Louis Zukofsky," *Sulfur,* 18 (1987), 110–51, 129.

Pound, Ezra. *The Cantos of Ezra Pound.* United Kingdom, New Directions Publishing Corporation, 1998.

Sielke, Sabine. *Fashioning the Female Subject: The Intertextual Networking of Dickinson, Moore, and Rich.* United States, University of Michigan Press, 1997.

Wallace, Stevens. *The Necessary Angel: Essays on Reality and Imagination.* Vintage, 1951.

Williams, William Carlos. "Introduction to The Wedge," *Selected Essays.* New Directions, New York, New York, 1969.

**Where the Unconscious Monsters Are:
A Feminine Surrealist Guide to Andrei Codrescu's Outside
by Kendra Noelle Richard**

Breton, André. *Manifeste du surréalisme (Manifestoes of Surrealism)*. Éditions du Sagittaire, 1924.

Codrescu, Andrei. *The Disappearance of The Outside: A Manifesto for Escape*. Addison-Wesley Co., 1990.

—. *The Disappearance of The Outside: A Manifesto for Escape*. Ruminator Books, 2001.

—. *The Posthuman Dada Guide: Tzara & Lenin Play Chess*. Princeton University Press, 2009.

Tzara, Tristan. *Manifeste Dada (Dada Manifesto)*. Dada Vol. 3, 1918.

Surrealism and the Suggestion of the Unconscious by Andrei Codrescu

Codrescu, Andrei. *Surrealism and the Suggestion of the Unconscious*, Jack Kerouac School of Disembodied Poetics Audio Archive, 1988, https://archive.org/details/Andrei_Codrescu_lecture_Surrealism_unconsciousness_July_19 88_88P028

Breton, André. *Manifeste du surréalisme (Manifestoes of Surrealism)*. Éditions du Sagittaire, 1924.

—. *The Disappearance of The Outside: A Manifesto for Escape*. Addison-Wesley Co., 1990.

Deleuze, Gilles. *Foucault*. Éd. Du Minuit, 1986.

—. *Foucault*. University of Minnesota Press, 1988.

Jackson, Lears T J. *No Place of Grace Antimodernism and the Transformation of American Culture,* 1880 - 1920. Pantheon Books, 1981.

Surrealism & Humaneness by Diana Lizette Rodriguez

Mayer, Bernadette. *Memory*. 1971. Siglio Press, 2020.

Poetry Foundation. "Bernadette Mayer." Poetry Foundation, www.poetryfoundation.org/poets/bernadette-mayer. Accessed 19 Dec. 2020.

Siglio Press. "Press Release for Memory by Bernadette Mayer." http://sigliopress.com/book/memory/. Accessed 29 Dec 2021.

On Experimental Techniques in Writing by Bernadette Mayer

Mayer, Bernadette. *On Experimental Techniques in Writing [1/2]*, Jack Kerouac School of Disembodied Poetics Audio Archive, 1978, https://cdm16621.contentdm.oclc.org/digital/collection/p16621coll1/id/311/rec/11

—. *On Experimental Techniques in Writing [2/2]*, Jack Kerouac School of Disembodied Poetics Audio Archive, 1978, https://cdm16621.contentdm.oclc.org/digital/collection/p16621coll1/id/312/rec/28

Artaud, Antonin. *The Theatre and Its Double*. Grove Press, 1958.

Breton, André. *Nadja*. Translated by Richard Howard. Grove Paperback, 1971.

Breton, André and Phillipe Soupalt. *Magnetic Fields*. 1920. Translated by Charlotte Mandell. NYRB Poets, 2020.

Coolidge, Clark. *Polaroid*. Adventures in Poetry/Big Sky, 1975.

Duchamp, Marchel. *The Bride Stripped Bare by Her Bachelors, Even*. New York: Viking, 1973.

Motherwell, Robert. *Dada: Painter and Poets*. New York, Wittenborn, Schultz, Inc, 1951.

—. *Dada: Painter and Poets*. Second edition. Belknap Press of Harvard University, 1981.

Raymond, Marcel. Excerpts from *From Baudelaire to Surrealism*. *Dada: Painter and Poets*. Second edition. Edited be Robert Motherwell Belknap Press of Harvard University, 1981.

Satie, Erik. "The Day of a Musician." *Dada: Painter and Poets*. Second edition. Edited by Robert Motherwell. Belknap Press of Harvard University, 1981.

Shakespeare, William, "Sonnet 105." *Shake-speares Sonnets: Never Before Imprinted*. London: Thomas Thorpe, 1609.

Stein, Gertrude.

— .*Lectures In America*: "Poetry and Grammar." 1935.

— .*The Autobiography of Alice B. Toklas*, New York, Harcourt, Brace and Company, 1933.

— .*Stanzas in Meditation*. *The Yale Gertrude Stein: Selections*. Edited by Richard Kostelanetz. New Haven: Yale University Press, 1980. Print.

— ."*What Are Masterpieces, and Why Are There So Few of Them?*" Lecture, 1936.

Tzara, Tristan. *How I Became Charming, Delightful and Delicious.* December 19, 1920. *Dada: Painter and Poets.* Second edition. Edited by Robert Motherwell. Belknap Press of Harvard University, 1981.

—.“Dada Manifesto 1918,” *Dada: Painter and Poets.* Second edition. Edited by Robert Motherwell. Belknap Press of Harvard University, 1981.

—.“Lecture on Dada. (1922),” *Dada: Painter and Poets.* Second edition. Edited by Robert Motherwell. Belknap Press of Harvard University, 1981.

Williams, William Carlos. *Spring and All.* Frontier Press, 1970.

Acknowledgements

Embodied Unconscious is the living archive of our literary and writerly community. The anthology was first inspired by a mere MFA assignment during the Jack Kerouac School's Summer Writing Program in 2020 where we were asked to transcribe a piece from the Naropa University Audio Archive. Inspired by the scholarship of years prior and their continued urgency and relevance, we embarked to constellate this discourse. I am immensely grateful to Jeffrey Pethybridge, Swanee Astrid, and Anne Waldman for sparking this project and serving as constant guides and support throughout its creation. Without them, it simply would not be. I would also like to thank our professors and mentors from the Jack Kerouac School—J'Lyn Chapman, Michelle Naka Pierce, Sarah Richards Graba, and Andrew Schelling—who have been essential and inspirational in our growth as writers, scholars, and teachers and were generous with their support of this publication.

As the anthology rises from the Naropa Audio Archive, I am eternally thankful to Anne Waldman and Allen Ginsberg for having the vision to create it and securing its legacy and accessibility to all students of the Jack Kerouac School and beyond. Its wisdom and fabric of creative community are invaluable.

The Naropa Audio Archive contains lectures, classes, readings, and panels from the Jack Kerouac School and Summer Writing Program's vivid history, containing presentations from some of the most influential contemporary writers, poets, and artists. Its collections are available to all online at Naropa University's Audio Archive website: https://cdm16621.contentdm.oclc.org/. Specific lectures featured within the anthology are noted within the Works Cited section.

Cover art is "Surreal Scene" by Mina Loy, courtesy of Roger Conover, for the Estate of Mina Loy.

Anthology Contributor Bios

Amy Bobeda holds an MFA from the Jack Kerouac School of Disembodied Poetics where she serves as director of the Naropa Writing Center and teachers pedagogy and processed-based art. She's the author of *Red Memory* (FlowerSong Press), *What Bird Are You?* (Finishing Line Press), *mi sin manitos* (Ethel Press), and a forthcoming project from Spuyten Duyvil. She runs Wisdom Body Collective with a bunch of rad women and can be found on Twitter @amybobeda.

A.M.B. Brennan is a writer and poet who remembers many mountains; along with her husband and cat, she dreams of becoming an orchard or forest guardian and is learning new ways to understand her own roots. A recent MFA graduate of the Jack Kerouac School of Disembodied Poetics, she is currently located within the traditional homelands of the Na-Fiat and Tue-I Pueblos.

C. M. Chady holds her BA in Anthropology from Washington University in St. Louis and her MFA Creative Writing and Poetics from Naropa University's Jack Kerouac School where she was the Anne Waldman Fellow. She is the Founder and Editor-in-Chief of the experimental literary magazine *Tiny Spoon,* in addition to serving as a member of Wisdom Body Collective, who recently published *More Revolutionary Letters: A Tribute to Diane di Prima.* Formerly, she was the Editor-in-Chief of **apo-press*, Editor-in-Chief of *Bombay Gin,* and Managing Editor of *River Styx.* Her work spans multiple genres, including poetry, fiction, and hybrid forms. She has been published nationally and internationally in literary journals. More of her publications and work can be found on her website cmchady.com.

Ada McCartney is a poet, performer, and teaching artist. She is author of *Occupied Territory* (Kith, 2023), *cunt* (In Process, 2021), and an editor of the anthology *More Revolutionary Letters: A Diane di Prima Tribute* (Wisdom Body Collective, 2021). McCartney earned an MFA from the Jack Kerouac School of Disembodied Poetics at Naropa University and a BA from Kalamazoo College. She hosts the POETRY THEATRE podcast for the Femme On Collective and collaborates on occasional publishing projects with the Wisdom Body

Collective. Her writing appears in *Corporeal, en*gendered, Plants and Poetry Journal, The Bombay Gin, Phoenix Dance Observer,* and elsewhere. Connect with her on Instagram/Twitter @aa_mccartney or via www.aamccartney.com

Marlie McGovern is an essayist and educator. Her first book, *A Body Made of Eyes* was published by Wisdom Body Collective. She teaches writing at Naropa University's Jack Kerouac School and at the Colorado School of Mines. Her practiced-based research in embodied poetics is informed by a decade of teaching yoga and meditation. Marlie holds an MFA in Creative Writing & Poetics from Naropa University and an MA in Arts Administration from New York University.

Stephanie Michele is an artist, writer and humanist. She serves as an Editor-in-Chief and Founder of *Tiny Spoon Lit Mag*, an experimental magazine and community haven for misfit writers. She received her MFA from The Jack Kerouac School of Disembodied Poetics and once stole CA Conrad's wine glass from a party. Her work has been recently published or is forthcoming in *The Denver Quarterly, F3LL Magazine,* and *The Dillydoun Review.* She is also a writer, editor, and graphic design guru for the Wisdom Body Artist Collective. Find her on Instagram: @shinesunshine_ as well as Medium @stephaniemich.

Kendra Noelle Richard holds a BA in Writing and Theatre from Loyola University Maryland, and an MFA in Creative Writing and Poetics from the Jack Kerouac School of Disembodied Poetics at Naropa University. She was a Lighting Designer and Technician for music, theatre, and dance for 15 years—and she is currently the Tutoring Coordinator in the LEP at the University of Denver. She lives a magical Colorado life filled with nature and poetry.

Diana Lizette Rodriguez is a United States Mexicana artist born in San Antonio, Texas. Rodriguez is a graduate of Naropa University studying in the Jack Kerouac School of Disembodied Poetics and Visual Arts department. Rodriguez is an experimental artist, poet, and filmmaker. Rodriguez has published her work in *Womanly Magazine, Asymptote, Unstamatic,* the *Hong Kong Review,* and others. Her films have been featured in programs in

Mexico City and at the Performance Space in New York City. She published her chapbook, *Alicia*, through Sour Patch Press which Rodriguez founded. Rodriguez works with other poets & artists to publish their works.

EMILY TRENHOLM is a teacher, writer, editor, and maker from Minneapolis, Minnesota. She recently earned her MFA in Creative Writing & Poetics from Naropa University's Jack Kerouac School. Currently she teaches literature & creative visioning at a micro-college in Viroqua, Wisconsin called Thoreau College. She is a proud member of the artist collective Wisdom Body Collective, which recently published *More Revolutionary Letters: A Tribute to Diane di Prima*. More of her work can be found on her website: emilytrenholm.com

CHLOE TSOLAKOGLOU is a Greek-American writer who grew up in Athens, Greece. She obtained her MFA from the Jack Kerouac School, where she served as the Anselm Hollo Fellow, and she is a PhD student at Columbia University's English and Comparative Literature program. Her work has been published or is forthcoming by *The Adroit Journal, PANK, Denver Quartely's FIVES,* and elsewhere. Chloe's writing has also been nominated for various prizes, such as Best of The Net. You can find more of her poems, prose, and translations at fridaycowgirl.com

KATHY TUN is a Burmese/Rakhine writer, editor, and artist based in Chicago, IL. She specializes in film and digital photography, along with the occasional ballet dance move. She is also currently writing short films and learning how to be a filmmaker. Kathy earned her MA in English from the University of Illinois Chicago.

Index

A

B

C

D

K

L

M

N

O

P

R

S

T

U

V

W

Z